The Legacy of Dell H

ENCOUNTERS: Explorations in Folklore and Ethnomusicology
A *Journal of Folklore Research* Book

The Legacy of Dell Hymes

Ethnopoetics, Narrative Inequality, and Voice

Edited by Paul V. Kroskrity and Anthony K. Webster

INDIANA UNIVERSITY PRESS

Bloomington and Indianapolis

This book is a publication of

Indiana University Press
Office of Scholarly Publishing
Herman B Wells Library 350
1320 East 10th Street
Bloomington, Indiana 47405 USA

iupress.indiana.edu

The paper used in this publication meets the minimum requirements of the American National Standard for Information Sciences—Permanence of Paper for Printed Library Materials, ANSI Z39.48-1992.

Manufactured in the United States of America

Library of Congress Control Number: 2015948433

1 2 3 4 5   21 20 19 18 17 16

Contents

The Legacy of Dell Hymes

Introducing Ethnopoetics: Hymes's Legacy

voice
inequality

THIS VOLUME ADDRESSES the legacy, enduring impact, and future reach of Dell Hymes's ethnopoetics project. The authors take up various strands of Hymes's ethnopoetic interests and reveal how this focus on verbal art, far from being a marginal pursuit of the occasional Americanist, is actually central to many contemporary issues in folklore, linguistics, and linguistic and cultural anthropology. Indeed, a growing number of scholars have pushed for a rethinking of the importance of ethnopoetics research, from its concerns with language documentation and endangered languages to tacit forms of power that erase or deny local ways of speaking (see Blommaert 2009; Dobrin 2012; Kataoka 2012). All the essays in this volume take up the Hymesian legacy in their concerns with ethnopoetics, voice, and narrative inequality as matters of central concern to anthropology and folklore.

Though anthropologists in the Boasian tradition had already made the verbal art texts of various cultures a staple of cultural analysis, they were more concerned with these texts as sources of cultural evidence than as works of verbal art. Against this historical backdrop, Hymes began publishing pioneering studies of Native American verbal art in 1958 that related their linguistic and rhetorical forms to new appreciations of their aesthetic form and cultural significance. He first called this type of work *anthropological philology* but later rebranded the field of study that emerged under his and Dennis Tedlock's (1972, 1983) influence as *ethnopoetics*. While Hymes's (1981, 2003) early work in ethnopoetics focused on poetic devices in Native American verbal art, his later (1996) work also engaged with a variety of narrative traditions and explored fundamental issues of "narrative inequality" and "voice." This was not, however, a breakthrough for Hymes, but rather a continuation of a longstanding concern with the inequalities of languages (Hymes 1973).

As a method and theory of analysis of verbal art, much work over the last several decades has combined what has often been called a Hymesian approach (based on the patterned use of discourse particles) with the approach used by Tedlock (based on the prosody and pause structuring of actual performance). The distinction made between Hymes's and Tedlock's approaches was and continues to be misleading because it ignores the complexity of both. Hymes (2003, 36), for his part, famously—quoting Kenneth Burke—urged that linguistic anthropologists and linguists "use all there is to use" when it came to the analysis of verbal artistic traditions. Work by William Bright (1984), Sally McClendon (1977), Paul V. Kroskrity (1985, 1993), Joel Sherzer (1987, 1990), and Anthony Woodbury (1985, 1987) has shown that the perspectives of Hymes and Tedlock might be usefully combined to attend to the whole of the expressive resources of a narrator or community. Indeed, as Woodbury (1985, 1987) has argued, the interaction between various ways of poetically organizing verbal art can be communicatively and aesthetically meaningful.

Hymes, an astute student of Americanist anthropology, traditionalized his ethnopoetic work with that of Franz Boas ([1911] 1966), Edward Sapir ([1921] 1985), and the founders of linguistic anthropology (see Hymes 1999). Hymes's approach finds potent expression in Boas's ([1911] 1966, 58) claim:

> When the question arises, for instance, of investigating the poetry of the Indians, no translation can possibly be considered as an adequate substitute for the original. The form of rhythm, the treatment of language, the adjustment of text to music, the imagery, the use of metaphors, and all the numerous problems involved in any thorough investigation of the style of poetry, can be interpreted only by the investigator who has equal command of the ethnographical traits of the tribe and of their language.

This sentiment is repeated in Boas's (1917, 7) opening statement in the *International Journal of American Linguistics*:

> Indian oratory has long been famous, but the number of recorded speeches from which we can judge the oratorical devices is exceedingly small. There is no doubt whatever the definite stylistic forms exist that are utilized to impress the hearer; but we do not know what they are. As yet, nobody has attempted a careful analysis of the style of narrative art as practiced by the various tribes. The crudeness of most records presents a serious obstacle for this study, which, however, should be taken up

seriously. We can study the general structure of the narrative, the style of composition, of motives, their character sequence; but the formal stylistic devices for obtaining effects are not so easily determined.

This was the work that Hymes engaged in from the late 1950s onward. And, indeed, "Reading Clackamas Texts" (Hymes 1981) is a landmark in the study of stylistic devices that were often ignored or misrecognized by earlier researchers. As Robert Moore (this volume) points out, Hymes's fascination with line-structuring and with hierarchical relations of twos and fours and threes and fives seems to have pushed him toward a structuralism that he rightly decried (Hymes 1985).

Ethnopoetics is—or should be—concerned with more than simply poetic lines, such as individual creativity and careful attention to linguistic details. Paul Friedrich (2006) and Jan Blommaert (2006a) have offered useful evaluations of ethnopoetics. As Blommaert (2009, 268) writes, "Ethnopoetic work is one way of addressing the main issue in ethnography: to describe (and reconstruct) languages not in the sense of stable, closed, and internally homogeneous units characterizing parts of mankind, but as ordered complexes of genres, styles, registers, and forms of use." Such a perspective must engage not only individual speakers but also the languages they use and the connections they make. Blommaert (2009, 271) also adds, "Ultimately, what ethnopoetics does is to show voice, to visualize the particular ways— often deviant from hegemonic norms—in which subjects produce meaning." Hymesian "voice" is thus both a creative and a political accomplishment. It is concerned with individual narrators who can voice cultural, linguistic, and rhetorical preferences in the accomplishment of their verbal art. It is about how the narrator succeeds in making "oneself understood in one's own terms, to produce meanings under conditions of empowerment" (Blommaert 2009, 271). But this empowerment presupposes sufficient political and economic support to foster rather than silence or suppress voices, particularly those of counterhegemonic others. The recognition of voice is central to this volume. As Friedrich (2006, 228) notes in his review of ethnopoetics, "ethnopoetics tends to relativize knowledge, to recognize its subtlety." This relativization is akin to what Blommaert (2009, 259) describes as Hymes's democratization of voice by providing linguistic resources necessary for indigenous and other voices to be heard. This is certainly a crucial aspect of what Hymes (1996, 60) envisioned as the "mediative" role that linguistic anthropologists, folklorists, and linguists might provide, especially to marginalized groups, rather than the "extractive" stance that is often the academic norm.

If only because many individuals never have the opportunity to narrate in their chosen "voice," Hymes's notion of narrative inequality supplies a critical resource for examining the gulf between linguistic and narrative potential, on the one hand, and the reality of actual practice on the other. For Hymes, "narrative inequality" derives from the fact that certain ways of speaking, certain ways of telling a narrative are dismissed and marginalized. His early ethnopoetic research attended to the variety of ways of telling a story in Native American traditions and the linguistic resources that were interwoven between form and content. For Hymes, recognition of voice was the outcome of such understandings. This was the central thrust of Hymes's ethnopoetic work{the recognition of voice. As Hymes (1996, 64) argued,

> two ingredients of a vision are longstanding. One is a kind of negative freedom, freedom from denial of opportunity due to something linguistic, whether in speaking or reading or writing. One is a kind of positive freedom, freedom for satisfaction in the use of language, for language to be a source of imaginative life and satisfying form. In my own mind I would unite the two kinds of freedom in the notion of *voice*: freedom to have one's voice heard, freedom to develop a voice worth hearing.

Ethnopoetic analysis can challenge received assumptions about the nature of language and the ways that individuals engage in and use languages; that is, they can challenge "narrative inequality" not as a potential inequality but an actual inequality (Hymes 1996, 207–13) and recognize "voice." Whether these challenges arise from ethnopoetic research on the narrative structuring of asylum seekers (Blommaert 2006b), or the narrative achievements of African American school children using African American English (Hymes 1996), or the poetic accomplishments of Navajo poets writing and performing in Navajo English (Webster 2011), or the artistry of Native American verbal art (Hymes 1981; Tedlock 1983; Kroskrity 2012a; Webster 2009), such work has often combined close attention to linguistic structuring in the service of recognizing voice and in destabilizing "narrative inequality." In the studies above as in those in this volume, finding new patterns of organization is a critical aspect of not only understanding these narratives as works of art but also of communicating their social and cultural value. As Hymes (1996, 219) observed, "To demonstrate its [narrative patterning] presence can enhance respect for and appreciation of the voices of others." Translations and other attempts to understand and represent such voices, with appropriate fidelity to their artfulness, carry on this Hymesian tradition in various ways and depart from Boas's assumption that indigenous language texts were somehow untranslatable or that such translations were superfluous (Berman 1992, 157). Edited volumes such as *Voices from the Four Directions* (Swann 2004), *Inside Dazzling Mountains: Southwest Native Verbal Arts* (Kozak 2012), and *Telling Stories in the Face of Danger* (Kroskrity 2012b) confirm the important educational role that ethnopoetic projects can perform for indigenous and mainstream readers alike. As an ongoing part of this ethnopoetic endeavor, many essays in this volume attend both to close attention to linguistic structuring and to the ways such devices and structurings have been misrecognized or devalued.

This volume, though ultimately traceable to the pioneering and inspirational role of Hymes, has its own material history and origin myth. In a very real sense, this artifact that you can hold in your hands or examine as an online textual image was talked into existence. Like many outstanding ideas—and perhaps a fair number of not-so-good ones—this volume began in a bar room conversation between the editors about the proper way to appreciate a departed colleague and mentor. This particular bar was in New Orleans, a short walk from the hotels that served as the site for the 2010 annual meeting of the American Anthropological Association (AAA). We traded stories about how Hymes's ethnopoetic work had influenced us professionally and had inspired us to emphasize the study of verbal art in our own research.

When Webster was a graduate student at New Mexico State University in the mid-nineties, his advisor Scott Rushforth suggested he read some Hymes. Rushforth had expected that Webster might read *Foundations in Sociolinguistics* (1974) or some articles on the ethnography of speaking. Instead, Webster picked up *"In Vain I Tried to Tell You"* and became hooked on ethnopoetics and linguistic anthropology. His MA thesis concerned the ethnopoetics of the Chiricahua Apache narrator Samuel E. Kenoi. Hymes was also gracious in sending Webster a nineteen-page letter in May 1998 containing suggestions, comments, and encouragement for Webster's ethnopoetic analysis of Chiricahua Apache. Joel Sherzer, Webster's dissertation advisor at the University of Texas at Austin, was a student of Hymes at the University of Pennsylvania and further encouraged Webster's engagement with ethnopoetics. While Webster has met some anthropologists who were turned off of linguistic anthropology by *"In Vain I Tried to Tell You"*, it continues to be a source of inspiration in his own work. His current work with Navajo poets speaks to that continuing engagement.

For Kroskrity, too, Hymes's influence began in graduate school, when he was at Indiana University as the last student of C. F. (Carl) Voegelin, who had also been Hymes's dissertation advisor. As Kroskrity transitioned from the study of comparative literature to linguistic anthropology, Hymes's work became especially relevant as a guidepost to keeping a focus on the linguistic creativity and social significance of verbal art. As with Webster, Kroskrity enjoyed a correspondence relationship with Hymes, who generously commented on several of his articles. In addition, Kroskrity met with Hymes at various AAA meetings over the years, where they discussed such topics as the ethnopoetics of Tewa songs and stories, the history of linguistic anthropology, and the multiple connections of language and identity.

Motivated by a desire to honor one aspect of the life's work of a mentor who had profoundly influenced our research, we interpreted the call for papers for the next annual meeting of the American Anthropological Association—with the meeting theme "Traces, Tidemarks, and Legacies"—as an obvious invitation for a session on Hymes's ethnopoetic legacy. Our trial abstract drew so many positive responses from colleagues that we were able to organize a double session. This edited volume includes most of the original authors from that session (absent only are Amy Shuman and Daniel Suslak) and preserves the linkages between articles and discussants that were part of the 2011 session in Montreal.

Our division of essays into sections replicates the session organization. Our first section, "Listening For Voices," consists of five essays. Robert Moore's "Reinventing Ethnopoetics" expands on Hymesian ethnopoetics by developing new analytic tools and transcription practices that are useful for studying contemporary transformations of narrative in multilingual speech communities undergoing language shift and obsolescence. This alternative approach, grounded in Moore's work with Kiksht (the language that Hymes is most often associated with) and English and the narrators who moved between such putative codes, seeks to reorient ethnopoetics from a recuperative focus on past narrative practices to a conceptual framework that enables field researchers to take into consideration the shifting linguistic environments in which narration continues to take place in the present. Alexander D. King's "The Patterning of Style: Indices of Performance through Ethnopoetic Analysis of Century-Old Wax Cylinders" reminds us of the value of such recuperative ethnopoetics by exploring the value of Hymes's theory of ethnopoetics through an analysis of two Koryak stories recorded during the winter of 1900–1901. King, a student of Hymes at the University of Virginia, shows that such close analysis uncovers the voices of individual storytellers as well as aesthetic sensibilities found across texts and narrators.

M. Eleanor Nevins and Anthony K. Webster then turn to issues of misrecognition and describe how ethnopoetics and the ethnography of speaking can allow for opportunities of intertextual recognition of voices. Nevins's essay, "'Grow with That, Walk with That': Hymes, Dialogicality, and Text Collections," takes up Hymes's contributions to dialogic anthropology by comparing two accounts of Apache lives, one spoken by Lawrence Mithlo to Harry Hoijer and published in a 1938 text collection and another spoken by Eva Lupe to Nevins in 1996. For Nevins, also a student of Hymes at Virginia, considerations of genre and addressivity enable a latter-day recognition of terms of mediation utilized by persons like Mithlo and Lupe to address researchers in ethnographic dialogues. Anthony K. Webster's essay, "'The Validity of Navajo Is in Its Sounds': On Hymes, Navajo Poetry, Punning, and the Recognition of Voice," takes inspiration from Hymes's ongoing interest in presentational and expressive devices in ethnopoetic research. Webster combines ethnography of speaking and ethnopoetics to suggest how an understanding of Navajo punning (frequently misrecognized as semantic confusion) and a Navajo expressive device aid in the understanding of the poetry of Navajo poet Rex Lee Jim. Kroskrity's contribution, "Discursive Discriminations in the Representation of Western Mono and Yokuts Stories: Confronting Narrative Inequality and Listening to Indigenous Voices in Central California," extends the themes of ethnopoetic misrecognition and narrative inequality. Kroskrity's essay examines instances of what he terms "discursive discriminations" in the representation of indigenous Californian narratives collected and analyzed by salvage-era language and folklore scholars. Using his own recent ethnographic research on Western Mono, Kroskrity provides what Hymes has called "mediative" research designed to decolonize the misrecognitions of scholars who failed to see beyond the ethnocentric limitations of their schooled literacy and their preoccupation with "text" rather than performance. Richard Bauman then provides both a reflection on his own history with Dell Hymes and a commentary on the essays in this section. He concludes by discussing the importance of "voice" for language-oriented research.

Our second section, "Ethnopoetic Pathways," includes three essays that explore and extend Hymesian advances for language revitalization, translation, and religious language. In "The Poetics of Language Revitalization: Text, Performance, and Change," Gerald L. Carr and Barbra Meek explore some of the promising implications and applications of Hymes's ethnopoetics for various First Nations communities engaged with language revitalization projects in the Yukon. Drawing on Hymes's "breakthrough into performance," the authors analyze the ways several communities have drawn on verbal art texts as a source of language instruction, noting in particular an example of dramatically performed narratives that enable critical intertextual linkages between past, present, and future heritage language community members. Sean Patrick O'Neill's essay, "Translating Oral Literature in Indigenous Societies: Ethnic Aesthetic Performances in Multicultural and Multilingual Settings," also draws from research in language revitalization contexts. O'Neill moves our attention to the need to appreciate the delicacy and importance of translation, particularly for the indigenous communities of Northwestern California. Based on research involving translation across such distinct languages as Yurok, Hupa, and Karuk, O'Neill extends Hymes's work by showing examples of compartmentalizing and syncretic narrative practices that clearly show the influence of multilingualism and storytelling ideologies. David W. Samuels's essay, "Ethnopoetics and Ideologies of Poetic Truth," examines the ethnopoetics of religious rhetoric deployed by Lutheran missionaries working with the San Carlos Apache. He traces both Hymes's and the missionaries' ethnopoetic linkage of poetry and religious truth to medieval origins in ethical discourses of Christianity that link orality, performance, representation, and truth. Charles Briggs then provides a lively and provocative commentary on the three essays that comprise our second section. He challenges us to think about both questions of mobility as they relate to ethnopoetics, but also to the issue of colonial relativities.

Having introduced this edited volume, we invite you to join our distinguished discussants in reading and commenting on the essays and, in so doing, to not only appreciate the legacy of Dell Hymes but to extend it.

References Cited

Berman, Judith. 1992. "Oolachan-Woman's Robe: Fish, Blankets, Masks, and Meaning in Boas's Kwakw'ala Texts." In *On the Translation of Native American Literatures*, edited by Brian Swann, 125–62. Washington, DC: Smithsonian Press.

Blommaert, Jan. 2006a. "Applied Ethnopoetics." *Narrative Inquiry* 16 (1): 181–90.

———. 2006b. "Ethnopoetics as Functional Reconstruction: Dell Hymes' Narrative View of the World." *Functions of Language* 13 (2): 255–75.

———. 2009. "Ethnography and Democracy: Hymes's Political Theory of Language." *Text & Talk* 29 (3): 257–76.

Boas, Franz. (1911) 1966. "Introduction." In *Handbook of American Indian Languages and Indian Families of America North of Mexico*, 1–79. Lincoln: University of Nebraska Press.

———. 1917. "Introductory." *International Journal of American Linguistics* 1 (1): 1–8.

Bright, William. 1984. *American Indian Linguistics and Literature*. Berlin: Mouton de Gruyter.

Dobrin, Lise M. 2012. "Ethnopoetic Analysis as a Resource for Endangered-Language Linguistics: The Social Production of an Arapesh Text." *Anthropological Linguistics* 54 (1): 1–32.

Friedrich, Paul. 2006. "Maximizing Ethnopoetics: Fine-Tuning Anthropological Experience." In *Language, Culture, and Society,* edited by Christine Jourdan and Kevin Tuite, 207–28. Cambridge: Cambridge University Press.

Hymes, Dell. 1958. "Linguistic Features Peculiar to Chinookan Myths." *International Journal of American Linguistics* 24 (4): 253–57.

———. 1973. "Speech and Language: On the Origins and Foundations of Inequality among Speakers." *Daedalus* 102 (3): 59–88.

———. 1974. *Foundations in Sociolinguistics*. Philadelphia: University of Pennsylvania Press.

———. 1981. *In Vain I Tried to Tell You: Essays in Native American Ethnopoetics*. Philadelphia: University of Pennsylvania Press.

———. 1985. "Language, Memory, and Selective Performance: Cultee's 'Salmon Myth' as Twice Told to Boas." *Journal of American Folklore* 98 (390): 391–434.

———. 1996. *Ethnography, Linguistics, Narrative Inequality: Toward an Understanding of Voice*. New York: Taylor and Francis.

———. 1999. "Boas on the Threshold of Ethnopoetics." In *Theorizing the Americanist Tradition*, edited by Lisa Valentine Philips and Regna Darnell, 84–107. Toronto: University of Toronto Press.

———. 2003. *Now I Know Only That Far: Essays in Ethnopoetics*. Lincoln: University of Nebraska Press.

Kataoka, Kuniyoshi. 2012. "Toward Multimodal Ethnopoetics." *Applied Linguistics Review* 3 (1): 101–30.

Kozak, David L. 2012. *Inside Dazzling Mountains: Southwest Native Verbal Arts*. Lincoln: University of Nebraska Press.

Kroskrity, Paul. 1985. "Growing with Stories: Line, Verse, and Genre in an Arizona Tewa Text." *Journal of Anthropological Research* 41:183–99.

———. 1993. *Language, History and Identity: Ethnolinguistic Studies of the Arizona Tewa*. Tucson: University of Arizona Press.

———. 2012a. "Growing with Stories: Ideologies of Storytelling and the Narrative Reproduction of Arizona Tewa Identities." In *Telling Stories in the Face of*

Danger: Language Renewal in Native American Communities, edited by Paul V. Kroskrity, 151–83. Norman: University of Oklahoma Press.

———, ed. 2012b. *Telling Stories in the Face of Danger: Language Renewal in Native American Communities*. Norman: University of Oklahoma Press.

McLendon, Sally. 1977. "Cultural Presuppositions and Discourse Analysis." In *Linguistics and Anthropology Georgetown University Round Table on Languages and Linguistics*, edited by Muriel Saville-Troike, 153–89. Washington, DC: Georgetown University Press.

Sapir, Edward. (1921) 1985. *Culture, Language, and Personality: Selected Essays*. Edited by David G. Mandelbaum, with an epilogue by Dell H. Hymes. Berkeley: University of California Press.

Sherzer, Joel. 1987. "Poetic Structuring of Kuna Discourse: The Line." In *Native American Discourse: Poetics and Rhetoric*, edited by Joel Sherzer and Anthony Woodbury, 103–39. Cambridge: Cambridge University Press.

———. 1990. *Verbal Art in San Blas*. Cambridge: Cambridge University Press.

Swann, Brian. 2004. *Voices From the Four Directions: Contemporary Translations of the Native Literatures of North America*. Lincoln: University of Nebraska Press.

Tedlock, Dennis. 1972. *Finding the Center*. New York: Dial.

———. 1983. *The Spoken Word and the Work of Interpretation*. Philadelphia: University of Pennsylvania Press.

Webster, Anthony K. 2009. *Explorations in Navajo Poetry and Poetics*. Albuquerque: University of New Mexico Press.

———. 2011. "'Please Read Loose': Intimate Grammars and Unexpected Languages in Contemporary Navajo Literature." *American Indian Culture and Research Journal* 35 (2): 61–86.

Woodbury, Anthony. 1985. "The Function of Rhetorical Structure: A Study of Central Alaskan Yupik Eskimo Discourse." *Language in Society* 14:153–90.

———. 1987. "Rhetorical Structure in a Central Alaskan Yupik Eskimo Traditional Narrative." In *Native American Discourse: Poetics and Rhetoric*, edited by Joel Sherzer and Anthony Woodbury, 176–239. Cambridge: Cambridge University Press.

ANTHONY K. WEBSTER is Associate Professor of Anthropology at the University of Texas at Austin. He is the author of *Explorations in Navajo Poetry and Poetics* (2009) as well as numerous articles on Navajo poetry, language, and culture.

PAUL V. KROSKRITY is Professor of Anthropology and Chair of American Indian Studies at UCLA, where he has taught since earning his PhD in Anthropology from Indiana University in 1978. He has authored numerous works including *Regimes of Language* (2000) and *Telling Stories in the Face of Danger* (2012).

1   Reinventing Ethnopoetics

ASSESSING THE LEGACY of Dell Hymes (1927–2009) in ethnopoetics should entail assessing ethnopoetics more broadly, as a "legacy" in its own right within American cultural and linguistic anthropology since the 1960s. For indeed, ethnopoetics in the broad sense emerged more as a movement than as another subfield of (linguistic) anthropology, and it emerged at the same time and among the same generational cohort that produced *Reinventing Anthropology* (Hymes 1972), "the 'anti-textbook' of anthropology's then mid-career political Left" (Silverstein 2010, 935). Like *Reinventing Anthropology*, ethnopoetics—the term was coined in 1968 by Jerome Rothenberg (Quasha 1976, 65)—emerged in the context of a generational struggle between practitioners working in a number of different but overlapping fields of inquiry and expressive practice: academic anthropology, folklore, literary criticism, poetry, and what we now call performance art. Today we are separated from this period by at least two (demographic) generations, hence the need to ask, in the conclusion below, what parts of this legacy are still usable and active for students of narrative and other discourse practices today.

As a set of activities centered on verbal genres mostly of non-Western, nonliterate peoples, ethnopoetics is rather unlike the other anthropological specializations whose names likewise begin with *ethno-* and which used to be grouped under the heading of "ethnoscience": ethnobotany, ethnozoology, ethnoastronomy, ethnomedicine, and so forth. Most of these take as their subject matter (lexically) explicit, formal knowledge about domains of human activity and/or perceptual experience (plants, animals, celestial bodies, etc.), the nomenclature of which had already been formalized within Western, unprefixed "science" when the anthropologists came a-calling.

But at least in its Hymesian mode, as verse analysis, ethnopoetics has not primarily involved the ethnographic study of nonliterate

11

peoples' explicit ideas *about* narrative, as reflected, perhaps, in native terminologies. It has, rather, been an intervention into the presentational (printed) form of texts, a way of arranging the transcript of an event of oral narration so as to reflect or recuperate the true rhetorical architecture of denotational text, and in so doing to recover "the literary form in which the native words had their being" (Hymes 1981, 384; see Blommaert 2009, 271).

There are two implicit claims here: one is that it is possible to arrive at a single final arrangement of a transcript that reflects on the page *the* rhetorical or poetic structure of an(y) oral performance; another is the idea that in doing so, a scholar has restored or recovered a native voice. Whatever one thinks about the validity of these claims, there is no doubt that Hymes was committed to both of them. Indeed, one can observe a fundamental shift in Hymes's own work on materials in Chinookan (and an increasing number of other languages): from a focus on the event-bound interactional dynamics of narrative as *performance* (e.g., Hymes [1975] 1981), he moved to a focus on the rhetorical architecture of denotational *text*. To clarify matters, it might help to identify two distinct senses of the term:

ethnopoetics$_1$ ethnographic investigation of ideas about and evaluations of individual narrative performances and/or naration in general in the community from which the source texts emerge, including native vocabulary pertaining to parts of narratives (e.g., titles) and acts of narration (e.g., *verba dicendi*), and especially including information on (named) speech genres, their performance conditions, etc.;

ethnopoetics$_2$ "the recuperative restudy of the textual organization of originally oral literary forms of Native American and other peoples so as to make patent and to explicate their rhetorical power as verbal art." (Silverstein 2010, 933)

Ethnopoetics$_1$, then, fits more easily into the set containing ethnobotany, ethnozoology, and similar (sub)fields; it also overlaps with another field of which Hymes was a founding figure, the ethnography of speaking (or of communication; see Hymes 1962, 1964). Ethnopoetics$_2$ is focused on texts themselves, their rhetorical architecture and presentational form.

Hymes made signal contributions to ethnopoetics$_1$ in his work from the 1950s into the 1970s (e.g., Hymes 1959, 1966, [1975] 1981), but concentrated almost exclusively on ethnopoetics$_2$ after his discovery in the mid- to late 1970s of the principles of what he called "verse analysis." More succinctly:

> ethnopoetics$_1$ "study of the oral poetics of indigenous peoples and
> ethnopoetics$_2$ their literary monuments." (Silverstein 2010, 936n3)

As will become clear, I think this dichotomy is a false one; it is nevertheless helpful in organizing the discussion, partly because it was, as I also hope to suggest, never adequately resolved in Hymes's own work.

My purpose in this essay is to build upon Hymes's contributions to ethnopoetics, and to propose a set of transcription and text-formatting practices for capturing on the page dimensions of the poetic structure of oral narration that are not reflected adequately or systematically in Hymesian verse analysis. My broader aim is to contribute to the development of an analytic framework that can enable field researchers to take into consideration the shifting linguistic environment in which narration takes place. The material comes from my own fieldwork with speakers of Kiksht (Wasco-Wishram Chinookan), the language and the textual tradition that absorbed so much of Hymes's prodigious scholarly and creative energies. In the conclusion I take a brief look at ethnopoetics conceived in broadly cultural terms and try to place Hymes's work within it.

Contrapuntal Coyote Stories

During the 1980s, over several summers of fieldwork at Warm Springs Reservation in central Oregon, I became acquainted with Mrs. Lucinda Smith (née Scott), a fluent Wasco speaker then in her eighties; the circumstances of our first meeting are described elsewhere (Moore 1993, 213ff). With her late husband Alfred Smith, she had raised a large family and helped to run a cattle-ranching operation of considerable size located on an allotment of high sagebrush prairie about twenty miles to the west of "the Agency," as the reservation's main population center is known.

In 1983 I found her living with a recently divorced grown son in a small, detached house on "the Senior Citizens' loop," a cul-de-sac of

1970s-era federal housing built atop a small hill a stone's throw from the Agency. Attached to the house was a carport beneath whose roof sat a large, gleaming late-model Buick sedan, which she had recently bought at a dealership in the nearby off-reservation town of Madras, Oregon, paying for it with wads of cash retrieved from a beaded bag. She didn't drive; the Buick was there so that one or another of her adult children could drive her, in regal fashion, to Portland or Yakima to visit relatives or go shopping. Her son worked for a tribally owned timber company and was away ("in the woods," as she put it) from before dawn until late afternoon each day. I would come to her house once or twice each week in the early afternoon, usually bearing some small gift of fresh fruit or other edibles. We would sit at her kitchen table or side by side on her sofa; she knew I was interested in her language, and sometimes we engaged in the standard kind of linguistic elicitation or related activities.

Since she had spontaneously narrated (in English) an episode about Coyote the first time we met, I knew that she was not only conversant in the mythology, but also willing and able to assume responsibility for narrating it (Bauman 1977; Hymes [1975] 1981), and so between 1983 and the time of her death in 1986 I recorded her narrating the Wasco Coyote cycle in full on four separate occasions. Later, I discovered that Michael Silverstein had recorded another complete (and quite long) version of her Coyote cycle in 1972, when she still lived "up the ranch."

Coyote cycles—loosely connected series of episodes centering on the trickster-transformer figure Coyote and "telling how [he] traveled all the way up the Columbia river, transforming monsters and instructing the people in the various arts of life" (Sapir 1907, 542)—will be familiar to students of American Indian mythologies of the region (cognate episodes are attested for nearby Sahaptin- and Salishan-speaking groups), and familiar as well to readers of Hymes's many studies of Chinookan narrative traditions (e.g., Hymes [1975] 1981). Though not cosmogonic in the strict sense, Coyote cycles recount how the world as we know it took its current shape. The setting of the episodes is

> a time antedating the present one when animals walked about as men, though having approximately the same mental and, to a large extent, physical characteristics as now. At that time, when there were no Indians, properly speaking, in the country, but only anthropomorphic animals, many things were not as they should be, and, in order to make the country

fit for habitation by the Indians destined to hold it, it was necessary for a culture-hero or transformer to rectify the weak points in creation. (Sapir 1907, 542)

If Coyote in the guise of culture-hero or transformer "is distinctly the benefactor of mankind," Coyote in trickster mode is "often . . . conceived of as cunning, deceitful, and gluttonous," an "insufferable marplot" who is "at the same time . . . indescribably obscene" (543).

Mrs. Smith's renditions of the Coyote cycle turned out to be different in a number of ways from the texts I had encountered in the canon—for that is the proper word—of Chinookan mythology as represented in the work of Franz Boas (1891, 1901), Edward Sapir (1909), Melville Jacobs (1958), David French (1958), and others, to say nothing of the then-recent work of Hymes in ethnopoetics (e.g., 1981). In Mrs. Smith's tellings, for instance, Coyote the culture-hero or transformer was nowhere to be found. Rather, the deceitful, gluttonous, insufferable marplot was everywhere, and many of the episodes featured deeds that might well qualify as "indescribably obscene," were they not in fact described in fairly direct terms (and often, in two languages) by my interlocutor—an octogenarian, matriarch, and staunch Presbyterian.

In addition, Mrs. Smith did not localize the various episodes in her Coyote cycles to specific, named sites along the Columbia River. Such localizations are common in the Wishram Coyote cycle recorded by Sapir (1909) and in the closely cognate Clackamas cycle recorded by Jacobs (1958). But Mrs. Smith belonged to one of the first generations of people who were born and raised on the Warm Springs Reservation, one hundred miles south of the Columbia River; unlike many men, who might have spent part of every year on the river (during fishing season), she remained on the reservation virtually all of her life, as she explained in response to a direct question from Michael Silverstein in 1972:

MS: *Last summer you were telling me that* qanučk ['myth'] *about* isk'úlia kʷadau ikʷálali ['Coyote and the Dangerous Being']

LS: ikʷálali? [The Dangerous Being?]

MS: *Yeah. Where wás that on the ríver, do you know that?*

LS: *Huh-uh. I don't éven know. The people that used to líve 'long the ríver, I guess théy know about thát. But I never live around thére, my folks, well, they all moved out hére and we [were] raised here.*

MS: *Oh, so when they used to tell you a* qanǔck, *they didn't téll you where that wás.*

LS: *No, they never tell me where, they just sáy it, 'n that's áll. Well, wé never think nothing like that would éver be ásked, where they wére, or where.*[1]

The third—and most obvious—difference between these narratives and those in published collections was the fact that in all four versions of the cycle she recounted for me, Mrs. Smith alternated between narration in Kiksht and English. My facility and fluency in Kiksht improved over time, and there is much less English in the two versions from 1984—and still less in the 1985 version—than there is in the 1983 telling. However, when I brought a (non-Kiksht speaking) female friend along to visit Mrs. Smith in 1986, the story was almost entirely in English again (with many of the more risqué incidents glossed over quickly, if not eliminated). The version she recounted for Silverstein in 1972—perhaps not surprisingly, given the season (winter) and Silverstein's obviously high level of fluency in Kiksht—was almost entirely in Kiksht, though not without a number of English-coded asides.

Close examination of the full corpus of Mrs. Smith's Coyote cycles reveals that her narrative code-switching follows a general pattern: presentation of the direct speech of characters (including Coyote) is given in Kiksht, with or without a directly quoted English equivalent; narration of characters' movements and nonspeech behaviors may be in Kiksht or in English; metanarrative asides and other out-of-frame remarks are most often in English (see Moore 1993 for a detailed analysis).

In all—and I think the corpus of Mrs. Smith's narrations, spanning a fourteen-year period, provides a basis for assessing her narrative style—we can see that her Coyote cycles were presented in a manner that we might call contrapuntal. The musical analogy is far from perfect, but it is meant in part to recall Karl Reisman's (1974, 114) discussion of "contrapuntal conversation" in the West Indies:

> In a brief conversation with me, a girl called to someone on the street, made a remark to a small boy, sang a little, told a child to go buy bread, etc., all the while continuing the thread of her conversation about her sister.

Is it possible to reconcile such a contrapuntal style of narration with the requirements of Hymesian verse analysis? Verse analysis, it will be recalled, focuses on uncovering in a monologic text lineaments of verse structure whose "recurrence at all levels of organization . . . makes the pattern seemingly inescapable and convincing," with the result that "at each level at which the pattern applies, it segments and organizes the material without discontinuity, without leftovers" (Hymes 1977, 440).

Consider the following brief episode from the first time Mrs. Smith narrated the Coyote cycle for me, on August 25, 1983. The passage is reproduced below in (1a) more or less as it appears in my field notebook (with errors corrected, of course).

(1) From Lucinda Smith, "Raccoon and Coyote," August 25, 1983

(1a) As "prose"

a:ġ[a]+aštúy[a]⁺aštúya, *they'd come to—what was it first? Oh! They come to*
[Now the-two would be going along, going along . . .]

some tróut, físh, swimmin' 'round, swimmin' 'round. á:ġa dauda anugʷigáya!
[Now I'll grab these!]

akádaqi dau[a]⁺anaglgáya, alma naim[a]⁺anx̱lmùx̱mà *Coyote says.*
[I'll grab this trout, then I alone will eat it!]

Raccóon knows hów to catch 'em, hím! Hé just catch 'em éasy!

He'd láugh at him. kinwá:: *he tried to sneak úp.*   au, kínwa alik'iłx̱iyá::,
                    [Vainly . . .]   [Yes, vainly he'd crawl,]

akádaqi ačàglgáya. ã::nġad aksùbnáya, alaiġldáqłqa.
[he'd grab (at) a trout. She'd already jump, she'd leave him.]

aġa p'á::l[a]⁺ isk'úlia kʷaba. *His gúts ráttlin'. Hungry!*
[Now Coyote stopped there.]

Right away one notices much elision of adjacent identical vowel segments across word boundaries (marked here with square brackets and a plus-sign in superscript); one also notes the rapidity and apparent seamlessness of Mrs. Smith's alternation between languages.

Now consider the same passage, presented in the style of Dennis Tedlock (e.g., 1983). In (1b) below, line breaks are determined solely on the basis of pauses and/or breath groups. I have employed capitalization to indicate relatively louder utterances (or syllables) in English, and a larger font size for relatively louder syllables in Kiksht; markedly quieter utterances are given in a smaller font, and one fleeting bit of allegro narration in near-falsetto is presented in superscript; to signal rhetorically lengthened (i.e., nonphonemic) vowels here I use multiple alphabetic symbols rather than a mark for length. All the lines are positioned flush left, in part to emphasize the relentless linearity of this mode of ethnopoetic presentation. In (1b), then, I try to represent what Mrs. Smith *sounded like* as she narrated the passage.

(1b) As Tedlockian oral poetry

aaġ⁺ aštúy[a]⁺ aštúya *they'd come to*—
[Now the two would be going along, going along . . .]

What was it first?

Oh!

They come to some TROUT, FISH, ˢʷⁱᵐᵐⁱⁿ' 'ʳᵒᵘⁿᵈ ˢʷⁱᵐᵐⁱⁿ' 'ʳᵒᵘⁿᵈ

á:ġa dauda -ktyɛna-
[Now these whatchacallem]
anugʷigáya!
[I'm gonna grab 'em!]
akádaqi dau[a]⁺ anaglgáy[a]⁺ alma naim[a]⁺ anx̱lmùx̱mà!
[I'll grab this trout, then I alone will eat it!]
Coyote says.

RacCOON knows HOW to catch 'em, HIM!

HE just catch 'em EASY!

He'd láugh at him.

kinwaaa *he tried to*
[Vainly ...]

sneak úp.

au, kínw[a]⁺ alik'ił x̱iyaaa -ktyɛna- akádaqi ačàglgáya.
[Yes, vainly he'd crawl, whatchacallit, he'd grab a trout.]
ãã ãnġad⁺ aksùbnáya, alaiġldáqłqa.
[She'd already have long since jumped (away), she'd leave him.]
aġa p'áaal[a]⁺ isk'úlia kʷaba.
[Now Coyote was all alone there, he quit.]

His gúts ráttlin'.

Húngry!

Several features leap out from this presentation: first, many of the poetic "lines" here—determined on the basis of prosody alone—feature more than one verb. The discourse particle *aġa* 'now' appears in line-initial position (as one would expect on the basis of Hymesian principles), but in one case (in the fifth line) it bears a marked stress on its first syllable. Finally, what should be done about the discourse particle *au* 'yes' that begins the fifteenth line?

In (1c) below I present the same passage, now as the output of Hymesian verse analysis. The reader will notice first that all of Mrs. Smith's English has been quietly excised (and one line of Kiksht has been supplied, inside square brackets). Rhetorical vowel length is marked (now with a colon), but Mrs. Smith's frequent elisions of adjacent identical vowels across word boundaries are not, creating the appearance of a text carefully enunciated at dictation speed. In keeping with the methods of Hymesian verse analysis, lines are divided according to the principle of one verb (or predicate) per line, despite the fact that a majority of Mrs. Smith's prosodic lines in this section contain more than one verb.

(1c) As Hymesian measured verse

a:ġa aštúya,	Now the two would go,
aštúya,	they'd go,
[aštúgʷaqʷam itkádaqi].	[they'd come to some trout].
"á:ġa dauda anugʷigáya!	"Now I'll grab these!
"akádaqi daua anaglgáya,	"I'll grab this trout,
"alma naima anẋlmùẋmà."	"then I alone shall eat it."
kínwa alik'iɬẋiyá::,	Vainly he'd crawl,
akádaqi ačàglgáya.	he'd grab (at) a trout.
ã::nġad aksùbnáya,	She'd have already jumped,
alaiġldáqɬqa.	she'd leave him.
aġa p'á::la isk'úlia kʷaba.	Now Coyote stopped there.

Notice how perfectly the textual arrangement exemplifies the three- and five-line verse patterns discovered by Hymes in his work on

Chinookan narratives: two verses of three lines each, both with *aga* in line- and verse-initial position, and a final verse of five lines, with the pivotal middle line serving both as "outcome" of the first triad and "onset" of the second.

Finally, below in (1d) is the same passage one more time, now in the format I eventually devised to cope with Mrs. Smith's contrapuntal style of narration. The transcription format used below (and in other publications, e.g., Moore 1993, 2009) arranges the discourse into three tiers or columns of indented type in an attempt to render visually patent the fact that there seem to be (minimally) three distinct speech-event modalities constantly in play in the transcript: (1) a bilingual conversation between Mrs. Smith and me about linguistic and other details of the story at hand; (2) Mrs. Smith's narration of the plot events of "Raccoon and Coyote" in the third person; and (3) her use of directly quoted speech to present the utterances of the characters in the story.

The leftmost column or tier of transcription represents interlocutory speech deictically grounded in the immediate event of speaking (E^s in the notation of Jakobson [1957] 1990); included here are my own responses and reactions, along with the audience-like reactions provided by the narrator herself and various asides, excurses, and metanarrative comments directed to me as Mrs. Smith's interlocutor and co-conversationalist. The second column represents narrative discourse given in the third person (and usually in the past tense): description of characters' movements, actions, and behaviors, and so on, including *verba dicendi* and other methods used by the narrator to frame the directly quoted utterances of the story's characters (E^s/E^n). The third column from the left contains only the directly quoted speech of characters ($E^s/E^n/E^{ns}$). Line breaks roughly represent pauses in speech, though no systematic attempt has been made to capture subtle differences in pause length.

In Goffman's (1981) terms, Mrs. Smith is the Animator, Author, and Principal of all INTERLOCUTORY speech given in the first (leftmost) column; she is the Animator and Principal of (nonquoted NARRATIVE) speech given in the second (middle) column; but in the third (rightmost) column of directly QUOTED character speech, Mrs. Smith functions only as the Animator—the character whose speech is presented is the Author and Principal.

(1d) As narration across multiple speech-event modalities

[INTERLOCUTORY (E^s)]
   [NARRATIVE (E^s/E^n)]
      [QUOTATIONAL (E^s/E^n/E^{ns})]

LS: a:ġ⁺ aštúy[a]⁺ aštúya *they'd come to—*   90
      [Now the two would be going along, going along . . .]

What was it first?   91
Oh!   92
They come to some tróut, fish, swimmin' 'round swimmin' 'round.   93

      "á:ga dauda -ktyɛna-   94
      ["Now these, whatchacallem,]
      "anugʷigáya!   95
      ["I'm gonna grab 'em!]

RM: *mm*   96

LS: "akádaqi dau[a]⁺ anaglgáy[a]⁺ alma naim[a]⁺   97
      anx̣lmùx̣mà!"
      ["I'll grab a trout, then I alone will eat it!"]

      Coyote says.   98

RM: *uh-huh, uh-huh.*   99

LS: *Raccóon knows hów to catch 'em, hím!*   100
      Hé just catch 'em éasy!   101
      He'd láugh at him.   102

      kinwá:: *he tried to*   103
      [Vainly . . .]

      sneak úp.   104

      au,   105
      [Yes,]

      kínw[a]⁺ alik'iłx̣iyá::, -ktyɛna-,   106
      [Vainly he'd crawl, whatchacallit,]

RM: ã::   107
      [Ye::s]

LS: akádaqi ačàglgáya.   108
      [He'd grab a trout.]

ã::nġad[+] aksùbnáya,   109
[She'd already have long since jumped (away),]

alaiġldáqɬqa.   110
[she'd leave him.]

aġa p'á::l[a][+] isk'úlia k[w]aba.   111
[Now Coyote stopped there, he gave up.]

His gúts ráttlin'.   112

RM: *mm*   113

LS: *Húngry!*   114

The format adopted here allows one to observe Mrs. Smith tacking back and forth between her footing in the here-and-now (E[s]) of the bilingual conversation with me, and her role as the primary producer of the there-and-then (E[s]/E[n]) of the story, within which is located a second here-and-now, that of the characters as co-conversationalists (E[s]/E[n]/E[ns]). These three footings or speech-event modalities are kept formally distinct at some points, and formally merge with one another at other points, but in an orderly way.

Rather than offering a final and definitive representation of the true rhetorical architecture of textual form, the format adopted here is designed explicitly to foreground those points in a narrative performance where its own categories break down, bringing our attention to those places where the boundary between a narrating voice and the voice of a character becomes hard to draw (Bakhtin [1934–35] 1981). In line 98 above, for example, the framing line *Coyote says* is given in English, suggesting that it could belong to interlocutory speech addressed to me in the event. I have, however, assigned it here to the narrative speech column. In a similar way, we notice that in line 105 Mrs. Smith seems to preface a passage of narrative description with *au*, 'yes'. Here, the availability of multiple versions of the same story by the same narrator provides clarification: every time she narrated this incident, Mrs. Smith had trouble retrieving the Kiksht verb meaning 'crawl' ([ ][3]-√*k'iɬxi*); here she slows down noticeably in line 103, after *kinwa* ('in vain'), pausing for an instant, then inserting the English *he tried to / sneak up*. After a second very brief pause she has retrieved the word, says (to herself) *au* ('yes!'), and proceeds.

Even more important, this format allows us to see how speech in each of the three modalities can serve as a metadiscourse with respect to speech in the others. It is possible, for example, to step out of the narrative modality (E^s/E^n) and back into the conversation (E^s) to comment on the story and/or the characters, perhaps in a language like English that one shares with one's interlocutor—indeed, this practice is common and ever-present in many if not all storytelling traditions, and it is centrally involved in on-the-spot translations, glossing of particular words, and so on; it also figures when narrators are filling in "background information" and doing speech repair (see Başgöz 1986 for a Turkish case). Mrs. Smith's metanarrative coda to the passage presented above, for example—*his guts rattlin' / Hungry!*—provides a nuanced gloss of the complexly interrelated senses of the Kiksht particle *p'ala* in the immediately preceding narrative discourse, which can mean 'he stopped, came to rest; relented; gave up; quit'.

The next example (2), taken from the second episode of Mrs. Smith's 1983 Coyote cycle, shows that it is also possible to "translate" a directly quoted passage and simultaneously to comment on it in a way that makes clear that the narrator qua co-conversationalist (in E^s) is merely the Goffmanian Animator of character speech (in E^s/E^n/E^{ns}). In this episode of the Coyote cycle (as Mrs. Smith told it), Raccoon and Coyote come upon five girls—five sisters—jumping in and out of the water on the opposite bank of the Columbia River. The girls are scantily clad in buckskin:

(2) From Lucinda Smith, "Coyote and the Five Sisters" August 25, 1983

> [INTERLOCUTORY (E^s)]
>   [NARRATIVE (E^s/E^n)]
>   [QUOTATIONAL (E^s/E^n/E^{ns})]

"ank'iɬxiyá:: alma kʷaba anɬ-ktyɛna- ["I'll crawl over there, and I'll whatchacall]	195
"X'mànX'mán anXuxʷa iɬnəmškš ɬaxiaič!" ["I'll finger the genitals of those women!"]	196
RM: *mhm, mhm*	197
LS: *He mean he'll,*	198
uh, féel them 'róund.	199

Mrs. Smith's translation in lines 198–99 here—glossing a particle-verb construction (X'mànX'mán []$_2$-[]$_3$-u$_6$-√x̂$_7$ '[]$_2$ finger the genitals of []$_3$')—achieves by a kind of inversion of indirect free style (*style indirect libre*) a perfect insulation of the two speech-event roles: when Coyote is being directly quoted, it is he, not Mrs. Smith, who is speaking (and 'meaning') various indescribably (almost) obscene things.

It is also possible to comment on the conversational matrix (E^s) of the storytelling event from within the world inhabited by the characters, treating that event and its participant alignments as an object-language to be regimented, as it were, by the characters as co-conversationalists. A clear example of this emerged the following summer (1984), when I persuaded Mrs. Smith to narrate the Coyote cycle again for me, starting from the beginning. This time the opening episode, "Raccoon and Coyote," contained a new element:

(3) From Lucinda Smith, "Raccoon and Coyote," July 10, 1984

[INTERLOCUTORY (E^s)]
  [NARRATIVE (E^s/E^n)]
    [QUOTATIONAL (E^s/E^n/E^{ns})]

LS: galixčúix.
        [He (Coyote) came down (river).]

RM: ã:
        [Ye:s.]

LS: a:::ġa   65
        [No:::w]

        iak'áima!
        [He's all by himself!]

        kʷapt gàliguqám –ktyɛna-
        [Then he met up with whatzisname,]

        iq'álalas,
        [Raccoon,]

     —*thát's Raccóon.*

RM: ã   70
        [Yes.]

LS: a:ġ[a]⁺ gačiùlxámx̣,
        [No:w he told him,]

            "kdáya nak'áima ngušgíwal!"
            ["Hey, I'm going along all by myself!"]

And then—

And then iq'álalas gačiulxàmẋ,
[And then Raccoon told him,]

    "áwia náika dáya dáuka nak'áima!   75
    ["I'm all by myself too!]

    "tẋ—kánatẋ makʷšt pu it—itẋúya,
    ["The two of us should go along together,]

    "p[u]⁺àġa kikláyx wá:ʔau −aktyɛna- idwáča!"
    ["It would make a much nicer whatchacall, story!"]

RM: mm!
LS: ãhã
    [Yes.]

    i*Raccoon* gačiúlxam, iq'álalas gačiúlxam;   80
    [Raccoon told him, Raccoon told him;]

    isk'úlia:
    [Coyote (says):]

        "ã:::!
        ["Oh ye:::s!]

    "daxká dàẋdau q'áẋš nuẋt, idwáča!
    ["That's just what I want, stories!]

RM: ã:!
    [Ye:s!]

As can be seen from this small (but representative) sample, Mrs. Smith's July 1984 version of the cycle was narrated much more densely—and rapidly—in Kiksht than the 1983 version we have been sampling so far. It is also narrated in the Kiksht "remote past" tense (verbs prefixed with *ga-* before consonants, *gal-* before vowels), the normatively appropriate tense for myth narration. The 1983 telling, by contrast, was narrated in the "future-conditional" (*a-* before consonants, *al-* before vowels)—hence my translations: not 'they went', but 'they'd go'; not 'he jumped', but 'he'd jump', etc. The future-conditional is the appropriate tense to use when telling *about* a myth, summarizing the plot, as opposed to *telling* it; it's a way of telling someone what would be happening in a story, were one to tell it.

Wanting to check my transcription, and needing help with translation, the day after Mrs. Smith recounted the cycle from which item (3) above is taken, I played the tape recording for another of my colleagues and teachers on the reservation, Mrs. Alice Florendo (see Moore 2009 for a text from her). When we reached the passage quoted above I had to shut off the tape recorder so that she could recover from an almost convulsive fit of laughter: "She's talking about *you*, you know!" Mrs. Florendo explained, as soon as she was able to regain her composure (lines 82–83 above).

Though not terminologized (so far as I know) in Kiksht ethno-poetics₁, the passage here recalls an Arizona Tewa narrative technique discussed by Paul V. Kroskrity (1985, 196) and termed "carrying it hither" (*-ma:di-ma'a*): a set of techniques for "situating the narratives for the present audience," by, for example, "situating the narratives in known geographical locales, elaborating or editing episodes as part of recipient designing, and other details that contribute to the audi-ence's sense of immediacy by virtue of the narrator's reshaping of old texts to new contexts."

Discussion

Clearly, these narrations from Mrs. Smith—replete with code-switching and all manner of "extraneous" metanarrative asides to her inter-locutor—represent something other than "full performance" (Bauman 1977; Hymes [1975] 1981). These are not transcripts of ritual speech acts performed over winter nights to an audience of adults who already knew the plots of all the stories, or to children who were made to "bathe in ice water" if they fell asleep, as they inevitably did (Silverstein 1996); this is talk between Mrs. Smith and me, sitting at her kitchen table or side by side on the "daveno" (sofa) with the tape-recorder between us, in her senior citizen's house at Warm Springs, on long summer after-noons. In situations like these, the boundary between performer and "audience"—so central to folklore study (e.g., Bauman 1977)—turns out to be permeable and up for negotiation, as Mrs. Smith frequently breaches "the fourth wall" and addresses me directly.

Jacobs, writing about his fieldwork with the Clackamas Chinook narrator Victoria Howard, opined that

> the change in emphasis from a meticulously correct presentation for a
> wholly native audience to informing an outsider about a story which he
> had never heard tied in with acculturative disintegration. . . . [Mrs. How-
> ard's] task with me was to tell a story, not to tell it with all its trappings. . . .

In Mrs. Howard's time, stories were stories rather than plays which everyone present also knew. (Jacobs 1959, 223)

Jacobs's point here about "acculturative disintegration" could be rephrased in more reflexive language: what we observe in these transcripts is the transformation of a narrative speech genre in the context of community-wide conditions of language shift and replacement, and in more specific conditions that partly reflect long-term interactions between Mrs. Smith (and other Chinookan elders) and a succession of anthropological linguists, most notably in the present instance Hymes himself (starting in the 1950s) and Silverstein (starting in the 1960s).

To review: Mrs. Smith's Coyote cycles present a number of new or anomalous features when viewed against the background of what is known about "traditional" Chinookan myths of this type: episodes featuring Coyote as culture-hero or transformer are notably absent—the Rabelaisian trickster is dominant; the episodes are not localized to specific sites (including geologic formations) along the Columbia River, though they are presented as having taken place there; finally, and most obviously, Mrs. Smith's distinctive narrative style emerges in the complex but orderly intertwining of quoted and nonquoted speech, narrative and metanarrative discourse, English and Kiksht. What is more, it is clear that from Mrs. Smith's point of view, they are not myths at all, but "stories."

Below in (4) are the native-language labels for major narrative genres in Kiksht. The term for *myth*—a genre for which the Coyote cycle would be the exemplar—is the unprefixed and unanalyzable noun stem *qánučk*, shown in (4a), which takes a masculine-singular cross-referencing pronominal (-*i*-) in the verb. The *verbum dicendi* that goes with this noun is built on the semantically "light" verb root $\sqrt{\dot{x}}$ 'be, make, do', in a ditransitive construction, so that, to translate the Kiksht idiom, one "does" a myth (for someone).

The term roughly translatable as 'tale' (4b) is an invariably plural noun (with it_3- 'plural' prefix) that is transparently a deverbal nominalization, made from a verb construction that denotes the act of 'bringing (an object) forth from an enclosure'—hence my literal gloss 'recollection'. The speech act involved in the telling of a tale or recollection would be denoted by the verb given in (4b), with absolutive$_3$ inflection for speaker, and dative$_4$ inflection for hearer.

But Mrs. Smith's narrations belong to neither of these categories—they are, as can be seen from the passage quoted above in (3), *stories*:

the noun is *id-wáča*, an invariably plural form that has broad semantic range, taking in 'stories' as things one has heard, as well as gossip, information, and, perhaps most saliently, 'news.' Etymologically the noun is related to the body-part term for 'ear'—hence, to gloss the noun etymologically, one might offer 'hearsay' as a rough English equivalent. The Wishram lexical files (begun by Sapir, and massively expanded by his student Walter Dyk) contain a neologism for 'telegraph wires' that is built on this noun, structurally glossable as 'news-carriers'. *Qanučkmax̣* can only be told on winter nights, before an audience of children and adults (who would already know the plots); *idwáča* can be imparted by anyone, to anyone, at any time.

(4) Labels for major narrative genres in Kiksht[2]

(a) qánuǔk (pl. qánuǔk-max̣)   'myth(s)'
   verbum dicendi: $[]_2$-$[]_3$-$[]_4$-l_5-u_6-$\sqrt{\dot{x}^w}_7$
                         '$[]_2$ "do" [(myth)]$_3$ for$_5$ $[]_4$'

(b) it-q'íx̣ik'alx̣   'tales' (lit., 'recollections')
   verbum dicendi: $[]_3$-$\dot{x}$a-$[]_4$-l_5-$\sqrt{k^w \dot{l}i}_7$-$\check{c}k_8$
                         '$[]_3$ recount something to$_5$ $[]_4$'

(c) id-wáča   'stories'; 'news'; 'gossip'; 'information'
   verbum dicendi: $[]_2$-$[]_3$-$\sqrt{\dot{x}^w}_7$-l_8
                         '$[]_2$ be saying to $[]_3$'
   possessive: id$_3$-$[]_4$-wáča
                         '$[]_4$'s story'

Mrs. Smith was utterly consistent in using the term *idwáča* as the label for the stories she told me. In July of 1984, for example, as I was gently coaxing her to re-tell the Coyote cycle for me, this is how she responded, just before launching into the beginning of the narrative:

(5) Before beginning narration, July 10, 1984

LS: *Talk Wasco?*

    O:h.

    Well, whát will I téll you 'bout?   50

RM: isk'úlia?
    [Coyote?]

LS: isk'úlia?
[Coyote?]

O:h.

au, iagámla idíawač[a]⁺ isk'úlia!
[Yes, Coyote's story (is) no good!]

RM: [laughs]   55

On that same occasion, she crafted a remarkable formulaic ending to
close off the narration of an episode concerning Coyote's encounter
with a child-stealing ogress; note here the hybrid of "oral" and "literate" story-final formulae (she intones the phrase *The End* just as if she
were finished reading a bedtime story to a child), and the metaphoric
reference to Coyote's story (*idíawača isk'úlia*) as a physical object with
a definite 'edge' (*kəmkit*):

(6) Ending of "Coyote and Adat'alhia," July 10, 1984

LS: daya káux ͣau gaiuxk'ʷá.
[This Owl went home.]

ağá yaẋda
[And finally now, that,]

sa::q'ʷə.
[is (absolutely) all (of it).]

Thé Énd.

kʷapt sáq' yaẋdau kəmkit idíawač[a] isk'úlia.
[Then that (is) the very (outer) edge of Coyote's story.]

That's what I knów now.

Conclusion

The reinvention of ethnopoetics proposed here is intended to enable
the study of discourse practices in multilingual speech communities
undergoing the dramatic socioeconomic transformations associated
with language shift and obsolescence. Like all heuristic devices, it
should be evaluated for what it allows the reader to see, or whether
it enables the reader to learn more. But because the transcription
format proposed here is superficially so similar to that of Hymes in

its appearance on the page, it may be useful to sharpen the contrast between the intentions, and the effects, of the two approaches.

Introducing his analysis of a Hopi text, Hymes (1992, 47) remarked, "Experience of a number of Native American traditions, and of narrative traditions in some other languages, including English, has led to a conception of a narrator as weaving together two threads. One is a thread of incident, what is going to happen, and the other is a thread of form, how what happens is to be given shape." The dialectic between narratable content and rhetorical form that Hymes puts front and center here has certainly been central to the development of European and modernist (ethno)poetics and literary culture, as has been the concern with what is going on in the mind of the narrator or literary artist. The relevance of this to the verbal traditions of other peoples, however, has not so much been argued for as it has been taken for granted.

One cannot help but notice in Hymes's later ethnopoetic work an increasing sense of certainty: "Again and again, an analysis of form leads to recognition of larger relationships, to deployment in the service of balance and point. One is able to recognize with some degree of accuracy just what parts a narrative has" (1992, 50). At the same time, there is a move toward universalism, deploying a notion of narrative competence that is clearly modeled on the Chomskyan notion of linguistic competence:

> The principles of narrative performance are not limited to any language, cultural tradition or area, but rather are universally human. We must imagine children as being born with the capacity to acquire mastery of such form. Local circumstance will determine the particular groupings acquired—two and four, three and five, or some other. Local circumstances will also condition the degree of mastery acquired. As with grammar, so with discourse: not everyone has access to all that has come to be done with it, or is given encouragement to extend its range. . . . When texts come from a culture grounded in oral tradition and a narrative view of life, it is not surprising to find text after text that shows rewarding artistry. (Hymes 1987, iii)

Indeed, Hymes (1992, 50) explicitly claims that the formal structures revealed by verse analysis "involve competence. It is a competence that probably is largely out of awareness, like the competence that enables us to deploy complexities of syntax we could not ourselves analyze."

As a heuristic, the format I propose may prove useful as a research tool because it deals not in abstractions of narratable content (onset, ongoing, outcome) arranged in a numerically regimented rhetorical scaffolding (i.e., verse structures based on pattern numbers). Rather, it highlights explicit distinctions between speech-event modalities grounded in language-universal principles: mechanisms enabling direct and indirect quotation exist in every language, along with *verba dicendi*. In speech communities undergoing language shift and other forms of sociolinguistic transformation, quotation can become a crucially important resource in negotiating the interpersonal politics of language "choice" (see Moore 1988, 1993, for development of this point).

To segment or resegment a narrative into lines, the smallest unit of narrative verse analysis, Hymes relied heavily on particles translatable into English as 'now', 'and then', etc., and on the principle of one verb (or predicate) per line; thus, narrative structure at the level of the (Hymesian) line devolves upon a chunk of language exactly coextensive with a proposition—the foundation of truth-functional semantics in a long European (and classical) tradition of philosophical discussion of language. For the grouping of lines into verses and stanzas, Hymesian verse analysis relies on summaries of narratable content, employing a technique clearly inspired by the modernist literary theories of Cleanth Brooks and Robert Penn Warren—"exposition, complication, climax, denouement" (Brooks and Warrren 1949)—a debt that Hymes acknowledges in many places and creatively explores (e.g., Hymes 1981, 106, 225).[3] The larger units that Hymes calls scenes are clearly determined on the basis of the classical (European) ideal of unity of time, place, and participants.

Rendering the denotational content of a narrative text as a repeating pattern or (to use a visual metaphor) an all-over design akin to a Navajo rug or a Klikitat basket captures one dimension of aesthetic form;[4] my argument here is that this view, while grounded in verbal structures that are perfectly patent, turns out to be incomplete. Insofar as we wish to move beyond the idea that we are dealing with a literature realized in oral performance, we need to see how poetic structures in discourse not only emerge in contexts of verbal interaction, but also help to (re)shape those contexts in particular ways. We need, in other words, a transcription format that enables us to represent on the page these situated aspects of poetic form that unfold in "the interaction order" (Goffman 1983).

The positive proposal is that we should, as a first approximation, attempt to organize our presentations of the texts "on the page" to reflect the way that narrators and their interlocutors deftly shift their footings (Goffman 1981) during a storytelling encounter, both with respect to each other and with respect to the story being told. We need to capture these indexical dimensions of the event-bound functionality of speech, because they reveal another dimension of poetic patterning. The ethical and political entailments of this alternative proposal include a sustained attention to the ethnographic encounter as a cultural episode in its own right—an orientation articulated early on (before "verse analysis") by Hymes himself, most notably in "Breakthrough into Performance" (Hymes [1975] 1981), and explored further by Tedlock (1983), Richard Bauman and Charles L. Briggs (2003), and many others.

Finally, what of ethnopoetics as a literary and cultural movement? If, as seems to be the case, it was at least in part an effort to destabilize or subvert certain conventional pieties of the literary establishment through the introduction of the verbal arts of ethnic and racial "others" (in translation), then perhaps it should be studied alongside the development of World Music (Feld 2000) and the emergence into the global art market of Australian Aboriginal painting (Myers 2002).

Jerome Rothenberg, the coiner of the term *ethnopoetics*, explains in a 2009 interview his own view that ethnopoetics

> is not a way of making poetry, but rather a way of talking about poetry, both the practice and the theory of poetry, as it exists in different cultures, with a certain emphasis on cultures without writing or in which oral poetry and poetics seemed to be dominant. *And all of this was as much of a challenge to a conservative poetics as was the work of the most radical experimenters among us. It also tied to the quest for "a primary human potential" by allowing us to start with a serious search across the spectrum of cultures.*

The time may be ripe for the kind of reconsideration and critical analysis proposed here for ethnopoetics as an intellectual, political, and poetic project. Ethnobotany, for example, has assumed a new kind of importance in the contemporary moment, especially insofar as it now aims not only to offer an account of how the natives (incorrectly) interpret the natural world, but also to demonstrate how such "Traditional Environmental Knowledge" (TEK) can help "us" make discoveries that may lead to scientific (or pharmaceutical) breakthroughs.

And so the prefix *ethno-* is not merely a mark of irreducible cultural difference, but a positive source of value for a whole set of rather differently positioned observers and experts: linguists, poets, musicians—and now, biologists. A long Western artistic and now scientific tradition of finding (or creating) value in the *ethno-* seems to emerge again and again at the intersection of similar cultural concerns, albeit at different social and cultural "sites." Many of these concerns, for example, coalesce in the discourse of language *endangerment* (e.g., Hill 2002; Moore 2006; Moore et al. 2011)—a term that again cuts across the linguistic-cultural-biological divide.

Reinventing ethnopoetics along the lines suggested here entails recognizing that we are dealing with verbal genres that are being transformed under conditions of language shift—and that we have been all along (as the quote from Jacobs above suggests). Lucinda Smith wasn't "doing" (performing) myths for me, she was telling me stories (*idwáča*). Ethnopoetics reinvented would recognize that there is another layer or modality of poetic patterning beyond the level of denotational text, one that inheres in the kind of recurring yet orderly shifts of footing that characterize Mrs. Smith's narrative style. We need an approach to speech genres in transformation that allows us to represent on the page the way that narrators and their interlocutors navigate among speech-event modalities and role-fractions in story-telling events. This alternation of footings, grounded in three distinct but overlapping participation frameworks, is crossed or overlain by an alternation between two languages: one language on its way out, the other on its way in.

Lucinda Smith was bracingly unsentimental about all of this. Untouched by the identity politics that was just then reshaping local consciousness of ancestral languages at Warm Springs, placing them in a regime of value mediated by culture and heritage, she simply said that she stopped speaking Wasco when she realized that there was nobody left to talk to. "I'm the Last of the Mohicans, I guess," she once remarked with a sardonic grin.

Acknowledgments

This essay originated as an invited contribution to the panel "Ethno-poetics, Narrative Inequality, and Voice: On the Legacy of Dell Hymes," held at the Annual Meeting of the American Anthropological Association in Montreal on November 18, 2011. I'm grateful to the panel organizers, Paul V. Kroskrity and Anthony K. Webster, for their kind invitation; to the discussants, Charles Briggs and Richard Bauman, for their very useful comments; and to the audience on that occasion for their questions and comments. Some of this material was again presented on March 2, 2013, to a group of graduate students in the Faculty of Humanities, University of Copenhagen; I thank the students and my hosts on that occasion—J. Normann Jørgensen, Martha Sif Karrebaek, Lian Malai Madsen, and Janus Møller—for much stimulating discussion. The current version has benefited greatly from extensive written commentaries by Jef Van der Aa and James Slotta, and from an extremely helpful eleventh-hour intervention from Nancy Hornberger. The comments of an anonymous referee for the *Journal of Folklore Research* and the patience and support of its editor, Jason Baird Jackson, have been a great help. Errors and infelicities that remain are my sole responsibility.

Notes

1. Field recording of Michael Silverstein, January 6, 1972; I thank Silverstein for generously granting me access to his field materials.
2. Cf. Silverstein 1984, 147–52.
3. The literary critic Kenneth Burke (e.g., 1925) loomed much larger in Hymes's intellectual (and personal) life than did Brooks and Warren, as is well known. A fuller treatment would address the impact of Burke's ideas on Hymes's ethnopoetics more generally, and on his development of the "onset/ongoing/outcome" scheme in particular.
4. See, for example, the "profiles" that Hymes attached to his verse analyses of later years.

References Cited

Bakhtin, Mikhail. (1934–35) 1981. "Discourse in the Novel." In *The Dialogic Imagination*, edited by Michael Holquist, 259–422. Austin: University of Texas Press.
Başgöz, İlhan. 1986. "Digression in Oral Narrative: A Case Study of Individual Remarks by Turkish Romance Tellers." *Journal of American Folklore* 99 (391): 5–23.
Bauman, Richard. 1977. *Verbal Art as Performance*. Prospect Heights, IL: Waveland.
Bauman, Richard, and Charles L. Briggs. 2003. *Voices of Modernity: Language Ideologies and the Politics of Inequality*. Cambridge: Cambridge University Press.
Blommaert, Jan. 2009. "On Hymes: Introduction." *Text & Talk* 29 (3): 241–43.
Boas, Franz. 1894. *Chinook Texts*. Bureau of American Ethnology, Bulletin 20. Washington, DC: US Government Printing Office.
———. 1901. *Kathlamet Texts*. Bureau of American Ethnology, Bulletin 26. Washington, DC: US Government Printing Office.
Brooks, Cleanth, and Robert Penn Warren. 1949. *Modern Rhetoric*. New York: Harcourt, Brace.
Burke, Kenneth. 1925. "Psychology and Form." *The Dial* 79:34–46.

Feld, Steven. 2000. "A Sweet Lullaby for World Music." *Public Culture* 12 (1): 145–71.

French, David. 1958. "Cultural Matrices of Chinookan Non-casual Language." *International Journal of American Linguistics* 24 (4): 258–63.

Goffman, Erving. 1981. "Footing." In *Forms of Talk*, 124–61. Philadelphia: University of Pennsylvania Press.

———. 1983. "The Interaction Order." *American Sociological Review* 48 (1): 1–17.

Hill, Jane. 2002. "'Expert Rhetorics' in Advocacy for Endangered Languages: Who Is Listening, and What Do They Hear?" *Journal of Linguistic Anthropology* 12 (2): 119–33.

Hymes, Dell. 1959. "Myth and Tale Titles of the Lower Chinook." *Journal of American Folklore* 72 (284): 139–45.

———. 1962. "The Ethnography of Speaking." In *Anthropology and Human Behavior*, edited by Thomas Gladwin and William C. Sturtevant, 13–53. Washington, DC: Anthropological Society of Washington.

———. 1964. "Toward Ethnographies of Communication." *American Anthropologist* 66 (6.2): 1–34.

———. 1966. "Two Types of Linguistic Relativity (with Examples from Amerindian Ethnography)." In *Sociolinguistics*, edited by William Bright, 114–67. The Hague: Mouton.

———, ed. 1972. *Reinventing Anthropology*. New York: Pantheon.

———. (1975) 1981. "Breakthrough into Performance." In *"In Vain I Tried to Tell You": Essays in Native American Ethnopoetics*, 79–141. Philadelphia: University of Pennsylvania Press.

———. 1977. "Discovering Oral Performance and Measured Verse in American Indian Narrative." *New Literary History* 8 (3): 431–57.

———. 1981. *"In Vain I Tried to Tell You": Essays in Native American Ethnopoetics*. Philadelphia: University of Pennsylvania Press.

———. 1987. "A Note on Ethnopoetics and Sociolinguistics." *Working Papers in Educational Linguistics* 3 (2): i–xxi. http://www.gse.upenn.edu/wpel/sites/gse.upenn.edu.wpel/files/archives/v3/v3n2Hymes.pdf.

———. 1992. "Helen Sekaquaptewa's 'Coyote and the Birds': Rhetorical Analysis of a Hopi Coyote Story." *Anthropological Linguistics* 34 (1–4): 45–72.

Jacobs, Melville. 1958. *Clackamas Chinook Texts.* Vol 1. Indiana University Research Center in Anthropology, Folklore, and Linguistics, Publication 8. Bloomington: Indiana University Research Center in Anthropology, Folklore, and Linguistics.

———. 1959. *The Content and Style of an Oral Literature. Clackamas Chinook Myths and Tales*. Viking Fund Publications in Anthropology, No. 26. Chicago: University of Chicago Press.

Jakobson, Roman. (1957) 1990. "Shifters, Verbal Categories, and the Russian Verb." In *On Language,* edited by Linda R. Waugh and Monique Monville-Burston, 386–92. Cambridge, MA: Harvard University Press.

Kroskrity, Paul V. 1985. "Growing with Stories: Line, Verse, and Genre in an Arizona Tewa Text." *Journal of Anthropological Research* 41 (2): 183–99.

Moore, Robert. 1988. "Lexicalization vs. Lexical Loss in Wasco-Wishram Language Obsolescence." *International Journal of American Linguistics* 54 (4): 453–68.

————. 1993. "Performance Form and the Voices of Characters in Five Ver-
    sions of the Wasco Coyote Cycle." In *Reflexive Language: Reported Speech and
    Metapragmatics*, edited by John A. Lucy, 213–40. Cambridge: Cambridge
    University Press.

————. 2006. "Disappearing, Inc.: Ways of Writing in the Politics of Access to
    'Endangered Languages.'" *Language & Communication* 26:296–315.

————. 2009. "From Performance to Print, and Back: Ethnopoetics as Social
    Practice in Alice Florendo's Corrigenda to 'Raccoon and His Grandmother.'"
    Text & Talk 29 (3): 295–324.

Moore, Robert, Sari Pietikainen, and Jan Blommaert. 2011. "Counting the
    Losses: Numbers as the Language of Language Endangerment." *Studies in
    Sociolinguistics* 4 (1): 1–26.

Myers, Fred R. 2002. *Painting Culture: The Making of an Aboriginal High Art*. Durham,
    NC: Duke University Press.

Quasha, George. 1976. "The Age of the Open Secret: A Writing Piece on Ethno-
    poetics, the Other Tradition, and Social Transformation." *Alcheringa/
    Ethnopoetics* 2 (2): 65–77.

Reisman, Karl. 1974. "Contrapuntal Conversations in an Antiguan Village." In
    Explorations in the Ethnography of Speaking, edited by Richard Bauman and Joel
    Sherzer, 110–24. Cambridge: Cambridge University Press.

Rothenberg, Jerome. 2009. "The Cream City Interview, Part One: Ethnopoetics,
    Artaud & Cruelty, McClure & Chomsky, Paul Celan, etc." January 4. Interview
    by Chad Faries and Brent Gohde. Online at http://poemsandpoetics.blogspot
    .com/2009/01/cream-city-interview-part-one.html. Originally published in
    The Cream City Review 25 (1–2), Milwaukee, Summer 2001.

Sapir, Edward. 1907. "Preliminary Report on the Language and Mythology of the
    Upper Chinook." *American Anthropologist* (new series) 9 (3): 533–44.

————. 1909. *Wishram Texts*. Publications of the American Ethnological Society,
    2. Leiden: Late E. J. Brill.

Silverstein, Michael. 1984. "The Culture of Language in Chinookan Narrative
    Texts; or, On Saying that . . . in Chinook." In *Grammar Inside and Outside the
    Clause*, edited by Johanna Nichols and Anthony C. Woodbury, 132–71. Cam-
    bridge: Cambridge University Press.

————. 1996. "The Secret Life of Texts." In *Natural Histories of Discourse*, edited
    by Michael Silverstein and Greg Urban, 81–105. Chicago: University of Chi-
    cago Press.

————. 2010. "Dell Hathaway Hymes." Obituary. *Language* 86 (4): 933–39.

Tedlock, Dennis. 1983. *The Spoken Word and the Work of Interpretation*. Philadelphia:
    University of Pennsylvania Press.

ROBERT MOORE received a BA in Anthropology from Reed College
(Portland, OR) and a PhD in Anthropology and Linguistics from the
University of Chicago. He is a Lecturer in Educational Linguistics at
the Graduate School of Education, University of Pennsylvania.

2   The Patterning of Style: Indices of Performance through Ethnopoetic Analysis of Century-Old Wax Cylinders

ETHNOPOETICS IS PREDICATED on the understanding that form and content are so intertwined that it is impossible to disentangle one from the other. Ethnopoetic analysis thus requires learning the grammatical structures of a story's original language in order to carry out the necessary close reading of the text. One cannot approach anything like a full analysis of a story without attempting to understand person marking, the tense-mode-aspect system, or other basic grammatical forms and relations in the language of origin. Franz Boas certainly understood this axiom, as is clear from his insistence on the publication of texts in the original language with interlinear glosses as well as free translations. Dell Hymes moved beyond the crib of Boasian linguistics with an attention to quality translations (1981, 2003). I use *translations* in the plural because the movements are across several frames simultaneously: from one lexico-grammatical frame to another, from one cultural frame to another, and from an oral frame to a written one. The three translations of code, context, and mode are intertwined, of course, as form and content are inseparable. Commentary and criticism of Hymesian ethnopoetics has tended to dwell on the last frame shift—from speech to written verse organized by threes and fives or twos and fours. Translation is more than just choosing the right words or rendering an exotic tongue into English with the right effect. Hymes's work demonstrates that translation is both possible and desirable.

Hymes consistently argued that the representation of oral narratives on the page in lines, verses, stanzas, and scenes (and sometimes larger units as well) was important in order to index a performative competence rarely conscious in the mind of the performer, but nonetheless real and present in the organization of the text. Writing is a visual medium of language, and thus one should pay attention to the visual presentation of the words on a page if one is going to write previously "invisible" oral narratives. Hymes's work with mute texts recorded by Edward Sapir, Melville Jacobs, and others has led critics to argue that his ethnopoetic theory is ill suited to recorded materials; they suggest that acoustic paralinguistic elements such as pause, intonation, loudness, voice quality, etc., are more appropriate for indicating to the translator a strophic poetic organization without recurrent patterns (e.g. Tedlock 1983, 55–61).[1] However, the work of Virginia Hymes (e.g., 1987, 1994, 1995) and experiments such as those by William Bright (1979) belie such criticism of Hymes's ethnopoetics of measured verse. With reference to my own work on Koryak oral narratives recorded onto wax cylinders during winter 1900–1901, I argue that ethnopoetic analysis provides the best vehicle for capturing performative acoustic qualities. Below I discuss two Koryak storytellers outstanding for their dynamic and lively performative qualities, and I show that ethnopoetic versification can index not only recurrent patterns, but also body movements and gestures. In the conclusion I suggest that Hymesian ethnopoetics is best thought of as political activism through translation. Rather than maligned as an obscure theory or tedious method, Hymes's approach should be seen as anthropolitical linguistics, a method that incorporates a theory of language and a theory of culture more sophisticated than most people realize.

Boasian Attention to Oral Literature

My interest in Koryak oral narratives is rooted in a Boasian appreciation for the value of literature in understanding culture—whether my own or one very alien to me. In his early programmatic essay "The Aims of Ethnology," Boas ([1888] 1940, 634) was already asserting that "every primitive people has had a long history"—an insight he gained from careful attention to the stories he collected from Native Americans. The essay was published about ten years after his participant-observation work in Baffinland, where he learned about Inuit lifeways and, in particular, Inuit perceptions of the ice and land (Cole 1999). By then he had already shifted to his (in)famous method of text gathering, working in British Columbia and Washington State to record texts from elder men and women who could talk about the old days and relate myths and legends.

Boas's theory of culture is connected to the identification of patterns observed in texts and material artifacts. For Boas, the culture of Native Americans was found to a large degree in oral texts; thus, he believed, fieldworkers should write down the words of knowledgeable Indians and produce text-artifacts (Darnell 1998, 279–81). The production of text-artifacts (henceforth just *texts*) was part of a theoretically motivated methodology that Boas developed and insisted upon for Jesup Expedition fieldworkers (Berman 1996; Boas 1911; Vakhtin 2001).[2] These texts served multiple purposes for Boas, and it was crucial that the texts "preserve for future times a truthful picture" through a careful rendition of the speech upon paper ([1907] 1974). He was after a recording of the phonetics, lexicon, and grammar of undocumented languages; he wanted to inscribe an oral tradition into a literary one; and he wanted an objectification of cultural patterns for further analysis and comparison (Stocking 1992). These text "objects" were by and large transcriptions of folklore and oral literature (Jacknis 1996).

One of the many points of agreement between Dennis Tedlock's (2006) work and that of Dell Hymes (2003, 72) is the importance of publishing these texts using ethnopoetic analysis. Even those critical of Boas's text collecting admit the importance of these texts for understanding the cultures of the North Pacific (e.g., Harkin 2001, 94). Every culture has authors and poets who are recognized as being particularly adept with language, metaphor, and storytelling. The literature they produce is the foundation of the humanities and required study for anyone interested in those cultures. Boas believed (and I agree) that oral cultures needed linguists and folklorists to transcribe oral arts in order to preserve that artistry and offer access to a wider public. In his 1905 letter to William H. Holmes, then director of the Bureau of American Ethnology (BAE), Boas ([1905] 1974, 122) stressed the documentary importance of the text:

> I do not think that anyone would advocate the study of antique civilizations or, let me say, of the Turks or the Russians, without a thorough knowledge of their languages and of the literary documents in these languages; and contributions not based on such material would not be considered as adequate.

This was part of an argument for supporting the publication of original texts with linguistic analysis and translation. In this particular instance, he was sharing John Swanton's frustration that Holmes had agreed to publish only fourteen of Swanton's texts. This documentary function of the anthropologist was so important to Boas that he stated clearly, "I let this kind of work take precedence over practically everything else, knowing it is the foundation of all future researches" ([1905] 1974, 123).[3] Just because Haida and Koryak storytellers did not write was no cause to prejudge them as inferior to Homer or Sophocles. I believe that it is impossible to make any significant judgments or comparisons with literature from other cultures without first transcribing the performances of Koryak storytellers, and I agree with Boas's position that the most serious study requires knowledge of the original language; thus, publication of transcriptions remains essential. Unfortunately, these "performances" published in Boasian text collections were usually tediously slow sessions in which storytellers dictated to a barely or noncomprehending linguist-scribe. Boas and his students were aware of the shortcomings of dictation, but it was an important and productive method for writing down oral performances nonetheless (Boas 1925, 491–92; Darnell 1992; Stocking 1992, 90–91). He did occasionally take advantage of the most advanced sound recording technology available to him, and he mentions phonograph recordings as one way to compensate for the distortions of dictation (Boas 1914, 376; Stocking 1992, 91).

Waldemar Bogoras and Waldemar Jochelson were hired for the Jesup North Pacific Expeditions in northeast Asia to collect materials and artifacts from the Chukchi and Koryak, and they received detailed instructions and training by Boas in New York before starting their work (Vakhtin 2001). Bogoras had lived about a decade among Chukchi speakers and had considerable knowledge of the language, while Jochelson had been exiled to the Kolyma River to the west and had lived in closer contact with Yukaghir people. Since Chukchi is similar to Koryak, the two men agreed that Bogoras would be responsible for all the linguistic investigations of Chukotka and Kamchatka together. Bogoras collected texts in Chukchi, Koryak, and Itelmen. He published a grammar of Chukchi that simultaneously described all three languages; the similarities between Koryak and Chukchi are clear. Bogoras's (1910) *Chukchi Mythology* has nearly 150 pages of narratives, songs, and other folkloric materials in interlinear translation with the original Chukchi, followed by fifty pages of narratives presented only in English. The slim collection *Koryak Texts* (Bogoras 1917) has only 106 pages of Koryak language material with translations, although this is followed by a helpful glossary, a feature missing from *Chukchi Mythology*. Jochelson's (1908) ethnography *The Koryak* is dominated by 250 pages of Koryak narratives and their analysis, although only English summaries are presented. Boas was disappointed by Jochelson's folklore methods, as he used a field translator to write down the stories (presumably) in Russian as they were being told in Koryak.[4] Boas's low opinion of Jochelson's method is clear as he continues his letter to William Holmes (part of a plea for the BAE to fund the publication of all of John Swanton's Haida and Tlingit texts):

> We can accept undigested collections of translated traditions only in cases, where for one reason or other the collection of the original was impossible. I have permitted collections of this kind, for instance the Koryak, because on account of the remoteness of the tribe, a full collection of traditions in the original would have required years and more money than I had. I think, however, that in our own country a collection of translated traditions is not up to the standard of excellence that we must demand for the publications of our best institutions. (Boas [1905] 1974, 123)

I share Boas's frustration. Jochelson's notes have been lost, so we do not even know how the published versions compare with the versions noted down in the field. When I took photocopies of *The Koryak* (Jochelson 1908) and *Koryak Texts* (Bogoras 1917) to Kamchatka, some Koryak speakers familiar with the Latin alphabet could read the original Koryak in the latter and enjoy the stories, many of which are no longer told in Kamchatka. I have not been able to translate Jochelson's English versions of Koryak tales into Russian, unfortunately. As most Koryaks have shifted to speaking Russian, these collected texts have been mostly ignored in their land of origin. Recording oral literature and publishing facing-page translations are the scholarly interventions these source communities value the most. During my postdoctoral research trips to Kamchatka in 2001 and 2011, when I was working mostly on mythology and ritual practice, people told me that they wished more anthropologists and folklorists would document just that.[5] Some scholars may still deride such work as salvage ethnography supported by "mere antiquarian sentiment," as A. R. Radcliffe-Brown put it. I rather side with Edward Sapir and his rejoinder that such texts are "priceless linguistic document[s]" (in Darnell 1992, 41).

In "Stylistic Aspects of Primitive Literature," an essay published in 1925 in the *Journal of American Folklore*, Boas lays out his theory of anthropology as a discipline of the humanities. While he operated with some ethnocentric assumptions about poetry and prose, his insights into the qualities of oral narratives are worth noting, as Hymes discussed in his essay "Boas on the Threshold of Ethnopoetics" (2003). I agree with Hymes that Boas is wrong in his assumption that song is poetry and that narrative, even oral narrative, is therefore prose. Hymes (2003, 29–30) points out that Boas "was an empiricist who had to overcome the ways in which cultural assumptions could distort perception and interpretation." One great assumption that Boas overcame was that Indians, and "primitives" in general, do not have literature and verbal arts, let alone poetry of any kind. I would like to note that Boas ([1925] 1940, 491) does make the observation that Native American oral narratives differ considerably in form and style from "the printed literary style": the former are "based on the art of oral delivery and [are], therefore, more closely related to modern oratory." The twentieth century saw the dramatic decline of formal oratory and the study of rhetoric as a distinct expressive genre, at least in North American schools.[6] In earlier times, the study of rhetoric was a cornerstone of education, and it explicitly connected Western civilization in Europe and North America to the classical civilizations of Greece and Rome. To claim that Indian tales have patterns of form and style similar to classically trained orators is another example of the typically Boasian assertion that so-called primitive cultures produce works of art that demand the world's attention. Hymes reiterated this point time and again because it still needed (and needs) to be made at the turn of the twenty-first century. Boas ([1925] 1940, 491–92) acknowledged the shortcomings of nonfluent linguists transcribing stories onto paper, resulting in a "crippled version." If we identify shortcomings in Native American literatures, the fault may mostly lie with the anthropologists and linguists inscribing them into notebooks and publishing them in Bureau of American Ethnology bulletins, as Hymes repeatedly points out in his retranslations of Northwest Coast narratives. Still, one should not underestimate the beautiful literature preserved in those publications, waiting only for a sensitive reader to listen to the oratory (Bringhurst 2009, 331–34).

Boas's grand universalizing goal was equally scientific and political. He recognized that a proper understanding of oral narratives required an acknowledgement of the role of individual taste and creativity with traditional patterns. In "Stylistic Aspects of Primitive Literature" and elsewhere, Boas debunked the idea that Native American literature was at a more primitive stage of development, inevitably progressing toward genres and forms found in Europe (like epic or proverb) but absent in Native America. Traditional tales were not unchanging: "Primitive culture is a product of historical development no less than modern civilization" ([1925] 1940, 496–97). Hymes (2003, 11) pushes that legacy forward with clear statements such as his assertion, "Again and again, people whom some whites would have seen only as impoverished and uneducated have been found to be creative and articulate, to have rich minds, minds both retaining stories and continuing to think them." Equally political is Hymes's (2003, 11) argument that such beautiful traditions and examples of great art come from "thoughtful, motivated individuals, seeking narrative adequate to their experience, surviving and renewing." This is an argument that Hymes made for fifty-some years, detailing the narrative artistry of people like Victoria Howard, Charles Cultee, and Louis Simpson. He has many fellow travelers, of course, publishing the oral literature of Native Americans, including Robert Bringhurst (1999), Nora and Richard Dauenhauer (1987, 1990), Brian Swann (1994, 2004), Dennis Tedlock (1972), and Michael Uzendoski and Edith Felicia Calapucha-Tapuy (2012), just to name a few examples. However, Boas's original point that Native Americans and other indigenous people have languages and literatures as good and important as those of any other civilization still needs to be made repeatedly and loudly (Bringhurst 2006, 15–17).

Using All We Have

Hymes cogently argues that his approach to ethnopoetics is not restricted to silent texts, nor is it attentive solely to particles or grammatical patterning, which is why he titled his most programmatic essay "Use All There Is to Use" (2003). Aural qualities of intonation, pause, and other aspects of voice quality from an audio recording can help identify the ethnopoetic shape of a narrative—and while the vast majority of texts produced by Boasian anthropologists do not include audio recording, Boas did encourage the use of audio technologies For instance, he equipped the Jesup Expedition researchers with Edisonphones, a move that reflected Boas's larger interest in music and ethnomusicology and followed from his own use of cutting-edge technology to record 150 wax cylinders of material from British Columbia (Keeling 2001, 279–80). The Edisonophone can be described as the first generation of audio recording technology. It was purely mechanical and (unlike vinyl records) used no amplification. The recording material was delicate, but the apparatus and supplies were smaller and lighter than those needed for photography. The model commonly available in 1900 had a clamp-on cover, giving it the size and appearance of small sewing machine, and each wax cylinder could hold just over three minutes of sound.

Apparently Jochelson and Bogoras took prerecorded cylinders of music to Siberia, for Jochelson (1908, 426–27) reports that

> our phonograph made the most striking impression wherever we went. Often a hundred persons would crowd into the house where we put up our phonograph, and gather around it in a ring. Some of the lads watched the phonograph in action with an interest as intense as if they were about to penetrate the mystery of the box which could utter words and sounds. . . . Naturally, they were especially pleased to hear the box repeat Koryak tales and songs. Of the musical records they liked particularly the reproduction of the xylophone and of negro melodies. They preferred solo to orchestral records. . . . They appreciate a good voice and skill in beating the drum. They will sit and listen for hours to singing accompanied by the drum.

Figure 1 shows a Chukchi man in Marinsky Post (now Anadyr, Chukotka) during one of Bogoras's recording sessions. The man is speaking (or shouting) into the recording trumpet, which is mechanically connected to a steel stylus that carves the sound recording into the soft wax cylinder. The playback apparatus used a bamboo stylus and a shorter and broader trumpet. I quote Jochelson at length because the passage demonstrates the seriousness his Koryak interlocutors gave to the problem of recording sound performances. Even if the men and women whose voices were recorded did not understand the recording technology in terms of wave mechanics, they did appreciate the care needed to achieve a quality recording. It is clear that speakers understood they had to address the box directly while singing a song or telling a story in order for it to record the words and sounds properly. While one of the stories does have very low volume and was spoken very quickly, the other recordings achieved a fair audio quality given the constraints of the technology. The clear sound quality testifies to the performers' interest and cooperation in the recording process.

I first learned about these recordings (Bogoras and Jochelson 1901–2), which are located at the Archives of Traditional Music at Indiana University in Bloomington, as part of my work for Virginia Hymes in her course on Native American languages at the University of Virginia.

FIGURE 1

A Chukchi man records a wax cylinder using an Edisonophone at Mariinsky Post (present-day Anadyr) in 1900. Image #2727 American Museum of Natural History Library.

The project involved combing databases and metabibliographies for all extant sources documenting, describing, and analyzing Koryak language. The recordings are controlled by the American Museum of Natural History (as custodian of all results of the Jesup Expedition), so after securing permission from AMNH via fax and sending my check to Bloomington, I received an audiocassette copy of the ten-inch reel recording of the nineteen wax cylinders with Koryak material. Thirteen of the cylinders record songs, some clearly by shamans (and one or two powerful ones, according to people in Kamchatka).[7] The other six cylinders contain five narratives, one of which is split over two cylinders. This longest story narrates a whale festival sponsored by Amamqut, a primary Koryak culture hero. The language of all the cylinders comes from maritime Koryaks living on the western coast of Penzhina Bay, also called Nymlans, from the word for villager. They call themselves *Koryaks*, but also use the term *Nymylans* to distinguish themselves from reindeer-herding Koryaks traditionally living in the interior areas.[8] When I played the tape for people in Kamchatka, most Koryak speakers in the south and east poorly understood the language of the recording except for a few words. Although several people tried to write down some of the words they understood, I was not able to get a full transcription of the material until I met Nina Nikolaevna and Vasili Borisovich Milgichil, who live in the village of Manily on the northeast corner of Penzhina Bay. Vasili Borisovich is from Paren, and Nina Nikolaevna comes from the village of Mikino (now abandoned), which was on the west coast of Penzhina Bay about halfway between Paren and Manily. Together they embody the two variants of Koryak recorded on these wax cylinders. Nadezhda Mikhailovna Plepova, working as a teacher in the village of Paren in 1998, was also very helpful in checking and correcting the texts in the Paren dialect of Koryak.[9]

The first story I discuss here is spoken in the Paren variant of Nymylan Koryak and the second was recorded in Kamenskoye, which was near the mouth of the Penzhina River not far from present-day Manily.[10] The dialect of Kamenskoye differs slightly from that of Paren and seems to be more or less the same as that from Mikino. The first prominently features a birth (henceforth, "A Man Is Born" from the very clear line *qlavol gaitolen*, "a man is born") and the second is the tale "Amamqut's Whale Festival" (also my title).

"A Man Is Born," by Ki-una (attributed)

As Vasili Borisovich translated "A Man Is Born," he and his wife acknowledged that several of the words are very strange. I have underscored these problematic words in the facing-page translation in the appendix, particularly the verbs translated as "have sores on their ears" and "have dirty hands." The Milgichils and others interpreted the first scene, marked with roman numeral I, as ritual preparation for the birth. Two of the most dangerous times in one's life are as a neonate and immediately after death. At these times one is defenseless against the predation of kalaw (sing. 'kala'), usually invisible and always anthropophagous beings that kill by consuming human souls. A key method of diverting kala and other spirit attacks upon neonates is to talk of shit and other unpleasantries instead of the beautiful new baby. Scene II is the announcement of the birth; scene III is the cutting of the umbilical cord; and the final scene, IV, is the naming of the newborn. Prompted by my interpreters, I understood the story to be a narration of ethnographic custom, a dramatic statement representing common practices surrounding childbirth.

Jochelson (1908, 100) complains that despite women giving birth in two different villages while he and his wife were there, his wife was never invited to attend so "that she might become acquainted with the Koryak methods of midwifery." When I reread his statement after the birth of my first son in 2003, I wondered at the man's crazy presumption that the "natives" would ever want a strange woman lurking voyeuristically during a birth. Nevertheless, he did obtain substantial details of Koryak beliefs and practices surrounding childbirth, naming, and neonatal care of child and mother, undoubtedly from interviews. Although I can find no direct comment by either Jochelson or Bogoras about this recorded birth narrative, it supports Jochelson's ethnographic descriptions.

In interpreting "A Man Is Born," and following the example of Bright (1979) and the teaching of Virginia Hymes (1987, 1994, 1995) and others, I combine an analysis of lexical and grammatical patterning with attention to pause, intonation, and voice quality. I am convinced that oral narratives are best represented on the page as verse. Lines are combined into larger units (verses, stanzas, scenes) following consistent patterns. I mark verses by successive indentations when several lines constitute a single verse. Scenes, acts, and the narratives themselves are defined by the onset of a problem and its eventual resolution. These openings and closings operate at many levels, producing patterns of bracketing and symmetry. These patterns were most likely unconscious in the mind of the storyteller, but they are no less real for their implicitness.

The fascinating thing for me is that this narrative is by no means a straightforward third-person account of a woman giving birth. What we have instead is a three-and-one-third-minute one-woman show. The narrator is theatrical in her performance, with the effect achieved almost entirely through quoted speech. The last line of II.C ("They left, they came up") may or may not be quoted speech. The second line of III.B ("They cut off the cord") is the only line that is clearly not quoted speech. My initial interpretation was that the narrator takes the roles of village women preparing for the birth, the expectant mother, the crying baby, and assorted relatives looking for equipment and attempting to determine the baby's proper name.

In an experiment with Flash digital animation tools, I produced a prototype of an animated text formatted as an ethnopoetic edition of

the transcript with a loose interlinear translation.[11] The animation is
a blue box that appears around a word or phrase as it is pronounced.
When one plays the animation, the audio recording plays and the
reader can see the lines, verses, and stanzas while hearing the sound
of each line as it is performed. Although my execution of the animation file left much to be desired (such as handy play and pause but-
tons!), and an alternative software tool may be more appropriate, it
was a success in demonstrating the possibility of using digital media
to integrate the sound of the performance with Hymes's measured
verse. Most importantly, such a presentation obviates any argument
over obscuring one aspect of the narrative poetics (performative or
measured) in sacrifice to highlighting another. Animated typography
allows one to listen actively to the text as one simultaneously hears the
performance and sees the larger ethnopoetic patterning reflected in
the textual formatting.

"A Man Is Born" is an excellent example of a text in which the
ends of lines index pauses in the performance, although not always.
Parallelism in intonation and repetition of particles are also important in defining some key units, especially stanza B of the first scene.
This story is remarkable for the consistent use of the first-person perspective. There are no verbs of speaking (e.g., "he said"). I dispense
with quotation marks in the transcription and translation because
nearly all of the words are direct speech. The narrative reads more
like a stage script than a story.[12] The common Koryak word *vahayok*
('so then', 'soon'), which always occurs at the beginning of lines and
often marks the start of a verse or stanza, is nowhere to be seen. I rely
on changes in topic to mark the beginnings of stanzas, and scenes are
distinguished by larger shifts in topic. Scene II is marked by the introduction of a new intonation contour, one of calling out, as opposed to
the normal intonation of the first stanza of scene I and the chanting
intonation of stanza I.B.

Scene III is a comedic interlude reminiscent to my mind of the
Three Stooges. It could also be defined as a theme in Albert Lord's
(1960) sense. This scene is also found in the story "Ermine People II"
by Paqa, published by Bogoras (1917) and retranslated in ethnopoetic
form in my "Raven Tales from Kamchatka" (King 2004).[13] The humor
comes from the fact that the knife used to cut the umbilical cord is
one of the most sacred objects in a household. It is literally tied to a
bundle of charms and idols that symbolize all the people born into

that household and that materialize connections among people, generations, and (in the case of reindeer herders) deer. Thus it is hilarious to suggest someone misplacing such a thing and having to look for it by querying a string of people as to its whereabouts. Stanza A in scene III consists of four verses, each identified as a verbal exchange. Stanza B is a final couplet describing the cutting, mostly through direct speech, but with one line of description.

The last scene of the recording, IV, describes an initial attempt to identify the correct name of the newborn. Koryaks believe that ancestors are reincarnated in their descendants. My translators chuckled at the performance in the recording, where the woman alternated between the roles of crying baby and adults attempting to guess his name. Normally the returning ancestor would make his or her identity known to the expectant mother by visiting her in a dream and telling her. Other forms of divination by an expert in such matters were also commonly used then, as they are now. Looking at the baby and guessing resemblances is one method, but as we see here, it is not very effective. The baby's crying shows that the names suggested are incorrect. The cylinder ends before we get the correct name, but I would guess that this is the last scene. This patterning of twos and fours is common to other Koryak narratives I have analyzed (King 2004).

Although my Koryak interpreters understood this story as little more than a theatrical performance of a birth, this scene prompted Richard Bauman (pers. comm.) to suggest a reassessment of the story as another version of "Ermine People" (Bogoras 1917; King 2004; Jochelson 1908, 203–4). The Milgichils and others explained to me that the dancing and insults in scene I are a ritualized account of preparing for a birth, which must not be discussed overtly lest one attract the attention of a soul-eating kala hungry for a vulnerable newborn. Early in my analysis, I noted that the story includes a scene remarkably parallel to one in a story narrated by Paqa from Kamenskoye about Ermine People, where Ermine Woman gives birth (Bogoras 1917, 63–67; King 2004). When I later checked all of the names in this story against those published in *Koryak Texts* (Bogoras 1917), I found none repeated save one—Ermine Man (Imchenemtəlhanak). My interpreters insisted that the names were names and that they did not need translating. Evingto is a common name among Koryaks.[14] When children fall ill, they may have their names changed to something unpleasant, such as Shit-bag, to deceive the sickness-causing kala and get it to give up its attack. Thus it is conceivable for an ordinary human to be called Imchenemtəlhanak, but in "A Man Is Born" this character is the one who has the sacred knife, indicating that it is his household and perhaps even his son that was born. We cannot know if scene I is an exchange between Ermine Woman and Beetle People or Great Raven's people, but it is most likely one or the other, following the pattern of all other instances of the Ermine story published by Bogoras and Jochelson. While discourse surrounding birth is full of circumspection and euphemism, there is no evidence of ritual abuse of the mother. It makes much more sense to understand scene I as abuse by the Beetles or Great Raven's people to get Ermine Woman to go away, although they seem to have regrets at causing hurt feelings in stanza D. In other instances of Ermine People stories, they are driven off by others because they stink. Scene II thus begins with Ermine Woman being called back to help her sister with a cradle. Scene III shows the father cutting the newborn's umbilical cord, and scene IV is cut off before Grandma Ermine can suggest that the newborn is probably her deceased husband reincarnated, a common situation.

The narrator of "A Man Is Born" may very well be Ki-una of Big Itkana. It is clear that the version here (Bogoras and Jochelson 1901–2) is not a recording of Paqa. First of all, the language is in the Paren or (more likely) Itkana dialect, and Paqa was from Kamenskoye. Second, the order of scenes is different. A story presented in *The Koryak* (Jochelson 1908, 203–4), called simply "Ermine People" and told by Ki-una of Big Itkana, has a similar structure. Following that story, scene I of "A Man Is Born" parallels the opening paragraph in which Ermine Woman goes to visit the Beetles and they insult each other while dancing until Ermine Woman cries from hurt feelings. Then she is called back home because her sister gave birth, as in scene II here. Ki-una's story in the 1908 publication differs slightly from "A Man Is Born": the printed version describes Ermine People cooking shit soup (literally) to serve to Great Raven's people, and it also lacks the "where is the knife" routine. However, the published version does include a call for the sharpening stone as we have here; further, the naming scene comes before the umbilical-cord-cutting scene and ends successfully when Old Ermine Woman suggests the name of the boy's grandfather, which the baby agrees to with a laugh (Jochelson 1908, 204).

Itkana is about a half-day's travel south of Paren and those people spoke the same dialect, as did those in the village of Kuel, a half-day's travel north of Paren; if the wax cylinder recording is a separate performance by Ki-una, that would explain the presence of words strange to Vasili Milgichil, who grew up in Paren. Itkana was hit hard by flu epidemics in the early Soviet era and the survivors were soon moved to neighboring Paren, as were residents of Kuel. The unfamiliar words may be more typical of Itkana speech and mark its difference from speech common to Paren. However, this story may also have been recorded in Kuel, as was at least one other story.[15]

Possibly Ki-una is the one who told the story to Jochelson and his translator Vilkhin with great verve. The text published in *The Koryak* (Jochelson 1908) may be the result of Vilkhin adding the verbs of speaking and disambiguating the narrative as he orally interpreted the Koryak to Russian in a way that adds those and other words absent from the cylinder record of "A Man Is Born." We do not know for sure if Jochelson made the Koryak recordings or if Bogoras performed that task. In any case, the narrator of cylinder 4534 (Bogoras and Jochelson 1901–2) is clearly a master storyteller. From Jochelson's account we can assume that she understood what was required of her and that the cylinder could only record short stories. Thus I conclude that the recording is a condensed version of "Ermine People" that Ki-una told to Vilkhin and Jochelson, where the birth of the child and not the interaction with Great Raven's people lies at the core of the narrative.

I could go into much greater detail unpacking the form and content of this narrative performance. Here I want to emphasize two things: the appropriateness of ethnopoetic versification and the artistry of the performer. The parallelism and patterning of different intonations suggest the organization of lines into verses. The theme of "looking for the knife" also lends support for Hymes's (2003, 11) argument that narratives exist beyond performance even as they are emergent through them: "To say that stories exist only in performance is to say that between performances narrators do not think." Perhaps a better way to put the matter is to observe that stories are *manifested* through performances, as we cannot know what is inside people's heads. Most importantly, *this* performer is a masterful actor. She puts on a one-woman show, taking on all the parts. She inhabits the different characters in a forceful and dynamic manner that caused my translators to shift in their chairs following the chanting rhythm of stanza I.B. The pauses do organize the action in this narrative; that is certainly clear, but not always. If one strictly followed pausing as a method for marking lines, the symmetry in I.C would be obscured and the verses in III.A would not be clear. These symmetrical relations were most likely not conscious to the performer, but they are not my invention. The verse patterning in III.A may have been more conscious in the mind of the speaker, as the verses are defined by four dialogic exchanges. In this, we can follow Hymes's attention to literary criticism and acknowledge that texts contain much significant meaning beyond the intentions of the author.

"Amamqut's Whale Festival" by Aqaŋŋaw

The second story I want to discuss is "Amamqut's Whale Festival," recorded on cylinders 4545 and 4546, because it also has remarkably performative qualities, unlike the other four stories recorded (Bogoras and Jochelson 1901–2). Bogoras includes a version of this story in his collection of texts (1917, 45–50). The Koryak woman Aqaŋŋaw in Kamenskoye on the northern shore of Penzhina Bay told this and two other stories published in *Koryak Texts*, and a version of "The Whale Festival" credited to "Aqan" was also published in translation by Jochelson (1908, 265–66).[16] Since all versions of this tale seem to be from Aqaŋŋaw in Kamenskoye and we know from prefatory remarks in Russian that the cylinders were recorded in Kamenskoye, I think it safe to attribute this recording to her with certainty. Bogoras's published transcription of the tale differs in many ways, especially with regard to word order and usage, indicating that it is most likely a retelling dictated either before or after the audio recording. Aqaŋŋaw must have impressed Bogoras considerably, because he continued the story onto a second cylinder. The first cylinder ends in the middle of I.H, as indicated in square brackets, and I designate the following stanza also as I.H because Aqaŋŋaw begins the second cylinder with a line analogous to that beginning I.H on the first cylinder. Thus we see that stanzas are real units; the interrupted narrator resumed her story at the beginning of the stanza that was cut off and not at some other point.

The artistry of Aqaŋŋaw is equal to that of Ki-una, but the form differs considerably. Aqaŋŋaw employs the word *vǝhayok* several times to mark the beginning of a verse, as I found Paqa doing in narratives dictated to Bogoras. Aqaŋŋaw uses a mix of reported speech, quoted speech, and description to advance the story and develop characters. Unique to Aqaŋŋaw's style is frequent use of the word *ǝñŋǝhan* 'thus, so, like that'. My first attempts at versification tried to use it as an initial particle, but the results were a mess. When I thought of it as a final particle to lines, patterns became more regular, although the word clearly occurs in the middle of lines, too. The Milgichils hesitated at first to specify all the occurrences of this and similar words because they thought of them as semantically empty. Vasili Borisovich, in particular, pointed out to me that they were clearly associated with gestures. As I reviewed the transcript over and over again with Nina Nikolaevna, who speaks the relevant variant of Koryak, Vasili Borisovich would sometimes act out the gestures that he imagined Aqaṇṇaw performing as he listened to the audio recording of her voice. He held his arms close to his body with the elbows bent out, gesturing with open palms as if his lower arms were raven wings performing the action in stanza II.B. As he re-acted Aqaṇṇaw's performance, all of us in the room began to laugh. It was hilarious and I deeply regret not videotaping the transcription session to get his marvelous rendition of the story. My point is that Koryaks definitely understand Aqaṇṇaw's narrative to be a dramatic performance, and in this case the gestures are audible through the use of what some folklorists and anthropologists would term "filler" words. In particular, instances of *əñŋəhan* co-occur with a more normal voice intonation and complementary with Aqaṇṇaw's use of character voices. Character enactments of this kind are most noticeable in stanzas I.H and II.B, when Raven Woman is speaking. My translators focused mostly on Aqaṇṇaw's dramatic voice quality, and they would chuckle and imitate her voice quality while we were drinking tea or doing other things.

Although they consciously wanted to dismiss *əñŋəhan* as not meaning anything, this word functions as a lexical deictic to the drama as much as the character voice indexes characters. If we look at lines 55, 63, 81, 86, and 88, we see that use of the word *əñŋəhan* serves to intensify a description of action, locating the narrative in a very present "here and now" of performance in the storyworld.[17] Following comments from Nina Nikolaevna and Vasili Borisovich, *əñŋəhan* most likely co-occurs with gestures by the narrator. She is acting out stabbing a dog in the heart, tying things down, and so on as she speaks the word *əñŋəhan*. It serves as a metadeictic in this transcription. It points toward gestures that point toward imaginary objects that exist only in the storyworld. Transcribing these "meaningless" words is important for recovering key features of the performance that make the story come alive and immerse narrator and audience in the storyworld.

The concept of "somatic poetry" (Uzendoski 2008; Uzendoski and Calapucha-Tapuy 2012) has been useful for drawing my attention to the corporeal aspects of storytelling for both performer and audience. Somatic poetry is a way of understanding the bodily inhabitation of a story. My problem is how to understand deictic words that native speakers would rather throw away than actively consider. These deictics index the bodily gestures and other performative qualities in the audio recordings originally made on wax cylinders. The indexical meaning of these deictics is powerful but not fully conscious: I witnessed Vasili Borisovich's embodiment and reenactment of Aqaṇṇaw's story during his repeated listening and retelling, despite his insistence that the deictic words were unimportant to the task of transcription. The story, and thus indirectly the long-dead storyteller, came to inhabit his body through careful listening. These stories can come alive and inhabit the body of anyone with the skill and patience to listen carefully—and they will be rewarded, no shaman required (Bringhurst 1999).[18]

The patterning of the verbal indices of the narrator's patterned gestures and other performative actions in these tales fit together with other aspects of ethnopoetic patterning, such as the use of words that mean 'and then', changes of topic, and grammatical parallelism. While particles often mark the beginning of lines, these gestural deictics often mark the ends of lines. In Aqaṇṇaw's case the somatic indices appear in the guise of words and particles that have little or no semantic meaning. Hymes anticipated this idea in a 1995 classroom presentation and discussion of Deaf storytelling, where the transcript of measured verse included parenthetical notes of gestures by the ASL storyteller that some might have ignored as "nonsemantic." In one scene the storyteller repeatedly tugged at his waistband as his entire body enacted one character for just a second at a time at regular intervals (see also Farnell 1990, 2009; Sutton-Spence 2010). I suggest the term *somatic index* to refer to a patterned connection of verbal elements and gestural elements that work to structure a narrative, such as those presented with the Koryak word *əñ̩əhan*.

Conclusion

Boas's attention to indigenous literature was part of his project to capture a larger cultural context, and there is clearly a lot of fascinating ethnographic material embedded in the silly, farcical stories I've discussed here. A Boasian exegesis of either would go on for dozens of pages, explaining the cosmological, mythic, ritual, and social facts implied in the characters and their actions.[19] Here I have focused on the aesthetic and performative aspects of these two stories to highlight the individual artistry of the two women who recorded them onto wax cylinders in the winter of 1900. I often heard Hymes quip that linguistics is too important for anthropologists to ignore and language is too important to leave to the linguists. I think he would agree that the same is true for literature and poetry.

Like his friend and classmate Gary Snyder, Dell Hymes studied literature and anthropology in equal measure as an undergraduate. Snyder has penned significant works of poetry, philosophy, and cultural commentary based on his personal experiences among different peoples of the world. While not always overtly political, Snyder's poetry and prose sing of the beauty of ordinary life, everyday experiences, and values of common people who are otherwise usually invisible. Hymes's oeuvre likewise stems from youthful experience with Oregon Indians, loggers, and farmers. As Jan Blommaert (2006, 2009) has argued, Hymes's work at the juncture of anthropology and linguistics has been concerned with language in use in a way that highlights the social injustice and power differentials that stand behind and are reproduced by patterns of language uses and evaluations of a language and its speakers.

In his teaching and conversations, Hymes made clear that he saw his work as a direct and logical progression of a line of inquiry initiated by Boas and continued by Sapir. His legacy has been to take forward the Boasian call to study the literature of Native Americans and document other oral artistic forms (Boas [1907] 1974, 1925; Stocking 1974). This essay builds upon a theory of voice lying at the intersection of obscure linguistics and activist politics, providing an example of anthropolitical linguistics, to use the term coined by Anna Zentella (1997). The linguistics seems obscure because it entails a close reading of little-known languages such as Clackamas Chinook, Sahaptin, and Koryak. The work is political because simply taking verbal art in these languages as serious literature is to challenge the hegemony of languages represented in the work of artists like Byron, Borges, and Blok. Hymes's legacy for anthropologists is the lesson that a humanistic approach, sharing more with literary criticism and poetry translation than with new kinship studies or political agency theory, is necessarily one of radical activism for people who are most often at the bottom of any economic, social, or political hierarchy: the peoples of the Fourth World.

Hymes's work is not in vain, since many of us have received the message. Part of the problem in convincing others of the value of Hymes's method lies in the difficulty of the methods of comparative literature, as Lord (1960) identified in his work on Serbo-Croatian epics. A close reading of literature requires knowledge of the original language, and this is hard. It is hardest with languages such as Kiksht or Koryak, which have few speakers; those who do remain are far away from the critics and command a dwindling audience. Nonetheless, increasing numbers of scholars in folklore, anthropology, and literature are taking an active interest in serious criticism of the oral literature of indigenous peoples. I was delighted to contribute to a recent edited collection of literary criticism that considers literatures of the circumpolar north (Langgård and Thisted 2011). That work and the collection of which this essay is a part show that we can learn much about Literature from the careful study of oral storytelling. Printing is a prestige mode of discourse, to be sure, and I follow Hymes's belief that adapting oral literature to a prestige mode of discourse is both an analytic exercise worth undertaking in order to aid our (anglophone, but also russophone) understanding, and a political move to empower people often oppressed (partly) through association with disparaged ways of speaking.

Hymes (2003, 323) wrote that there is "a need for anthropologists and folklorists to understand their field as philology—to return to manuscript sources, to discover what has been excluded, rearranged, normalized, misunderstood," but he did not teach ethnopoetics as philology. He taught it as literature, cross-coded as an English class and taken by African American students in Charlottesville in much higher numbers than anthropology and linguistics classes typically were, at least when I was at the University of Virginia in the mid-1990s. The sound recordings studied here serve as the "field notebooks" that lie behind publications such as Bogoras's *Koryak Texts* (1917). As Hymes taught and wrote, examining field recordings (whether on cylinder or in a notebook) reveals much that was lost in the first publishing process.

The ethnopoetically formatted transcripts of the two stories discussed here (see appendices) reveal many indices of somatic and performative patterns that contribute to a richer understanding of the tales and their tellers. Repeated chant or nonsense words, the use of apparently "empty" deictics, and many of the pauses made between words fit into a regular patterning dominated by couplets and sets of four. The use of twos and fours dominates all the oral narratives in Koryak I have analyzed so far. Kamchatka in 1900 is far in time and space from the Amazon in 2000, yet Uzendoski and Calapucha-Tapuy (2012) and I have found that somatic poetry is best represented on the page in Hymesian measured verse. Hymes's theory of ethnopoetics is just as relevant to the full and proper understanding of audio- and video-recorded oral narratives as it is to the philological reinterpretation of silent texts.

Acknowledgments

Research for this essay was funded in part by the following sponsors: Summer Scholars Fellowship, California State University, Chico; Summer Stipend, National Endowment for the Humanities (USA); Principal's Interdisciplinary Fund, University of Aberdeen; Research Grant, Carnegie Trust for the Universities of Scotland (UK). I learned much from Hymes in his graduate seminars and as I worked on my master's and doctoral theses. I am delighted that this essay is part of a special collection honoring his legacy, and I would like to thank Anthony Webster and Paul Kroskrity for the invitation to participate in the 2011 American Anthropological Association (AAA) session that was its genesis. I also want to thank Richard Bauman, Jan Blommaert, and an anonymous reviewer for helpful comments on previous drafts of this essay. The appropriateness of using measured verse to format and organize transcriptions and translations of recorded oral narratives is not a lesson I initially learned from Dell, however; I learned it from Virginia Hymes. In 2009 I co-organized with Eve Danziger a panel at the Philadelphia AAA meetings in honor of Virginia's teaching. It was there that I first presented my analysis of "A Man Is Born" and demonstrated the proof-of-concept for digitally animate text. Thus, this essay honors Virginia's legacy, as well as Dell's.

Appendix

"A Man Is Born," possibly by Ki-una

Patterning of style in Koryak wax cylinder #4534 (Bogoras and Jochelson 1901–2)

I.A. Məhayŋačeyła.
　　Təlalagahas.
　　Mey ełhaw mətyallamək.
　　Mənhayŋačellyamək.

　B. Unn, hot! hot! hot! hot! hot! hot!
　　　Inčew–we eł–aw–we !
　　　　kak–veł–ŋa–vo !
　　　Inčew–we eł–aw–we !
　　　　čan–əʕat–məñ–gi–ŋa–vo !
　　　Unn, hot! hot! hot! hot! hot!
　　　Inčew–we eł–aw–we !
　　　　kakek–məł–ve–ŋa–vo !
　　　Unn, hot! hot! hot! hot! hot!
　　　Inčew–we eł–aw–we !
　　　　čeñʕek–mił–giy–ŋa–vo !

　C. əčču–ham, inčew–we eł–aw–we !
　　　halat–ke–ŋa–vo–ge !
　　　Pagətgət–ke–ŋa–va !

　D. I-i-i-i-i-i-i-i !
　　　əčču–muʕ amgayivatəŋ.
　　　　　　　　　Qhenqew.
　　　Muyu net isgi niwtuyu,
　　　　"Inčew ełhaw čeñhekmiłgiŋavo
　　　　kakkəkməłveŋavo."
　　　Muyu ele əyhediwkenənmuyu,
　　　　　　　　toskəŋ ʕopta.

II.A. *Ayŋawnawot gayayta* !
　　　Qaytakalŋən gekmiŋellin.
　　　Ayŋa–vən–ŋa–vən–te.
　　　Ayŋawot, inhe geyete !
　　　Qin qaytakalŋən qəgit
　　　　gekmiŋellin, kmiŋetətkən.
　　　Kiməŋayočgin emen gannyaytata.
　　　Avon–ŋo ŋi–ŋa–han !

I.A. Let's sing
　　We came
　　Hello women we came
　　Let's sing

　B. Unn, hot! hot! hot! hot! hot! hot!
　　　Those women
　　　　Ear cleaning spoon!
　　　Those women
　　　　have dirty hands
　　　Unn, hot! hot! hot! hot! hot!
　　　Those women
　　　　have sores on their ears
　　　Unn, hot! hot! hot! hot! hot!
　　　Those women
　　　　have dirty hands

　C. They, Those women
　　　stink of shit!
　　　They stink!

　D. I-i-i-i-i-i-i-i ! [crying]
　　　They're teasing.
　　　　　　　　　Stop it.
　　　We talked about you now,
　　　　"These women have dirty hands
　　　　ears with sores."
　　　We aren't teasing you, OK
　　　　　　　　already

II.A. *Ayŋawnawot come home!*
　　　A brother was born.
　　　With Ayŋa-vən-ŋa-vən.
　　　Ayŋawot, come quickly!
　　　So a brother indeed was born, a
　　　　　　　　child was born
　　　A bassinet, need to bring it home.
　　　Avon–ŋo quic–ker !

B. Inhe əmen Ayŋəŋavəen
　　　　　　　gayayta !
Ɣala–čun–ma–vənte
goñat–vaŋ–gəm–ma–vo.
Inhe qin əmen gayayta.

C. Əŋa.
Ɣam emčekmiŋenŋe
　　　　　　ayŋačinmaləŋ.
Yavas Ɣam yeleŋmənlalamək.
ƏnɁe tavanlagas.
Təlalalay yalkewlay.

D. Əŋa! Ewŋavək gekmiŋellin.
čənno gaytolen ?
Qlavol gaytolen!

III. A. Əŋa, Toyəkethawən.
Menno, ŋayen, nika–qun
　　　　　　　kiləčvineŋ?
Pnakvon, kiləčvikin,
　　　　　　　　pnakin.
Vitavałaŋənok?
Elle gimək.
Megivałaŋənak, anam ?
Gaimat, nətkenek
　　　　　　Heviŋtonak.
Ele qigi gaimat
　　　　　Imčenemtəlhanak
Awwa wutənno.

B. Qəkeləsvelagətka.
Nekiləsvigahan. Eqqe
Ehet, ham qəkəltəlagətka.

IV. Əŋe tusqəhet ham kmiŋən
　　　　　miknu anam čitəŋ?
Nikenu, ham anam
　　　　　　Vethavałaŋəno.
Əŋa! əŋa! əŋa.
Kmiŋən nəme česŋatətkən.
Nətkenu, am, nitgaɁan
　　　　　Hevəŋtono.
Əŋa! əŋa!
　　　Haqaypəshatətkən . . .

B. Quickly need Ayŋəŋavəen to go
　　　　　　　home!
Shit is all ov–er the ba–by's bot–tom
like a pine–cone.
Quickly need to go home.

C. Waaa.
Probably the newborn is
　　　　　　　crying.
Later we'll probably go there.
Quicker, they already left.
They left, they came up.

D. Waaa! Ewŋavək gave birth to a child
Who was born?
A man is born!

III. A. Waaa, they are looking for it.
Where is, that whats-it, the
　　　　　　umbilical cord knife?
The sharpener, to cut the
　　　　　umbilical cord, to sharpen it.
Does Vitavalangen have it?
No, I don't have it.
Megivalangen has it, probably?
Maybe, that one, Hevingto
　　　　　　　has it?
Yeah-no! maybe Ermine-man
　　　　　　　has it?
Yes, here it is!

B. Cut off the umbilical cord.
They cut off the cord.
Now, so, tie it off.

IV. So then, here is the baby,
　　　　　what shall we name him?
OK then, so, probably
　　　　　　Vethavalangeno.
Waa! Waa! Waa
The baby is crying again.
Maybe he, uh, is called
　　　　　Hevengtono.
Waa! Waa!
　　　He doesn't want it . . .

"Amamqut's Whale Festival"

Wax cylinders #4545 and #4546 (Bogoras and Jochelson 1901–2)

I.A. Amamqut, əno **ənəŋəʕan** gaŋvoyge.
    Əñŋəʕan ʕat gaŋvolen ənki valayke.
    Gayuŋzułinaw ənki.
    Gañẅatallen, ganəpkiyaylin.
    ʕat gamlawŋəvolenaw. (5)

B. Vəʕayok, inačəqzat gellin.
    Əməŋ ganumakawlinaw Čawčəvaw,
        əməŋ Wekətgəmkəkʕen,
            əməŋ Yaygočawŋakətəno, Wačəŋawatəno.
    ʕam gamlawŋəvolenaw. (10)

C. "Tok, Wekətgən qəmlawge!"
    "Yeqin yeqqe ivəkke? Ənannekeŋe eleyke ʕətvel,
    Wakə či-ki či-ki či-ki!
    Əlləlʕa giniwlin,
        —Tumgun kavačotqo noqəŋqo gayoʕa! Ənno gaito. (15)
    Añanak giniwlin,
        —Tumgun kavačotqo noqəŋqo gayoʕa! Ənno gaito.
    Wakə či-ki či-ki či-ki!"

D. Eh, Kłu gaŋeŋtolen,
    "Čemeč ənəŋʕaŋ əŋinəyek məčawʕuyičən kavačočŋo ən (20)
                                     gačvičuvəlinaw,
        zina nətvan."
    Gaʕiŋalin, gaŋekəlawlən.

E. "Ənzawot Zayočačŋawut tok gənza qəmlawgi."
    "Ii! Ya!"
    Gaŋvolen zatgipalnik gallalʕalin. (25)
    "Waa, woto qaytigət.
    Ottoyo kamłełəŋ małkalekolqalvuvategən gataykəlina.
        Qaytigapiłaqo gantəgevalenaw.
    ʕətʕək gayqəntema nəyataykəŋqin.
        Ənki tigətpiłaqu, aaa–aaa–aaa" (30)

    [coughs]
F. En ŋayen ganikalin.
    Ənpəqlavol gaŋeŋtolen Quyqiñaqu,
    "En tumgənəčginaw yamayŋagičŋən itəlʕan gantoŋvallen
                                  nanʕayŋavikon."
    En gəmlaŋ ŋayen vasqən ganikalin ənke gaŋvolen
        gəmlaŋ zepa zatgipawŋəkon. (35)

I.A. Amamqut, so **thus** he began.
    Thus, here, he was living.
    They hunted whales here.
    They dragged them home, carried them home.
    Here they started dancing.   (5)

  B. So then, the ritual songs began.
    All the Chawchus came together,
      all of the Magpie People,
        All of the Fox People, Raven People.
    So they started dancing.   (10)

  C. "Well, Magpie, dance!"
    "What then can I say? Here I am so inept,
      Waka chi-ki chi-ki chi-ki!
      Mother always said,
        —Take from the bottom of others' full traps! Take out the fish. (15)
      Grandmother always said,
        —Take from the bottom of others' full traps! Take out the fish.
      Waka chi-ki chi-ki chi-ki!"

  D. Um, Klu says,
    "Now it's clear how we see these fish sacks are already   (20)
                      torn up,
      what's left."
    It flew off, embarrassed.

  E. "Now Fox-woman, go on, you dance."
    "Yes! Alright!"
    She began to sober up, she had eaten the mushroom.   (25)
    "Waa, here are small skiis.
      A wooden frame and beautifully decorated seal skins.
        Small skis are set up.
      Like a dog has done it [chewed them up].
        Here are small skis, aaa–aaa–aaa."   (30)

    [coughs]
  F. There he did it.
    An old man told Quyqiñaqu,
      "She is at friends and reveals how they raise their
                      young."
    She did another one [mushroom] and here she began
      again she was still sobering up.   (35)

"Gəmmalo učuču ŋavigəm.
    Gəmmalo učuču ŋavigəm."
Ŋe! Gaŋikəlalin ŋano-kok!
Amamqutənak giwlin,
    "Emeč močgənan mətyoʕekən tiguwə en gatilagačviču̵linaw."   (40)
E! Gaŋiykəlalen,
    galqəlin.

G. "Tok-qun wekətgən gənñaq qəmlawge."
    "Aŋikəlka ŋe zaqinzyak taʕivək, aŋikəlka,
        Waki-ki-ki-ki-ki-ki-ki-kiii-kiii-kiii!   (45)
        Gəmək melgetəŋ ŋa, otəqlaveɬ məyavan ənki nəwatkətken, twa–aa."
    "Ənənu tmginaw itəlʕu ananmaynotgigino."

H. "To Wačvəŋawet gənñaq qəmlawge."
    "Qoʕo! Qoʕo! Qoʕo! Qoʕo!
        Gəmək zelʕalenak . . ." [cylinder ends]   (50)

H. E! Wačvəŋawət **ǝ̃ŋǝ̃ʕan** gaŋvolen mlavək.
    "Gəmək zelʕalənak tamgaɬ anam masunam tamzeləʕənok.
    Qoʕo! Qoʕo! Qoʕo! Qoʕo!"
    "Ənnen gənan, ŋazim, gəmnan kenanwalelŋavəŋ."
En **ǝ̃ŋǝ̃ʕan** ʕat ənnin gamalʕanqawlin, **ǝ̃ŋǝ̃ʕan**.   (55)

I. Eloŋ vəʕayok ganikalin, Amamqut gaŋtolen **ǝ̃ŋǝ̃ʕan**.
    "Ənki Watkitgiŋawtu wayike,
        Amkun-am, ellʕan qəqoleyava, Amamqut qəyava.
        ʕətʕiʕatgiɬŋo!"
    "Uyŋe tita muyu gətgəzepnuka.   (60)
        Qinam nutak mətəlgolayken uyŋe tita anaɬgi-
                                            əpnuka,
        liqay ʕətʕəzipnuka."
E, gəmlan gaziŋalinat gaŋikəlalenat, **ǝ̃ŋǝ̃ʕan**.

II.A. Vəʕayok goŋvolen nika Ziɲiʕaŋawut,
    "Əŋe! ʕətʕəŋinawaŋatək. Miknak ninaʕalen?"   (65)
Wačvəwŋat,
    "ʕat gəmmo."
Yeloŋ gəŋtolenat.
Gaŋvolenat ʕətʕənwañŋatək, **ñŋǝ̃ʕan**.

B. ʕat, vəʕayok, Wačvəŋavətənak ləlalŋən gaytolen.   (70)
Ŋewət eki,
    "Ləlalŋən amənno-qi?
        Miŋki təpkuykən?
        Metke wutčuk?
            Ənki-vat."   (75)

"That's me, a little female animal.
  That's me, a little female animal."
Oi! She was ashamed right there!
Amamqut said,
  "Definitely, we walk up and the skis are already torn up."   (40)
Yes! She became embarrassed,
  and left.

G. "Well, go on Magpie, now you dance."
  "How embarrassing, how they talk about me, embarrassing,
    Waki-ki-ki-ki-ki-ki-ki-kiii-kiii-kiii!   (45)
    At my fire, I mean, a wooden man sings and walks through here, twa-aa."
  "So that's how other people raise their children."

H. "Well, Raven-Woman, now you dance."
  "Qo-ho! Qo-ho! Qo-ho! Qo-ho!
    My sister's husband . . ." [cylinder ends]   (50)

H. Yes! Raven-Woman **thus** began to dance.
  "My sister's husband and I togehter, that is, where we wiggle our spines.
    Qo-ho! Qo-ho! Qo-ho! Qo-ho!"
  "Here you, I mean, you are entertaining."
  Yes, and **thus** here, she finished, **thus**.   (55)

I. Here, soon, he did it, Amamqut came out, **thus**.
  "Here Magpie-Woman here,
    Amkun-am, girl sing, sing about Amamqut.
      Eating dog-skin scrapings!"
  "Never, we do not eat dog-skin scrapings.   (60)
    Even in the tundra when we are slaughtering wild animals we
                        never eat hide scrapings,
      especially not dog hide scrapings."
  Yes, again she flew off embarrassed, **thus**.

II.A. So then she began, Zingihangawut,
  "Oi! I need to sacrifice a dog. Who will hold it?"   (65)
  Raven-Woman [said],
    "Here, I will."
  They went out there.
  They began to slaughter a dog [for sacrifice], **thus**.

B. Here, so then, Raven-Woman plucked out an eye.   (70)
  She says with surprise,
    "The eye, where'd it go?
      Where is it?
        Maybe here?
          Here it is."

Zičʕetʕətʕəmək tilgətənpoykənak.
"Metke wutku-qi?
    wutku nəpəqən."

C. E! Winve   Ziŋiʕaŋawut galəʕəpetkəytelen.
    "Wəčəwo ganəlŋəŋvota   (80)
        Ačikin ənən-qun, **əngəʕan**, genenayŋən gəmnan tənpəčavon."
    "Tok, zyakuqotva,
        Wuččin zeləgətvan mənumkevon gəmnan.
            Wuččin zeləgətvan yəʕaqačguŋavəŋ, yəʕaqatkeŋvoŋ."
    E! Gənumkewlin yəmlamgegəŋka gulguwlin, ənkəŋ yulʕən.   (85)

D. Vəʕayok gaplətkulinaw **ənəŋəʕan** ʕat.
    Inačeqzyatok.
    Čawčəvaw gayaytəŋvolenaw, gayənginaŋalinaw, **əññəʕan**.
    Imkultaw imtikčəʕu genomalenawe.

    Tok aččič neʕalle.   (90)

Notes

1. Dennis Tedlock has been the most persistent and vociferous champion of a strophic approach to ethnopoetics, which ignores grammatical, thematic, and lexical patterning of verses and stanzas in favor of a poetic linearization following pause and intonation patterns (see Tedlock 2006). Other scholars are implicit in their criticism, as they simply ignore Hymes's approach of ethnopoetic versification in favor of a strophic format following pause and intonation (e.g., Dauenhauer and Dauenhauer 1987, 8–10; Ridington 1994; and many other works compiled in Swann 1994).

2. Michael Silverstein and Greg Urban (1996) make a useful distinction between "texts" (the "said" of discourse) and "text-artifacts" (the transcription of the "said"). The contributions to that edited 1996 volume, as well as publications by William Hanks (1996) and Silverstein (2004, 2006), cogently lay out a theory of language and communication in which texts are much more than the stuff of writing. While I am in agreement with such a semiotically sophisticated theory of language and language use, I find the term *text-artifact* cumbersome for my purposes in this essay. I use the term *text* only to refer to written records and transcriptions, which are distinguished from performances (instantiations of entextualization) and stories.

3. Although Holmes never did publish all of John Swanton's Haida texts, Swanton's work was not in vain. It has provided material for several volumes of literature published by Bringhurst (1999), Ghandl and Bringhurst (2000), and Skaay and Bringhurst (2001).

(7   She points at the vertebrae with her wing.
    "Maybe over here?
       Here it is."

C. Yes! Accidentally [Raven-Woman] sprayed Zingihangawut in the face.
    "Don't pay any attention   (80)
      Now that, **thus**, the thing you're looking for, I burst it."
    "Well, OK,
      I will hide that eye.
        That eye will rot, it will stink."
    Yes! She hid it under the stairs, buried it, to eat it [later].   (85)

D. So then they finished, **thus**, here.
    They finished doing it [the ritual].
    Chavchuven got ready to go home, quickly they loaded their sleds, **thus**.
    All the dry goods were tied up with seal skins

    All done, the end.   (90)

---

4. Jochelson (1908, 15) describes his method: "Nicholas Vilkhin, a Russianized Koryak of the settlement of Gishiginsk, assisted me on the spot in recording and translating the myths. . . . He has equal command of the local Russian dialect and the Koryak language, and is more intelligent than two or three other Russianized Koryak who also live there." Since Jochelson's fieldnotes are lost, we do not know if Vilkhin was writing in Koryak or Russian or if Jochelson was merely writing down a Russian summary-translation while Vilkhin acted only as interpreter. Jochelson could have made fieldnotes in German or English, as well.

5. In May 2012 I was awarded a grant by the Hans Rausing Endangered Language Documentation Programme to record Koryak stories and other verbal genres and produce an annotated multimedia database, which will also include previous field recordings made over the course of the previous 110 years. For more information see http://elar.soas.ac.uk/deposit/koryak-140247/.

6. From what I can tell, rhetoric seems to be absent from schools in Britain, too. It may lurk in some private schools or the occasional university classics department, but the formal study of rhetoric and oratory is certainly not mainstream, in contrast with its importance in anglophone education around the world a century or so ago.

7. Keeling 2001 discusses the songs at length and provides musical notation for two of the Koryak cylinders.

8. Nymylan is also used as a synonym for Alutor, which is a language distinct from but closely related to Koryak. Alutor lies geographically on the Pacific, and the Nymylans along Penzhina Bay do not refer to themselves by that name. The Penzhina Bay Nymylan Koryak language is poorly documented, aside from

Bogoras 1917 and a few Russian publications, such as Milgichil 2003. While the *Ethnologue* (Lewis 2009) and Fortesque (2005) group Penzhina Nymylan with the Koryak spoken by reindeer herders, as opposed to language of the Alutors, I suspect that it is more likely to be intermediate of the two, along a spectrum of variation. I am investigating this in my current research.

9. Dr. Valentina Romanovna Dedyk has helped me greatly in the morphological and syntactic analysis of these texts and is my first Koryak teacher. Her husband Igor Olegovich Dedyk helped me digitize the audiocassette recordings, applying filter and time-expansion effects that aided transcription. Many other Kamchatkans have also listened to these recordings and examined my transcriptions with Russian interlinear translations and made useful comments.

10. The Kamenskoye of 1900 should not be confused with present-day Kamenskoe, which is located about fifty kilometers up the Penzhina River. Present-day Kamenskoe was originally called Kul'tbaza (Culturebase) and founded in the 1920s by the Soviets to improve contact with nomadic reindeer herders. The old Kamenskoye may be near the site of what is now called Kamenki, located a few miles west of Manily. This closed village is now used as a seasonal fishing camp, but one can still see the rotting remains of the traditional semi-underground houses. In 1900 Penzhina Bay was dotted with about two dozen small villages, all within an easy walk of one another. Over the course of the twentieth century, the Soviets closed down all these villages except Paren and consolidated the population in Manily.

11. I debuted the Flash animation at a session in honor of Virginia Hymes at the 2009 annual meetings of the American Anthropological Association in Philadelphia. It is available at http://www.koryaks.net/language/flashexperiment.html.

12. One reviewer wondered if the speaker could have been using masks or other props to change characters in addition to gestures. I find that very unlikely. First, masks are used only in a narrow range of ritual activities in Koryak culture, according to both Jochelson (1908) and my own observations. Second, use of a mask would have muffled the voice on the recording. Finally, I have never myself seen or even heard of any instances of Koryak storytellers using props. I will investigate the question more explicitly in future research.

13. While this work was not published until 2004, the bulk of the analysis was done in 1994 and 1995, before I went to the field and long before "A Man Is Born" was transcribed.

14. Evingto is also a good example of a name not simply translated. It may mean either 'Beautiful Departed' or 'Departing Wolf', but the meaning is not immediately apparent to most Koryak speakers (Valentina Dedyk, pers. comm.).

15. Cylinder 4538 (as numbered by the Indiana University Archives of Traditional Music) opens with a Russian man naming the storyteller and indicating the place as Kuel. Cylinder 4545 announces a story told in Kamenskoye.

16. Aqaŋŋaw's other stories published by Bogoras are "Gull-Woman and Cormorant-Woman" and "Ingiangawhut and Kilu's Marriage with Fish-Man." The suffix *–ŋaw* is a feminine ending common on women's names. Jochelson may have dropped it, thinking that it was unnecessary in English, but that could make the name masculine in some cases. For example, Wachaŋa is a woman while Wachok is a man.

17. My use of the term *storyworld* comes from David Herman (2002).

18. Uzendoski and Calapucha-Tapuy (2012) further develop the concept of somatic poetry to analyze Uzendoski's experiences of physical malaise and healing that are related to understanding Quechua stories and storytelling practices in the Ecuadorian Amazon. Uzendoski, Calapucha-Tapuy, and I are all talking about poetry in terms of verbal expressions represented as lines; on that we agree fully. Our difference is perhaps in their need to make sense of the embodiment of an understanding of stories in everyday life versus my desire to understand the role of these two women's bodies in their performances.

19. For a particularly elegant and comprehensive example of such Boasian analysis, see Snyder's (1979) examination of a single Haida myth.

References Cited

Berman, Judith. 1996. "'The Culture as It Appears to the Indian Himself': Boas, George Hunt, and the Methods of Ethnography." In *Volksgeist as Method and Ethic: Essays on Boasian Ethnography and the German Anthropological Tradition*, edited by G. W. Stocking Jr., 215–46. Madison: University of Wisconsin Press.

Blommaert, Jan. 2006. "Ethnopoetics as Functional Reconstruction: Dell Hymes' Narrative View of the World." *Functions of Language* 13 (2): 255–75.

———. 2009. "On Hymes: Introduction." *Text & Talk* 29 (3): 241–43.

Boas, Franz. (1888) 1940. "The Aims of Ethnology." In *Race, Language, and Culture*, 626–38. Chicago: University of Chicago Press.

———. (1905) 1974. "The Documentary Function of the Text." In *A Franz Boas Reader: The Shaping of American Anthropology 1883–1911*, edited by G. W. Stocking Jr., 122–23. Chicago: University of Chicago Press.

———. (1907) 1974. "A Truthful Picture for Future Times [letter to Henry W. Tate, March 28, 1907]." In *A Franz Boas Reader: The Shaping of American Anthropology 1883–1911*, edited by G. W. Stocking Jr., 124. Chicago: University of Chicago Press.

———. 1911. "Introduction." *Handbook of American Indian Languages*. Bulletin of the Bureau of American Ethnology, vol. 40. Washington, DC: US Government Printing Office.

———. 1914. "Mythology and Folk-Tales of the North American Indians." *Journal of American Folklore* 27 (106): 374–410.

———. (1925) 1940. "Stylistic Aspects of Primitive Literature." In *Race, Language, and Culture*, 491–502. Chicago: University of Chicago Press.

Bogoras, Waldemar. 1910. *Chukchee Mythology*. Leiden: E. J. Brill.

———. 1917. *Koryak Texts*. Leiden: E. J. Brill.

Bogoras, Waldemar, and Waldemar Jochelson. 1901–2. "[Soviet Union, Siberia, 1901–1902]." Sound recording. 136 cylinders. 54-149-F ATL 18011–18019, Archives of Traditional Music, Indiana University, Bloomington, IN.

Bright, William. 1979. "A Karok Myth in 'Measured Verse': The Translation of a Performance." *Journal of California and Great Basin Anthropology* 1 (1): 117–23.

Bringhurst, Robert. 1999. *A Story as Sharp as a Knife: The Classical Haida Mythtellers and Their World*. Vancouver: Douglas and McIntyre.

———. 2006. *The Tree of Meaning: Language, Mind, and Ecology.* Kentville, Nova Scotia: Gaspereau.

———. 2009. *Everywhere Being Is Dancing: Twenty Pieces of Thinking.* Berkeley, CA: Counterpoint.

Cole, Douglas. 1999. *Franz Boas: The Early Years 1858–1906.* Seattle: University of Washington Press.

Darnell, Regna. 1992. "The Boasian Text Tradition and the History of Anthropology." *Culture* 12 (1): 39–48.

———. 1998. *And Along Came Boas: Continuity and Revolution in Americanist Anthropology.* Amsterdam: J. Benjamins.

Dauenhauer, Nora, and Richard Dauenhauer. 1987. *Haa Shuká, Our Ancestors: Tlingit Oral Narratives.* Seattle: University of Washington Press.

———. 1990. *Haa Tuwunáagu Yís, for Healing Our Spirit: Tlingit Oratory.* Seattle: University of Washington Press.

Farnell, Brenda. 1990. *Plains Indian Sign-Talk: Action and Discourse among the Nakota (Assiniboine) People of Montana.* Bloomington: Indiana University Press.

———. 2009. *Do You See What I Mean? Plains Indian Sign Talk and the Embodiment of Action.* Lincoln: University of Nebraska Press.

Fortesque, Michael. 2005. *Comparative Chukotko-Kamchatkan Dictionary.* Berlin: Mouton de Gruyter.

Ghandl, and Robert Bringhurst. 2000. *Nine Visits to the Mythworld.* Lincoln: University of Nebraska Press.

Hanks, William F. 1996. *Language and Communicative Practices.* Boulder, CO: Westview.

Harkin, Michael. 2001. "(Dis)pleasures of the Text: Boasian Ethnology on the Central Northwest Coast." In *Gateways: Exploring the Legacy of the Jesup North Pacific Expedition, 1897–1902,* edited by Igor Krupnik and William W. Fitzhugh, 93–107. Washington, DC: Smithsonian Institution Press.

Herman, David. 2002. *Story Logic: Problems and Possibilities of Narrative.* Lincoln: University of Nebraska Press.

Hymes, Dell H. 1981. *"In Vain I Tried to Tell You": Essays in Native American Ethnopoetics.* Philadelphia: University of Pennsylvania Press.

———. 2003. *"Now I Know Only So Far": Essays in Ethnopoetics.* Lincoln: University of Nebraska Press.

Hymes, Virginia. 1987. "Warm Springs Sahaptin Verse Analysis." In *Native American Discourse.* edited by Joel Sherzer and Anthony Woodbury, 62–102. Cambridge: Cambridge University Press.

———. 1994. "How Long Ago We Got Lost: A Warm Springs Sahaptin Narrative." *Anthropological Linguistics* 34 (1–4): 73–83.

———. 1995. "Experimental Folklore Revisited." In *Fields of Folklore: Essays in Honor of Kenneth Goldstein,* edited by Roger D. Abrahams, 160–68. Bloomington, IN: Trickster.

Jacknis, Ira. 1996. "The Ethnographic Object and the Object of Ethnology in the Early Career of Franz Boas." In *Volksgeist as Method and Ethic: Essays on Boasian Ethnography and the German Anthropological Tradition,* edited by G. W. Stocking Jr., 185–214. Madison: University of Wisconsin Press.

Jochelson, Waldemar. 1908. *The Koryak*. Memoirs of the American Museum of Natural History, vol. 10, parts 1–2: The Jesup North Pacific Expedition. Leiden: E. J. Brill.

Keeling, Richard. 2001. "Voices from Siberia: Ethnomusicology of the Jesup Expedition." In *Gateways: Exploring the Legacy of the Jesup North Pacific Expedition, 1897–1902*, edited by Igor Krupnik and William W. Fitzhugh, 279–96. Washington, DC: Smithsonian Institution Press.

King, Alexander D. 2004. "Raven Tales from Kamchatka." In *Voices from the Four Directions*, edited by Brian Swann, 3–24. Lincoln: University of Nebraska Press.

Langgård, Karen, and Kirsten Thisted, eds. 2011. *From Oral Tradition to Rap: Literatures of the Polar North*. Nuuk, Greenland: Ilisimatusarfik/Forlaget Atuagkat.

Lewis, M. Paul, ed. 2009. *Ethnologue: Languages of the World*, 16th ed. Dallas: SIL International. http://www.ethnologue.com/.

Lord, Albert. 1960. *The Singer of Tales*. Cambridge, MA: Harvard University Press.

Milgichil, Nina N. 2003. *Nyiingtyqin Ngilngyn. (The Magic Rope). A Tale by Vera Amchekh*. Edited by Yukari Nagayama. Illustrated by Liudmila M. Gileva (Khelol). Kyoto: Nakanishi Printing.

Ridington, Robin. 1994. "Dunne-za Stories [Dunne-za]." In *Coming to Light: Contemporary Translations of the Native Literatures of North America*, edited by Brian Swann, 176–89. New York: Random House.

Silverstein, Michael. 2004. "'Cultural' Concepts and the Language-Culture Nexus." *Current Anthropology* 45 (5): 621–52.

———. 2006. "Old Wine, New Ethnographic Lexicography." *Annual Review of Anthropology* 35:481–96.

Silverstein, Michael, and Greg Urban. 1996. "The Natural History of Discourse." In *Natural Histories of Discourse*, edited by Michael Silverstein and Greg Urban, 1–17. Chicago: University of Chicago Press.

Skaay, and Robert Bringhurst. 2001. *Being in Being: The Collected Works of Skaay of the Qquuna Qiighawaay*. Lincoln: University of Nebraska Press.

Snyder, Gary. 1979. *He Who Hunted Birds in His Father's Village: The Dimensions of a Haida Myth*. Bolinas, CA: Grey Fox.

Stocking, George W., Jr. 1974. "The Pattern of Boas' Fieldwork." In *A Franz Boas Reader: The Shaping of American Anthropology 1883–1911*, edited by G. W. Stocking Jr., 83–86. Chicago: University of Chicago Press.

———. 1992. "The Boas Plan for the Study of American Indian Languages." In *The Ethnographer's Magic and Other Essays in the History of Anthropology*, 60–91. Madison: University of Wisconsin Press.

Sutton-Spence, Rachel. 2010. "The Role of Sign Language Narratives in Developing Identity for Deaf Children." *Journal of Folklore Research* 47 (3): 265–305.

Swann, Brian, ed. 1994. *Coming to Light: Contemporary Translations of the Native Literatures of North America*. New York: Random House.

———. 2004. *Voices from Four Directions: Contemporary Translations of the Native Literatures of North America*. Lincoln: University of Nebraska Press.

Tedlock, Dennis. 1972. *Finding the Center: Narrative Poetry of the Zuñi Indians*. New York: Dial.

———. 1983. *The Spoken Word and the Work of Interpretation*. Philadelphia: University of Pennsylvania Press.

———. 2006. Review of *"Now I Know Only So Far": Essays in Ethnopoetics,* by Dell Hymes. *American Anthropologist* 108 (1): 246–47.

Uzendoski, Michael. 2008. "Somatic Poetry in Amazonian Ecuador." *Anthropology and Humanism* 33 (1–2): 12–29.

Uzendoski, Michael, and Edith Felicia Calapucha-Tapuy. 2012. *The Ecology of the Spoken Word: Amazonian Storytelling and Shamanism among the Napo Runa*. Urbana: University of Illinois Press.

Vakhtin, Nikolai. 2001. "Franz Boas and the Shaping of the Jesup Expedition Siberian Research, 1895–1900." In *Gateways: Exploring the Legacy of the Jesup North Pacific Expedition, 1897–1902,* edited by Igor Krupnik and William W. Fitzhugh, 71–89. Washington, DC: Smithsonian Institution Press.

Zentella, Anna. 1997. *Growing up Bilingual: Puerto Rican Children in New York*. Malden, MA: Blackwell.

ALEXANDER D. KING is Senior Lecturer in Anthropology at the University of Aberdeen (UK). He has been researching Koryak language and culture since 1995. His current project is documenting the dialectical variety of Koryak, funded by a major documentation programme grant from the Hans Rausing Endangered Language Documentation Programme.

3   "Grow with That, Walk with That": Hymes, Dialogicality, and Text Collections

THIS ESSAY REFLECTS upon Dell Hymes's contribution to dialogic anthropology and to the interpretation of Americanist text collections. I will show how Hymes's concerns for communicative relativity, genre, and poetics enable new understandings of dialogic relations hidden in the documentary record of the Americanist tradition and in ethnographic research encounters more broadly. Dennis Tedlock (1979) and Bruce Mannheim have identified dialogism as a way to address what they describe as the "phenomenological critique" of anthropology (Mannheim and Tedlock 1995, 3; cf. Fabian 1971). They find promise in bridging the theoretical concerns of Bakhtin with the Americanist tradition's documentary practice of transcribing stories, songs, speeches, and other long stretches of indigenous consultants' speech. While I follow them in these respects, I expand the role they assign to the ethnography of speaking. The latter is limited, in their view, by its reliance on synchronic structure and a static, normative relation of competence drawn between individual and collective.

I would complicate that account in two ways. First, taking up Bakhtin's (1986) later writings, I note the necessary role he assigned to repeatable conditions of utterance with respect to milieu, inclusive of the norms, genres, and idiomatic competencies that he assigned to "language system." For Bakhtin, accounting for the repeatable is necessary if one is to recognize utterances in context and achieve what he described as "precision" in understanding. Hymes's concern with the relativity of communicative competence across speech communities makes it possible to consider the role of contrasting language systems to the production and interpretation of texts situated between communities. Some provision for difference is necessary to achieving precision in our understanding of encounters between researchers and the people they work with (cf. Briggs 1986). To illustrate the importance of

71

contrasting language systems to the task of recognizing utterances and persons in anthropological fieldwork, I turn to examples of collected Apache language texts. I identify an Apache speech genre termed *bá'hadziih* at play across two historically separate transcribed performances. I show how a consideration of that genre allows for greater precision in interpreting these texts, which are otherwise cast in the literature within the disciplinary genres of the researcher. I argue that recognizing local genres used to address others has implications for the complex role of language documentation in the mediation of communities (cf. Nevins 2013).

This essay also explores ways in which Hymes (1975) more directly anticipates dialogism and its implications for anthropological research. First, Hymes shows in "Breakthrough into Performance" (1975) that addressivity—the shifting orientations indigenous contributors come to assume with respect to their interlocutor in ongoing interaction with researchers—bears upon the documentation of tradition in significant ways. Second, Hymes's lifetime of work tacks back and forth between honoring what he took to be tradition—that of his academic discipline and that of his ethnographic consultants—and resisting the implicit temporal bracketing that "tradition" entails when considered from the perspective of the modern (Latour 1993).

Dialogic Emergence of Culture

The introductory essay to Mannheim and Tedlock's *The Dialogic Emergence of Culture* (1995) provides a point of orientation for defining dialogic anthropology and why it might matter to disciplinary futures, with special implications for linguistics and folklore studies. According to the authors, dialogism radicalizes and clarifies the "phenomenological critique" of anthropology (Mannheim and Tedlock 1995, 3), which understands fieldwork as a negotiated intersubjective relation between researchers and their interlocutors (Fabian 1971). However, the negotiated, contingent nature of the relationship "in the field" is bounded off and obscured in the process of writing and publishing, that is, in the process making a circulating object of that research (cf. Latour and Woolgar 1979). When writing up findings, the researcher orients to a different field of intersubjective negotiation: that of her disciplinary colleagues. From that position, she employs a suite of disciplinary tools that translate traces of prior negotiations that had occurred over a history of interaction with field consultants (e.g., transcriptions of consultants' speech, field notes, recordings, memories) into objects of representational knowledge to be circulated among colleagues and a broader readership.[1] The disjuncture between these two fields of intersubjective negotiation is made political by their implicit conflation in the authorial role assumed by the researcher in disciplinary discourse. Further questions of political asymmetry arise when the researcher, as expert, represents her field site across multiple institutional loci in a manner not accessible to the same degree to her consultants or to other members of the community to which the researcher's claims extend.

Mannheim and Tedlock draw upon the writings of Bakhtin to pose dialogism as a vantage point from which to place encounters with interlocutors in the field and in the disciplines on distinct but commensurable footing:

> The dialogical critique of anthropology radicalizes the phenomenological critique, refusing to privilege disciplinary discourse and instead locating it on the same dialogical ground as other kinds of discourse. . . . But the point is not that the writings of returned field-workers should consist solely of "native texts." . . . Rather, we would argue that the voices of these texts and transcripts should remain in play rather than being pushed into a silenced past. The disciplinary voice still has its place within a multivocal discourse, but this voice now becomes provisional right on its face rather than pretending to finality. (1995, 3)

They note also that researchers are not the only parties to fieldwork encounters that produce objectifications (a point also made by Bauman and Briggs [1990], Webb Keane [1995, 2007], and Michael Silverstein and Greg Urban [1996]). Objectifications—texts of various sorts, including stories, songs, names, and gifts of food or clothing—are composed, presented, exchanged, reflected upon, and circulated by both parties to a research encounter over the course of their involvement. Dialogism promises to locate both entextualized utterances emergent among interlocutors during fieldwork and those texts that researchers compose for their disciplinary colleagues on the same plane without conflating them or reducing one to another. Each occupies a different position along what Bakhtin (1986, 69) described as "very complexly organized chain of other utterances."

If the objective is to render the researcher's disciplinary voice as provisional in relation to the voices of interlocutors "in the field," then the prospect of alternative voices must be entertained and in some way provided for. For this reason Mannheim and Tedlock present the

Americanist tradition, with its attention to transcripts of native speech in text collections, as a promising disciplinary lineage. They note in the historicism of Boas and Sapir a compatibility with the Bakhtinian notion of dialogic emergence, in which spoken life is reducible neither to intentions of individual subjects nor to the reproduction of an objective socio-cultural system. However, in their account, the promise of the Americanist tradition was interrupted by the death of key figures, notably Sapir, and by subsequent disciplinary ruptures occasioned by the ascendance of the Chomskyan program in linguistics and the turn to British structural-functionalism in American cultural anthropology. For a generation, linguists and cultural anthropologists pursued separate projects and constructed separate objects of study. These were separate but parallel, in that both fields modeled their objects of study as synchronic structures with homologous, iterative relations between individuals and the structures they reproduce (Mannheim and Tedlock 1995, 4–6).

Mannheim and Tedlock assign Hymes and the ethnography of speaking a constructive but limited role in moving the discipline toward dialogism. The movement toward ethnography of speaking followed on the heels of the division just described. Hymes addressed that division by inviting scholars to work together across disciplinary boundaries to establish correlations between their respective objects: linguistic form and social-situational functions (Gumperz and Hymes 1991; Hymes 1964, 1974b). However, Mannheim and Tedlock (also Tedlock 1979, 398) describe the ethnography of speaking as limited in its relevance to dialogism because of what they identify as its reliance upon synchronic structure:

> Sociolinguistics, particularly under the rubric of the "ethnography of speaking" (Hymes 1974), has gone a long way toward reestablishing a working relationship between the sciences of language and of culture. . . . As they continue their respective researches, the particular ground on which they now find themselves meeting face-to-face is the vastly rich one of discourse analysis, and that is where it is becoming clear that despite their apparent differences, they share a common heritage. As Johannes Fabian (1979, 19) would argue the point, they tend to subordinate action, which takes place in "real time and history," to synchronic structure. The locus of this structure remains the individual, and the usual focus of analysis and comparison is the utterances of individual

(but purportedly typical) performers whose audiences are reduced to a marginal role. (Mannheim and Tedlock 1995, 6)

While it may not be fair to say that audience is "reduced to a marginal role" in the ethnography of speaking, the larger difference from dialogism they identify seems justified. Hymes's notion of communicative competence, posed as a counterpart to Chomsky's notion of (linguistic) competence, retains the latter's focus upon the individual's facility with given rules. As Barbara Johnstone and William Marcellino (2010) point out, Hymes did build a sort of dynamism into the speech community with assumptions of variation, or uneven distribution, of competencies among individuals. However, others have noted that distributions of competencies have differential consequences for their bearers with respect to norms that are attributed to the speech community as a whole or that are in some sense shared (Patrick 2008). The speech community and the individual bearers of communicative competencies within it are differently scaled domains of cultural reproduction, modeled as systemically organized diversity, where orientation to norms or to contrasting norms across contrasting speech communities (Gumperz 1982) is the difference that makes a difference. Even in defining "speech events" as a unit of descriptive focus, the terms of description are weighted toward conventional norms of various sorts, to which individuals bear an implicitly iterative orientation, playing given roles as performers, audiences, and the like (Hymes 1962). Historicism, or what Tedlock and Mannheim (1995) describe as the "emergence of culture" through dialogic action, in which each action (even an action apparently identical to another) is in an important sense unrepeatable, is not built into the model.

Hymes seems to have been aware of differences between the ethnography of speaking and projects advocated by Bakhtin's circle, as evidenced in his (appreciative) comments published on the jacket cover of the 1973 English print edition of Voloshinov's *Marxism and the Philosophy of Language*:

> In this one book a reader can discover the ideas of Bakhtin and his circle about language, not as a conceptual metaphor, but as that aspect of human life which is in fact the subject matter of a cumulative science. Its critical account of the state of linguistic thought in the first decades of the century is all that a sociological or Marxist critique can and should

be: not a stereotyped application of received categories, but an attempt
to think through from the foundation the consequences of taking social
interaction, not the abstract individual speaker, as starting point.

Hymes describes an ultimate compatibility between what he implicitly
casts as the "cumulative science" of linguistic anthropology (and sociolinguistics) and the Bakhtinian circle's attempts "to think through"
the same problem "from the foundation." In what follows I pick up
Hymes's thread while also following Mannheim and Tedlock in invert-
ing the relationship implied by Hymes between dialogism and the
"cumulative science" developed through the ethnography of speaking
and ethnopoetics, and I suggest ways that the body of Hymes's work
contributes to and anticipates dialogic anthropology.

Why Dialogic Anthropology Needs
Ethnography of Speaking

As noted above, Mannheim and Tedlock are justified in identifying an
implicit reliance upon synchrony and collective normativity in Hymes's
formulation of the ethnography of communication. However, they
fail to do justice to other respects in which Hymes anticipates some
of the concerns of dialogism and lays a foundation for their exploration. Communicative competence as defined by Hymes corresponds to
what Bakhtin described as "language" or "language system," which he
took to be a necessary precondition for dialogic relations. As Bakhtin
(1986, 117) stated, "Dialogic relations presuppose a language." The
given norms, rules, and conventions investigated through ethnography
of speaking therefore stand as necessary means for any utterance:

> And so behind each text stands a language system. Everything . . . re-
> peatable and reproducible, everything that can be given outside a given
> text (the given) conforms to this language system. . . . [It] proves to be
> material, a means to an end. (1986, 105)

In consonance, Hymes also casts already-given communicative norms,
the subject matter of the ethnography of communication, as "means of
speech." Far from conflicting with the goals of a dialogic anthropology,
the subject matter of the ethnography of communication stands to
dialogic relations as a necessary precondition.

Bakhtin devoted most of his writings to the interpretation of elite
literary art (cf. Bakhtin 1981). Mannheim and Tedlock, as they adapt

dialogism to anthropology, trace a lineage from Bakhtin to Roman Jakobson that suggests a progression from the study of elite texts to a focus on the more vernacular:

> For Bakhtin, the epitome of the multivoiced discourse is the novel, and he sets up the Homeric epic, which he deems monophonic, as both its opposite and its historical predecessor (1981, 4–40). Meanwhile (and unlike Jakobson) he completely overlooks the ordinary folktale, which is more widespread (and probably older) than the epic. (Tedlock and Mannheim 1995, 17)

I take Mannheim and Tedlock's invocation of the folktale here to be emblematic of the many other vernacular discourse genres (Bauman 2004, 2008; Bauman and Briggs 1990) that merit attention if an account is to be made of something as broad as "the dialogic emergence of culture," either among its bearers, or in the composition of ethnographic scholarship. And this is where Hymes's contributions merit more notice.

Jakobson may not have overlooked the folktale, but he did not spearhead a comparative investigation of vernacular forms of discourse. For that, following Silverstein (2010), it is necessary to trace the lineage a little further, from Jakobson to Hymes:

> [Hymes] drew particular inspiration from the Praguean structural-functionalism of Roman Jakobson's (1896–1982) componential view of speech events and the "poetic function" underlying message form. But he reworked these ideas, again and again, in a conceptual vocabulary attuned to anthropology's particular interest in the diversity of cultures and of systems of social value and socialization. (Silverstein 2010, 936)

Here, in a manner consistent with Mannheim and Tedlock, Silverstein places Hymes astride linguistic and anthropological structural-functionalisms. However, he also recognizes Hymes for developing a body of comparative work across diverse communities and speech situations. Hymes, in his own work and through his stewardship of the journal *Language in Society*, extended the ethnographic study of language systems to include vernacular styles and genres that had been previously neglected or outside the purview of scholarship. Hymes described the purpose of the ethnography of speaking as contrastive, where the goal was to bring into view differences in patterns of speaking that had previously gone unnoticed because they had been assimilated to the researcher's own tacit communicative norms.

Therefore, a primary argument of this essay is that by fostering comparative studies of means of speech Hymes contributed to what Bakhtin in his later writings described as "precision" in the "human sciences" of anthropology, folklore, and linguistics. Precision here is compatible with that Boasian mixture of empiricism and relativity that permits one to "surmount the otherness of the other without transforming him into purely one's own" (Bakhtin 1986, 169). Hymes's effectiveness in mobilizing a cohort of interdisciplinary scholars to embark on comparative studies of vernacular discursive forms established a necessary (if not sufficient) foundation for a dialogical anthropology addressed to relations of historical, linguistic, and cultural difference. Below, in my treatment of Apache-language bá'hadziih speeches, I will show how attending to contrasting means of speech, as these are applied to research encounters by consultants as well as researchers, enhances the precision with which we can "bring the means of depiction close to the subject of depiction" (Bakhtin 1986, 111) in our interpretation of archived texts as well as in our composition of ethnographic representations.

Text Collections

Throughout his career Hymes reflected upon and reinterpreted the Native American language text collections of the Americanist tradition. In his 1974 address to the Second Golden Anniversary Symposium of the Linguistic Society of America, delivered before an audience that included Carl Vogelin and Mary Hass, Hymes pointed to Levi-Strauss's use of Americanist text archives and to the desirability of further renewal of these texts through reinterpretation:

> The mode of interpretation most actively pursued today is the interpretation of texts. Levi-Strauss has made the world aware of riches hidden in the old unwieldy volumes of the Jesup North Pacific Expedition, and the BAE. Much more remains to be disclosed: structure and meaning that can be found only through close control of the language of the texts. . . . The norms implicit in native language texts are commonly both aesthetic and moral, and current judgments of the propriety of form and conduct may shed unexpected light on texts generations old. (Hymes 1983, 124)

By mentioning "norms implicit in native texts," Hymes appears to extend the concerns of the ethnography of communication to the reinterpretation of established text collections. However, his writings in the latter half of his career reflect a selection and narrowing of focus, from the full range of concerns introduced with the ethnography of communication to his understanding of the poetic function (following Jakobson 1960, 1980) in spoken form and written presentation (e.g., Hymes 1981, 2003).

Ethnopoetics and Measure

Hymes argued that linguistic details of the performances represented in text collections bore aesthetic and moral significance. With ethnopoetics he concentrated on the poetic form of oral narrative and its presentation on the printed page. He re-presented the oral narratives of text collections, transforming the block paragraphs of earlier editions (e.g., Hoijer 1938) into lines, verses, stanzas, and scenes in order to better translate what he took to be an implicit relation between storyteller and anticipated audience. For cross-lingual translation Hymes advocated maintaining close ties between source transcription and translated forms, especially with regard to discourse particles, verbs of speaking, and other qualifying evidentials, maximizing fidelity to the native language text over and above the folkloric narrative style expectations of English-language readers.

Hymes observed that oral narratives tend to be composed according to an expected measure of parallel clauses and of more inclusive discursive units, which he treated as verses, stanzas, and scenes. He described these relations as "measured verse" to distinguish them from "rhythm" or "meter." Measured verse "projects the principle of equivalence from the axis of selection to the axis of combination" (Jakobson 1960, 358), not through syllabic rhythms but through grammatical and discourse-grammatical parallelisms (Jakobson 1980, 87; Sapir 1921, 89). By comparing texts from different collections, Hymes found that measure trended consistently in some ethno-narrative traditions. For some he found pairings of two and quads of four, while others focused on groupings of three and five. And finally, he also found that the typical measure for an ethnopoetic tradition was in many cases analogically coherent with the "pattern number" of other sorts of ritual action. An example from Apache practices would be the correspondence of repetitions of four in oral narratives to those songs repeated with controlled variation to four directions in Traditionalist ceremonies, or to stylized progressions over four explicitly comparable actions in narrative sequences (see Nevins et al. 2004, 2013). With "measured verse" Hymes brought to the oral narratives of text collections a concern for relations between speaker and imagined audience in figurations of narrative action and in tacit requirements for "fulfillment of expectation."

Communicative Relativity and (Mis)Recognition

In this section I return to some of Hymes's work that predates ethnopoetics to suggest the relevance of other concerns he defined through the ethnography of speaking (especially speech genre) to the project of listening to the voices represented in text collections. Text collections emerge from research encounters between persons whose respective involvements in chains of utterances are either historically separate or made distinct through disciplinary training. Each party to the research encounter (and other encounters between historically separated persons) is embedded in different sets of givens, and those historical differences are relevant to how any track record of mutual involvement they establish is likely to be interpreted by each party. A longstanding theme of the Americanist tradition germane to Bakhtin's (1986, 169) project of "surmounting the otherness of the other without transforming him into purely one's own" is that the historical, enculturated condition of any person limits her capacity for recognizing others on their own terms. This includes the mode of action those others undertake in their utterances of a given "text." In a work titled "Two Types of Linguistic Relativity," Hymes called for the investigation of cultural difference in communicative action:

> It is the contention of this paper that the role of language may differ from community to community; that in general the functions of language in society are a problem for investigation, not postulation. . . . My contention is that people who enact different cultures do to some extent experience distinct communicative systems, not merely the same natural communicative condition with different customs affixed. Cultural values and beliefs are in part constitutive of linguistic reality. (1966, 116)

Here, rather than confine relativity to categories and their implications for worldview (referential function), Hymes considers differences of communicative function. This provides scaffolding for more complex textual translations. That is, translation may involve more

than matching like element (or text) to like element, while keeping
the presumed function of those elements constant. Instead, Hymes
suggests that translation should also be attuned to communicative
relativity. Subsequent scholarship that elaborates upon this concern
includes work on discourse genres (Bauman 2004; Bauman and Briggs
1990, 2003; Hanks 1987), on language (or semiotic) ideologies (Keane
2007; Kroskrity 2000, 2004; Rumsey 1990), and on contrasting modes
of semiotic action (Rosaldo 1982; Wagner 1981). Following Hymes
(1981, 263–64), Bauman and Briggs (1990), and Silverstein (1996), I
extend a consideration of functional relativity approached through
speech genres to the interpretation of collected texts. I take speech
genres to be cultural means for addressing and figuring relations to
others. This perspective highlights the dual role of texts as disciplinary
objects and as forms of strategic address to a researcher and to imagined audiences by a speaking subject.

Equivocal Convergence of Indigenous and Disciplinary Discourse Genres: The Case of Bá'hadziih

To illustrate these issues, here I compare two recorded accounts of
Apache lives. Lawrence Mithlo spoke the first to Harry Hoijer on the
Mescalero reservation in the 1930s (Hoijer 1938).[2] Eva Lupe spoke
the other to me in the community of East Fork on the Fort Apache
reservation in 1996. Despite a sixty-year separation between the two
performances, and despite differences in the historical experiences of
Chiricahua Apaches (see Opler and Kenoi 1938) and White Mountain
Apaches, there are striking similarities between the two speeches. I
propose that the parallels are the result of commonalities in Lupe's
and Mithlo's respective placements as Apache (*ndee*) in a history of
colonial encounter with White people (*ndah*). Also, both speakers
were situated in leadership roles with respect to communities where
knowing how to speak for others (*bá'hadziih*) was part of the linguistic
repertoire of community leaders.

Outside of performances recorded during research sessions, expressions of bá'hadziih occur across many social contexts, from Traditionalist ceremonies (Nevins and Nevins 2009, 2013) to Christian
testimony (M. Nevins 2010) to political speeches. As a way of speaking, it is a means of transforming otherness to plausible familiarity
by temporalizing the relation between oneself, one's own group, and

the participating others in specific ways. However, the similarities between Lupe's and Mithlo's speeches are not only due to expectations associated with that speech genre: they also stem from the genre's application by Apache persons situated in parallel fashion with respect to a history of colonialism (Webster 1999). Thus, these two speakers employ parallel means of speech to engage with the otherness of the researcher and with the politics of the ethnographic encounter.[3]

A consideration of bá'hadziih oratory as a discourse genre associated with Apache leaderships makes a difference to how we approach these texts. This is because both speakers use bá'hadziih to alter their relation to the addressed researcher and imagined non-Indian audience. More specifically, both speakers temporalize Apache relations with White people in a way that contrasts with the modernist action of the documentary text collection. According to Bauman and Briggs (2003), linguistic documentation and the language ideologies associated with these practices have played a key role in the discursive construction of modernity. Linguistic text collection applied to indigenous or other politically marginalized speakers is a technocratic means through which researchers attempt to fix, or record for posterity, a traditional past associated with them. Composing the past in this way entails an imagined future assumed to be different in kind from that past. By identifying the voices of indigenous, minority, and other politically marginalized speakers with the traditional past, documentation constructs the modern. In this way the notion of tradition and its objectification through documentation are directly constitutive of modern time consciousness.

By contrast, my purpose is to attend to Mithlo's and Lupe's speeches, not as straightforward descriptions of a stable object we might call "the Apache past" but as a different kind of temporalizing speech addressed to the researcher. The temporalizing action of bá'hadziih consists in bringing previously unrealized prior states to bear upon ongoing relations between the speaker's group and others in the audience, posing new possibilities for mutual futures (see Nevins and Nevins 2013). The commonalities between Mithlo's and Lupe's speeches afford a glimpse of the means by which this temporalizing action is accomplished. First, both speakers mark a difference in point of view between themselves and others in their audience, in this case marking the researcher as a "White person." Following this, both speakers address what they take to be the appearance of their own group's past from that other (in this case "White people's") imagined point of view. Then the speaker establishes that there is something about their past that had been hidden from view but that the speaker now reveals to be true. And finally, the speaker poses this newly revealed truth to both parties as a mutual enabling precedent that bears implications for possible relations between them going forward. The following excerpts from both speeches demonstrate these commonalities.

1. Establish and mark difference in perspective. First, the speaker evokes established differences in perspective between the parties. For both Mithlo and Lupe, this is a difference between *ndee* (Apache/Indian) and *ndah/i*^{n}*daa* (White people). Here is how Mithlo begins his speech:

'Iłk'idá, i^n*daaí 'it'ago hąhé łá daolaahát'édadą,*
[Long ago, at a time long before there were many White men,]

>*^{n}Déí 'ił'ango 'ádaahooghéí díík'eh joogobago daahi*^{n}*dáná'a.*
>[all of the different ones who are called Indians lived poorly, they say.]

'Íyąąda k'adi, Chidikáágo hooghéí 'ásht'į.
[But anyhow, I am one of those called Chiricahua.]

Shin^n*déí, biłn*^{n}*dénshłį́í,*
[My people, those people with whom I live,]

>*dásídá'át'égo 'iłk'idá daahi*^{n}*dáná'aí baanałdaagosh*^{n}*di.*
>[I shall tell you exactly how they are said to have lived long ago.]

Lupe begins her speech this way:

Díí ndaahíí hágot'éégo doníina
[This White person, how it was long time ago]

"Nágowągohíí baago shiłnágo" shiłndi, 'ákoo
["Tell me all about all it" she said to me, and so]

2. Pose image of one's own group from the other's point of view. Near the beginning of each speech, both speakers describe a view of their own group as it might appear in the gaze and gossip of White people. Both speakers reflect a history of politically asymmetrical encounters

with Whites by elaborating themes of material poverty and ignorance.
For example, Mithlo said:

Daanahitsóyéí dáleezhíighe'yá daahindáná'a.
[Our grandfathers lived in the dirt, they say.]

Dátł'ohná beekooghạshị dá'ádaa'ílaa.
[Their houses were made only of grass.]

Tł'oh bégoos'eelyá naasjé.
[They lay on grass that had been spread out.]

Ch'ide yá'édị.
[There were no blankets.]

Beekooghani yá'édị.
[There were no tents.]

Dooha'shị ła'jóláhát'éda.
[None could be secured anywhere.]

'Iban 'ádaat'éí gotł'aazhị k'édaadeesdizná'a.
[Things like deerskin were wrapped about them, they say.]

Naagołtịgo, tóí gok'izhị nkeedanlị.
[When it rained, the water flowed down upon them.]

Zas naałtịgo, zasí gokázhị naadaałtị.
[When it snowed, the snow fell on them.]

Hago, dákọọná daagoch'ide.
[In the winter, only the fire was their blanket.]

And Lupe:

Dá''ostagyóó 'onékał łehni', ádách'itishé.
[We used to go to school when we were little.]

Bus dohwaada.
[There was no bus.]

Daní' 'onékaa łehni'.
[We used to walk.]

Zhot'éé nagołt'ịịh.
[It would be really raining.]

Ch'ih binádasiłdíígo onékaa łehni'.
[We used to walk with a blanket draped over us.]

Ná'íícho hat'í' 'ágodzééhí dohwaa bé dá'ǫǫzida.
[We don't even know what 'jacket' was.]   (restrained crying)

Áná zhǫt'éé dáńdí łehni', iłdó'...
[And we used to be just poor...]

Both speakers portray their own group at a relative disadvantage
with respect to the gaze of White people. Both fill in the unknowing,
unsympathetic view of themselves from the imagined gaze of White
people with their own emotional stances, implicitly inviting empathy
and moral alignment. Here is Mithlo:

'Iⁿdaanałíí goostáńdiłtałí hah'áálgo, díík'ehnyá
[White men, carrying six-shooters, from this]

   ⁿdédáłeendasijaaí beenaał'a'áládá.
   [by means of them you (dual) could make slaves of a whole camp
   of Indians.]

'Ágołdishⁿdí:
[I say thus to them:]

   "Naał'a'ánahałaaí nahí Chidikáágo hongéí doobaayándzįda.
   ["We who are called Chiricahua are not ashamed that you (singular) made us slaves.]

   "Han k'aa nahá'ágólaaná'ań 'áńá yaayáńzįhálí."
   ["Perhaps whoever is said to have made arrows for us is ashamed."]

Later in the speech, after listing foodstuffs such as wood rats and burros, he makes a similar declaration:

'Ádíídíí díík'eh nahidáń.
[All of these (were) our food.]

'Áí nahí doobaayándzįda.
[We are not ashamed of that.]

Dá'ághát'égo, nahidáń nahá'ájílaaná'a.
[In that way, they made our food for us, they say.]

Jooba'éⁿdéłáí yee'isdahóóka.
[Many poor people lived by means of it.]

Mithlo expresses an emotional orientation to the view of the Apache
past from the imagined perspective of White people (*iⁿdaa*), in a

masculine idiom of denial and counter-assertion against the looming suggestion of shame.

Lupe establishes a parallel stance in the following passages:

Kodííbi 'áshich'íshí íbiye'hóó,
[When I was small]

> *zhǫ t'édat'iyéhyóó łehni', nokée baa dowhaada łaí*
> [we used to be very poor, when we were little and we didn't have any shoes, and]

> *diyáágo zhó'dágowǫ t'ééda'chǫǫ' éízhǫ.*
> [all our clothes were just ruined and wearing out.]

Łeh náshijeí łehni' íí schoolyóó daa.
[That's what we used to wear to school.]

Diyáágé naketano ndah da'idééhgo. éí beena ółtag.
[Those White people used to give just some clothes, and then, that's what we'd wear to school.]

Dółghaiyé nóhwił nakih 'i shódohwaa hayóó háń init'įįh binída émá.
[We used to ride, two at a time, on a donkey, nobody used to tease us for that.]

And later in her speech:

íyóówóyóóhíí bikeé dikáhá nádaidéé łehni'
[We used to get shoes too from those same people]

> *dǫǫzht'éé ádikeé.*
> [they weren't good but I had to wear them]

Nchǫǫ 'égat'éé.
[They weren't good.]

Dohaa deez ndíhí dikée dadohwaada.
[The shoes were not the right size.]

Dohaa k'ehgot'éégo bikee dayóó ts'onts'a degá hágo bee ánóch'itaá be nách'oghah bee.
[You don't have to be shy about it, you have to leave it on and then walk around with it.]

Zhǫ tédant'íhyóó nagh'áh azhǫ́.
[We were raised just poor.]

Here, as in Mithlo's speech, Lupe counters the possibility of shame at the ill-fitting, donated shoes with the assertion that "you don't have to be shy about it." And she expresses her pain in the context of poverty with restrained crying. Both speakers first present an unsympathetic (objectified) view of an Apache past from the imagined gaze of *ndah*. And both speakers attempt to destabilize that view by filling it in with what it is like to be the subject, or sufferer, of that gaze.

3. Reveal what was hidden, but already there. In a third rhetorical move, both Mithlo and Lupe reveal something previously unperceived about their pasts, implicitly inviting their audiences to orient to that newly revealed past as something that might alter the way in which they orient to one another. In the penultimate section of his speech, Mithlo reveals a state of affairs he casts as not having been realized by the addressed *'iⁿdaa,* or White people:

'Ádą 'iłk'idą, joogobago daajiⁿdáná'a.
[At that time long ago, they lived poorly.]

Ndah ⁿdéí 'isdzą́ą́yóí biche'shkéne gózhǫ́go yaahihⁿdíná'a.
[But Apache women taught their children well, they say.]

    [. . .] *"Shishke'é, doo'jódzįda.*
    [. . . "My child, one does not curse.]

"Doháń k'eshíⁿdiida.
["One hates no one.]

"Doháń bich'įįlójigoda.
["One behaves foolishly to no one.]

"Doháń baajadloda.
["One laughs at no one.]

"Dohyáabaajó'įįlee'át'édań goshinsį.
["One treats with respect those to whom one can do nothing.]

"Yóósń Tóbájiishchinéń bichįį'itédahdlii.
["Pray to God (and) Child of the Water.]

"Áń dá'gobiłk'eh gok'ehgodaanⁿdá.
["We live because of those two.]

"Niigosjáńi yáí 'ágoił'į."
["They made the earth (and) the sky."]

daayiiłⁿdíná'a.
[they said to them, they say.]

[. . .] *'Iⁿdaanałį́, dákogo,*
[. . . You who are White people, then,]

> *díídíí 'iłk'idą́ ⁿdé doo'ikónzįdaí gólį́ ndah,*
> [even though these ancient people knew nothing,]

> *dá'át'égo kooghą gótǫ́ǫ́yéí goos'ą́í bighe'yá*
> [still, inside their poor camps,]

> *dá'át'égo gózhǫ́go biche'shkéne yaahihⁿdíí,*
> [still, they taught their children in a good way,]

> *nahí doobégonasįda.*
> [you do not realize this.]

Similarly, in the penultimate passage of her speech Lupe depicts a new realization about a prior state. She says:

Dat'įshdí tł'égó shichóstííńí dohwaada dobí ná'daghą́.
[I used to be kind to my grandfather because he doesn't see.]

Shimaa bikįh nadááhyóó,
[When he used to come to my mom's house,]

> *bits'il got'áá nasgis łéne*
> [I used to wash his hair]

Hankerchief dách'ęę łehda nits'óo sé bátánizgis.
[When he used to carry around a dirty handkerchief, I used to wash it for him too.]

Soap bee bátánísgis baa clean ánáslé godaá iłts'os.
[I used to wash it with soap and then give it back to him.]

Dííjįįyóó yich'odahńdii' ashłį́ nágonsee
[Today I was thinking about how it was good that I did that for him.]

With "Today I was thinking about" she poses a new realization. And like Mithlo, she draws the new realization about her own group's past in terms of familial acts of sustenance.

4. Use newly revealed precedents to pose a mutual anticipatory stance. Finally, in a fourth move characteristic of this genre, at the end of their speeches Mithlo and Lupe both make a direct appeal, a sort of exhortation, to their interlocutors. To the extent that both speakers make a newly revealed reality perceivable, they also make it possible for that perception to impress itself upon the audience, orienting the researcher and White people more generally to the prior acts of sustenance that have just been revealed and therefore allowing those prior acts to speak anew to the present and to shape ongoing and future actions. However, in this respect Mithlo seems to assume a more robust divide than does Lupe. He says:

Danghéí, chiⁿdáí, gok'azí, goosdoí, joobaí, díík'eh goniiⁿłt'é ndah,
[Though hardship, hunger, cold, heat, poverty all overmastered them,]

    Yóósń Tóbájiishchinéń goche'shkéneí beebich'įįyájiłti.
    [they talked to their children about God (and) Child of the Water.]

Bikooghąí baajoogobááyéégo naagoos'ą ndah,
[Though their camps were everywhere poor,]

    bighe'shį saanzhóní híⁿdínzhóní yeeyádaałti.
    [they inside of them spoke by means of good words (and) good thoughts.]

Yeenaatsékees.
[They thought by means of them.]

Yee'aahihⁿdíná'a.
[They taught by means of them.]

'Ádíídíí díík'eh dáándí.
[All of this is true.]

Dálóó'stso téjółgayé daahiiłghał nałdishⁿdíí dásí'ághát'égo dááⁿdí.
[It is true just as that which I told you (about) our eating wood rats (and) burros is true.]

With marked syntactic parallelism among lines and by evoking the names of holy persons *Yóósń* and *Tóbaájiishchinéń,* Mithlo aligns himself with ritual speech and prayer and challenges the listener to make a parallel alignment. He does so across the difference in perspective that in the last line he suggests may yet persist.

    Mithlo's negative assertion "You do not understand" is underscored through successive contrasts between the poverty of Apache families as viewed from afar set against the moral worthiness of sustaining acts viewed from within Apache homes. The argumentative quality of his closing statements suggests that he was aware that he was working against the assumptions and purposes of the interview with Hoijer. And this suspicion is born out in the manner in which Mithlo's speech is presented in the text collections. Hoijer titled the speech "Old Apache Customs," which implies that what is presented is neutral information about the Chiricahua Apache past rather than an explicitly moralizing and argumentative address by an Apache leader to the researcher and to White people more generally. The ethnological frame is not complicated by a visible acknowledgment of Mithlo's authorship; the speaker's name does not appear with the text but is tucked into a paragraph in the collection's introduction. And finally, when annotating the speech, Hoijer does not acknowledge or respond to Mithlo's direct address or counter-assertions.

This is not to condemn Hoijer. More explicit consideration of Mithlo's contributions would have worked against the disciplinary conventions of the time (Bauman and Briggs 2003). Rather, my purpose in highlighting these circumstances is to demonstrate changes in the discipline that we can attribute at least in part to the legacy of Hymes and especially to his stewardship of the ethnography of communication. Not all manifestations of dialogue are the same, and the ethnography of speaking paves the way for recognizing utterances from our interlocutors in the field that draw upon different givens—different taken-for-granted participant roles, different modes of action—and that pose different political entailments. Accounts of dialogicality emergent in research encounters should be informed by awareness of the specificity of the researcher's genre expectations as well as recognition of local genre and style choices made by field consultants who provide researchers with source materials.

Returning to Lupe, she also ends her speech by posing for her audience a mutual anticipatory stance. She adapts a prayer formula that is otherwise described in the literature as *sa'ạh naghaaí bik'eh gózhǫ́ǫ́* 'maturation and growth, walking with it so that goodness/health is forthcoming' (Basso 1966, 1996; Farella 1990; Farrer 1991; Hoijer 1938; Witherspoon 1977). She uses this formula to pose the sustaining familial action that she described between herself and her grandfather as a basis of moral relations more generally and as a precedent that she exhorts her entire audience to follow (the verb stems that connote the prayer formula appear in bold):

*Dándii, kíł **gózhǫ́ǫ́**, baa **dózhǫ**, 'abegoz'ǫh ch'agé ch'**oghaał** gołda*
[Truly, you should do good for people, grow with that, walk with that]

> *"niłgózhǫ́" baa ch'adii 'ídágo . . .*
> [so that "it's good with you" is what people say about you . . .]

Doníina, dołjį́į́n
[Long time ago, those days]

> *lą́ni' bich'osdii na*
> [I used to help a lot of people back then]

> *dágową*
> [all of them.]

Lupe's attention in the passage to *ch'adii 'ídágo* 'what people say about you' both reflects and models an outward orientation to the anticipated perspective and evaluation of others that the listener is exhorted to take up. And like Mithlo, she stresses morally valorized actions constitutive of family and extending outward from there. In this case her ethnographer interlocutor was a woman younger than herself. Here she poses herself in the role of moral example and teacher and her own past as having a shaping influence on the ongoing actions of both in their relations moving forward.

I have connected both Lupe's and Mithlo's accounts to the speech genre bá'hadziih in order to suggest an orientation and purpose to the project they are engaged in with the researcher. I have also suggested that their project stands as an alternative to the given orientation of the researcher and of the researcher's disciplinary audience. Attention to commonalities in the progression of both speeches, implicitly compared against commonalities both speeches share with bá'hadziih in other contexts, reveals an alternative rhetoric at play in the research encounter, one that exists alongside the motivating concerns of the researcher. When understood through the frame of bá'hadziih, each speaker can be recognized as making a bid to recast that encounter in terms not anticipated by their interlocutors and not reducible to the production of knowledge about an Indian past. Instead, each reveals something that the speaker poses as previously not apparent to the researcher and suggests the possibility of newly realized mutual commensurability that extends from that revelation. In their address to the researcher, both speakers depict prior sustaining acts that bear upon the present encounter. And because these prior acts are both

Dynamic speech events.

morally recognizable and concretely sustaining, they stand as links
in the ongoing chain of dialogic action that extends to the present
encounter, and they continue to have the power to shape possible
relations moving forward.

Hymes on the Threshold of Dialogicality

The discussion in the preceding section, while addressed to reinterpreting text collections, has less to do with Hymes's prolific work on
measured verse than with his landmark essay "Breakthrough into
Performance" (1975). Here Hymes discusses recording sessions he
conducted with Phillip Kahclamet and Hiram Smith, comparing
the texts they produced to prior texts collected by Sapir and Curtis.
Throughout the chapter Hymes destabilizes the notion that text
collections are simply records of cultural or traditional knowledge.
Instead, he demonstrates that ethnographic recording sessions are
dynamic unfolding speech situations to which consultants progressively address themselves, taking differences between themselves and
their anthropological interlocutors into account. Hymes shows that
addressivity in research encounters considered from the standpoint
of ethnographic subjects plays a structuring role in the composition
and status of documentary texts. He describes successive shifts in the
stances taken by Smith and Kahclamet with regard to "what the speaker
thinks the hearer capable of understanding" (Hymes 1975, 19). He
shows how, over the course of their interviews, both men adopt different stances with respect to tradition. At times they explain tradition,
at times they remember it, and at times they perform it.

Hymes does appear to maintain the assumption that all parties to
the research interview are concerned with documenting "tradition."
Yet by involving his readership in unfolding acts between audience
and performer, Hymes obviates the identification of tradition with
cultural objects alienated from persons and performances:

> Much that has been published, I think, has . . . treat[ed] tradition as
> something known independent of its existence as something done. . . .
> This shows how much we tend to expropriate the traditions as *objets
> d'art* or as documents for scholarship, how little we have attended to the
> persons whose traditions they are. . . . Details as to performer, audience,
> and setting presumably were accidental. The irony is that a more exact
> science and method make accidental details essential. (Hymes 1981, 132)

He treats Smith and Kahclamet not only as bearers of tradition, but also as speaking subjects addressing themselves to an other (the researcher). He advocates for a "more exact science and method" in which such "accidental" details of historical spoken interchanges are accorded a central place in the account. My intention with this essay has been to extend this concern via an attention to genre, temporality, and dialogic action.

Once the stance and purpose of speakers come into focus, the temporal action of language documentation is thrown open to new possibilities. Performance of tradition in Hymes's account is an act whereby tradition breaks through the veil of the past into history and the contemporary:

> It should be clear that analyses of the sort attempted in this study—analyses of the conditions and character of events involving known persons, who accept responsibility not only for knowledge but also for performance—entail a thoroughgoing break with any standpoint which divorces the study of tradition from the incursion of time and the consequences of modern history. Such standpoints condemn the study of tradition to parochial irrelevance and deny those who would help to shape history necessary insights into their situation. By bracketing the traditional, and stopping there, such standpoints conceal the need to breakthrough into performance in our own time. (Hymes 1981, 134)

Performance here is not only about assuming responsibility to an audience; it is also about placing the speaker in the flow of action, as someone who "would help to shape history." Dialogicality—performing with addressees in mind, with the purpose of shifting their orientations to horizons of possibility—allows us to square Hymes's concern with speaker stance with his moral commitment to locating ethnographic *agency* subjects as agentive voices making bids to shape the flow of history. I have presented Mithlo's and Lupe's use of the bá'hadziih to demonstrate something of how such bids have been made.

Dialogicality, Speech Genres, and Addressing Others

In "Breakthrough into Performance," Hymes brings a consideration for variation in ways of speaking to his analysis of documented texts. With this essay I further elaborate the relationships between these two interests. I have taken a notion associated with the ethnography of communication—speech genres—and added to this a *inviting new intersubjective alignments.*

consideration for oratorical genres as means of speech addressed to persons figured as other (following Nevins and Nevins 2013). Further, I have shown how ethnographic and linguistic consultants deploy local genres like bá'hadziih that are used as means for addressing other others in their spoken exchanges with researchers. This draws upon a broader linguistic anthropological literature in which genre has been reformulated from a concern with conventional discursive forms to bundles of rhetorical strategies tuned to specific conditions of addressivity (see Briggs and Bauman 1992; Hanks 1987; Harding 1987) constitutive of persons, lived realities, and their ongoing relations with one another. Bá'hadziih, as we have seen, fits some of the genre expectations of language and culture documentation but is not reducible to them. Bá'hadziih reflects a different set of semiotic ideological assumptions (Keane 2007; Kroskrity 2000, 2004; Rumsey 1990), in which temporality as a ground of intersubjective orientation is configured differently. With bá'hadziih, prior acts are not treated as stable, mutually visible objects, but as partially known opacities whose meanings are suggestively latent, waiting to be revealed (cf. Merlan and Rumsey 1991, 224–35), and whose revelation invites new intersubjective alignments.[4]

A number of differences are introduced with the turn from ethnography of speaking to dialogic anthropology. What was approached by the researcher as biography (in my recording with Lupe) or an account of the Chiricahua preinternment past (in Hoijer's recording of Mithlo), can also be seen as persuasive speech addressed to researchers. Mithlo's and Lupe's choices to speak as they did to researchers were not normative in any simple way. Bá'hadziih 'speaking for others' on the reservation was not something everyone did, and those who attempted it risked controversy, scrutiny, and gossip. Even when employed in more conventionalized contexts, such as during ceremonial gift exchanges or as Christian testimony (Nevins 2010b), bá'hadziih was described by my consultants as provoking the sometimes hostile gaze of others and their gossip (ch'idii). It is a risky way of speaking and is used in anticipation of persons whose difference and distance from one another is already established and marked. Understanding these two collected texts as examples of bá'hadziih reveals not the reproduction of culture, but rather the emergence of plausible personal relations—or, in Wagner's 1981 term, their "invention"—in gambits made by historical, culturally embedded persons. The goal is not to reproduce the past but to draw new realizations about it in order to suggest yet further possibilities for ongoing moral relations.

Another difference introduced with the turn from ethnography of speaking to dialogicality is that historicity with respect to bá'hadziih describes not only spoken actions recorded, transcribed, and published in the documentary time of researchers and disciplinary audiences, but it also describes temporal orientations actively negotiated through what speakers present of new deferred realizations (de Reuse 2003; cf. Dobrin 2012) of prior acts and their consequences for future relations with yet other participants extending outward from the research encounter.

I also hope to have demonstrated that a dialogic concern for speech genres as strategies for addressing others might, as Hymes suggested, "shed unexpected light on texts generations old." Speech genres approached with a concern for otherness provide an entry to alternate modes of dialogue at play in communities. Research encounters stand as just one of many relevant contexts in this regard. For instance, in the bá'hadziih that accompany ceremonial exchanges, the speaker "speaks for" an extended family or clan with which he is identified to an audience that includes members of his own family as well as persons belonging to an unrelated family or clan. Similarly, in the bá'hadziih that occur in connection with Apache Independent Christian churches, also described as "testimony," the speaker speaks on behalf of *Ánashog*, or persons identified as Christian, to an audience that includes those whose Christianity is in doubt (or those who doubt the speaker's Christianity) (M. Nevins 2010). Bá'hadziih addressed to encounters with researchers, and with prospective audiences of *ndah*, exist on a continuum of these and other locally recognizable actions that permit indigenous persons to form and reform their extended relations (cf. Merlan 2005; Rumsey 2006). In this way an address to a researcher is modeled on addresses to other others, whether these are members of other clans or other claimants to Christianity.

Returning to Mannheim and Tedlock's discussion, investigation of local ways of addressing persons and agents figured as "other" affords a more precise phenomenological appraisal of ethnographic research in the broader mediation of communities, inclusive of indigenous and disciplinary audiences. The discursive entities performed, remarked

Researcher constitutive of action

upon, reported upon, and respoken by indigenous speakers, and those corresponding texts that are documented and circulated in disciplinary terms among researchers, act as boundary works (Hanks 1986; Keane 1995) with equivocal significance across contrasting but mutually articulated regimes of meaning. Research encounters stand to other encounters constitutive of local communities and persons as parallel, and as similar in kind, with the researcher participating in and partially constitutive of that action, whether she is aware of it as such or not. Similarly, indigenous speakers are party to the constitution of disciplinary networks and to their articulation with the broader socio-political order. Research encounters involve indigenous speakers and researchers in actions with implications and consequences for their respective communities that neither party can entirely foresee.

The Dialogic Emergence of Indians and White People

In this penultimate section, to illustrate the potential embedded in text collections for investigations into the "dialogic emergence of culture" and to come a little closer to Hymes's longstanding concern with the ethnopoetics of Native American oral narrative, I present a brief cosmological narrative, also performed by Mithlo for Hoijer and published in the same 1938 text collection. In the narrative Mithlo portrays a series of events through which differences between Iⁿdaa and ⁿDee were established. Relations between White people and Indians emerge in this story out of contrasting relations between two brothers: Naaghéé'neesghánéń 'He Overcomes Evils' and Tóbájishchinéń 'Child of Water'. This story is part of a long cycle and occurs after the two brothers have already defeated a series of dangerous beings who had been making it impossible for human beings to live on the surface of the earth.

One given condition assumed by the narrator is that Naaghéé'-neesghánéń and Tóbájishchinéń figure as brothers in cosmological stories across many Apache communities, but that the roles attributed to them, and the moral alignments associated with those roles, differ depending on the speaker's affiliations. Most salient to this telling is the contrast between White Mountain Apache and Chiricahua Apache. Naaghéé'neesghánéń is associated with White

Mountain Apache and figures as the hero of their creation cycles, within which *Tóbájishchinéń* is often cast as a cowardly little brother. Within Chiricahua Apache creation cycles, however, *Tóbájishchinéń* plays the role of hero, with *Naaghéé'neesghánéń* cast as a cowardly or lazy big brother.

Although the story that follows is told from the perspective of a Chiricahua speaker, it is sardonic with respect to the comparison between the two brothers and what this entailed for Chiricahua futures. *Tóbájishchinéń* is shown to make sympathetic but ill-informed choices for the Chiricahua, choosing bows and arrows over guns (because "the making of these is understood") and verdant hunting grounds over an apparently barren hill. *Naaghéé'neesghánéń*, choosing for White people, secures for them the greater benefit in opting for guns and the apparently barren hill that opens to reveal riches that *Tóbájishchinéń* had not been able to see, namely, domesticated animals and mechanical industry. This contrast reflects historic relations between the two Apache groups with respect to the US Army. In the conflicts surrounding the so-called Apache wars, many White Mountain Apache men acted as military scouts. White Mountain leaders like Alchesay were able to negotiate stable relations between emplaced Apache clans and the US military stationed at Fort Apache, and they held onto much of their land. Chiricahua Apache, however, as a concession to settler outrage following Geronimo's multiple escapes from San Carlos, were forcibly removed from Arizona and lived as prisoners of war in internment camps in Florida and Oklahoma for more than twenty years. Mithlo had been a child when his family was forcibly removed (with the assistance of White Mountain Apache scouts) from Arizona. So the fact that *Naaghéé'neesghánéń* chooses for White people in this story reflects their mutual affiliation from the perspective of Mithlo and other similarly displaced Chiricahua persons.

In homage to Hymes, I have altered the presentation of the Apache language source text and the English translation from Hoijer's version, making tighter correspondences between Apache language discourse particles and hearsay constructions (in bold in the Apache language text) and their counterparts presented in English. I have also arranged the narrative in verse and stanza format according to what I take to be apparent relations of parallelism, cohesion, and disjuncture between lines and stanzas.

A.

K'adi nii'íkáee 'ił'ango bindáayeedaa'ighą́ą́'í
díík'eh naajiistsee**ná'a**.

K'adi ndé 'ágojilá**ná'a**.
Goshtł'ish ndé k'éhát'égo naaki 'ájílaa**ná'a**.
'Isdzáń 'iłdǫ́ naaki k'eht'égo 'ájílaa**ná'a**.
Haodzígo 'ájílaa**ná'a**, dík'eh.

Nágo, ndéshį́ 'isdzáńdó:
    "Nahí ndé hinahédaał."
        gołjindí**ná'a**.
    "Nahí 'iłdǫ́ naadinałt'éí 'indaa hinahédaał."
        gołjindí**ná'a**.

B.

'Ákoo káni'jíńłdéél**ná'a**.
Tóbájishchinéń ndéne yáná'dii'įįgo,
    Naaghéé'neesghánéń 'indaa yáná'dii'įįgo;
    'iłtįį k'aabił kánjíń'įį**ná'a**.

Nágo Tóbájishchinéń Naaghéé'neesghánéń
    bił'iłaanaagot'aash**ná'a**.
""ⁿDí 'iłtsé ná'n'įį."
    iłjidihndí**ná'a**.

Dá'óós'ago Tóbájiishchinéń k'aaí ndé
                    yánáinłjee**ná'a**.
"'Ádíídíínábégózį̇ 'ájílágo."
    ndí**ná'a**.

'Ákoo Naaghéé'neesghánéń 'iłtįį bich'ą́ná'shn'įįí
    dooyáłtidahe náintą́**ná'a**.

C

'Ákoo, k'adi, dził naaki
    kánjíńłdeel**ná'a**.

Łi'íyá bikáee gońłch'il**ná'a**.
nDé bidáńí, dá'ákodeeyá nánt'į́į́: bįįí, dziłátaazheí—díík'eh biká'
                                    gólį̇**ná'a**.

Ghashį́go dziłsi'ą́í dooyáabiká'gólį̇daná'a.
Dádiłk ǫǫ dego si'ą́íbąą, Tóbájishchinéń hich'ą́ná'n'įį**ná'a**.

Nágo Naaghéé'nesghánéń 'áí dziłí bich'ą́ná'shn'įịní 'indaa yánáin'įį**ná'a**.

Nágo 'áí dził dooyáabaagólį̇daní
    'iłch'ą́'ádzaa**ná'a**.
'Áí bighe'shį̇, łíní, dzaandeezí dásídanzhǫ́níná,

A.

Now all of those different ones on earth who killed
with their eyes; had been vanquished, **it's said.**

Now he was to create human beings, **it's said.**
He made two mud [figures] just like men, **it's said.**
He also made two just like women, **it's said.**
He made them capable of speech, **it's said**, all of them.

And so, [to one] man and woman:
"You two will be called Indians."
he said [to them], **it's said.**
"You others, you two will be called White people."
he said to them, **it's said.**

B.

From there he set down [things] for them, **it's said.**
Child of the Water choosing for the Indians
He Overcomes Evils choosing for the White people;
he put down a gun and a bow and arrow, **it's said.**

And so, Child of the Water [and] He Overcomes Evils
quarreled with each other, **it's said.**
"You choose first."
each said to the other, **it's said.**

A little later Child of the Water chose the bow and
arrow for the Indians, **it's said.**
"The making of these is understood."
he said, **it's said.**

From there He Overcomes Evils, the gun that
remained, not saying anything, he picked it up, **it's said.**

C.

From there, now, two mountains
he put down for them, **it's said.**

One was covered with vegetation, **it's said.**
The Indians' food, wild growing things: deer, wild
turkeys—all of these were on it, **it's said.**

The other mountain that lay there had nothing living on it, **it's said.**
Because it lay absolutely barren, Child of the Water chose the other, **it's said.**

And so, He Overcomes Evils chose for White
people the mountain that the other had left, **it's said.**

And so, that mountain that had nothing living on it spread apart, **it's said.**
That one, from inside it, horses, the very best mules,

náa'tsílíí, dibéhéí, góochíí, taazheí
—díík'eh ch'énádaaheesáná'a.

Kát'égo 'indaaí ndéíbił
   baa'shdóó'įiná'a.

'Áíbee ndéí 'ádíídíí dá'ákodeeyá nádánt'íí díík'eh
   yeehindáná'a.
"Bįį'ádaat'éí, dziłátaazheí, dá'ákodeeyá daagólį,
   yeehindádaał."
   jindíná'a.

"'Indaaí, naa'iziigo, ná'nłt'íí hich'áshį hindádaał."
   jindíná'a.

D
'Ákoo 'indaaí 'áałjíndíná'a.
"'Iłch'á'aandahyá—díídíí tógonásga'í hananyá
   —'iłch'ágonałídaał.
   Dáhaaee 'iłiyaałtsééłee, naagonałdzoodaał—
   ndéń 'indaań bił."
   goołjindíná'a.

———————————————

    As a narrative presented in a research encounter, this story shares
with bá'hadziih what Hymes (via Burke) might term a "rhetoric of
motives." What I want to suggest, though, is that the motives reflected
in this text indicate dialogic relations between Mithlo and Hoijer as
participants in a spoken exchange, transposed onto and reflected in relations between the principal characters of the story. Like bá'hadziih,
the key rhetorical progression in the story moves from "what was apparent but partial" to "what was not apparent but nonetheless true and
consequential." The audience is alert to the partiality and limitations
of Child of Water's perspective and to differences hidden to him but
apparently not hidden to his brother. The two parties to the research
exchange are linked in commensurate terms through these past brothers but also differentiated from one another in consequential ways.
Note also that this is not an essentializing narrative of difference, but
one that relies upon accident,[5] partiality of understanding and perception, and the unfolding, interactive emergence of consequential
differences in perspective.

cattle, sheep, pigs, chickens—
—all of these came out, **it's said**.

In that way, with White people and Indian people,
   things were given to them, **it's said**.

Using that, the Indians live on those wild growing
   things, **it's said**.
"All varieties of deer, turkeys, [and] the things that are
   wild will they live on."
      he said, **it's said**.

"White people, working, will live on cultivated food."
      he said, **it's said**.

D.
From there he spoke thus to the White people, **it's said**.
"Very far apart—on the other side of this ocean
   —you will live from one another.
   Whenever you see one another, you will fight—
   Indian with White man."
      he said to them, **it's said**.

Conclusion

In a chapter devoted to considering Boas's contributions to ethnopoetics, Hymes (2003, 16) makes an observation about how temporal
relations are drawn in disciplinary histories:

> Some years ago I was asked to read an impressive manuscript on intel-
> lectual foundations for linguistic anthropology. I found myself slotted
> into a narrow genealogical niche. The manuscript was wide-ranging,
> for the most part, but for the period into which I was slotted for con-
> sideration omitted most of what I remembered as having mattered. I
> felt compelled to reconstruct for several pages what to me had been
> circumambient horizons of what to the writer was only a notch on a line
> from past to present.

What bothered Hymes was finding his voice rendered as a tempo-
rally bracketed object, "a notch on a line from past to present." His
counterproposal was that we might do better by attending to horizons
of expectation projected by earlier scholarship—a subject-relation

rather than an object-relation to the now. In this, Hymes was making an argument that bears some similarities to those advanced by Mithlo and Lupe in their speeches to anthropologists.

In bá'hadziih, temporal framing is shown to be an interactional achievement (and a specific intersubjective strategy) that establishes possibilities for mutual orientation among parties to an ongoing exchange. Through the application of bá'hadziih, research encounters were cast as special instances of exchange (or attempted exchange). The alternatives posed by Lupe and Mithlo throw the interactional accomplishment of prior disciplinary practices into relief in a way that complements critiques of temporal bracketing in the construction of ethnographic, folkloristic, and linguistic objects (Bauman and Briggs 2003; Errington 2008; Fabian 1983). A consideration of Mithlo's and Lupe's uses of bá'hadziih teaches us that just as a dialogic approach to culture prompts us to expect that our interlocutors in the field will produce "objects" (texts, etc.) with respect to the research encounter, so too are they likely to constitute particular modalities of subject with respect to that encounter. Lupe's and Mithlo's applications of a temporalizing strategy otherwise characteristic of bá'hadziih cast the production of linguistic, folkloristic, and anthropological knowledge as yet another such strategy, but oriented to (and productive of) a different horizon of politically freighted intersubjective expectation.

Mithlo's and Lupe's arguments are consistent with a statement from Hymes concerning the accumulated materials of the Americanist tradition:

> Success may depend on acceptance of a responsibility to the materials because they represent languages that are "American," not simply in the sense of pertaining to a hemisphere or country, but in the sense of pertaining to members of our own communities, both local and scholarly, in which the languages and materials retain social function. . . . The Americanist tradition, having begun as the study of languages of a fading past and far west, will find fruition as the study of the language of citizens. (Hymes 1983, 121)

I want to suggest that we consider one of the fruits of Hymes's long career to be that he encouraged the discipline to develop better means of listening to the strategies employed by anthropological consultants and more precise means of recognizing alternate purposes in new and old transcripts of native speech (cf. Blommaert 2009). In this way Hymes, as a leading figure in the elaboration of the Americanist tradition, establishes necessary precedents for dialogic anthropology 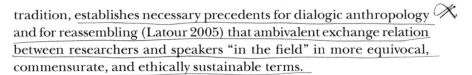 and for reassembling (Latour 2005) that ambivalent exchange relation between researchers and speakers "in the field" in more equivocal, commensurate, and ethically sustainable terms.

Acknowledgments

Funding for research on the Fort Apache reservation was provided by the Wenner Gren Foundation, the Phillips Fund of the American Philosophical Society, and the Jacobs Research Fund of the Whatcom Museum. Writing this essay was made possible by a summer stipend from the College of Liberal Arts at the University of Nevada, Reno. I am grateful to these organizations for their support. This essay has its origins in a paper given as part of "Ethnopoetics, Narrative Inequality, and Voice: On the Legacy of Dell Hymes," a panel organized by Paul V. Kroskrity and Anthony K. Webster for the 2011 Annual Meetings of the American Anthropological Association in Montreal. The argument presented here concerning bá'hadziih was originally developed in collaboration with Thomas J. Nevins regarding the speeches that accompany gift exchanges in Traditionalist ceremonies. It is extended to exchanges with researchers here. My argument concerning genre and dialogism developed from engagement with discussant commentary provided by Richard Bauman at the 2011 panel. The essay as a whole has benefited from critical engagement and editorial guidance from Kroskrity and Webster and from the comments of an anonymous reviewer. It also benefits from extended discussions with Webster on the history of research relations among Mescalero and Chiricahua Apache and from conversations with Amy Shuman, Bauman, and Kroskrity on disciplinary history. And of course the essay would not be possible without Eva Lupe, Dell Hymes, and the record created by Lawrence Mithlo, Harry Hoijer, and Morris Opler. I am grateful to all of these persons and to the other panelists in the session for their contributions and inspiration.

Notes

1. Thomas Nevins explores the contrast between these intersubjective fields in a 2010 article about different deployments of textuality and "knowing others" at Fort Apache.

2. This interview took place fourteen years before Hymes began his studies with Hoijer at UCLA.

3. What follows is an abbreviated version of an analysis is given in more detail in *Lessons From Fort Apache: Beyond Language Endangerment and Maintenance* (M. Nevins 2013, 128–45). The texts excerpted here can be found in their entirety on pages 229–49.

4. See Nevins and Nevins 2013 for a more fully drawn ethnographic treatment of *bá'hadziih* given in exchanges between families during a girl's coming of age ceremony.

5. In his ethnological notes published with Hoijer's texts, Opler reports on comments from Chiricahua about this story, to the effect that this series of choices constituted the only mistakes Child of Water ever made.

References Cited

Bakhtin, M. M. 1981. *The Dialogic Imagination: Four Essays.* Edited by Michael Holquist. Translated by Caryl Emerson and Michael Holquist. Austin: University of Texas Press.

———. 1986. *Speech Genres and Other Late Essays.* Translated by Vern W. McGee. Edited by Caryl Emerson and Michael Holquist. Austin: University of Texas Press.

Basso, Keith. 1966. *The Gift of Changing Woman.* Bureau of American Ethnology Bulletin 196. Washington, DC: Smithsonian Institution.

———. 1996. *Wisdom Sits in Places: Language and Landscape among the Western Apache.* Albuquerque: University of New Mexico Press.

Bauman, Richard. 2004. *A World of Others' Words: Cross-Cultural Perspectives on Intertextuality.* Malden, MA: Blackwell.

———. 2008. "The Philology of the Vernacular." *Journal of Folklore Research* 45 (1): 29–36.

Bauman, Richard, and Charles L. Briggs. 1990. "Poetics and Performance as Critical Perspectives on Language and Social Life." *Annual Review of Anthropology* 19:59–88.

———. 2003. *Voices of Modernity: Language Ideologies and the Politics of Inequality.* Cambridge: Cambridge University Press.

Blommaert, Jan. 2009. "Ethnography and Democracy: Hymes's Political Theory of Language." *Text & Talk* 29 (3): 257–76.

Briggs, Charles L. 1986. *Learning How to Ask: A Sociolinguistic Appraisal of the Role of the Interview in Social Science Research.* Cambridge: Cambridge University Press.

Briggs, Charles L., and Richard Bauman. 1992. "Genre, Intertextuality, and Social Power." *Journal of Linguistic Anthropology* 2 (2): 131–72.

de Reuse, Willem. 2003. "Evidentiality in Western Apache (Athabaskan)." In *Studies in Evidentiality,* edited by Alexandra Y. Aikenvald and R. M. Dixon, 79–100. Amsterdam: John Benjamins.

Dobrin, Lise M. 2012. "Ethnopoetic Analysis as a Resource for Endangered-Language Linguistics: The Social Production of an Arapesh Text." *Anthropological Linguistics* 54 (1): 1–32.

Errington, Joseph. 2008. *Linguistics in a Colonial World: A Story of Language, Meaning and Power*. Malden, MA: Blackwell.

Fabian, Johannes. 1971. "Language, History, and Anthropology." *Philosophy of the Social Sciences* 1:19–47.

———. 1983. *Time and the Other: How Anthropology Makes Its Object*. New York: Columbia University Press.

Farella, John R. 1990. *The Main Stalk: A Synthesis of Navajo Philosophy*. Tucson: University of Arizona Press.

Farrer, Claire R. 1991. *Living Life's Circle: Mescalero Apache Cosmovision*. Albuquerque: University of New Mexico Press.

Ferg, Alan, ed. 1988. *Western Apache Material Culture: The Goodwin and Guenther Collections*. Tucson: University of Arizona Press.

Gumperz, John, ed. 1982. *Language and Social Identity*. Cambridge: Cambridge University Press.

Gumperz, John, and Dell Hymes, eds. 1972. *Directions in Sociolinguistics: The Ethnography of Communication*. New York: Holt, Rinehart, and Winston.

Hanks, William. 1987. "Discourse Genres in a Theory of Practice." *American Ethnologist* 14 (4): 668–92.

Harding, Susan. 1987. "Convicted by the Holy Spirit: The Rhetoric of Fundamental Baptist Conversion." *American Ethnologist* 14 (1): 167–81.

Hoijer, Harry. 1938. *Chiricahua and Mescalero Apache Texts*. Chicago: University of Chicago Press.

Hymes, Dell H. 1962. "The Ethnography of Speaking." In *Anthropology and Human Behavior,* edited by Thomas Gladwin and William Sturtevant, 13–53. Washington, DC: Anthropological Society of Washington.

———, ed. 1964. *Language in Culture and Society: A Reader in Linguistics and Anthropology*. New York: Harper and Row.

———. 1966. "Two Types of Linguistic Relativity (with Examples from Amer-Indian Ethnography)." In *Sociolinguistics: Proceedings of the UCLA Sociolinguistics Conference, 1964,* edited by William Bright, 114–67. The Hague: Mouton.

———. 1974. "Ways of Speaking." In *Explorations in the Ethnography of Speaking,* edited by Richard Bauman and Joel Sherzer, 433–51. Cambridge: Cambridge University Press.

———. 1975. "Breakthrough into Performance." In *Folklore: Performance and Communication,* edited by Dan Ben-Amos and Kenneth Goldstein, 11–74. The Hague: Mouton.

———. 1981. *"In Vain I Tried to Tell You": Essays in Native American Ethnopoetics*. Philadelphia: University of Pennsylvania Press.

———. 1983. *Essays in the History of Linguistic Anthropology*. Amsterdam Studies in the History of Linguistic Science, vol. 25. Amsterdam: John Benjamins.

———. 2003. *Now I Know Only So Far: Essays in Ethnopoetics*. Lincoln: University of Nebraska Press.

Jakobson, Roman. 1960. "Closing Statement: Linguistics and Poetics." In *Style in Language,* edited by Thomas Sebeok, 350–77. Cambridge, MA: MIT Press.

———. 1980. "Poetry of Grammar and Grammar of Poetry." In *Poetry of Grammar, Grammar of Poetry, Volume III of Selected Writings,* edited by Stephen Rudy, 87–135. The Hague: Mouton.

Johnstone, Barbara, and William M. Marcellino. 2010. "Dell Hymes and the Ethnography of Communication." In *The SAGE Handbook of Sociolinguistics,* edited by Ruth Wodak, Barbara Johnstone, and Paul E. Kerswill, 57–67. London: Sage.

Keane, Webb. 1995. "The Spoken House: Text, Act, and Object in Eastern Indonesia." *American Ethnologist* 22 (1): 102–24.

———. 2007. *Christian Moderns: Freedom and Fetish in the Mission Encounter.* Berkeley: University of California Press.

Kroskrity, Paul V. 2000. "Regimenting Languages: Language Ideological Perspectives." In *Regimes of Language: Ideologies, Polities, and Identities,* edited by Paul V. Kroskrity, 1–34. Santa Fe, NM: School of American Research Press.

———. 2004. "Language Ideologies." In *A Companion to Linguistic Anthropology,* edited by Alessandro Duranti, 496–517. Malden, MA: Blackwell.

Latour, Bruno. 1993. *We Have Never Been Modern.* Cambridge, MA: Harvard University Press.

———. 2005. *Reassembling the Social: An Introduction to Actor-Network Theory.* London: Oxford University Press.

Latour, Bruno, and Steven Woolgar. 1979. *Laboratory Life: The Construction of Scientific Facts.* Princeton, NJ: Princeton University Press.

Mannheim, Bruce, and Dennis Tedlock. 1995. "Introduction." In *The Dialogic Emergence of Culture,* edited by Dennis Tedlock and Bruce Mannheim, 1–32. Urbana: University of Illinois Press.

Merlan, Francesca. 2005. "Explorations towards Intercultural Accounts of Sociocultural Reproduction and Change." *Oceania* 75 (3): 167–82.

Merlan, Francesca, and Alan Rumsey. 1991. *Ku Waru: Language and Segmentary Politics in the Western Nebilyer Valley, Papua New Guinea.* Cambridge: Cambridge University Press.

Nevins, M. Eleanor. 2010. "The Bible in Two Keys: Traditionalism and Apache Evangelical Christianity on the Fort Apache Reservation." *Language and Communication* 30 (1): 19–32.

———. 2013. *Lessons From Fort Apache: Beyond Language Endangerment and Maintenance.* Hoboken, NJ: Wiley-Blackwell.

Nevins, Thomas J. 2010. "Between Love and Culture: Misunderstanding, Intertextuality and the Dialectics of Ethnographic Knowledge." *Language and Communication* 30 (1): 58–68.

Nevins, Thomas J., and M. Eleanor Nevins. 2009. "'We Have Always Had the Bible': Christianity and the Composition of White Mountain Apache Heritage." *Heritage Management* 2 (1): 11–33.

———. 2013. "Speaking in the Mirror of the Other: Dialectics of Intersubjectivity and Temporality in Western Apache Discourse." *Language and Communication* 33 (3): 296–306.

Nevins, M. Eleanor, Thomas J. Nevins, Paul Ethelbah, and Genevieve Ethelbah. 2004. "He Became an Eagle: A Contemporary Western Apache Oral Narrative." In *Voices of the Four Directions: Contemporary Translations of Native American Oral Literature,* edited by Brian Swann, 283–302. Lincoln: University of Nebraska Press.

Nevins, M. Eleanor, Paul Ethelbah, and Genevieve Ethelbah. 2013. "Ndah Ch'ii'n: A Western Apache Journey between Worlds." In *Inside Dazzling Mountains:*

Southwest Native Verbal Arts, edited by David L. Kozak, 197–240. Lincoln: University of Nebraska Press.

Patrick, Peter L. 2008. "The Speech Community." In *The Handbook of Language Variation and Change,* edited by J. K. Chambers, Peter Trudgill, and Natalie Schilling-Estes, 573–98. Oxford: Blackwell.

Opler, Morris, and Samuel E. Kenoi. 1938. "Chiricahua Apache's Account of the Geronimo Campaign of 1886." *New Mexico Historical Review* 13 (4): 360–86.

Rosaldo, Michelle. 1982. "Things We Do with Words: Ilongot Speech Acts and Speech Act Theory in Philosophy." *Language in Society* 2 (2): 193–223.

Rumsey, Alan. 1990. "Wording, Meaning, and Linguistic Ideology." *American Anthropologist* 92 (2): 346–61.

———. 2006. "The Articulation of Indigenous and Exogenous Orders in Papua New Guinea and Beyond." *The Australian Journal of Anthropology* 17 (1): 47–69.

Sapir, Edward. 1921. *Language: An Introduction to the Study of Speech.* New York: Harcourt, Brace.

Silverstein, Michael. 1996. "The Secret Life of Texts." In *Natural Histories of Discourse,* edited by Michael Silverstein and Greg Urban, 81–105. Chicago: University of Chicago Press.

———. 2010. "Dell H. Hymes." *Language* 86 (4): 936–39.

Silverstein, Michael, and Greg Urban. 1996. "The Natural History of Discourse." In *Natural Histories of Discourse,* edited by Michael Silverstein and Greg Urban, 1–17. Chicago: University of Chicago Press.

Spicer, Edward. 1962. *Cycles of Conquest: The Impact of Spain, Mexico, and the United States on Indians of the Southwest 1533–1960.* Tucson: University of Arizona Press.

Stasch, Rupert. 2009. *Society of Others: Kinship and Mourning in a West Papuan Place.* Berkeley: University of California Press.

Strathern, Marilyn. 1988. *The Gender of the Gift: Problems with Women and Problems with Society in Melanesia.* Berkeley: University of California Press.

———. 1999. *Property, Substance, and Effect: Anthropological Essays on Persons and Things.* London: Athlone.

Tedlock. Dennis. 1979. "The Analogical Tradition and the Emergence of a Dialogical Anthropology." *Journal of Anthropological Research* 35 (4): 387–400.

Voloshinov, V. N. 1973. *Marxism and the Philosophy of Language.* Translated by Ladislav Matejka and I. R. Titunik. New York: Seminar.

Wagner, Roy. 1981. *The Invention of Culture.* Chicago: University of Chicago Press.

Webster, Anthony K. 1999. "Lisandro Mendez's 'Coyote and Deer': On Reciprocity, Narrative Structures and Interaction." *American Indian Quarterly* 23 (1): 1–24.

Witherspoon, Gary. 1977. *Language and Art in the Navajo Universe.* Ann Arbor: University of Michigan Press.

M. ELEANOR NEVINS is Assistant Professor of Sociology and Anthropology at Middlebury College. She is the author of *Lessons from Fort Apache: Beyond Language Endangerment and Maintenance* (Wiley-Blackwell 2013). Her articles have been published with *Language in Society, Journal of Linguistic Anthropology, Language and Communication,* and *Heritage Management* (renamed *Heritage and Society*).

4 "The Validity of Navajo Is in Its Sounds": On Hymes, Navajo Poetry, Punning, and the Recognition of Voice

If we are to understand a fair part of linguistic change, comprehend the use of language in speech and verbal art, take account of all the varied speech play in which a competent speaker may indulge, and to which he can respond, we must study his real and lively sense of appropriate connection between sound and meaning.

—Dell Hymes (1960, 112)

WHILE DELL HYMES'S (1981, 1996b, 1998, 2003) conception of ethnopoetics often seemed overly focused on recognition of structuring patterns of discourse and their hierarchical relations (e.g., lines, verses, stanzas, acts), another recurring theme in Hymes's (1979; 1981, 65–76; 1984, 174–76; 1996a; 1998, 19–20; 2000, 299–300; 2003) ethnopoetic work was his concern with expressive or presentational features of language. This focus was most masterfully and famously taken up in his essay "How to Talk Like a Bear in Takelma" (Hymes 1979, later revised in Hymes 1981).[1] But as the epigraph illustrates, a concern with expressive features was presaged by his earlier work on the "nexus between sound and meaning" in English sonnets (Hymes 1960, 111). Implicit and often explicit in this work was a critique of a linguistics discipline overly enamored with reference that ignored or erased such expressive features in linguistic descriptions (and thus promoted a monotelic view of language—see Hymes 2000, 334 and 1968, 362).

Inspired by Hymes's ethnopoetic analysis of expressive and presentational features, this essay takes as its point of departure a poem written in Navajo by contemporary Navajo poet Rex Lee Jim; the poem uses the velar fricative [x] as an expressive feature that indicates an affective stance toward the actions and actors in the poem. This affective stance is one of "lacking control," which is an important distinction in Navajo (linguistically and culturally). Not all scholarship on Navajo language has attended to this feature: in the mid-twentieth century, Gladys Reichard documented it, while Edward Sapir and Harry Hoijer systematically erased the feature from their linguistic descriptions of Navajo, as did missionaries who saw confusion instead of speech play in Navajo punning. Here I look at the use of phonological iconicity and punning as an important component of Navajo verbal art, placing Jim's poem within a larger context of Navajo verbal aesthetic practice. In the conclusion, I take up the implications discussed in the previous sections and interweave Hymes's concern with presentational features with his concern about inequality and voice. I suggest how some Navajo educators see the insertion of the velar fricative into written Navajo as a spelling error rather than an expressive option. Thus a Western language ideology enchanted with reference and standards has crept into Navajo evaluations of Navajo poetry and poetics. I argue that Hymes's legacy of ethnopoetics is a challenge to a monotelic vision of language and literacy, that is, one focused on a singular semantico-referentialist function of language (see Hymes 2000, 334), and that scholars need to continually reengage with that vision if we are to satisfy Hymes's call for the recognition of voice.

Two hallmarks of ethnopoetic research have been careful attention to linguistic details often overlooked in more "formal" or "theoretical" models of language, and an appreciation for the role of the linguistic individual (Becker 1995; Hymes 1981, 2003; Johnstone 1996; Tedlock 1983), especially as close attention to linguistic details reveals aesthetic practices. A third goal of ethnopoetics should be to recognize local aesthetic judgments about poetic forms (see Mitchell and Webster 2011). Specifically, in this essay I will discuss Jim's poem in relation to the images it evokes for Blackhorse Mitchell, a Navajo poet (among other things). I am not offering an interpretation of what Jim meant by this poem. Many Navajos that I have worked with have been reluctant to speculate on the whys or whats of a given poem or poet; instead, they offer interpretations based on the images evoked by a poem (Webster 2009). In general, ideal Navajo poets do not force an interpretation onto the reader or listener, nor should the listener or reader force an interpretation onto a poet. This ethos is an important feature of what one might term Navajo ethnoliterary criticism, and it resonates with a wider Navajo ethos of *t'áá bí bee bóholníih* 'it's up to her/him to decide'. This ethos also echoes with the use of punning in Navajo poetry, as puns allow the listener imaginative options of interpretation.

Poetry

The poem that is the focus of this essay comes from Rex Lee Jim's all-Navajo collection *saad* (which glosses as 'word, language'). The book was published in 1995 by the Princeton Collection of Western Americana. It is important to note that the entire book is in Navajo, including the page numbers and the title page. The untitled poem we are concerned with here can be found on page *tádiin dóó bi'qq tseebíí* 'thirty-eight'. I have seen Jim perform this poem on the Navajo Nation and recorded it on three different occasions.[2] At such performances, the book is for sale by Jim, but I have not found the book available at other venues on the Navajo Nation and in the surrounding area that sell Navajo books of poetry (see Webster 2009). Later in this essay, I will discuss Jim's performance of this poem in Window Rock, Arizona, on July 18, 2001. Here I first present the poem, along with a translation I worked on in consultation with Blackhorse Mitchell.

na'ashchxiidí	The badger's
bíchxįįh	nose
ní'deeshchxidgo	stretched round
ni'iihchxįįh	shitting
chxqq' bee	with shit
nániichxaad (Jim 1995, 38)	is full

In its brevity and its dense use of sound, this poem is very much like the other poems in *saad* (see Webster 2006). Indeed, in 2001 when I interviewed Jim about the book at his Diné College office in Tsaile, Arizona, he told me that "sounds were very important." I will discuss in the next section Jim's penchant for using what I will call sound affinities and phonological iconicity (sounds echoing sounds) in his poetry. "Sound affinity" owes a debt to Dwight Bolinger's (1940) concept of "word affinities," and the idea of "phonological iconicity" has been developed from David Samuels's (2001) discussion of Western Apache punning (see also Webster 2009, 2010b).

The first thing to note about Jim's poem is that each line includes the sound *-chx-*, which can be described as a voiceless palatal affricate (here written <ch>) and a velar fricative (here written <x>). This is a form of consonantal rhyme, here based on the consonant cluster at the beginning of the verb or noun stem. I should also note that the consonant cluster stem initial of *chx-* in this poem is optional in both spoken and written discourse. All of the forms in this poem that have this consonant cluster can also appear without the velar fricative [x].

As a first approximation of a Navajo ethnopoetics concerned with ethnoliterary criticism, I would suggest that the expressive use of *-x-* in this poem resonates or echoes with the *-x-* that is normally found in expressions like *nichxǫ'í* 'it is ugly, disorderly, out of control' or *hóchxǫ'* 'ugly, out of control, disorderly'. Things that lack control, according to some Navajos, are things that need to be returned to order or control or beauty (*hózhǫ́*). Jim not only repeats the sound *-x-* throughout the poem, but in fact creates a consonantal rhyme by repeating the consonant cluster *-chx-*. This is the very consonant cluster found in the verb stem *-chxǫ'* 'ugly'. The velar fricative resonates across a number of lexical items, including some that are more prototypically found with the velar fricative (e.g., *hóchxǫ'*). Jim underscores this sound affinity or phonological iconicity by repeating the consonant cluster *-chx-* throughout the poem. Note that phonological iconicity is a resemblance between words or consonant clusters, where sounds echo off of each other.

Expressive and poetic features based on phonological iconicity—from puns to poetry—are much appreciated by some Navajo (see below; see also Webster 2009, 2010b); thus, Jim's use of the velar fricative is a richly layered and textured poetic accomplishment in this context. To see how, I turn now to comments offered by Mitchell as we went through the poem, and supplement his observations with comments that I have elicited from other Navajos. I rely on Mitchell's discussion for a number of reasons. First, like Jim, Mitchell is a poet. Second, like Jim, Mitchell is a medicine man (though they do not do the same chantway).[3] Third, like Jim, Mitchell has spent a fair amount of time thinking about the Navajo language. Fourth, Jim and Mitchell have known each other for many years.

The introduction of *na'ashchxiidí* 'badger' with the velar fricative indicates a pejorative affective stance towards this character. As Mitchell noted in a phone conversation in 2010, without the *-x-* the badger might be from a storybook or Disney DVD: "these animal characters in those movies, there is no ugliness, it's nice and clean movies." But the -x- introduces a pejorative sense, as well as a sense of the badger being out of place, ugly, and uncontrolled. First, the verb stem here is -chid 'to move hands and arms in a non-controlled manner'. As has been widely noted in the literature, behaving (and speaking) in a controlled manner is a basic tenet of Navajo philosophy (Reichard [1950] 1963; Witherspoon 1977; see also Rushforth and Chisholm 1991, 146–48). Thus, it is not surprising that some Navajo verb stems indicate controlled action (e.g., -nííh 'to move hands and arms in a controlled manner'), while others indicate that the actor does things in a non-controlled—but not uncontrolled—way (e.g., -chid 'to move hands and arms in a non-controlled manner'). Second, the addition of the -x- in conjunction with -ch- suggests, because it evokes the -chx- sound in hóchxǫ', that not only are the hands, arms, or paws moving in a non-controlled manner, but they are moving in an *un*controlled manner. Badger lacks control.

Let us turn to the second line, bichxį́į́h 'its nose'. Reichard ([1950] 1963, 142), as I will discuss below, translated the stem –chxį́į́h as 'muzzle'. In conversations at his home outside Shiprock, New Mexico, and in conversations over the phone and via email, all between 2010 and 2012, Mitchell has variously tried to explain the expressive work done by -x- through lexicalizing it into English, using phrases like 'big nose', 'fat nose', 'dried and cracked', and 'ugly nose' to describe the expressive quality of the line bichxį́į́h. Another Navajo that I worked with on this poem suggested 'protrusion'. The velar fricative expresses a pejorative stance toward Badger's nose, while the conso-nant cluster -chx- evokes—through phonological iconicity with the verb stem -chxǫ'—an out-of-control-ness or ugliness as well. If the character na'ashchxiidí is uncontrolled in behavior, he is uncontrolled in appearance as well.

The third line of ní'deeshchxidgo, which Mitchell translated as "stretched round," was elaborated by Mitchell as follows: "its nose is widened out," "its nostrils, horrible looking," "the rim of its nose is open wide," and "it's expanding its nose, getting big." I would suggest that na'ashchxiidí's nostrils are flaring in a "horrible" and hence uncontrolled manner. The -x- in combination with -ch- evokes again the sense that Badger's behavior is uncontrolled and "ugly" (hochxǫ').

The next line—ni'iihchxįįh—suggests that Badger is taking a "nasty shit." It is a "shit" that "smells awful." It might be the case that Badger has lost control of his bowel movement and has become incontinent.

This seems suggested, anyway, in Mitchell's comment that Jim's chosen linguistic form connoted "shitting around"; another Navajo commentator suggested "shits all over." In either case, it is a vile shit that Badger is taking. This is, of course, affirmed in the fifth line. Here we find *chxąą' bee* and, as noted above, the use of the *-x-* here indicates that Badger's defecation is, as Mitchell described to me at various times, "too much," "like you filled up the toilet bowl," "dirty," "nasty"; furthermore, it "smells awful."

This brings us to the final line: *náníichxaad* 'to become full (bulge or swell) with food' or as Mitchell translated it, "is full." In our conversations, Mitchell has variously explained that the use of *-x-* here indicates that Badger "overate," "ate till it was too full," "its belly became too round," "ate till they became ugly with a round belly hanging out," and "ate more than it needs." He further observed, "We shouldn't overeat, we shouldn't have a round stomach." The velar fricative here suggests an affective stance both augmentative and pejorative, that is, *-x-* in conjunction with *-ch-* seems to indicate that Badger ate in an uncontrolled manner; that it ate too much, much more than it needed. And the consonantal rhyme of *-chx-* in each line forefronts that sound and suggests—through phonological iconicity—a felt connection with the verb stem *-chǫ'*. Note finally that the vowel that follows the velar fricative in this poem moves from a high front vowel /i/ (*na'ashchxiidí*) to a low central vowel /a/ (*náníichxaad*). In producing this vowel while reading down the poem, the mouth physically gets more open and rounder, thus replicating—iconically—the very fullness of *náníichxaad*.

While Mitchell stressed to me that each listener of this poem would get "a different image, a different picture," and that Jim was "creating a descriptive picture" and "playing around with words" in this poem, Mitchell did note that, for him, the poem suggested that "we don't think about what we are doing, we don't know what we become." *Na'ashchxiidí* is not behaving in a proper manner, and according to Mitchell the *-x-* seems to add to the view that Badger does not "think about what it is doing." Badger is not paying attention to what it is doing to itself. Badger is out of control, eating too much and eating its own vile shit. It is, quite literally, "full of shit." For Mitchell and for me, this poem suggests that some people are not paying attention to what they are doing to themselves. They are, like Badger, acting out of control and doing ugly things.

This poem, written as it is in Navajo, seeks an audience of Navajos. However, literacy in Navajo is still relatively restricted among Navajos, most of whom come to this poem not as a text artifact, but rather as an oral performance. Mitchell has pointed out to me that Jim does not always pronounce the velar fricative in the first line when he performs, though all subsequent lines do include the expressive feature. In such cases, it would appear that it is not Badger who is out of control, but Badger's actions. Note that when reading the poem, the -x- is always available as part of the experience of the poem. When it is performed by Jim, the velar fricative is optional. When I have seen Jim perform this poem, most notably in July 2001 in Window Rock, Arizona, to a primarily Navajo audience (including Mitchell), most listeners laughed during this poem. There is, indeed, something absurd about Badger acting in such an uncontrolled manner, becoming satiated from its own shit, its nostrils flaring. Here it is useful to remember, as Barre Toelken and Tacheeni Scott (1981, 86) suggest, that for some Navajos, "any kind of extreme like . . . gluttony . . . is considered the kind of weakness that must be cured by ceremony, and is often in the mean-time subject to laughter." Thus, it also appears that Jim is encourag-ing Navajos to think about their own actions, their own behavior. He asks them to reflect on the possibility that they too are acting without thinking, letting their bellies get too large—that, in Mitchell's words, "we don't know what we become."[4]

Linguistics

Given the meanings associated with the expressive use of the velar fricative in Navajo, some consideration of the feature's historical documentation by linguists is in order.[5] In an early paper, Reichard (1948) called attention to what she called "aspiration." In describing this expressive device (more accurately, use of a velar fricative) as an "augmentative" form, she noted that "a more forceful action, a state exaggerated in size or quantity, or a pejorative may be expressed by aspirating the voiceless stem initial so strongly as to form a conso-nant cluster" (1948, 15). In Reichard's (1951) mammoth and impor-tant grammar of Navajo, she listed a number of contrasting pairs of stems where the addition of "aspiration" changed not the semantico-referential meaning of the words, but rather the expressive implication of those forms (for example, from neutral to pejorative). In Table 1, I

TABLE 1

Unmarked Navajo form	Gloss	-*x*- marked Navajo form	Gloss and commentary
-sał	move like a feather	-sxał	heavy object (e.g., a person) moves like a feather, gracefully. (Mitchell said that the insertion of the velar fricative here would be appropriate for describing the "light fall of the first snow on the ground." Conversations with Navajo consultants suggest that the distinction is between something "floating" and [with the -x-] something [heavier] "floating" and "falling.")
-si	make numb	-sxi	paralyze, deaden
sǫ'	star	sxǫ'	a fearful star
-sǫs	glitter like copper	-sxǫs	glitter like a red star (Mitchell describes this as a glittering "deep pink.")
-tsaaz	grow big	-tsxaaz	grow very large
-chah (-cha)	cry	-chxah (-chxa)	scream
chąą'	manure, excrement, feces	chxąą'	excrement (vulgar) (Mitchell suggested this was not so much 'vulgar,' but rather had the sense of being "smelly" and "nasty.")
-chin	have, exude odor	-chxin	have strong odor
-chįįh	nose	-chxįįh	muzzle
-chǫ'	bad	-chxǫ'	wicked, essentially bad
-łaał	hate	-łxaał	be exasperated

present a number of the pairs she identified (Reichard 1951, 141–42). I have amended the forms to present them as they are currently written in Navajo orthography and I have added Mitchell's remarks about some of these forms in parentheses. One can see that two of the forms that Jim uses in his poem are also included in Reichard's list: *-chį́įh* versus *-chxį́įh* and *chąą'* versus *chxąą'*.

Reichard was not the only linguist to call attention to the use of this expressive feature, though she was the only one to fully engage the topic. In 1943, Robert Young and William Morgan (1943, 142) noted in *The Navaho Language* that "a depreciative sense is injected by inserting gh after an unaspirated, or x after an aspirated consonant. Thus, sǫ', star; sxǫ', that such and such star; dził, mountain; dzghił, that such and such mountain; dzą́ądi, here; dzghą́ądi, here (with an intonation of disgust or displeasure)." Later, in their own mammoth dictionary, they wrote, "Also h used as a depreciative-augmentive in certain stems is written x, as in łitsxo, orange (łitso, yellow), t'áá 'ałtsxo, absolutely all (t'áá 'ałtso, all), hółchxon, the place stinks (hółchon the place stinks—less emphatic)" (1987, xiv). Mitchell once glossed *łitsxo* as 'dirty yellow' for me (see also Landar et al. 1960, 381–82). In their 1992 *Analytical Lexicon of Navajo*, Young and Morgan also note that a number of stems seem to "occur more frequently" with the *-x-* form. For example, the verb stem *-chǫ'* 'bad, ugly, sulk, dirty, filthy' "occur[s] most frequently in intensive form, with *-x-* (CHXǪ' in lieu of CHǪ')" (1992, 96). Likewise, the verb stem *-tsxas* 'whip, lash' seems to always occur with the *-x-* (Reichard 1948, 16; Young and Morgan 1992, 592). The verb stem *-chosh* 'rumpled, disheveled, bushy' also "often appears in intensive form as CHXOSH" (Young and Morgan 1992, 95). I have noted these verb stems (*-chxǫ', -tsxas, -chxosh*) because they occur in other poems in Jim's *saad*, always with the *-x-*.

To recall a point made by Hymes (2003), because the use of *-x-* as an expressive feature does not change semantico-referential meaning, the form can also be ignored. Reichard makes this point in reviewing previous collections of Navajo textual materials: "The Sapir-Hoijer [1942] texts do not differentiate the regular forms from the augmentatives because they treat both types of initial as a single phoneme" (1948, 17). In Hoijer's 1974 *A Navajo Lexicon*, for example, he never includes the *-x-* on any of the verb stems noted above. Thus, the verb stems are *-chǫ'* 'bad, ugly, ill-natured, evil' (1974, 220), *-chosh* 'unevenly cut, ragged' (219), and -*tsas* 'whip' (182).[6] Indeed, Hoijer also misses the distinction between *łitso* 'yellow' and *łitsxo* (conventionally glossed as 'orange' but also with a sense of 'so-and-so yellow' or 'dirty yellow') (1974, 186; on Hoijer's work, see also Nevins, this volume). Thinking velar fricatives unimportant because they did not contribute to the semantico-referential meaning of a lexical item, Hoijer did not include them in his lexicon.

Indeed, Sapir and Hoijer (1967, 7) go so far as to dismiss Reichard's discussion concerning the use of -*x*- to indicate an "augmentative" or a "pejorative" sense. They claim that it is a "nondistinctive feature" and can therefore be excluded from the serious work of describing Navajo morphology and phonology. In Leonard Faltz's (1998) insightful discussion of the Navajo verb, he spends a good deal of time discussing the verb stem -*cha* 'cry' without noting that there is an optional expressive form with the velar fricative -*chxa* 'scream, cry without control, wail' (see Reichard 1951, 142). Credit, then, must be given to Reichard, Morgan, and Young for recognizing the expressive work that the velar fricative does and for including it in their grammars and dictionaries. Not every linguist or anthropological linguist did.

While it is beyond the scope of this essay to explain why the uses of expressive features have been largely "neglected" (Nuckolls 2006, 39) in the linguistic literature, I would like to note two relevant points. First, as Samuels (2004a) has noted, many of our modernist assumptions about languages are based in a primarily referentialist view of language: the idea that language primarily refers to things in the world (see also Bauman and Briggs 2003). Expressive features of languages, especially those features based on iconicity (a resemblance of something to someone), for example, have been largely ignored or trivialized because they were deemed "prelinguistic" or "primitive" (see Farnell 1995; Nuckolls 1999; Samuels 2004a; Webster 2009). When a linguistic feature does not contribute to semantico-referential meaning it violates a basic assumption of Western language ideologies: language = reference. As Richard Bauman and Charles L. Briggs (2003) note, this particular ideology has sometimes been conflated as a totalizing feature of languages.

A second reason for inattention to expressive features, and related to the first, is that the shift in language documentation from a more phonetic-centered approach to a phonemic method has led to many expressive features simply not being recorded. Hymes (2003, 207) describes this shift from phonetics to phonemics as intimately tied to concerns about reference:

> Descriptive linguistics developed on the basis of the kind of contrast that underlies the phonemic principle. Only differences in referential or propositional meaning were addressed. The general term "language" was reduced to that one, basic dimension of language. . . . The phonemic principle led many linguists to omit features of the second sort [expressive meaning] from their recordings of texts from the 1930s onward. Recordings that included nonphonemic features were even thought of as "old fashioned" and of no scientific use.

Hymes goes on to note that "we want to be sure that features that were part of the teller's performance, conveying emphasis and attitude, are represented. . . . In Wishram and Chinookan languages, these features especially include vowel length, shift of stress, and vowel color." The phonemic view had the potential to obscure locally evocative ways of using language. To Sapir's credit, in his famous work on Nootka consonant play ([1915] 1985) he tended to record expressive features because he had not yet decided on the phonemic inventory of the language. Later linguists and linguistic anthropologists would ignore such nonphonemic or expressive features because they did not fit a narrow view of "grammar."

Punning

Having provided the context for documenting the expressive use of the velar fricative in Navajo, I now want to provide some ethnographic context for the poetic use of phonological iconicity and sound affinities in Jim's poem. We can broadly define this aesthetic practice as punning or what some Navajos call *saad aheełt'éego diits'a'* 'words that resemble each other by sound'. As the Navajo form suggests, punning is based on homophony or phonological iconicity, where words sound alike. It has long been noted that punning among Navajos is a particularly appreciated way of speaking and a form of verbal art (e.g., Cisneros et al. 2006; Hill 1943; Kluckhohn and Leighton 1962; Sapir 1932; Webster 2009, 2010a, 2010b; for comparative purposes see Liebe-Harkort 1979 and Samuels 2001, 2004b). Clyde Kluckhohn and Dorothea Leighton (1962, 260) make the following observation based on work in the 1940s and 1950s:

Homonymous words and syllables gives rise to the many puns in which the Navahos delight. For instance, *ha'át'íishą nílį* means either 'what is flowing?' or 'what clan are you?' and The People [Navajos] tell stories with many embellishments about this question's being asked of a man who was standing beside a river.

Elsewhere, I have described the punning practices of a number of Navajo poets and nonpoets alike (Webster 2009, 2010b). Rather than give a series of Navajo puns, here I would like to briefly discuss one interlingual pun in particular because it speaks to the ways that Navajo verbal art based on phonological iconicity can be erased due to a Western fascination with semantico-referential meaning. I then provide two further examples of Jim using punning in his poetry.

One day in April 2001, as a Navajo consultant and I were driving across the Navajo Nation, we passed several signs for a Christian revival meeting. My Navajo companion asked me why Anglo-Christians, especially missionaries, were overly focused on trees. Seeing that I was at a loss for a response, the consultant clarified that Anglo-Christians are always talking about *gad* 'juniper tree, cedar tree'. Here the pun arises from the homophony between *gad* and the English-language *god* [gáad]. This is an interlingual pun (Webster 2010b). Interlingual puns—puns that challenge the fixity of the boundaries of languages—are, following Kathryn Woolard (1998), bivalent, that is, they potentially sit uneasily in two linguistic codes. Note that the quickness of puns—the "now you see it, now you don't" quality—is rooted in the always-present ability to misrecognize a pun as not a pun (on "quickness," see Calvino 1988). As I describe elsewhere (Webster 2010a, 203–4), interlingual punning by Navajos in the context of the boarding school recitation of the pledge of allegiance was predicated precisely on that bivalency, the possibility of misrecognizing Navajo as English. Navajos took the chance that teachers and matrons would hear not a pun, but rather acquiescence.

Navajo linguist Ellavina Perkins has told me that the pun between *gad* and *god* has been around "for a while" (pers. comm., 2009). Indeed, in looking at Ethel Wallis's 1968 biography of the Protestant missionary linguist Faye Edgerton, we find Wallis claiming that some Navajos were "puzzled" by God's name, thinking the term was either *gad* 'juniper tree, cedar tree' (Wallis identifies the tree as a "cedar tree") or the onomatopoetic *gaagi* [gáagii] 'crow' (Wallis 1968, 6). Indeed, Wallis claims that "when Christmas came and a tall cedar tree was gaily decorated and set in front of the church, The People [Navajos] concluded he [sic] must be a plant" (6). For the Protestant missionaries in this context, the Navajos are unrepentant literalists. Note that the interlingual pun is most decidedly not meant to be taken literally. It works because of phonological iconicity, not literalism. It is verbal play based on sound that subverts the idea of semantic meaning as stable.

I would argue that Wallis's account betrays the missionaries' hyperconcern with reference and literalism (Nevins 2010; Samuels 2006). Indeed, Wallis (1968, 6) notes that the "native" Navajo term for *god* had too many "pagan" connotations. Incidentally, the Navajo term to which Wallis referred is *Diyin 'Ayói 'Át'éii* (*diyin* 'holy', *'ayói* 'exceedingly', *'át'éii* 'that which is'). This was the term coined by Catholic missionaries in consultation with Navajos (Bodo 1998, 4). It is an early example of a neologism; the term *Diyin 'Ayói 'Át'éii* is "native" only insofar as it is expressed using Navajo language. Perhaps the paganism the Protestant biographer Wallis was suggesting was the "paganism" of Catholicism?

Be that as it may, I strongly doubt that the conflation by Navajos of *god* and *tree* represents straightforward confusion. Rather, from my experiences, it seems more likely to represent playful punning in the face of naïve outsiders. We can think of such forms of punning as mischievous grammars. Navajos that I know enjoy the straight-faced put-on that tests the thresholds of gullibility. Like the Anglo anthropologists described by Américo Paredes (1977) who took Mexican-American put-ons as straightforward description because they matched certain (negative) received assumptions about those Mexican-Americans, the missionaries indexed here by Wallis often misrecognized speech play as being straightforward confusion on the part of Navajos because it matched expectations that Navajos would be "primitive" and "childlike." That Navajos might have been playfully challenging the missionaries' assertions of authority and knowledge seems to have been utterly missed. Indeed, Navajo verbal art, based on phonological iconicity, is erased by a Western fascination and obsession with literalism.

As noted above, such punning practices (based on phonological iconicity) can also be found in contemporary written Navajo poetry. Both Laura Tohe and Luci Tapahonso have used homophony and punning in their poetry (Webster 2009, 211–12). Jim uses this poetic device in poems other than the one discussed above. For example, in the following poem by Jim from the same collection, the first word can be heard at least two different ways and thus offers a complex range of understandings (see Webster 2006, 2012c):

na'asts'ǫǫsí	mouse
ts'ǫǫs, ts'ǫǫs	suck, suck
yiits'a'go	sounding
ííts'ǫ́ǫ́z (Jim 1995, 37)	kiss (Webster 2006, 39)

The first line, *na'asts'ǫǫsí*, is the conventional Navajo term for 'mouse', but it can be morphologically analyzed as 'the one who goes about sucking'. It is based on the ideophonic (sound symbolic) verb stem *–ts'ǫǫs* 'to suck, to kiss' (the independent ideophone is then used in reduplicated form in line two of the poem). However, not all Navajos that I have spoken with could identify the term's constituent parts. The last line is semantically ambiguous and can mean something akin to 'to kiss', 'to suck', or 'to perform a sucking ceremony'. The sucking ceremony is a curative ritual in traditional Navajo beliefs, in which a Navajo medicine man ritually sucks out an object that is causing harm to a patient. It is significant that the first line—*na'asts'ǫǫsí*—is homophonous with *náá'ásts'ǫǫs* 'to perform a sucking ceremony again' (with the semeliterative *náá-* 'again' + *'asts'ǫǫs* 'to suck, to kiss, to perform a sucking ceremony').[7] As Jim explained to me in June 2001, because the mouse is an "omen of evil, the spirit of death" in "traditional" Navajo beliefs and more recently has become associated with the deadly Hantavirus, the poem—through the initial homophony—takes on a rather ominous sense. Another way to translate the above poem, then, might be:

sucking again
suck, suck
sounding
a sucking ceremony is performed

In a video for the *Princeton Alumni Weekly*, Jim describes another poem that he wrote for the 250th-anniversary celebration of his alma mater as playing with the phonological iconicity or homophony between *ni* 'you' and *ni'* 'earth' (Delano 2010). Navajo poet Sherwin Bitsui has told me that one of the reasons he enjoys Jim's poetry is because it is "ambiguous." The punning provides multiple potential ways of imagining a poem and does not force a singular interpretation. Punning is an important feature of Navajo poetics and ways of speaking. It can be found in everyday conversations and in the poetry of contemporary Navajo poets. Such poetic practices are based on phonological iconicity and not on a narrow semantico-referentialist view of language.

The use of punning also resonates with the Navajo ethos of *t'áá bí bee bóholníih* 'it's up to her/him to decide' described at the beginning of this essay. As Louise Lamphere (1977, 38–41) notes, this ethos is an expression of Navajo views on autonomy (see also Chisholm 1996). Individuals have the right to make their own decisions. Puns, like the "indirect" forms of requests described by Lamphere (1977, 57), reinforce an individual's autonomy by relying on ambiguity. In form, then, they do not force a singular interpretation, but rather act as an invitation to imaginative processes. As some Navajos have indicated to me, overtly explaining something assumes the listeners do not have the proper mental capacity to discern something on their own. Explication infringes on the autonomy of the listener, with the added assumption that the listener has a deficient imagination. Puns display verbal dexterity, but they also invite mental engagement on the part of the listener/reader.

Conclusions

Finally, I want to take up the implications of the previous discussions, especially as they relate to Hymes's ethnopoetic work and his concern with social inequality (see also Blommaert 2009). In this essay I have attempted to give an ethnographically and linguistically informed interpretation of the use of the expressive feature -*x*- and the phonological iconicity evoked by the consonant cluster -*chx*-in a poem written in Navajo by Rex Lee Jim. Such ethnographically and linguistically informed interpretations are the basis of ethnopoetics. The first thing to note is that the -*x*- is an expressive option. Its inclusion marks a creative and poetic choice by Jim, one that suggests something about the ways to understand this poem. I have argued that the -*x*-indicates an affective stance toward the character and actions that occur in the poem. This stance is reinforced throughout the poem both by the repeated use of -*x*- and by the velar fricative's combination with -*ch*-; this consonant cluster is phonologically iconic with the consonant cluster in *hóchxǫ́* 'ugly, disorderly, out of control'. The affective stance that emerges in this poem, then, is not just one of augmentation or deprecation; rather, the implication is that Badger lacks control over its actions. Badger is not paying attention to what it is doing. This is an important distinction in Navajo both linguistically—where there are verb stems that differentiate between doing something in a controlled manner and doing things in a non-controlled manner—and culturally, where a premium is placed on acting in a controlled manner and where much ritual is associated with restoring order (*hózhǫ́*) to things that are disorderly (*hochxǫ'*) (see especially Witherspoon 1977). I note, however, that this is just one interpretation of the poem, developed in conversations between Mitchell and myself. Neither of us would presume to argue that it is the only interpretation. By including the velar fricative in the written poem, Jim has provided the possibility or option for readers to connect the consonant cluster -*chx*- with *hochxǫ'*. Jim was, as Navajos sometimes say when positively evaluating a narrative or poem, "giving an imagination to the listener" (see Webster 2009). Importantly, however, this giving of an imagination relies on the creative reflection of the listener. The poem is an invitation to reflect and think.

I also suggested that some linguists and linguistic anthropologists (among others) have not been overly concerned with the expressive features of languages. In fact, there has been a tendency to ignore such features because they do not aid semantico-referential meaning. We saw, for example, that Hoijer (1974; Sapir and Hoijer 1967) did not indicate the velar fricative in verb stems where the -*x*- either always occurs (-*tsxas*) or where it almost always occurs (-*chxǫ'*). An examination of Sapir and Hoijer's *Navaho Texts* (1942) for evidence of the uses of the velar fricative would be misleading at best: Sapir and Hoijer did not record that feature in their texts. Imagine, as is sometimes the case, if that volume were the only evidence of an indigenous language in use. Such texts would then reproduce a Western fascination with reference at the expense of local, feelingfully expressive features. The kind of ethnopoetic work that Hymes (1979) developed based on Sapir's Takelma materials is impossible in this instance, since Sapir and Hoijer erased the expressive use of the velar fricative in their 1942 publication.

Elision of the velar fricative is a continuing trend in Navajo language materials. The use of -*x*- as an expressive feature that indicates augmentation or deprecation is not directly discussed in Irvy Goossen's *Diné Bizaad: Speak, Read, Write Navajo* (1995; but see page xiv for an implicit suggestion that -*x*- indicates "intensity"). Likewise, there appears to be no explicit discussion of the use of -*x*- as an expressive feature in *Diné Bizaad Bináhoo'aah: Rediscovering the Navajo Language*, a 2007 text by Evangeline Parsons Yazzie and Margaret Speas. Both of these are important Navajo language textbooks, but neither discusses the use of the velar fricative as an expressive feature in Navajo. In the summer of 2011 in Shiprock, New Mexico, Mitchell, who has been a longtime Navajo language instructor, told me that he does not get to -*x*- when he is teaching Navajo. As he pointed out, there are so many things to teach and so many demands on teaching that decisions have to be made about what to include and what to exclude from his Navajo language class. One Navajo language teacher with whom I discussed some of Jim's poetry in 2001 went so far as to explain that Jim had misspelled some of the words with the velar fricative. In this volume and elsewhere, Paul V. Kroskrity describes such practices and orientations towards narrative forms as "narrative discriminations" and uses this phrase to evoke the dual force of aesthetics and the political (Kroskrity 2012, 151; see also Bourdieu 1986). Such narrative discriminations, in this case the devaluing of the use of the velar fricative, is clearly both an aesthetic consideration and also fully implicated in the politics of Western educational regimes of knowledge that devalue presentational forms in favor of the banally semantico-referential (see Basso 1990, 74).

I also placed Jim's use of phonological iconicity in this poem within a larger context of Navajo ways of speaking and aesthetics. This aesthetic is one based on implicit punning or *saad aheełt'éego diits'a'*. When one reads or hears a poem in Navajo by Jim, I would suggest (echoing Jim) that it is important to be attentive to the sounds highlighted in that poem—to look for the other words those sounds may evoke. Mitchell's command of Navajo and his own interests in the importance of the sounds of the language are, obviously, the crucial component for my interpretation here (and in other work he is my coauthor). Such creative uses of homophony are part of the "interwovenness" of Navajo, the ways that patterns of language features evoke and interanimate other aspects of language in use (see Woodbury 1998, 244).[8] I would add that this discussion of the poetic use of the velar fricative and consonantal rhyme, and the poem's active interpretation by Mitchell, suggest creative agency both in the production and reception of poetic forms (see Kroskrity 2010). But such aesthetic and poetic practices do not occur outside of social and political realities. Here again it is useful to think of narrative discriminations (Kroskrity 2012, and in this volume). As the pun between *gad* and *god* suggests, these narrative discriminations, which erase an aesthetic practice based on phonological iconicity or punning, have been a recurring theme. Euro-American outsiders and their institutions (schools and missions) have continually misrecognized or devalued Navajo poetic and aesthetic practices, from expressive features to puns to ideophones to Navajo English (see Webster 2009, 2011). Such uses of language, which run the very real danger of being marginalized, erased, and/or ridiculed, I have, of late, termed intimate grammars (Webster 2010a, 2011).

There is an irony here, of course. This Western fascination with literalism obscures the poetic uses of punning in the Western canon. William Shakespeare, an icon of Western literary imaginings, often used puns in his works (see Parker 1996, 2009). Likewise, Jim and I had a number of conversations in 2000 and 2001 in which Jim talked of his admiration for the work of Edmund Spenser, who is also known for his punning (Maley 2001). However, as Joel Sherzer (2002) and Samuels (2004a) have noted, punning in contemporary Euro-American society is not highly valued (see also Bauman and Briggs 2003). One can see this as a curious oversight of what Lawrence Levine (1988) describes as the process of elevating Shakespeare in the cultural hierarchy of the United States. While Shakespeare may have gone from "lowbrow" to "highbrow," punning did not similarly become a valued aesthetic practice. In fact, there is a tradition in Shakespeare scholarship of apologizing for Shakespeare's use of puns (see Johnson [1765] 1968, 74). Hymes was not unconcerned with punning in his ethnopoetic work,[9] nor, of course, was Sapir, who was quite influential to Hymes's thinking and early on described Navajo punning practices (Hymes 1987, 105; Sapir 1932). Jim's use of punning intertextually links to a Navajo poetic tradition of punning, but it also intertextually links to the punning practices of authors like Spenser and Shakespeare. If Jim's poem highlights an aesthetic feature of Navajo verbal art, it also chastises the devaluing of an aesthetic feature in English.

Here we must also confront Western views of literacy, which are fully implicated in a language ideology overly focused on the semantico-referential. Hymes (2003, 42) once noted that "we tend to forget that the usual way of writing languages on the page is one that implies, or, one might say, conceals, linguistic information." Echoing him, I would suggest that as the Navajo language becomes standardized in a written form that is not attentive to expressive forms, some Navajos may not realize that inserting the -*x*- is an expressive option—or they may find that by not indicating the use of such expressive features, those features have been devalued. Mitchell noted that today "people use -*x*- without thinking." Instead, Navajos may see words that normally are produced and written with the velar fricative (like *łitsxo* 'orange, dirty yellow') as merely how one spells the word—a minimal pair for semantico-referential meaning between *łitso* 'yellow' and *łitsxo* 'orange'—and not as a productive expressive feature. In fact, I have been told by some Navajo consultants that *łitsxo* means only 'orange'. Indeed, one Navajo/English dictionary sold at both the Tsaile and Shiprock campuses of Diné College lists *łitsxo* as meaning only 'orange', thus obscuring the expressive use of -*x*- to indicate 'so and so yellow' or 'dirty yellow' and creating a false equivalence between languages (Parnwell and Yellowhair 1989, 104). We can think of this process as the *vocabularization of language*, where languages are reduced to interchangeable labels for the world (see Meek 2010 and Silverstein 1979, 1981). Concomitantly, some Navajos may agree with the teacher that I talked to in 2001 and see the insertion of the velar fricative in other words, like *bichxį́į́h*, as a mistake. This is not an inherent problem of literacy, however; rather, it is a risk generated by a particular literacy that promotes a referentialist view of language at the expense of expressive features (Tedlock 1983), one predicated on a monotelic view of language (Hymes 2000, 299–300). An expanded view of literacy, an ethnopoetic view of literacy, one that acknowledges expressive and presentational features rather than trivializing them or relegating them to the status of nonlinguistic features, would be a literacy that might go some distance in the work of recognizing voice.

Essential to Hymes's ethnopoetic work was a concern with "voice," the ability to express something in a satisfying manner using all of one's expressive options (Hymes 1996b, 64; see also Blommaert 2009 and Kroskrity 2010). Expressive and presentational features of language seem crucial to his concern with voice because they are precisely the kinds of poetic and aesthetic practices that were erased, ignored, and/or marginalized. As Jan Blommaert (2009) argues, Hymes's concerns with ethnopoetics and inequality were intimately linked. Here I think it good to recall the two freedoms of voice that Hymes (1996b, 64) argued for: (1) a "negative freedom," that is, "freedom from denial of opportunity due to something linguistic, whether in speaking or reading or writing" (here we still see the marginalizing of expressive features as either nonlinguistic or spelling mistakes), and (2) a "positive freedom," or "freedom for satisfaction in the use of language, for language to be a source of imaginative life and satisfying form." Jim's poem seems an example of such positive freedom of voice. But not all Navajos recognize Jim's voice; instead many seem enamored by spelling standards.

Spelling standards, however, hinder us when we look at Jim's poem (or the poetry of John Clare or William Blake). Understanding Jim's poem means not just understanding the semantico-referential meanings behind those words, but also catching a glimpse of the expressive potentials of the use of -*x*- as an optional poetic device—a poetic device Jim chose to use in this poem—and listening for potential ambiguities and sound affinities evoked through phonological iconicity. It means recognizing Jim's voice, or, as some Navajos are fond of saying, "really listening" (see Webster 2012a). In our conversations, Mitchell has noted that Jim's use of -*x*- is "very descriptive" and helps in "giving a picture" to those who hear or read this poem; he also observed that Jim's poem "is very strong" because it inspires continued thought. Those are some of the qualities of an aesthetically pleasing Navajo poem; they evoke an image for the listener or reader to ponder (Webster 2009). Such expressive features may, as Mitchell went on to tell me, be hard for "White people" to understand. Or, more poignantly, it may be hard for those Navajos who have been educated in Euro-American institutions to understand. I believe this lack of understanding is predicated on a Western language ideology overly focused on semantico-referential meanings instead of the expressive and affective features of languages (Bauman and Briggs 2003; Samuels 2004a, 2004b; Webster 2009, 2010a).

Mitchell once explained to me, in critiquing the way some linguists and anthropologists approached Navajo, that "the validity of Navajo is in its sounds, not in the neat things it does." His statement suggests that a phonic view of Navajo should take precedence over a Westernized semantic view of language (Frisbie 1980; McAllester 1980; Reichard [1950] 1963).[10] Jim's poetry, which is intimately concerned with the sounds of Navajo and the ways such sounds echo, reverberate, and evoke affinities, stands as a testament to the validity of Navajo being in its sounds. Navajo is here, then, a language of sound and it is this acoustemology (Feld 1996) that makes real—validates—the language as a language that does—creates and enacts—something (Frisbie 1980; McAllester 1980; Reichard [1950] 1963). This is the "sound power" of Navajo that was first described by Reichard (1944, 51). Language—as a sounded phenomenon—is a creative force in the world. Ethnopoetics should be concerned with recognizing local expressive and poetic practices and, in doing so, in recognizing voice, which is intimately tied to such practices. This also means recognizing the politics of inequality in ethnopoetics and understanding the ways that people and their poetic practices are and can be devalued, trivialized, and erased. It is only in understanding ethnopoetics as fully imbricated in social and cultural milieus that we can, returning to a theme long espoused by Hymes, fully appreciate the artistry and implications of language performance. In so doing, we may come to recognize both the beauty and restorative potential of Jim's poetry.

Acknowledgments

I would like to thank Rex Lee Jim for a number of valuable conversations about Navajo poetry. I would also like to thank all the Navajo poets who have taken time to talk with him about their poetry and Navajo poetry more generally. Special thanks go to Blackhorse Mitchell for stimulating conversations about Jim's poetry and the Navajo language more generally; this essay has greatly benefited from his insights. An earlier version of this essay was presented in a session coorganized by Paul V. Kroskrity and me titled "Ethnopoetics, Narrative Inequality, and Voice: On the Legacy of Dell Hymes" at the American Anthropological Association meetings in Montreal, Canada, in November 2011. Thanks also to Paul Kroskrity, Aimee Hosemann, Richard Bauman, Joyce McDonough, Scott Rushforth, M. Eleanor Nevins, Sean O'Neill, Tony Woodbury, Joel Sherzer, Leighton C. Peterson, and David Samuels for useful comments on various iterations of this essay. Mistakes are still mine. Original funding for this research on the Navajo Nation during 2000–2001 was provided by the Wenner-Gren Foundation, the Philips Fund from the American Philosophical Society, and the University of Texas at Austin. More recent research on and around the Navajo Nation from 2007–12 was funded by a Faculty Seed Grant from Southern Illinois University at Carbondale, a Philips Fund Grant from the American Philosophical Society, and a Jacobs Grant from the Whatcom Museum. I would like to thank them all. My research on the Navajo Nation was conducted under permits from the Navajo Nation Historic Preservation Office, to which I am most grateful. Finally, this essay owes a profound debt to the work of Dell Hymes.

Notes

1. My own Hymes-inspired ethnopoetic analysis of a Navajo narrative told by John Watchman can be found in Webster 2012b.

2. In February 2012, Rex Lee Jim was vice president of the Navajo Nation and did not perform his poetry as he once did. Statements from 2001 included in this essay are from an interview we recorded in Tsaile, Arizona. The tape recording is in my possession.

3. Chantways are elaborate Navajo curing rituals. "Medicine man" is one of the ways that Navajos talk about those who perform Navajo chantways. There is an elaborate literature on Navajo chantways and here I merely gesture the interested reader to the groundbreaking work of Reichard (1944, [1950] 1963) and David McAllester (1980).

4. There is more to be said about the moral force of this poem; see Mitchell and Webster 2011 for an extended discussion.

5. Mitchell and I take up the details of documenting and linguistically describing the velar fricative at greater length in Mitchell and Webster 2011.

6. I have updated Hoijer's orthography to match the current Navajo orthography.

7. One Navajo consultant noted that there is also a sexual pun here based on the notion of "sucking" (see also Webster 2006, 42). In conversations with several Navajos about Jim's poetry, a number of such sexual puns were highlighted. Indeed, one Navajo language teacher decided against using Jim's poetry in class because of concerns about how some of the parents and grandparents might respond to such puns.

8. For Anthony Woodbury (1998, 257), interwovenness is one part of a larger pattern of "form-dependent expression" based "on a perception of nonarbitrariness in the relationship between form and function." Iconicity and indexicality would be the most obvious examples of this. Intralingual punning is an example of language-internal form-dependent expression. Note, however, that interlingual puns are also linguistic forms that are deeply implicated in the expressive economy of local groupness—but with a twist, because they are interwoven *across languages* through phonological iconicity. It is this twining of linguistic forms across languages and their expression of local groupness that is threatened by the current language shift on the Navajo Nation (see Webster 2010b). The language situation among Navajos is and has been one of heteroglossia, and interlingual puns are one response to that heteroglossic context (see also Webster 2009, 2010a; Field 2009).

9. Judith Berman's (1992) discussion of punning in a Kwakwa'ala narrative about Oolachan-Woman told to Franz Boas stands as a notable example of the insight that can be gained from combining ethnopoetic work with sensitivity to punning.

10. Many scholars have noted that literacy in Navajo has not taken hold (see McLaughlin 1992; Spolsky 2002; Webster 2012d). A variety of historical reasons has been offered—for example, that literacy has been associated with Western educational regimes and is often seen as suspect today by Navajos. I have made such an argument (Webster 2012d). However, here it might be useful to note that there is a significant literature about the importance of sound in Navajo (see Frisbie 1980; McAllester 1980; Reichard [1950] 1963; Webster 2009). Reichard (1944, 51) termed this concern with sound "sound power." Jim's and other poets' use of ideophony in their poetry may be related to this concern with sound in Navajo (see Webster 2009). It is possible that a Western literacy, focused as it is on semantics, runs counter to the view that "the validity of Navajo" lies in its sounds. Western-inspired literacy would then fundamentally misunderstand the nature of language and might fit uneasily with some Navajo language ideologies.

As Hymes notes, our literacy practices conceal linguistic information (2003, 42)—most importantly, its sounds. And while we tend to think that an alphabet represents sounds, what it represents are, at best, the abstract phonemes of a language—though, as is well known, English is inconsistent on this point. Such phonemes are in the service of semantic meaning based on minimal pairs and the like. Western literacy erases the sounds of a language for the phonemes of a language. Jim's poetry seeks to highlight the sounds of Navajo and to suggest meanings in the relations or echoes of sounds, not in the binary of phonemic minimal pairs, but in the evocation of sound affinities and phonological iconicity.

Notice, by the way, how the entire edifice of *emic* and *etic* based on the distinction between *phonemic* and *phonetic* (see Pike 1967) collapses when we realize that some Navajos are concerned not with the phonemes of a language, but with the phones of the language, interested not in phonemic contrasts, but in phonological iconicity.

References Cited

Basso, Keith. 1990. *Western Apache Language and Culture*. Tucson: University of Arizona Press.

Bauman, Richard, and Charles Briggs. 2003. *Voices of Modernity: Language Ideologies and the Politics of Inequality*. Cambridge: Cambridge University Press.

Becker, Alton. 1995. *Beyond Translation*. Ann Arbor: University of Michigan Press.

Berman, Judith. 1992. "Oolachan-Woman's Robe: Fish, Blankets, Masks, and Meaning in Boas's Kwakw'ala Texts." In *On the Translation of Native American Literatures*, edited by Brian Swann, 125–62. Washington, DC: Smithsonian.

Blommaert, Jan. 2009. "Ethnography and Democracy: Hymes's Political Theory of Language." *Text & Talk* 29 (3): 257–76.

Bodo, Fr. Murray. 1998. *Tales of an Endishodi: Father Berard Haile and the Navajos, 1900–1960s*. Albuquerque: University of New Mexico Press.

Bolinger, Dwight. 1940. "Word Affinities." *American Speech* 15 (1): 62–73.

Bourdieu, Pierre. 1986. *Distinction*. Cambridge, MA: Harvard University Press.

Calvino, Italo. 1988. *Six Memos for the Next Millennium.* New York: Vintage.

Chisholm, James. 1996. "Learning 'Respect for Everything': Navajo Images of Development." In *Images of Childhood,* edited by Philip Hwang, Irving Sigel, and Michael Lamb, 167–83. Hillsdale, NJ: Lawrence Erlbaum.

Cisneros, Ruth, Joey Alexanian, Jalon Begay, and Megan Goldberg. 2006. "The Language of Humor: Navajo." *Santa Barbara Papers in Linguistics,* vol. 18. Proceedings from the Ninth Workshop on American Indigenous Languages. http://www.linguistics.ucsb.edu/research/santa-barbara-papers#Volume18.

Delano, Bill. 2010. "Video: Poems by Rex Lee Jim '86." *Princeton Alumni Weekly,* November 3. http://paw.princeton.edu/issues/2010/11/03/pages/8440/index.xml.

Faltz, Leonard M. 1998. *The Navajo Verb: A Grammar for Students and Scholars.* Albuquerque: University of New Mexico Press.

Farnell, Brenda. 1995. *Do You See What I Mean: Plains Indian Sign Talk and the Embodiment of Action.* Austin: University of Texas Press.

Feld, Steven. 1996. "Waterfalls of Song: An Acoustemology of Place Resounding in Bosavi, Papua New Guinea." In *Senses of Place,* edited by Steven Feld and Keith Basso, 91–135. Santa Fe: School of American Research Press.

Field, Margaret C. 2009. "Changing Navajo Language Ideologies and Changing Language Use." In *Native American Language Ideologies: Beliefs, Practices, and Struggles in Indian Country,* edited by Paul V. Kroskrity and Margaret C. Field, 31–47. Tucson: University of Arizona Press.

Frisbie, Charlotte. 1980. "Vocables in Navajo Ceremonial Music." *Ethnomusicology* 24 (3): 347–92.

Goossen, Irvy. 1995. *Diné Bizaad: Speak, Read, and Write Navajo.* Flagstaff, AZ: Salina Bookshelf.

Hill, W. W. 1943. *Navajo Humor.* Menasha, WI: George Banta.

Hoijer, Harry. 1974. *A Navajo Lexicon.* Berkeley: University of California Press.

Hymes, Dell. 1960. "Phonological Aspects of Style: Some English Sonnets." In *Style in Language,* edited by Thomas Sebeok, 107–31. Cambridge, MA: MIT Press.

———. 1968. "Linguistics: The Field." In *International Encyclopedia of the Social Sciences,* vol. 9, edited by David Sills, 351–71. New York: Macmillan, Free Press.

———. 1979. "How to Talk Like a Bear in Takelma." *International Journal of American Linguistics* 45 (2): 101–6.

———. 1981. *"In Vain I Tried to Tell You": Essays in Native American Ethnopoetics.* Philadelphia: University of Pennsylvania Press.

———. 1984. "Bungling Host, Benevolent Host: Louis Simpson's 'Deer and Coyote'." *American Indian Quarterly* 8 (3): 171–98.

———. 1987. "A Pattern of Verbal Irony in Chinookan." *International Journal of the Sociology of Language* 65:97–110.

———. 1996a. "Consonant Symbolism in Kathlamet and Shoalwater Chinook." *University of Oregon Anthropological Papers* 52:163–71.

———. 1996b. *Ethnography, Linguistics, Narrative Inequality: Toward an Understanding of Voice.* Bristol, PA: Taylor and Francis.

———. 1998. *Reading Takelma Texts.* Bloomington, IN: Trickster.

———. 2000. "Sung Epic and Native American Ethnopoetics." In *Textualization of Oral Epics,* edited by Lauri Honko, 291–342. Berlin: Mouton de Gruyter.

———. 2003. *Now I Know Only That Far.* Lincoln: University of Nebraska Press.

Jim, Rex Lee. 1995. *saad*. Princeton, NJ: Princeton Collections of Western Americana.

Johnson, Samuel. (1765) 1968. "Preface to Shakespeare." In *The Yale Edition of the Works of Samuel Johnson, Volume VII: Johnson on Shakespeare*, edited by Arthur Sherbo, 74. New Haven, CT: Yale University Press.

Johnstone, Barbara. 1996. *The Linguistic Individual*. Oxford: Oxford University Press.

Kluckhohn, Clyde, and Dorothea Leighton. 1962. *The Navajo*. New York: Doubleday.

Kroskrity, Paul V. 2010. "The Art of Voice: Understanding the Arizona Tewa Inverse in Its Grammatical, Narrative, and Language-Ideological Contexts." *Anthropological Linguistics* 52 (1): 49–79.

———. 2012. "Growing with Stories: Ideologies of Storytelling and the Narrative Reproduction of Arizona Tewa Identities." In *Telling Stories in the Face of Danger: Language Renewal in Native American Communities*, edited by Paul V. Kroskrity, 151–83. Norman: University of Oklahoma Press.

Lamphere, Louise. 1977. *To Run After Them: Cultural and Social Bases of Cooperation in a Navajo Community*. Tucson: University of Arizona Press.

Landar, Herbert, Susan Ervin, and Arnold Horowitz. 1960. "Navaho Color Categories." *Language* 36 (1): 368–92.

Levine, Lawrence. 1988. *Highbrow/Lowbrow*. Cambridge, MA: Harvard University Press.

Liebe-Harkort, M. L. 1979. "Bilingualism and Language Mixing among the White Mountain Apaches." *Folia Linguistica* 13 (3/4): 345–56.

Maley, Willy. 2001. "Spenser's Languages: Writing in the Ruins of English." In *The Cambridge Companion to Spenser*, edited by Andrew Hadfield, 162–79. Cambridge: Cambridge University Press.

McAllester, David. 1980. "The First Snake Song." In *Theory and Practice: Essays Presented to Gene Weltfish*, edited by Stanley Diamond, 1–27. New York: Mouton.

McLaughlin, Daniel. 1992. *When Literacy Empowers: Navajo Language in Print*. Albuquerque: University of New Mexico Press.

Meek, Barbra. 2010. *We Are Our Language: An Ethnography of Language Revitalization in a Northern Athabaskan Community*. Tucson: University of Arizona Press.

Mitchell, Blackhorse, and Anthony K. Webster. 2011. "'We Don't Know What We Become': Navajo Ethnopoetics and an Expressive Feature in a Poem by Rex Lee Jim." *Anthropological Linguistics* 53 (3): 259–86.

Nevins, M. Eleanor. 2010. "The Bible in Two Keys: Traditionalism and Evangelical Christianity on the Fort Apache Reservation." *Language & Communication* 30 (1): 19–32.

Nuckolls, Janis. 1999. "The Case for Sound Symbolism." *Annual Review of Anthropology* 28:225–52.

———. 2006. "The Neglected Poetics of Ideophony." In *Language, Culture, and the Individual*, edited by Catherine O'Neil, Mary Scoggin, and Kevin Tuite, 39–50. Munich: Lincom.

Paredes, Américo. 1977. "On Ethnographic Work among Minority Groups: A Folklorist's Perspective." *New Scholar* 6:1–32.

Parker, Patricia. 1996. *Shakespeare from the Margins: Language, Culture, Context.* Chicago: University of Chicago Press.

———. 2009. "Shakespeare's Sound Government: Sound Defects, Polyglot Sounds, and Sounding Out." *Oral Tradition* 24 (2): 359–72.

Parnwell, E. C., and Marvin Yellowhair. 1989. *The New Oxford Picture Dictionary: English/Navajo Edition.* Oxford: Oxford University Press.

Pike, Kenneth L. 1967. *Language in Relation to a Unified Theory of the Structure of Human Behavior.* 2nd ed. The Hague: Mouton.

Reichard, Gladys. 1944. *Prayer: The Compulsive Word.* American Ethnological Society Monograph 7. Seattle: University of Washington Press.

———. 1948. "The Significance of Aspiration in Navaho." *International Journal of American Linguistics* 14:15–19.

———. (1950) 1963. *Navaho Religion: A Study of Symbolism.* New York: Bollingen Foundation.

———. 1951. *Navaho Grammar.* New York: J. J. Augustin.

Rushforth, Scott, and James Chisholm. 1991. *Cultural Persistence.* Tucson: University of Arizona Press.

Samuels, David. 2001. "Indeterminacy and History in Britton Goode's Western Apache Placenames." *American Ethnologist* 28 (2): 277–302.

———. 2004a. "Language, Meaning, Modernity, and Doowop." *Semiotica* 149 (1–4): 297–323.

———. 2004b. *Putting a Song on Top of It.* Tucson: University of Arizona Press.

———. 2006. "Bible Translation and Medicine Man Talk: Missionaries, Indexicality, and the 'Language Expert' on the San Carlos Apache Reservation." *Language in Society* 35 (4): 529–57.

Sapir, Edward. (1915) 1985. "Abnormal Types of Speech in Nootka." In *Selected Writings in Language, Culture, and Personality,* edited by David G. Mandelbaum, 179–96. Berkeley: University of California Press.

———. 1932. "Two Navajo Puns." *Language* 8:217–19.

Sapir, Edward, and Harry Hoijer. 1942. *Navaho Texts.* Iowa City: Linguistic Society of America.

———. 1967. *The Phonology and Morphology of the Navaho Language.* Linguistics 50. Berkeley: University of California Press.

Sherzer, Joel. 2002. *Speech Play and Verbal Art.* Austin: University of Texas Press.

Silverstein, Michael. 1979. "Language Structure and Linguistic Ideology." In *The Elements,* edited by Paul Clyne, William Hanks, and Carol Hofbauer, 193–247. Chicago: Chicago Linguistic Society.

———. 1981. "The Limits of Awareness." *Sociolinguistic Working Papers* 84. Austin: Southwest Educational Development Laboratory.

Spolsky, Bernard. 2002. "Prospects for the Survival of the Navajo Language: A Reconsideration." *Anthropology & Education Quarterly* 33 (2): 139–62.

Tedlock, Dennis. 1983. *The Spoken Word and the Work of Interpretation.* Philadelphia: University of Pennsylvania Press.

Toelken, Barre, and Tacheeni Scott. 1981. "Poetic Retranslation and the 'Pretty Languages' of Yellowman." In *Traditional Literatures of the American Indians,* edited by Karl Kroeber, 65–116. Lincoln: University of Nebraska Press.

Wallis, Ethel Emily. 1968. *God Speaks Navajo.* New York: Harper and Row.

Webster, Anthony K. 2006. "The Mouse that Sucked: On 'Translating' a Navajo Poem." *Studies in American Indian Literature* 18 (1): 37–49.

———. 2009. *Explorations in Navajo Poetry and Poetics.* Albuquerque: University of New Mexico Press.

———. 2010a. "On Intimate Grammars, with Examples from Navajo English, Navlish, and Navajo." *Journal of Anthropological Research* 66 (2): 187–208.

———. 2010b. "A Note on Navajo Interlingual Puns." *International Journal of American Linguistics* 76 (2): 289–98.

———. 2011. "'Please Read Loose': Intimate Grammars and Unexpected Languages in Contemporary Navajo Literature." *American Indian Culture and Research Journal* 35 (2): 61–86.

———. 2012a. "Blackhorse Mitchell's Beauty of Navajoland: Bivalency, Dooajinída, and the Work of Contemporary Navajo Poetry." *Semiotica* 189 (1–4): 97–131.

———. 2012b. "John Watchman's 'Ma'ii dóó Gólízhii'." In *Inside Dazzling Mountains: Southwest Native Verbal Art,* edited by David Kozak, 150–72. Lincoln: University of Nebraska Press.

———. 2012c. "Rex Lee Jim's 'Mouse that Sucked': On Iconicity, Interwovenness, and Ideophones in Contemporary Navajo Poetry." Paper presented at *Linguistic Society of America,* Portland, OR, January 7.

———. 2012d. "Who Reads Navajo Poetry and What Are They Reading? Exploring the Semiotic Functions of Contemporary Written Navajo." *Social Semiotics* 22 (4): 375–408.

Witherspoon, Gary. 1977. *Language and Art in the Navajo Universe.* Ann Arbor: University of Michigan Press.

Woodbury, Anthony. 1998. "Documenting Rhetorical, Aesthetic, and Expressive Loss in Language Shift." In *Endangered Languages,* edited by Lenore Grenoble and Lindsay Whaley, 234–58. Cambridge: Cambridge University Press.

Woolard, Kathryn. 1998. "Simultaneity and Bivalency as Strategies in Bilingualism." *Journal of Linguistic Anthropology* 8 (1): 3–29.

Yazzie, Evangeline Parsons, and Margaret Speas. 2007. *Diné Bizaad Bínáhoo'aah: Rediscovering the Navajo Language.* Flagstaff, AZ: Salina Bookshelf.

Young, Robert, and William Morgan. 1943. *The Navaho Language: The Elements of Navaho Grammar with a Dictionary in Two Parts Containing Basic Vocabularies of Navaho and English.* Phoenix: Education Division, US Indian Service.

———. 1987. *The Navajo Language.* Albuquerque: University of New Mexico Press.

———. 1992. *Analytical Lexicon of Navajo.* With the assistance of Sally Midgette. Albuquerque: University of New Mexico Press.

ANTHONY K. WEBSTER is Associate Professor of Anthropology at the University of Texas at Austin. He is the author of *Explorations in Navajo Poetry and Poetics* (2009) as well as numerous articles on Navajo poetry, language, and culture.

5   Discursive Discriminations in the Representation of Western Mono and Yokuts Stories: Confronting Narrative Inequality and Listening to Indigenous Voices in Central California

AT THE HEART of folklore's interest in oral traditions, traditional narratives provide critical resources for the mutually dependent projects of constructing selves and creating communities. But even though all human groups seem to display a penchant for stories, most also live in a world in which it is abundantly clear that not all stories are equally valued, supported, or permitted. This "narrative inequality," to use a concept created and championed by Dell Hymes (1996), calls attention to disparities of treatment and to disparate evaluations of stories. Oral versus literate, schooled versus unschooled, standard language versus minority language, and elaborated versus restricted code provide a sample of the dichotomies used not only in the ranking of narratives, but in the stratification of their speakers. As noted by Jan Blommaert (2009, 258), Hymes's "democratic" and ethnographically based "political" theory of language called for students of language and discourse to use their skills not to hierarchize language users but to offer resources to communities in what Hymes (1996, 60) termed a "mediative" manner that would enable them to better understand and use their linguistic and narrative diversity:

> The study of language has had a checkered career in the history just sketched. It became a self-conscious activity, and to a great extent has developed, as an instrument of exclusion and domination. The analysis of Sanskrit in ancient India, . . . of Greek and then Latin in the ancient Mediterranean, of nascent national languages in the Renaissance . . . were in the interest of cultural hegemony. Only in our own [twentieth] century, through the decisive work of Boas, Sapir, and other anthropologically oriented linguists (as components of the general triumph of methodological relativism in the human sciences), has every form of

135

> human speech gained the right, as it were, to contribute on an equal
> footing to what is known of human language.

This essay is an attempt to extend Hymes's important work on narrative inequality while critically engaging the sense of progress suggested in the quote above. While I do feel that the historical development of linguistic anthropology and adjacent fields has provided an increasing number of conceptual and analytical resources, I question whether linguistic scientists are consistently able to incorporate these cumulative advances into their actual scientific practice and into the kind of "mediative" resources that might be of use to actual speech communities.[1] In an effort to extend the notion of narrative inequality and make it a more useful tool for dealing with the indigenous narrative traditions of Central California, I want to honor Hymes in my own practice by applying an admittedly derivative concept of *discursive discrimination* (Kroskrity 2012a) to capture the simultaneity of aesthetic evaluation and the imposition of social hierarchies. In so doing, I want to focus on both the professional language ideologies (Kroskrity 2000) of anthropologists and linguists around the mid-twentieth century who were engaged in "salvage" research on Central California Indian languages and on the indigenous narrative practices that were erased by those salvage-era scholars.

My first goal, then, is to deconstruct the narrative discriminations of these scholars by disclosing the ethnocentric basis of their aesthetic taste and by exposing their professional practice of decontextualized appreciation, which would only further contribute to the discursive marginalization of the narratives (Kuipers 1998). My second goal is to contribute to a partial restoration of Yokuts and Western Mono voices by using textual, ethnographic, and multimedia resources that help provide an alternative, community-based understanding. Though unrelated, these two indigenous languages are from a common region, and both have been marginalized as a consequence of nation-state policies with which academic scholars have been compliant. Here I use Hymesian ethnolinguistic "voice," which, as characterized by Blommaert (2009, 271–72), provides a concept more flexible than Mikhail Bakhtin's "voice" and one more concerned with recognizing the narrative, generic, and linguistic preferences of speakers who are otherwise marginalized by hegemonic institutions.

Western Mono and Yokuts:
Hegemonic Erasure and Counterhegemonic Responses

Both Western Mono and Yokuts were traditionally spoken in California's central San Joaquin Valley and adjacent foothill areas. The two unrelated languages had been in significant contact for hundreds of years prior to exposure to Euro-Americans. Western Mono is from the Numic branch of the Uto-Aztecan language family, whereas Yokuts is generally regarded as a member of the Penutian language family (Mithun 2001, 567). Today the Western Mono, by their own reckoning, number 1,800 in North Fork, Auberry, and other Central California rancherias. This total includes perhaps twenty-five highly fluent speakers, all in the oldest generation, making it a severely endangered language according to Krauss's (2007) classification of endangered languages. I have treated elsewhere what there is no space for here—the history of language contact, shift, and ideological change in the region (Kroskrity 2009). Yokuts communities outnumbered those of the Mono in precontact times and continue to do so in the present. About forty different Yokuts communities (Gamble 1994, 1) once inhabited various locations in the Central Valley and spoke regional forms of the language in the Northern Valley (e.g., Chukchansi, Chawcilla), foothills (e.g., Choynimni), and Southern Valley (e.g., Tachi, Yawelmani). Today their descendants number about 2,600 and live in communities such as the Santa Rosa, Picayune, Table Mountain, and Tuolumne Rancherias, on the Tule River Indian Reservation, and in adjacent towns. Yokuts now has approximately twenty-five highly fluent speakers and is comparable to Mono in its current state of endangerment through shift to English (Hinton 1994, 32–33).[2] All the Western Mono and Yokuts language communities went from a classic residual zone in Nichols's (1999) sense—an adaptation involving multilingualism, seasonal movement, and intermarriage—to one that featured the aggressive spread of English, forceful suppression of indigenous languages, and a hegemonic pressure following a massive language shift that was facilitated in part by indigenous language ideologies that prioritized language as an adaptive tool (Kroskrity 2009). This massive language shift was imposed by hegemonic institutions that suppressed and stigmatized all indigenous language use—including forms of verbal art.

Early popular representations of these and comparable indigenous verbal art traditions, such as Judson's *Myths and Legends of California and the Old Southwest* ([1912] 1994) and Gifford and Block's *California Indian Nights* ([1930] 1990), contributed to discursive marginalization by fetishizing and appropriating their referential content as once-local lore now controlled by the dominant society. Such popular treatments recontextualized indigenous narratives solely in English translation and exercised the dominant society's cultural preferences by erasing locally valued rhetorical features such as "repetition" (Gifford and Block [1930] 1990, 43) and "long conversations" (Judson [1912] 1994, 15). Given the attempt to reach a general public, we can perhaps understand the deletion of what from the Native perspective would be regarded as essential features of performance. These deletions of indigenous rhetorical form and narrative practice in favor of those more familiar to the dominant society represented a form of discursive marginalization that closely paralleled the ideological erasure of California Natives' distinctive aesthetic and discursive perspectives as a necessary removal of an impediment to the appropriation of indigenous narrative traditions.[3] But rather than examine the representational practices of de- and re-contextualization of indigenous storytelling traditions designed with the primary goal of popularizing narrative content for a reading public, I want to devote attention to specific works on the Mono (and the neighboring Yokuts) written by professional academics for their peers and meant to address not just content but aesthetic and stylistic issues as well. I think these attempts at literary criticism of an oral tradition are an especially appropriate site for understanding the professional and other language ideologies that have further contributed to the discursive marginalization of these narrative traditions.

After more than seventy years, much has changed since Anna H. Gayton and Stanley Newman characterized what they called the "narrative style" of Yokuts and Western Mono myths and proceeded to supply what I will call a deficit image of these Central Californian indigenous traditions (Gayton and Newman [1940] 1964). Though this collaborative research was performed and published as part of the salvage research orchestrated by Kroeber and his colleagues at the University of California, the work continues to merit scholarly attention. Newman and Gayton's *Yokuts and Western Mono Myths* became at least semicanonical to the evolving subfield of linguistic anthropology.

The monograph's inclusion, in excerpted form, in *Language in Culture and Society* (Hymes 1964), arguably the first anthology in linguistic anthropology, both expresses Hymes's evolving interest in what he would call anthropological philology (Hymes 1981) and prefigures his scholarly quest to develop a notion of "style" (Hymes 1979) at a time when so many scholars were obsessed with grammatical order. It is important to remember the historical chronology of linguistics and linguistic anthropology and its impact on research on Native American narrative traditions. A tradition of textual collection had emerged since Boas's foundational work (e.g., Boas 1894; Boas and Hunt 1902), but scholars working around the mid-twentieth century did not have the benefit of several significant scholarly movements relevant to the study of narratives. These include (1) verbal art as performance (e.g., Bauman 1975); (2) ethnopoetics (e.g., Hymes 1981; Tedlock 1983); (3) the politics of poetics (Bauman and Briggs 1990; Briggs and Bauman 1992); and (4) the ethnography of communication. Salvage-era scholars labored under pervasive paradigms that emphasized acculturation and assimilation, and—quite significantly, I think—they regarded their "salvage" efforts as directed exclusively at academic elites and not at the communities whose linguistic and cultural heritage they collected and analyzed.[4] In Hymes's terms, their research was "extractive" rather than "mediative." Their goal was to make a purely academic contribution, to archive representations of languages that were rapidly vanishing. Their works were exclusively written for academic audiences and, given the expectation of Indian acculturation and assimilation, they could not imagine a future indigenous use or need for their publications.

But times have changed, and Native Californian communities have not vanished. Many have in fact engaged in various forms of language revitalization. The texts once designed exclusively for academics are now more readily available to contemporary communities. Given the comparative availability of their publications and comparable forms of cultural representation in the public space of the Internet and in the digital world more generally, it is important that the circulation of these texts back to heritage communities be accompanied by appropriate commentary that might rectify past inadequacies in representation and better provide resources for the contemporary consumption of these texts by academic audiences and especially by indigenous communities themselves.

Salvage Anthropology's Discriminating
Glance: Relativism or Racism?

It is not surprising that linguistic anthropological research performed during the salvage era would be found lacking by today's standards, both because it could not benefit from subsequent advances in the study of language use and because it did not consider contemporary communities as audiences. The two distinguished scholars whose research is examined here must be viewed within a historical context of both academic disciplines and national policies. A "salvage" anthropologist specializing in Central California groups like the Mono and a student of both Kroeber and Lowie at the University of California's Berkeley campus, Anna H. Gayton (1899–1977) was more familiar with trait-list ethnography and folkloristic motifs than she was trained in the study of language (Gayton 1948). Her Mono stories were, in her words, "taken in English" translation and submitted to the kinds of areal analysis of cultural elements common to studies of indigenous California and other Native American regional cultures more generally (Gayton 1935). Though her emphasis was on content and not based on a careful analysis of the Mono originals, Gayton nevertheless contributed a list of comparative observations that suggested the use of benchmarks derived from the literary qualities of expository or essayist discursive prose so highly valorized in academic settings (Collins 1996, 2009, 334). She would go on to a major career in folklore studies and became president of the American Folklore Society in 1950 (Boyer 1978). Certainly Stanley Newman (1905–84) was no less accomplished. A student of the "Sapir school" who followed his mentor from Chicago to Yale, Newman abandoned his early career in English composition and literature and committed to a professional focus on anthropological linguistics, earning his PhD from Yale on the basis of an outstanding dissertation that represented the grammar of Yokuts (Newman 1944; Darnell 1989; Silverstein 1989). His collaboration with Gayton was brief and consisted of his providing an annotated Yokuts text and a section on the "linguistic style" of Yokuts narratives. These sections were added to Gayton's synthetic discussion of "narrative style" for these two groups, plot summaries of the collected narratives, and a discussion of areal themes and motifs suggesting the influence of culture contact, perhaps as an attempt to better authenticate Gayton's analysis (Hymes 1970). For my purposes here, I occasionally combine the largely similar remarks of these two researchers, but it should be observed that all of Newman's remarks in his sections of *Yokuts and Western Mono Myths* were focused upon Yokuts and, though Gayton commented about stories in both languages, her only knowledge of them was gleaned from English-language translations.

Collectively, both scholars offered a putatively descriptive characterization that assumed the shape of contrastive expectations. Seven relatively negative characterizations of Central California indigenous narrative can be distinguished in the Gayton/Newman representation of Yokuts and Mono narratives. These include lexical deficiency, lack of figurative language, simplicity, redundancy, lack of explication, lack of variation, and lack of formal structure. Though it is easy to judge Newman and Gayton harshly for what looks like their ethnocentric English literacy-based judgments, a closer examination reveals that they were, comparatively speaking, attempting a relativism in their appreciation of distinct "narrative styles." Newman, for example, wrote:

> But by the same token, the stylistic features of English cannot appeal to the intuitions of a Yokuts native. To him English must appear erratic, lacking in those qualities of restraint and consistency that he finds in his own language. He will see no uniformity in the pattern of English sentences. . . . Behind this unevenness of expression there seems to be a strident and feverish energy obsessed with the need of expressing nuances that could best be left to contextual inference. (Newman and Gayton [1940] 1964, 377)

Relativism, I suppose, represents an improvement over treating discursive difference in a more discriminating manner, but though Newman achieves a measure of relativism by attempting to see English speakers' literacy-based expectations from another's perspective, neither he nor Gayton ever succeeds in imagining a systematic alternative in which the cluster of normally dispreferred traits would make sense.

Does an appeal to relativism rationalize a reluctance to search for an alternative pattern in structural form, performance practice, ethnographic detail, or speakers' own accounts? While I concede that advances in linguistic anthropology have considerably broadened the scope of our investigations and that it is unfair, in many respects, to judge these scholars by today's methodological and theoretical standards, I still find it completely appropriate to interrogate their

unwillingness to attempt an understanding of this array of dispreferred narrative norms. Classic statements on linguistic relativity by
Whorf that are contemporaneous with the study by Gayton and Newman clearly do not limit relativity to an isolation of difference, and they
offer an alternative model for displaying relativism. In works such as
"The Relation of Habitual Thought and Behavior to Language" (1939)
and "Science and Linguistics" (1940), Whorf did not merely detail the
lack of tense-aspect markers in Hopi or note the lack of a generalized
verb 'to clean' in Shawnee. Instead, Whorf also detailed the richness
of Hopi linguistic resources for representing the idea of preparation,
related this linguistic complex to Hopi ceremonial practice (1939), and
detailed the precise alternative coding of specific cleaning actions in
Shawnee (1940). But the relativism of Gayton and Newman is mute
with regard to locating an alternative pattern.[5] Is there something else
at work that makes sense of both their willingness to note difference
without understanding it and their contentment with displaying hegemonic narrative forms without also attempting to denaturalize them?

To better deconstruct their analysis and the apparently pejorative
foundation it rests on, we would need to examine all seven negative
claims; however, space limitations here will permit me to treat only
three partially overlapping claims: (1) repetition, or lack of structural
variation; (2) lack of richness of expression; and (3) lack of explanation.

Discursive Discriminations: (Artless) Repetition

Newman unpacks the "bareness" of Yokuts narratives when he explicates, "In these stories there is no tendency to indulge in elaboration
of concrete details. The notions expressed remain at a highly generalized level" (Newman and Gayton [1940] 1964, 373). Another key
manifestation of "simplicity and bareness," in the authors' minds, was
a preference for "repetition" rather than "variation." Here Newman
and Gayton fail to appreciate the orality of Mono and Yokuts narratives and thus misrecognize in their own textual artifacts the artistic
work of both structural parallelism, and dramatic repetition in orally
performed narrative, as mere "artless" repetition in entexted form.
Contrasting cultural perspectives, Newman compares Eurocentric
to Native Californian narrative aesthetics when he writes, "Although
we may regard variety as an absolute virtue of style and repetition
as a universal sin, it is obvious that Yokuts cannot be driven in this

direction. . . . When a notion is to be repeated there is no need to avoid verbal repetition" (Newman and Gayton [1940] 1964, 374). But such words both fail to appreciate the role of repetition in the parallelism of oral discourse and exaggerate its automaticity.

Let's examine this failure to appreciate repetition by considering an example from Chawchilla Yokuts, a story by Johnny Jones collected by Newman himself in 1931. I am relying on its interlinear representation in Geoffrey Gamble's (1994, 17) collection of Yokuts texts:[6]

1. *'ama' 'amin nophop 'amil'ay ne:ye:'ay 'amam, Sa:liki'ki put'uh.*
   And   his father   came   he:shook him wake up   son
   And his father came and shook him, "Wake up, my son!"
2. *'ama' 'ohom' 'okot'oy.*
   And   not   he:got:up.
   And he didn't get up.
3. *'ama' thawtham' nim puc'on wil'ay*
   And   is dead   my son   he-says
   And he said, "My son died."
4. *'ama' thah paxat'xo 'am'an*
   And   then mourned they
   And then they mourned.
5. *'ama' yuk'ulhal' thah'ama' puc'on 'amin tha:with'ay*
   And he was buried that one son   his   died
   And they buried that one—his dead son.
6. *'ama' he:te'*
   And that's all.
   And that is all.

Viewed strictly from a perspective that seems to regard English prose conventions as the appropriate benchmark, it is true that the concluding passage (lines 1–6 above) is repetitious and lacking in the syntactic diversity that is conventionally prescribed. But Newman and Gayton never explore whether this pattern conforms to an alternative aesthetic or whether the oral performance needs to be regarded as a shaping factor.

It is also noteworthy that these scholars were so preoccupied with the transcribed texts that they failed to relate the features of those texts to the oral performances that were recontextualized in them. Newman and Gayton's type of salvage linguistics did not attempt to collect narratives in culturally appropriate contexts, even when this was possible. And unfortunately none of the Yokuts and Mono consultants exhibited the refusal to cooperate with the linguist or ethnologist that was displayed to K. David Harrison (2007) by a Tuvan (Siberian) storyteller who sneered, "Do you expect me to tell stories to that thing?" (the linguist's tape recorder), requiring Harrison to assemble an improvised human audience by scouring the neighboring area before the consultant agreed to tell his stories. Thus it is no wonder that Newman and Gayton would misrecognize their text artifacts as "the stories" rather than viewing them, as we might today, as entextualizations of embodied performances of verbal art (Bauman 1975; Kroskrity 2009).

This privileging of schooled literacy over oral performance is remarkable since both Yokuts and Western Mono narratives demonstrate a very detectable pattern of textual cohesion created by repeated use of initial lexical items meaning 'and' and 'and then'. While Euro-American scholars in the pre-ethnopoetic period found little value in this type of repetition, my own ethnographically based research with Central California storytellers suggests that they, operating within a different discursive regime, regarded it as an authenticating feature of proper performance.

Western Mono storytellers employ a similar organizational style, creating a basic pattern of sentences linked by parallel use of the initial *onnoho-yaisi* 'and then'. The examples below (7–11) are taken from the story "Coyote and the Moles," performed in 1993 by Rosalie Bethel and audio- and video-recorded by me at that time (Kroskrity, Bethel, and Reynolds 2002).[7]

7. *Onnoho yaisi onnoho miya-t, niimi-boyo-naapaa miya-t.*
   Then and then go-TNS   Indian-trail-along go-TNS
   And then he went; he went along the Indian trail.

8. *Onnoho yaisi qwena'a-diya miya-t.*
   Then and far-also go-TNS
   And then he also went far.

9. *Onnoho yaisi na'mihoowi-t.*
   Then and tire-TNS.
   And then he got tired.

10. *Onnoho yaisi onnoho paya-ibo' huu'i-di*
    Then and then water-EMPH flow-TNS
    And then a little river was flowing there.

11. *Onnoho yaisi mannoho paya-na hibi-kus sunawi-t.*
    Then and there water-OBL drink-while think-TNS
    And then he thought that he would drink water there.

This passage occurs early in the story as Coyote is introduced and represented as waking up in the spring after his winter hibernation. Though Bethel uses this as her preferred linkage between story clauses, she also displays two instances of variation in the same story, each building from this basic pattern to create a meaningful and dramatic variation. In one instance, there is a stanza of four clauses with the first three all displaying the usual *onnoho-yaisi*. These sentences describe Coyote lying down and falling asleep. But in the fourth sentence the initial *mowaho* 'now' is used to surprise the hearer as Coyote is abruptly and mysteriously woken up.

Later in the narrative this alternation is exploited not to create the single-effect surprise but as a temporary replacement of 'and then' with 'now' to create an immediacy and intensity that is highly appropriate for that point in the narrative. Though accomplished with sentence-initial adverbs, the effect on narrative tempo and episode intensification is analogous to the use of tense variation in the narratives of American English-speaking storytellers (Schiffrin 1981). This intensity is used in describing a race between Coyote and Mole that is just reaching its climax. In this passage (lines 12–16), Coyote is tripped up by some tree roots as he nears the finish line, finally managing to rise up and run toward the goal, only to witness Mole pop up on the far side of the line.

12. *Mowahu iweehu hani'isU sumaiqaabina-t*
Now here why confuse-TNS
Now he became confused here.

13. *Tïpudi'i-wai-n tsinipipoosa'ïpa'i-t.*
escape-FUT-SUB flip-TNS
In trying to get free, he flipped over and over.

14. *Pidisi-yaisi mowa winikiya-t.*
finally and now stand-TNS
And finally he stood up

15. *Mowa onnohO miya-t.*
Now then go-TNS
And now he went.

16. *Mowahu yaisi a-tïwadïqa-qwee mowahu pïtihu-gaa-wai-s miyu-tsi' "AAAA, nii tï-ponaa-t!," inee-t.*
Now and it-finish-at now arrive-go-FUT-as mole-DIM "AAAA, I it-win," say-TNS
And now just as Coyote was approaching the finish line, Mole said, "AAAA, I won!"

Discursive Discriminations:
Lack of "Richness of Expression"

A second critique by Gayton and Newman is the supposed lack of metaphor and other richness of expression pertaining to descriptions of characters and settings. Newman finds metaphorical expressions such as *family tree* or *sharp appetite* to be generally lacking in Yokuts. In addition, he concludes that "the absence of nicety and richness of expression in Yokuts is not the symptom of meager grammatical resources; it is, rather, the result of willful selective forces within the language, for those resources which are the most powerful for the creation of meaning and the development of notional complexity in words are employed most sparingly" (Newman and Gayton [1940] 1964, 374). In this interpretation, the quest for simplicity—or what Newman elsewhere describes with much less restraint and in such value-laden terms as "drab," "colorless," and "monotonous"—is traceable not to grammatical shortcomings, but rather to an alternative aesthetic ideal (377). Again this literary and literacy-based bias in Newman's quest for textual richness—lexical treasures and original grammatical expressions—prompts him and most of his contemporaries to overlook the artful qualities of the spoken word.

To illustrate this point, rather than dissecting a dutifully transcribed text as if the entextualized form circumscribed the verbal artistry, here I will rely on a segment from a videorecorded telling of the story (Kroskrity, Bethel, and Reynolds 2002; Kroskrity 2009) that provides a glimpse of actual performance before an audience; the example suggests how amplitude, gesture, facial expression, pausing, and other aspects of dramatic performance contribute to the verbal art of Bethel's Mono storytelling. In an extract from "Coyote Races Mole" (lines 17–21, below), I attempt to represent prosodic features by distinguishing various levels of volume and by noting such important embodied communication as relevant body movements, facial expression, and gaze orientation. Though interested readers should consult the original recording to appreciate the details of this embodied performance, these examples can provide a sense of the communicative resources deployed by the storyteller. This segment is transcribed so that font differences encode amplitude changes. I follow the examples of Dennis Tedlock (1972, 1983) and Andrew Wiget (1987) in recognizing four amplitude levels: unmarked represents normal speaking

volume, but a *second*, THIRD, and *FOURTH* level of progressively increased volume are conveyed by case and italicization. Text written in
italicized upper case, for example, represents shouted speech. To this
range I add a *fifth* level, represented by underlined lowercase italics,
which indicates a whisper. In addition to this prosodic complication,
I also mark with latches points in the act of speaking that co-occur
with significant features of embodied communication.

17. *Mowahu-bo' yaisi* [*iyo a-poso'o-wi matahonee siwi-di*. [(Elevates both arms,
    moving both hands up and down)]
    Now-EMPH and here his-friend-PL there group-PROG
    And now his friends were forming a group (around him).
18. "[*WOOOOOO!*" [NITSADATAGI-QATI-GOI-T. [(Throws arms up to full
    extension, waving in celebration)] [(Smiles broadly)]
    "WOOOOOO" cheer-continue-they-TNS
    "WOOOOOO!" they all cheered.
19. [*Nohi tsau nama-t* [(Relaxes arms behind table; leans head forward with
    slight smile)]
    very good feel-TNS
    They felt very good.
20. *Uhu-bo' yaisi* [*isa' nasukwai-s ai-pudawa-s nasukwai-t*. [(Bows head with
    rolling motion with gaze directed downward)]
    that-EMPH and coyote shame-while them-look-while shame-TNS
    But that Coyote was ashamed, as he looked at them, he felt ashamed.
21. *Onnoho yaisi* [*onno na-ponaa-ku*. [(Eye gaze intermediate between
    camera and assembled audience to left)]
    Then and then PAS-beat-one
    And then (he knew) he was the loser.

Though the elapsed time of this performed segment was only twenty-
one seconds, it reveals a wealth of verbal artistry on the part of Mono
elder Bethel. In line 17, she begins the post-climax episode following
the victory by the moles. She first describes the energy and action of
friends rushing to celebrate with Mole using arm and hand gestures
to indicate a great deal of activity while she speaks fairly rapidly and
at an elevated volume. In line 18, she dramatically raises and waves
her arms in iconic celebration while providing an extended celebratory shout, representing the collective voice of Mole's friends. She
returns her arms in line 19 to a more at-rest position and lowers her
voice as she resumes her narrator role. But during her delivery of line
20 her voice sinks to a whisper as she looks downward and embodies
the shame and humiliation of Coyote. In line 21 she resumes normal

FIGURE 1
Rosalie Bethel shouts in the voice of Mole's friends, who celebrate his victory
(from her 1993 performance of "Coyote Races Mole"). This is a screen shot
from *Taitaduhaan* (Kroskrity, Bethel, and Reynolds 2002).

volume and returns her head to a more normal storyteller-as-narrator
position rather than iconically imitating the downcast gaze of the
Coyote character. This narrator gaze position enables her to attend
peripherally—though not through directional or mutual gaze—to her
assembled Mono-speaking audience. This is also significant strategi-
cally, since she has reached the conventional conclusion of this story
but is now monitoring for audience attention that will encourage her
to follow through with her plan to add an innovative ending—an explanatory coda (I will say more about this in the next section).

   To conclude this section, it seems clear that Newman and Gayton's
"richness of expression" as an evaluative criterion is especially ethno-
centrically and graphocentrically applied to privilege a literary and
literacy-oriented emphasis on lexical choice and innovative imagery
that is valued and expected by Western readers, though not by those
Mono and other Native Californian storytellers and listeners who still
connect with the discourse norms of their indigenous oral traditions.

By failing to recognize alternative aesthetic principles associated with this oral tradition, Newman and Gayton effectively erase a key source of its richness.

Discursive Discriminations: Lack of Explication

My third critique of Gayton and Newman concerns their claim of a supposed lack of explication in Western Mono. Both find Yokuts and Western Mono narratives lacking in detail regarding characters and cultural background. Gayton writes that there is

> no tendency to be explicit in regard to character or cultural features. If an episode has to do with several characters, the speaker or actor in each instance is not always named. The listener is expected to know who is talking or acting, for it is apparently assumed that he is already familiar with the details of the story. (Gayton and Newman [1940] 1964, 378–79)

This resembles an appeal to a notion like that of the "restricted code," in which there is a strong cultural preference for relying heavily on taken-for-granted, shared background knowledge (Bernstein 1977). On this point, I do not dispute Newman and Gayton's observation of difference, but I do reject their uncritical acceptance of the hegemonic normativity of what James Collins (1996, 2009) calls "schooled" literacy conventions and their failure to understand this practice within the context of Mono storytelling performance strategies.[8] Certainly one of the reasons storytellers sometimes do not specify who is speaking is that performance features like voice quality and facial expression often disambiguate such information. Beyond such performance features, Keith Basso (1990, 152–53) has eloquently described an Apache narrative aesthetic in which it is viewed as inappropriate to tell audience members what they already know or can readily figure out. Certainly a similar value appears to have prevailed among the Western Mono, since narrators did not typically provide morals or evaluative coda-type conclusions or even explanations of apparent incongruous endings.

One such story typically told without explanation is the story "Coyote Races Mole"—a story of a race in which the diminutive Mole somehow beats his much larger, and presumably faster, rival. I have personally heard five performances of this story over the course of two decades of fieldwork in Mono communities, and only one of those performances contained an explanatory ending. Bethel and other elders explained to me that endings containing moral conclusions were not customarily provided for two reasons. First, overt interpretations were omitted in order to show respect for those audience members who knew the details (and would be offended by being told something they already knew); second, less explicit endings would compel children (and other novices) who were hearing a story for the first time to ask their parents or older siblings questions. In earlier times, Western Mono narrators embedded their storytelling practices into a larger metanarrative discourse of "talk about stories." Children who did not understand how Coyote would be beaten in a race by a Mole could be "home-schooled" by their parents, older siblings, or other socializing agents by asking questions and getting answers in interactional asides.

As noted previously, however, the story I recorded from Bethel breaks with this historical norm. In comparing contemporary practices with those of older times and ultimately in rationalizing her own innovation of an explanatory coda, she told me in her home the evening after the performance, "Nowadays we can't rely on [families to explain stories], so that maybe our stories will have to tell it more completely since the children cannot always find someone to ask." This is what motivated her to include the explanatory coda below in her 1993 performance—a performance that amounted to a recontextualization of a story that was performed as a model indigenous-language pedagogical discourse before a collection of assembled North Fork Mono elders. At this event, Bethel performed "Coyote Races Mole" to demonstrate how Mono language stories might be adapted to the needs of younger audience members who lack either prior knowledge of the story or a personal network that would connect them to an informed elder capable of explaining that story.[9]

In the following passage (lines 22–31), Bethel takes a page from Bakhtin's (1986, 62) playbook in her creation of an instance of what he would call a "secondary genre" of conventional storytelling via her intertextual linking of story with metanarrative commentary. This passage is transcribed with less attention to prosodic and kinesic detail than the one above in order to concentrate on the propositional content of the coda.

22. [Uhu miyu-tsi' nihi tisumiya-daa-pI.
    [Leaving narrative posture, leans forward as if telling a secret]
    that mole-DIM very think-HAB-COMPL
    Contrary to expectations, that little mole had been very thoughtful.

23. Uhu mɨyu-tsi' ti-poso'o-hotU yaduha-s ihi sunawi-t.
    that mole-DIM own-friend-with talk-SUB he thought
    That little mole had talked with his friends and planned it.
24. "Ɨi-bo' 'a-wiya!,' a-inee-s, ii-bo'
    iga-gaa-wai"
    he-EMPH IMP-go, him-say-SUB you-EMPH
    enter-go-FUT.
    "When he says, 'GO!' you enter (the burrow)."
25. "Taaqwa-bo' yaisi sɨmɨ'-a a-na-wadiqa-qwee-dugu
    a-dɨgɨ'i-wai."
    We:INCL-EMPH and one-OBL it-PAS-finish-LOC-through
    him-place-FUT.
    "And we will place another one across the finish line."
26. "Mowahu yaisi isa' pitihuu-gaa-wai-s ɨi-bo',
    'Nii tɨ-wusu'a-t' inee-wai."
    Now and coyote arrive-go-FUT-SUB you-EMPH
    'I it-win' say-FUT.
    "And now just as Coyote approaches (the finish),
    you will say, 'I won.'"
27. "Taaqwa-bo' nasimi-tU mɨyu sɨmɨ'i-nisU sunawi-dɨ."
    We:INCL-EMPH all-SUBJ mole one-like appear-PROG.
    "We moles all look alike."
28. "Qadu'u yaisi uhu isa' sutabihi-duwa-t."
    NEG and that coyote know-can-TNS
    "And that Coyote cannot figure it out."
29. Uwamaqahuu ihiwɨ tɨ-ponaa-t.
    In:this:way they it-win-TNS
    That's how they won.[10]

In this passage, Bethel explicates how Mole (or actually, moles) won
the race. By using more than one mole, the group is able to position
a second mole across the finish line. That mole merely has to wait for
Coyote and anticipate his crossing the finish line. Though she could
have conveyed this entirely in the narrator's voice that she begins with
in lines 22–29, she artfully selects to perform part of the explanation
in previously unheard dialogue, with appropriate iconic gestures about
the placement of the mole and even a replay of the victory pose struck
by the "winning" Mole.

Bethel's analysis as an insider, as well as her innovation of explanatory story coda, suggests that Gayton and Newman's perception of a
lack of explication, in what Bakhtin would call the "simple" traditional

narrative, is actually their failure to recognize how Western Mono ideologies of intertextuality (Bauman 2004) shaped these narratives. As Richard Bauman and Charles L. Briggs (1990, 60) have noted, "a given performance is tied to a number of speech events that precede and succeed it." Relevant indigenous intertextualities would include how Mono and Yokuts traditional narratives were performed, the relationship between a story and other traditional stories that have been told, and the relationship between traditional stories and other kinds of narratives (and other cultural communications in which these stories are embedded). But neither Newman nor Gayton recognizes the importance of recipient-designing for children, the features that mark an oral performance orientation, or the way the stories are embedded in Mono metanarrative discourses (that is, Mono talk about stories and how they should be performed) as well as other forms of metanarrative commentary. Signficantly, such concerns have received little scholarly attention. But by erasing these and other connections to Mono and Yokuts social life through decontextualizing the resulting text artifacts and failing to adequately appreciate indigenous understandings of aesthetics and intertextuality, Gayton and Newman found in their own unexamined literacy-based and Western literary biases toward verbal art a readily available basis for invidious comparison and ethnocentric judgment.

Concluding Remarks

Like other essays in this volume honoring the work of Hymes, mine suggests the pivotal role of some of his many ethnopoetic contributions as a means of beginning to decolonize the Americanist scholarship of salvage-era researchers like Newman and Gayton, but also Harry Hoijer, Morris Opler, and Alfred Kroeber.[11] I would like to conclude by highlighting two items—both acknowledgments of Hymes's influence on this current project of decolonizing past research on indigenous California narrative traditions and on moving this research in the mediative direction Hymes championed, research designed to enable listeners in academic and/or Native communities to better attend to indigenous voices. The first item concerns my developing notion of discursive discrimination and the way aesthetic and socioeconomic evaluations often merge and saturate scholarly thinking by having one's zone of expert knowledge become profoundly influenced, and perhaps covertly so, by other more mundane cultural knowledge in the scholar's stock of knowledge at hand (Schutz 1967, 80–81). Applied to the case here, I am suggesting that while Gayton and Newman could rely on their expert knowledges in matters of motif and grammatical analysis, the task of turning to narrative and stylistic analysis invited them to fill a comparative vacuum of professional expertise by drawing upon much taken-for-granted knowledge that derived from their social milieu. Hymes's narrative inequality does a significant job in calling attention to the way narrative difference is managed, (re)produced, evaluated, and institutionally inscribed. But I think discursive discrimination plays a further role in emphasizing the inevitability of imposing standards, as well as the ease with which attempts to appreciate the discursive conventions of "others" are saturated with discursive expectations and evaluations that often prevent either an informed understanding or even a constructive representation. In the case of Gayton and Newman, the role of their own schooled literacy practices is particularly apparent in prestructuring their expectations about narrative form and content. One might also explore how professional ideologies of language deterred these scholars from either attempting to study narratives in more naturalistic contexts or producing materials that might be more recipient-designed for community consumption. Such observations suggest a possible interpretation regarding the profusion of negative characterizations in Gayton's and Newman's scholarship on Mono and Yokuts narrative, their unwillingness to look for alternative cultural patterns to explain anomalous traits, and their satisfaction with an empty relativism underlain by what I will call, following Jane Hill (2008), "covert linguistic racism."

Any accusation of racism is of course controversial, especially when the term is applied to the research of respected academic scholars who have outstanding reputations in their fields. It is therefore both important and necessary for me to clarify my use of *linguistic racism* and especially *covert linguistic racism*, because I am using these notions in accord with a recent school of thought within linguistic anthropology (e.g., Hill 2008; Meek 2006). This theoretical understanding of linguistic racism is different from more "mainstream" or vernacular (North) American usages in four ways. First, the theory of linguistic racism is founded on a constructivist rather than an essentialist understanding of racial categories that characterizes most vernacular theories. In the constructivist view, racial categories have been discursively produced rather than derived from imagined essential differences. So-called racial groups are trivially different from a biological perspective, yet these differences have been culturally magnified, reified, and naturalized by the articulation of racial categories.

While most vernacular understandings of racism neglect or minimize the role of linguistically constructed racial categories and their associated hierarchization, they also tend to emphasize explicitly racist vocabulary rather than attend to other linguistic practices and levels that are also involved in defamation and denigration. Racial epithets—like the so-called n-word—are perhaps the most conventionally recognized form of linguistic racism, but racial slurs are not the only means of invoking racial hierarchies. Hill has demonstrated how Anglo-Americans deploying Mock Spanish can use phonological features to signal appropriation of Spanish words (such as the place name Los Angeles) or how the pejorative use of Spanish terms, like *macho*, transforms a neutral representation of maleness (in Spanish) into something that is hyper-masculine, if not pathologically so. These forms of covert linguistic racism typically fly under the radar of most people's awareness because they are not construed as the kind of verbal attacks that racist epithets represent and because the boundary-creating projects (between "us" and "them") they contribute to are part of a larger but more subtle collective pattern.

This pattern also suggests a third contrast between everyday and linguistic anthropological theories of race. An important feature of American mainstream cultural notions regarding racism is their emphasis on intentionality. In this view, racism hinges on intentions and feelings in the heart of the speaker. If the speaker does not intend to discriminate or demean, then his or her speech is not racist, and since no offense was intended, recipients of racist discourse should simply excuse the act as a slip of the tongue. Clearly such a view is supported by American ideologies of personalism, with their strong emphasis on individualism. But such a view clearly backgrounds, even to the point of erasure, the harm done to minority groups when their language is mocked, appropriated, or otherwise denigrated. Is racist language only a matter of the speaker's intent, or is it also—and perhaps more importantly—a matter of its social consequences? We must remember that speakers do not fully determine the meanings of the words they speak and the impact they can have. This is rather a contextual and communicative matter decided in the process of interaction by all relevant participants.

A fourth contrast follows from the previous attempt to interrogate intentionality by calling attention to racist projects that go comparatively unnoticed because their features do not conform to vernacular understandings of racism. These observations illuminate the possibility of *covert* linguistic racism. Some readers might be inclined to dismiss my claim that salvage-era anthropological researchers engaged in linguistic racism, since the motives for documenting indigenous languages and cultures seem incompatible with these accusations. But the claim here is that social actors, in this case academics working in the salvage era/acculturation theory period, were unwittingly contributing to projects of linguistic racism that marginalized and denigrated the indigenous languages and cultures of Central California. Such a claim basically views these academics as engaging in scholarly practices that were highly compatible with an official national policy that emphasized the assimilation and acculturation of Native Americans. In addition, it views these scholars as reproducing academic versions of such popular Indian stereotypes as "primitivity" and "inevitable disappearance" (Deloria 2004, 10). These scholars were not willfully producing scholarship hostile to Native Americans; rather, they were unconsciously contributing to a racializing project in which their analyses played a small but significant part.

But racism and analogous efforts to exclude do not simply follow a singular model. Étienne Balibar (1991, 40), in his discussion of the interaction of nationalism and racism, has suggested the value of thinking about a "spectrum of racisms." The species of racism directed at indigenous people is likely to have a different character than that directed at other minorities, in part because of the political economy that underlies intergroup relations. Though there are aspects of linguistic racism, such as the development of the epithet "digger" (Hinton 1994, 165–79)—used to refer to California Indians who practiced traditional hunting and gathering economies—that suggest similarity to the racisms directed against African Americans and others, the racism directed at California Indians has some expected differences. Not surprisingly, hegemonic institutions and social actors have represented those people who have experienced the brutality of settler colonialist adaptations through different types of racializing discourses (Wolfe 1999). Settler colonialist nations and their citizens have a special need to rationalize their displacement and dislocation of indigenous communities. The construction of the disappearing, primitive Native both racializes California Indians and rationalizes their dispossession, marginalization, and erasure. Certainly, I am not claiming that Gayton and Newman were intentionally racist, but rather that they, by uncritically following certain academic and general cultural norms and expectations about Indian assimilation, participated in a racializing project directed at Native Californians and other Indians. By disentangling the discursive discriminations of Gayton and Newman, we can locate their evaluative expectations both in their ethnocentric reliance on standards of academic literacy and in their participation in marginalizing projects directed at Indians, projects that reflected a national policy of imposed assimilation and that had become integral to the professional socialization of academics who conducted "salvage" research among them.

It is possible to argue that the present emphasis on language endangerment and linguistic revitalization resembles salvage-era research in its emphasis on finality and emergency (Cameron 2007; Hill 2002; Kroskrity 2012b). Even though most anthropologists have moved beyond Boasian models that posited fragile relationships between language, culture, and social change, it is clear these models are all too alive and well in a variety of contemporary national and international contexts, where such beliefs and practices continue to have a negative influence (Cameron 2007; Moore 2006; Muehlmann 2008). Just as the Boasian model delegitimated projects of linguistic syncretism and pathologized social change, contemporary reincarnations of those organicist models now equate "authentic" language with state-endorsed regimes of linguistic purity (Muehlmann 2008) and require researchers and language communities who seek endangered-language funding to deploy tropes like the consubstantiality of language:culture:identity in the rhetoric of their grantsmanship (Moore 2006). And though the contemporary period features a discourse of language rights that was unthinkable during the assimilationism of the 1940s, today's multicultural policies—with their appeals to language rights—often amount to the imposition of a one-size-fits-all model that both flattens linguistic diversity and presupposes neoliberal norms of textual circulation that are anathema to communities whose linguistic cultures are predicated on a flow of information regulated by representatives of traditional regimes (Debenport 2010; Errington 2003; Whiteley 2003). Thus despite sweeping changes in national policy over the past seventy-five years, a case can be made that contemporary multiculturalism merely reproduces many of the problems for indigenous languages that can be found in assimilationist practices of the past.

But an important difference in contemporary projects of language documentation and language revitalization, and one that more sharply distinguishes such projects from salvage linguistics, is the existence of the very mediative goals that Hymes envisioned. Orienting not only to academic communities and to producing documentation to be deposited in archives for scholars, many contemporary researchers (native and nonnative) now include heritage language communities as research partners and envision them as a, if not *the*, target audience for their resulting products of language documentation. Freed from the trope of vanishing cultures and from grossly inadequate Boasian models of language and culture, some researchers have reopened the possibility of ethnography. For example, rather than dismissing contemporary Mono storytelling as inauthentic because its practitioners were bilingual, bicultural, and actively attempting to adapt their traditions to contemporary needs, I listened to indigenous elders, asked questions about storytelling discourses, and engaged in participant observation of storytelling performances in a variety of cultural contexts. Data gathered by listening to Native voices from the community—including those of Rosalie Bethel and Gaylen Lee (1998)—allowed me to see these storytellers and audiences as participants in a living culture (Kroskrity 2009) and to collaborate in the production of resources that would document, archive, and explicate a variety of verbal art performances (Kroskrity, Bethel, and Reynolds 2002). Though it is easy for scholars to engage in elite discourses about language revitalization that seem to prize epistemological sophistication and general theoretical refinement more than actual contributions to specific heritage language communities, Hymes's emphasis on the creation of mediative resources provides, in my view, a needed signpost indicating that research on indigenous verbal art can and does matter, not only in the academic community, but in indigenous communities as well.[12]

Listening to the expert voices of cultural members who are not merely producers of narrative texts but also capable of Native metacommentary enables contemporary scholars to explore other cultural discourses of narrative and to find alternatives to ethnocentric interpretation. Like M. Eleanor Nevins, Anthony K. Webster, and Sean Patrick O'Neill (this volume), I find in Hymes's contributions valuable resources for decolonizing past scholarship, recovering some of what it erased, and reinterpreting much of what it misunderstood. A key aspect of this process involves our recognition, as scholars, of the value of Hymes's ethnolinguistically and ethnopoetically inflected notion of "voice." Listening to such voices moves us closer to the Hymesian ideal of enabling indigenous speakers to be heard performing stories in their own voice. Blommaert (2009) has described Hymes's "democratic" theory of language and the special value of Hymes's distinctive notion of voice—the personally and culturally preferred ways of speaking, the languages, registers, and styles that convey the narratives with which we all construct ourselves and our communities. What I have attempted to convey here is that listening to the Native voices of Central California requires more than a preoccupation with those narratives alone. In accord with Hymes's ethnographic emphasis, such listening must extend into relevant areas of indigenous intertextuality (Bauman 2004) and the metacommentary of storytelling ideologies (Kroskrity 2012a)—domains that salvage ethnographers found epistemologically unavailable. Like Gerald L. Carr and Barbra Meek (this volume), I find great value in observing not only the theoretical importance of Bauman and Briggs's (1990, 60) understanding of intertextuality—how "a given performance is tied to a number of speech events that precede and succeed it"—but also its value in applied folklore, employed in the mediative manner outlined by Hymes. Carr and Meek explicate intertextuality's relevance to such important applications as language revitalization when they observe that the tying of past and future speech events involves linkages and mediation by social actors operating in the present.

Indeed, as Hymes (1979, 44) suggests, "One way to think about a society is in terms of the voices it has and might have." In developing his notion of voice and in calling attention to the narrative inequality that muffles and silences some voices, Hymes helped guide us to an appreciation of the diverse voices within our society and provided us with valuable tools to better understand, represent, and enable those voices to be heard.

Notes

1. Hymes (1996, 60) contrasts "extractive" linguistics with "mediative" in an attempt to represent different levels of engagement by linguists within the communities they are researching. Are linguists merely mining speech communities for linguistic patterns of variability or are they returning something of value that communities might use in their understanding of linguistic difference and variation? The contrast is at least as useful today as it was at the time of Hymes's original work.

2. These figures are extrapolations from a study by Leanne Hinton (1994, 27), but these estimates must now be reduced due to the death of many fluent elders. In that study, Hinton estimated forty-one speakers of Western Mono and sixty-four who could speak fluent Yokuts.

3. In using the term *ideological erasure,* I follow Judith Irvine and Susan Gal (2000) in targeting a specific type of semiotic process that simplifies a particular sociolinguistic field in order to create or collapse relevant social boundaries. In this case, the erasure assists in appropriating the content of indigenous oral traditions into the collective narrative of the nation-state by eliminating any distinctive cultural features that would suggest an alternative living tradition.

4. I interpret all these developments as moving scholars closer to decolonizing the translation and interpretation of Native American traditional narratives. For a different perspective on the ethnopoetics of Hymes and Tedlock, the interested reader should consider the work of Robert Dale Palmer (2003, 85), who says, "Hymes and Tedlock read their discovery of verse and poetry as a discovery of value, in effect implying that if Native story were not absorbed into the colonizing culture's notion of verse, it would not have as much value."

5. It should, however, be noted that Newman makes a provocative contrast between the grammatical potential of Yokuts for precision and delicacy. But he goes on to note a "stylistic" choice, presumably cultural, that favors simplicity, repetition, and drab representation (Newman and Gayton [1940] 1964). So he clearly does not locate the source of difference in inferior grammatical resources, but again seems not to want to understand or interpret the alternative aesthetic pattern.

6. My rendering of the Yokuts text follows the orthography used by Gamble (1994).

7. Western Mono is transcribed in the modified Americanist orthography used in Bethel, Kroskrity, Loether, and Reinhardt 1984 and in Kroskrity, Bethel, and Reynolds 2002.

8. The narrator's attempted conclusion here was not the actual last word of the performance. At this point, an audience member offers what he feels is an appropriate traditional collaborative conclusion that is rejected by the performer in her own final closing. See the full transcript of this in Kroskrity 2009, 203–4.

9. A more complete description and analysis of Bethel's recontextualized telling of "Coyote Races Mole" is beyond the scope of this essay, but is available to interested readers in Kroskrity 2009.

10. A more complete examination of the anthropology of literacy and its functions (e.g., Ahearn 2001; Besnier 1995), though clearly outside of the scope of this

essay, would continue the reflexive and ideological approach of James Collins (1996, 1998, 2009). Such research holds great promise in further disclosing the cultural biases of various academic literacies and the language ideologies that support them. Furthermore, such academic and folk theories of schooled literacy are at the heart of many popular language ideologies of linguistic evaluation, including one that views all languages without an indigenously developed script as inferior to written languages.

11. See, in this volume, M. Eleanor Nevins, Anthony K. Webster and Sean Patrick O'Neil on the work of Hoijer, Opler, and Kroeber respectively.

12. I think it is worth observing that the special significance of Hymes's works to anthropologists of verbal art is deeply rooted in his professional connections to the fields of folkloristics and education, which have a comparatively greater applied emphasis than that which is typical of most research in linguistic anthropology. This is also an appropriate time to assert that my appreciation of Hymes is not an uncritical one. While I have certainly celebrated the many contributions that I regard as resources for scholars and heritage language community members, I do recognize limitations in his work, such as his armchair research style and the reductive formalism that occasionally looms in some of his publications. Regardless of these and other limitations, Hymes still certainly ranks as one of the most inspirational historical figures in ethnopoetic inquiry.

References Cited

Ahearn, Laura. 2001. *Invitations to Love: Literacy, Love Letters, and Social Change in Nepal.* Ann Arbor: University of Michigan Press.

Bakhtin, M. M. 1986. *Speech Genres and Other Late Essays.* Edited by Caryl Emerson and Michael Holquist. Translated by Vern McGee. Austin: University of Texas Press.

Balibar, Étienne. 1991. "Racism and Nationalism." In *Race, Nation, Class: Ambiguous Identities,* edited by Étienne Balibar and Immanuel Wallerstein, 37–67. London: Verso.

Basso, Keith H. 1990. *Western Apache Language and Culture.* Tucson: University of Arizona Press.

Bauman, Richard. 1975. "Verbal Art as Performance." *American Anthropologist* 77 (2): 290–311.

———. 2004. *A World of Others' Words: Cross-Cultural Perspectives on Intertextuality.* Malden, MA: Blackwell.

Bauman, Richard, and Charles L. Briggs. 1990. "Poetics and Performance as Critical Perspectives on Language and Social Life." *Annual Review of Anthropology* 19:59–88.

Bernstein, Basil. 1975. *Towards a Theory of Educational Transmissions.* Vol. 3 of *Class, Codes, and Control.* London: Routledge

Besnier, Niko. 1995. *Literacy, Emotion, and Authority: Reading and Writing on a Polynesian Atoll.* Cambridge: Cambridge University Press.

Bethel, Rosalie, Paul V. Kroskrity, Christopher Loether, and Gregory A. Reinhardt. 1984. *A Practical Dictionary of Western Mono.* North Fork, CA: Sierra Mono Museum.

Blommaert, Jan. 2009. "Ethnography and Democracy: Hymes's Political Theory of Language." *Text & Talk* 29 (3): 257–76.

Boas, Franz. 1894. *Chinook Texts*. Bureau of American Ethnology, Smithsonian Institution. Washington, DC: US Government Printing Office.

Boas, Franz, and George Hunt. 1902. *Kwakiutl Texts*. Memoirs of the American Museum of Natural History 5:1. New York: American Museum of Natural History.

Boyer, Ruth M. 1978. "Anna Hadwick Gayton (1899–1977)." *Journal of American Folklore* 91 (361): 834–41.

Briggs, Charles L., and Richard Bauman. 1992. "Genre, Intertextuality, and Social Power." *Journal of Linguistic Anthropology* 2 (2): 131–72.

Cameron, Deborah. 2007. "Language Endangerment and Verbal Hygiene." In *Discourses of Endangerment*, edited by Alexandre Duchene and Monica Heller, 268–85. London: Continuum.

Collins, James. 1996. "Socialization to Text." In *Natural Histories of Discourse*, edited by Michael Silverstein and Greg Urban, 203–28. Chicago: University of Chicago Press.

———. 1998. "Our Ideologies and Theirs." In *Language Ideologies: Practice and Theory*, edited by Bambi B. Schieffelin, Kathryn A. Woolard, and Paul V. Kroskrity, 256–70. New York: Oxford University Press.

———. 2009. "The Place of Narrative in Human Affairs: The Implications of Hymes's Amerindian Work for Understanding Text and Talk." *Text & Talk* 29 (3): 325–45.

Darnell, Regna. 1989. "Stanley Newman and the Sapir School of Linguistics." In *General Amerindian Ethnolinguistics: In Remembrance of Stanley Newman*, edited by Mary Ritchie Key and Henry M. Hoenigswald, 71–88. Berlin: Mouton de Gruyter.

Debenport, Erin. 2010. "The Potential Complexity of 'Universal Ownership': Cultural Property, Textual Circulation, and Linguistic Fieldwork." *Language and Communication* 30 (3): 204–10.

Deloria, Phillip. 2004. *Indians in Unexpected Places*. Lawrence: University of Kansas Press.

Errington, Joseph. 2003. "Getting Language Rights: The Rhetorics of Language Endangerment and Loss." *American Anthropologist* 105 (4): 723–32.

Gamble, Geoffrey. 1994. *Yokuts Texts*. Native American Texts Series. Berlin: Mouton de Gruyter.

Gayton, Anna H. 1935. "Areal Affiliations of California Folktales." *American Anthropologist* 37 (4): 582–99.

———. 1948. *Yokuts and Western Mono Ethnography*. University of California Anthropological Records, vol. 10. Berkeley: University of California Press.

Gayton, Anna H., and Stanley S. Newman. 1940. *Yokuts and Western Mono Myths*. University of California Anthropological Records, vol. 5. Berkeley: University of California Press.

Gifford, Edward W., and Gwendoline Harris Block. (1930) 1990. *California Indian Nights*. Lincoln: University of Nebraska Press.

Harrison, K. David. 2007. *When Languages Die: The Extinction of the World's Languages and the Erosion of Human Knowledge*. New York: Oxford University Press.

Hill, Jane H. 2002. "'Expert Rhetorics' in Advocacy for Endangered Languages: Who Is Listening and What Do They Hear?" *Journal of Linguistic Anthropology* 12 (2): 119–33.

———. 2008. *The Everyday Language of White Racism*. Malden, MA: Wiley-Blackwell.

Hinton, Leanne. 1994. *Flutes of Fire: Essays on California Indian Languages*. Berkeley, CA: Heyday.

Hymes, Dell H. 1964. *Language in Culture and Society*. New York: Harper.

———. 1970. "Linguistic Method in Ethnography." In *Method and Theory in Linguistics*, edited by Paul Garvin, 249–325. The Hague: Mouton.

———. 1979. "Sapir, Competence, Voices." In *Individual Differences in Language Ability and Behavior*, edited by Charles. J. Fillmore, Daniel Kempler, and William S. Y. Wang, 33–46. New York: Academic Press.

———. 1981. *"In Vain I Tried to Tell You": Essays in Native American Ethnopoetics*. Philadelphia: University of Pennsylvania Press.

———. 1996. *Ethnography, Linguistics, Narrative Inequality: Toward an Understanding of Voice*. London: Taylor and Francis.

Irvine, Judith T., and Susan Gal. 2000. "Language Ideology and Linguistic Differentiation." In *Regimes of Language: Ideologies, Polities, and Identities*, edited by Paul V. Kroskrity, 35–83. Santa Fe: School of American Research Press.

Judson, Katherine B. (1912) 1994. *Myths and Legends of California and the Old Southwest*. Lincoln: University of Nebraska Press.

Krauss, Michael. 2007. "Classification and Terminology for Degrees of Language Endangerment." In *Language Diversity Endangered*, edited by Matthias Brenzinger, 1–8. Berlin: Mouton de Gruyter.

Kroskrity, Paul V. 2000. "Language Ideologies in the Expression and Representation of Arizona Tewa Ethnic Identity." In *Regimes of Language: Ideologies, Polities, and Identities,* edited by Paul V. Kroskrity, 329–59. Santa Fe: School of American Research Press.

———. 2009. "Embodying the Reversal of Language Shift: Agency, Incorporation, and Language Ideological Change in the Western Mono Community of Central California." In *Native American Language Ideologies: Beliefs, Practices, and Struggles in Indian Country*, edited by Paul V. Kroskrity and Margaret C. Field, 190–210. Tucson: University of Arizona Press.

———. 2012a. "Growing with Stories: Ideologies of Storytelling and the Narrative Reproduction of Arizona Tewa Identity." In *Telling Stories in the Face of Danger: Language Renewal in Native American Communities*, edited by Paul V. Kroskrity, 151–84. Norman: University of Oklahoma Press.

———, ed. 2012b. *Telling Stories in the Face of Danger: Language Renewal in Native American Communities*. Norman: University of Oklahoma Press.

Kroskrity, Rosalie Bethel, and Jennifer F. Reynolds. 2002. *Taitaduhaan: Western Mono Ways of Speaking*. CD-ROM. Norman: University of Oklahoma.

Kuipers, Joel C. 1998. *Language, Identity and Marginality in Indonesia: The Changing Nature of Ritual Speech on the Island of Sumba*. Cambridge: Cambridge University Press.

Lee, Gaylen D. 1998. *Walking Where We Lived: Memoirs of a Mono Indian Family*. Norman: University of Oklahoma Press.

Meek, Barbra A. 2006. "And the Injun Goes 'How!': Representations of American Indian English in White Public Space." *Language in Society* 35 (1): 93–128.

Mithun, Marianne. 2001. *The Languages of Native North America*. Cambridge: Cambridge University Press.

Moore, Robert E. 2006. "Disappearing, Inc.: Glimpsing the Sublime in the Politics of Access to Endangered Languages." *Language and Communication* 26 (3–4): 296–315.

Muehlmann, Shaylih. 2008. "'Spread Your Ass Cheeks': And Other Things That Should Not Be Said in Indigenous Languages." *American Ethnologist* 35 (1): 34–48.

Newman, Stanley S. 1944. *Yokuts Language of California.* Viking Fund Publications in Anthropology 2. New York: Viking Fund.

Newman, Stanley S., and Anna H. Gayton. (1940) 1964. "Yokuts Narrative Style." In *Language in Culture and Society,* edited by Dell H. Hymes, 372–82. New York: Harper.

Nichols, Johanna. 1999. *Linguistic Diversity in Space and Time.* Chicago: University of Chicago Press.

Palmer, Robert Dale. 2003. *The Invention of Native American Literature.* Ithaca: Cornell University Press.

Schiffrin, Deborah. 1981. "Tense Variation in Narrative." *Language* 57 (1): 45–62.

Schutz, Alfred. 1967. *The Phenomenology of the Social World.* Translated by George Walsh and Frederick Lehnert. Evanston, IL: Northwestern University Press.

Silverstein, Michael. 1989. "Singularly Like Our Ideal of a Scientist." In *General and Amerindian Ethnolinguistics: In Remembrance of Stanley Newman,* edited by Mary Ritchie Key and Henry M. Hoenigswald, 45–63. Berlin: Mouton de Gruyter.

Whiteley, Peter. 2003. "Do 'Language Rights' Serve Indigenous Interests? Some Hopi and Other Queries." *American Anthropologist* 105 (4): 712–22.

Tedlock, Dennis. 1972. *Finding the Center: Narrative Poetry of the Zuni Indians.* New York: Dial.

———. 1983. *The Spoken Word and the Work of Interpretation.* Philadelphia: University of Pennsylvania Press.

Whorf, Benjamin Lee. 1939. "The Relation of Habitual Thought and Behavior to Language." In *Language, Culture, and Personality,* edited by Leslie Spier, 75–93. Menasha, WI: Sapir Memorial Fund.

———. 1940. "Science and Linguistics." *Technology Review* 42 (2): 229–31, 247–48.

Wiget, Andrew. 1987. "Telling the Tale: A Performance Analysis of a Hopi Coyote Story." In *Recovering the Word,* edited by Brian Swann and Arnold Krupat, 297–336. Berkeley: University of California Press.

Wolfe, Patrick. 1999. *Settler Colonialism and the Transformation of Anthropology.* London: Cassell.

PAUL V. KROSKRITY is Professor of Anthropology and Chair of American Indian Studies at UCLA, where he has taught since earning his PhD in Anthropology from Indiana University in 1978. He has authored numerous works including *Regimes of Language* (2000) and *Telling Stories in the Face of Danger* (2012).

6   Discovery and Dialogue in Ethnopoetics

SOMETIME IN THE spring or summer of 1965, while I was working on my PhD at the University of Pennsylvania, I received a letter from Alan Dundes—a friend from my earlier days in Bloomington—alerting me that one of his Berkeley colleagues was moving to Penn and that I might be interested in what he had to say. That colleague was Dell Hymes. I was already finished with coursework and moving into dissertation mode, but, acting on Alan's advice, I went back to take a course that Hymes was offering to his new Penn constituency on the Ethnography of Symbolic Forms. That decision turned out to be a life changer, setting me on an intellectual path I have followed ever since.

At the time Hymes came to Penn, the ethnography of speaking—the line of linguistic anthropology that he was working with his former California colleagues to bring into being (Gumperz and Hymes 1964, 1972)—was still in its formative stages, and I was fortunate to get in on the development of this energizing line of inquiry fairly early (Bauman and Sherzer 1974, 1975). The collaborative engagement of folklorists in this enterprise, based in significant measure on our already established commitment to matters of genre and performance (see Hymes 1972), made the partnership with linguistic anthropologists especially attractive. The early seventies were the developmental heyday of what Robert Moore (this volume) calls *ethnopoetics₁*, in which verbal artistry as a situated and emergent accomplishment was a primary focus. To be sure, *ethnopoetics₂*, devoted to the poetic organization of performed texts, was also a part of this project; witness, for example, the inclusion of Dennis Tedlock's pioneering article on Zuni ethnopoetics in *Toward New Perspectives in Folklore* (1972), along with Hymes's (1972) foundational piece, "The Contribution of Folklore to Sociolinguistic Research." The two lines of ethnopoetics have continued to develop in tandem, though with some degree of divergence in central focus, emphasis, and outreach to adjacent disciplines. But the richness of the conjunctions between the two and the continuing productive-ness of Dell Hymes's synthetic vision are undeniable. One has only to consider the range of conceptual and analytical frameworks drawn from Hymes's work by the authors of the foregoing essays and their own various alignments to the full synthetic power of Hymes's work for corroboration.

I take up the essays individually, in sequence, highlighting what seem to me to be especially provocative aspects of the analyses they present, and concluding with some observations on voice. Regrettably, space will not allow for a comprehensive consideration of the complex and fertile arguments the authors develop in dialogue with the Na-tive people who told and retold the stories, the scholars who recorded them, and Hymes, who offered a challenging framework for engaging them. I can only offer instead one appreciative reader's preliminary response in the service of moving the dialogue along.

Robert Moore

From the vantage point of one who has been in on the development of the whole package from very early on, a broad and inclusive conception of ethnopoetics is not difficult to sustain. My unitarian tendencies and inclinations notwithstanding, though, it is true that *ethnopoetics* as a label for that branch of linguistic anthropology and folklore is dedi-cated to the discovery of the poetic organization of oral texts, their transcription and representation on the printed page, and their trans-lation into more widely accessible languages (see Blommaert 2006). Hence the foregrounding of particles and pauses, lines and verses, twos and fours, threes and fives, and so on. This is Moore's ethnopoetics$_2$, founded on what Hymes (1981, 309–41) heralded as "discovering . . . measured verse in American Indian narrative," the enterprise that absorbed his energies during the latter part of his career. "Discovery" is a key term here. By couching the analytical breakthroughs that con-stituted the foundation of ethnopoetics$_2$ in terms of discovery, Hymes meant to frame the project as representing something more than the findings of routinized analysis; rather, a game-changing, perspective-altering way of conceptualizing the texts, revealing their poetic form, and ultimately, through that analytical process, elucidating their cultural meaning. And there is no question that Hymes's discoveries were truly pathbreaking, opening up new territories in oral poetics and attracting large numbers of further explorers and new settlers into the territory.

After a while, though, the discoveries took on an air of *re*discovery—the routinized revelation of twos and fours and threes and fives—and began to forfeit the interest of readers who continued to be more energized by ethnopoetics$_1$, distinguished by "a focus on the event-bound interactional dynamics of narrative as *performance*" (Moore, this volume, p. 12) than by the normalization of ethnopoetics$_2$. Perhaps part of the problem was that Hymes's (2003, 11) "turning away . . . from speech events" became increasingly mentalist in its orientation, preoccupied with what was going on in storytellers' minds (36) and talking about competence in ways that resonated in disturbing ways with Chomskyian notions, as in "knowing tacitly an art of performance" (viii). An additional problem was that Hymes could come across as fairly prescriptive about his way of doing things, as when he wrote, "If organization into groups of lines is pervasive in oral narrative, then the editing of oral narratives for publication should take that into account" (311). At other times, though, Hymes professed greater openness to alternatives (e.g., Hymes 2003, 46).

And indeed, Moore has come up with an alternative mode of representation, one that returns the enterprise radically to the speech events that Hymes left behind. Moore's ingenious system for representing narration on the printed page foregrounds the emergent quality of entextualization in interaction, revealing the interplay of formal, pragmatic, and metapragmatic vectors in the production of narrative and interactional text. One of the most effective aspects of Moore's approach, in my view, lies in his useful synthesis of ethnopoetics with Erving Goffman's (1981, 124–59) notions of participant structures and footing and Roman Jakobson's ([1957] 1971) framework for sorting out the management of narrated and narrative events. Separating out the interlocutory speech of the ethnographic encounter, the narrative discourse that recounts the characters' actions, and the direct discourse of the dramatis personae while preserving the linear unfolding of the event really does reveal important things about how storytelling is accomplished. Moore's analysis—and representation—of his encounter with Lucinda Smith sheds especially productive light, for example, on a problem that looms large in Hymes's foundational "Breakthrough into Performance," what Hymes (1981, 87) termed "metaphrasis"—that is, "the interpretive transformation of genre." Hymes accounts for these transformations, manifested in the formal features of denotational texts, within the larger context of changes in the communicative economy of Chinookan culture. In his own integrative analysis of his interaction with Mrs. Smith, Moore discovers "another layer or modality of poetic patterning beyond the level of denotational text, one that inheres in the kind of recurring yet orderly shifts of footing that characterize Mrs. Smith's narrative style" (this volume). Mrs. Smith's navigation "among speech-event modalities and role-fractions," then, reveals metaphrasis under conditions of language shift not in terms of placing the denotational text in its larger cultural context, but in terms of *situated, dialogic practice.*

Alexander D. King

In the Koryak case explored by Alexander D. King, problems having to do with the interpretation of genre in conditions of language shift—including shifts in ways of speaking—again play a role. The old myths of Great Raven and the culture hero Amamqut are no longer told in Kamchatka, most Koryak people now speak Russian, and the classic published collection by Waldemar Bogoras (1917), with the texts rendered in Latin orthography, are largely inaccessible to them. Even King's Koryak-speaking consultants, distanced as they are from the living performance tradition and the generic features of traditional narrative forms, were not able to recognize the recording he labels "A Man Is Born" as an episode of the myth Bogoras (1917, 63–67) published as "Ermine People II." Accordingly, King and his consultants arrived initially at an interpretation of the recorded narrative as a descriptive account of childbirth among the Koryak, akin to those texts conventionally labeled "ethnological narratives" or "customs" in the classic Boasian collections (e.g., Sapir and Hoijer 1942, 260–333; Hoijer 1938, 45–47). Ultimately, however, by application of the tried-and-true Hymesian anthropological philology (Hymes 1981, 35–62), combining linguistic, literary, ethnographic, and text-historical perspectives, King was able to identify the recorded text as indeed a virtuosic performance of a key episode from "Ermine People," all that the limited affordances of cylinder recording technology would allow.

In my view, however, King's analysis of the second early recording, "Amamqut's Whale Festival," by Aqaŋŋaw, delivers much more interesting news, approaching the kind of discovery that Hymes achieved in elucidating the poetics of measured verse in Native American oral narrative. And here, the communicative competence of his Koryak consultants served King conspicuously well. In asserting that "the poetic purpose" of his ethnopoetic work "is to come as close as possible to the intended shape of the text in order to grasp as much as possible of the meanings embodied in this shape," Hymes (1981, 7) is compelled to acknowledge that for the kinds of older published texts from which he is attempting to recover that poetic patterning, "much will still escape. The gestures, voices, tunes, pauses of the original performance cannot be recovered." By contrast with print collections, though, the old cylinders with which King is working do allow for recovery of at least the acoustic features. One would expect, however, that the embodied features of performance would still remain beyond reach. But no. As King and his consultants reviewed the transcript while listening to the audio recordings, "Vasili Borisovich would sometimes act out the gestures that he imagined Aqanŋaw performing as he listened to the audio recording of her voice." The cues to those embodied aspects of the performance turn out to have been demonstrative adverbs, well known to students of deixis as being frequently accompanied by physical gestures. King remarks especially on Aquanŋaw's use of the word *əñŋəhan* 'thus, so, like that'. In its first two meanings, *əñŋəhan* is a connective, expressing a result or consequence of an antecedent reference. In its latter sense, however, it functions as a manner demonstrative, expressing the way an action is performed—'like this, in this way'—as in "she flew off embarrassed, **thus**," or "they loaded their sleds, **thus**." While the listener cannot be certain exactly how the action being described was expressed in movement, it is not difficult for the listener to recognize that the flying or loading of a sled is being enacted in some manner and to come up with an interpretively plausible image of the action.

King does not make a point, though, of the other significant demonstrative adverbs in the text, namely, *wutč* 'here' and *ənki* 'there', also frequently accompanied by deictic gestures. In stanza II.B., when Raven Woman says, after plucking an eye from the sacrificed dog,

"Where is it?
       Maybe **here**? [*metke wutčuk?*]
              Here [there?] it is." [*ənki-vat*]

She points at the vertebrae with her wing.
"Maybe over **here**? [*metke wutku-qui?*]
      Here it is." [*wutku nəpəqən*]

The gestures are implicated—and in one case, actually mentioned
("she points")—in the text, not lost. These gestures and enacted
movements accompanying demonstrative adverbs function in a
manner akin to quoted speech. The deictic center is the setting
in which the dramatis personae act in the narrated event, but by
being reenacted in the performance event, they serve to merge the
narrated and narrative events. This is the deictic function that Karl
Bühler ([1934] 2011, 140), in his pioneering study of deixis, termed
"imagination-oriented deixis" (*Deixis am Phantasma*). King's analysis,
prompted by the playful embodied enactments of his Koryak collabo-
rator, suggests the potential productiveness of searching for deictic
adverbs in the classic collections as a means of enriching still further
our understanding of the patterning principles that organize oral
narrative performance.

M. Eleanor Nevins

As suggested earlier, ethnopoetics is most commonly understood as
that branch of linguistic anthropology dedicated to the discovery of
the poetic organization of oral texts, their transcription and representation on the printed page, and their translation into more widely
accessible languages. Hence the foregrounding of particles and pauses,
lines and verses, twos and fours, threes and fives, and so on. But also
essential to ethnopoetics—and essential to the understanding of poetic organization—is the discrimination of what kinds of texts one is
dealing with, which is to say, what orders of texts the oral performers
are producing, their orienting schemas for the competent or virtuosic
production of entextualized discourse, and what kinds of texts their
audiences are hearing. That is why genre is a fundamental part of the
ethnopoetician's toolkit.

What I find especially exciting about M. Eleanor Nevins's essay is
that it reports on the discovery of a hitherto unrecognized Apache
genre, bá'hadziih, or 'speak for others'. In Nevins's account, bá'hadziih
turns upon a subtle temporalizing dynamic which "consists in bringing previously unrealized prior states to bear upon ongoing relations

between the speaker's group and others in the audience, posing new possibilities for mutual futures." Bá'hadziih can apparently stand alone or be incorporated into secondary genres like evangelical testimonies or political speeches.

Perhaps the most intriguing feature of the genre is that its participant structure incorporates an addressee figured as Other. In Lawrence Mithlo's and Eva Lupe's deployment of bá'hadziih, this feature amounts to more than simply the contextual adaptation of an indigenous genre to situations in which a white person is present, or even addressed. Bá'hadziih is remarkably well adapted to the contact zone, a means for dealing with the social exigency of addressing an interlocutor defined as being culturally different. The genre is built upon diversity, heterogeneity, difference. Accordingly, it is not surprising that Hoijer didn't recognize it, operating as he was with a conception of culture and of language that obscures—indeed, precludes—such heterogeneity, being founded instead on an ideology of uniformity and homogeneity, summarized concisely by Hymes (1968, 25) as "one language-one culture."

But even if Hoijer didn't recognize the genre, he recorded it "in text," as Paul Radin ([1933] 1987, 106–17) would say, that is, in Chiricahua, and in entextualized form. This circumstance points up yet again the ultimate productiveness of the Boasian philological approach, whatever may have been its attendant problems: collect texts in native languages and they will serve, as he said, as "the foundation of all future researches" (quoted in Stocking 1974, 480). The text in question is one of that species of texts that are included in so many Americanist text collections under the rubric of "customs" or "ethnological narratives" or some such—entextualized accounts of traditional indigenous practices. And lo and behold, an entextualized account of "Old Apache Customs" turns out to be an instance of bá'hadziih. Once you're attuned to it, with that ever-so-useful temporality of hindsight and Nevins's illuminating analysis, it's scarcely surprising that the genre should turn up in connection with the ethnographic elicitation of old customs. The ethnographic encounter is a quintessential site of Othering, characteristically cast in a past perfective indicative temporalizing framework, not open to a future progressive subjunctive set of relational possibilities. And by casting what Mithlo is recounting to him as "old" Apache customs, Hoijer plays right into his proper participant orientation: framing this information as over and done with, a closed account of a bygone culture. He doesn't realize—or at least he doesn't acknowledge—the retemporalizing and morally revalorizing thrust of Mithlo's discourse or its subjunctive reach into the future. Clearly, the "ethnological narratives" sections of the classic text collections would be very interesting to explore in genre-oriented terms for hitherto obscured generic organization.

But Nevins's rereading of this old text is only part of her method. Again, in good ethnopoetic fashion, she uses her own ethnographic dialogue with Lupe as a vantage point on past ethnographic work, to confirm the organization of both encounters. It's worth reminding ourselves, I think, that the close analysis of ethnographic dialogues has been foundational to ethnopoetics. Recall Hymes's (1981, 79–141) breakthrough formulation of the nature of performance in "Breakthrough into Performance," or Regna Darnell's (1974) pioneering unpacking of the emergent quality of storytelling in "Correlates of Cree Narrative Performance," or Michael Silverstein's (1996) subtle elucidation of the mythic framing of yet another of these "customs" narratives in "The Secret Life of Texts." Robert Moore's contribution to this volume is yet another case in point.

One last point. I can't resist acknowledging, though with only a brief nod, that in addition to her larger critique of Hoijer's epistemological stance and mode of engagement in his ethnographic work, Nevins also corrects his translation, again in good ethnopoetic fashion. Hoijer didn't translate the evidential suffix *ná'a* 'they say', but she not only sets out the translated texts in lines, she puts the 'they say' in as well.

Anthony K. Webster

Anthony K. Webster's essay develops Hymes's distinction between referential and expressive functions of language, outlined most fully in "Ways of Speaking" (Hymes 1974), where the contrasting terms are "referential" and "stylistic," and played out analytically in "How to Talk like a Bear in Takelma" (Hymes 1981, 65–76). Webster turns this distinction to an analysis of a poem by the contemporary Navajo poet, Rex Lee Jim. Hymes makes the point in "Use All There Is to Use" (2003, 42) that expressive features are often excluded from grammars, dictionaries, and transcriptions in text collections on the grounds that they are nonphonemic and do not affect referential meaning. Webster gives us an interesting survey of those students of Navajo who did find a place in their linguistic analysis for expressive features (including prominently Gladys Reichard, one of my heroines) and those who did not (including, yet again, Harry Hoijer).

Fortunately, Jim does his own writing and is unconstrained by the regime of the phoneme. He makes exuberant—though highly controlled—expressive use of the velar fricative <x> in his poem about the out-of-control Badger that Webster presents to us. Webster devotes the bulk of his analysis, then, to an explication of what kinds of expressive work <x> performs in the poem, especially in conjunction with the voiceless palatal affricate <ch>, the resultant consonant cluster thus conveying the sense that Badger lacks control over his actions. I won't recapitulate Webster's detailed analysis here. There are certainly lots of pithy arguments and points for thought in his essay. Let me just single out a few that I find especially interesting.

First, Jim establishes a pervasive patterning principle in his written poem, but allows himself the option of departing from it in oral performance. Remember, Bear doesn't always use the bear prefix <L> and Coyote doesn't always use the coyote prefix <s> (Hymes 1981, 68). What's going on here, then, is a very suggestive interplay between the oral and the written, which bespeaks a new order of literacy, viz., ethnopoetic literacy: "one that acknowledges expressive and presentational features rather than trivializing them or relegating them to the status of nonlinguistic features" (Webster, this volume, p. 126). More broadly, in this Navajo example, we have the cultivation of a new order of Navajo literature and literary artistry. Jim is fluent in Navajo, and his fluency includes—indeed, it rests upon—virtuosic command of Navajo oral aesthetics, in this case revolving around sound play, not only as a resource for poetic composition but also as a resource for performance. He is adept in written Navajo, with all that that competence presupposes: a writing system, schooling, and so on. But he also cultivates an appreciation of oral performance, as does his Navajo audience.

There is still more at play, though. Not only does Webster's essay report upon this new Navajo ethnopoetic *literacy*, but it also rests on a new order of Navajo *literary criticism*. As Webster indicates, his appreciation of Jim's poem builds upon a critical partnership and extended conversations with Blackhorse Mitchell, another Navajo poet, language teacher, and critic. This work bespeaks a community of poets who can recognize, explicate, and evaluate the nuances and virtuosity of each other's work. And it doesn't hurt to have an expert linguistic anthropologist and ethnopoetician like Webster to help convey the literary work to wider audiences. The potential significance of this complex of poetics and performance for language maintenance is clear. Sure, language maintenance programs demand grammars, dictionaries, and all that basic apparatus. But they also need poets and literary critics. The linguists are susceptible to prescriptive, code-based standards that view expressive play as deviant, even when it is virtuosically most under control: put in the expressive <x> and you're guilty of misspelling. It's the poets and performers, as Herder insisted a long time ago, who keep the language vigorously alive by keeping it lively. And, as Webster insists, it is precisely these players—in all senses of the word—who provide a critical corrective to the referentialist ideologies of the standardizers who would purify Navajo by denigrating or erasing the richness of sound symbolism, punning, and other forms of sonic iconicity that vivify Navajo verbal aesthetics, thereby silencing a vital quality of Navajo expressive voices.

Paul V. Kroskrity

Like Nevins and Webster—and Hymes before them—Paul V. Kroskrity uses the insights of ethnopoetics as a critical vantage point on the work of our Americanist forebears. This can be a tricky business. On the one hand, one wants to honor the first and second generation of Boasian workers for documenting the languages and texts on which so much of ethnopoetic work is founded, and even, on the part of some, doing it so well that we can discover things in those texts about which they had no clue. At the same time, we acknowledge a need for critical correctives where the early scholars missed the boat. And those critical correctives, we allow ourselves to hope, can also serve as the basis for remedies to conceptions and ideologies of language that underpin structures of social inequality.

Hymes, it seems to me, was conspicuously respectful, even reverent, when it came to evaluating the work of our Americanist predecessors, including our friend—and his teacher—Hoijer. In his treatment, generally speaking, those elders may not have recognized all that was going on or used all there was to use toward discovering and acknowledging the artistic excellence and beauty of Native American texts, but they are overall the good guys. They provide the wherewithal to counteract the forces of inequality, which reside elsewhere: in colonialist and racist ideologies, exploitive institutions, misguided policies, wrong-track linguistics. Hymes got red-in-the-face pissed off at me at a conference some years ago for suggesting that the sainted Boas, for all his liberal politics and monumental scholarly achievements—to which all honor is due—did ethically questionable things in his dealings with George Hunt (see Briggs and Bauman 1999).

Nevins's criticism is a bit stronger: Hoijer's misrecognition of what Mithlo was telling him and what the implications of that message might be bespeaks a colonialist mindset. Kroskrity goes much further still. He lambastes Stanley Newman and Anna Gayton as covert racists and as *agents* of the discursive marginalization of Yokuts and Western Mono people. Whoa!

I have to confess, Kroskrity's strong criticism took me aback. From my first encounter with Newman and Gayton in Hymes's *Language in Culture and Society* (1964)—commonly known as "the big red reader"—forty-five-plus years ago, Newman, at least, has stood high in my pantheon of ancestral heroes. His introduction to *Yokuts and Western Mono Myths*, "Linguistic Aspects of Yokuts Style" (1940a), ranks up there with Edward Sapir's *Abnormal Types of Speech in Nootka* (1915) as game changers in my worldview. What I took away from Newman's (1940a, 4) introduction was the pithy insight that a grammar "tells what a language can do but not what it considers worthwhile doing." So I went back to reread the introduction in light of Kroskrity's criticism. (Gayton's contribution is not nearly as interesting, consisting of areal and distributional and comparative motif-tracing).

By today's lights, it's not hard to see what Kroskrity is reacting to: Newman certainly does characterize Yokuts style in terms of what it lacks, what it doesn't do, where it is deficient. He is especially negative when it comes to the polysyndetic, additive organization that Kroskrity discusses as a core feature of Western Mono style: "Its [i.e., Yokuts'] favorite device for relating predications to one another is the particle 'ama', that can best be translated as 'and' or 'and then,' an element that achieves only the loosest and most ambiguous type of co-ordination. The great majority of sentences in a Yokuts text begin with this feeble co-ordinator" (Newman 1940a, 7). Actually, this kind of polysyndetic structure is a very widespread feature of oral narrative more generally, in the service of fluency and cohesion among other possible effects.

Newman's (1940b, 1–3) translation of the one Yokuts myth in the monograph does reveal the alternation with "now" that Kroskrity points to in Rosalie Bethel's Mono performance, but as he says, Newman takes no note of it. Kroskrity's own suggestion—that in performance, the polysyndetic organization sets up a cohesive, measured pattern of parallel structures, disrupted to narrative and aesthetic effect by the shift to "now" in line-initial position—is far more revealing and persuasive in light of what ethnopoetics has taught us and certainly rings true in terms of my own experience with oral storytelling.

One might also observe that taking the myths down in dictation, and in the summer, might have contributed to a stylistic flattening of the texts. Gayton (1940, 10) maintains that the summer issue is no big deal, but I believe that it could be. It has certainly made a difference in the recording of other Native American oral narratives. Dictation might also attenuate what appears to be a rich predisposition toward quoted speech in Yokuts, and, it appears, in Mono storytelling. In full performance, it might have been richer still. Early observers cut it out. Newman doesn't mention this stylistic feature, though there is clear evidence of it in the texts as we have them; Gayton (1940, 9) mentions it only in passing. But we all know how rich such direct discourse can be in performance, and how difficult it can be to capture in dictated texts.

Kroskrity's address of Newman's second negative characterization, lack of explication, is one of the most interesting and revealing aspects of his essay. The existence of an entire metacultural complex of practices in which children are supposed to inquire about meaning that may be unclear or ambiguous in the performed texts themselves, discovered in the course of Kroskrity's own dialogically open ethnographic work, is enormously suggestive. In functional terms, then, a referentially lean style may be a mechanism of socialization, a pedagogically oriented invitation to young auditors to ask the narrators for more information to fill in the gaps.

Voice

In closing, I want to say a bit about voice. It's one of the key terms in the title of this collection, and it figures to stimulating effect in the individual essays.

Hymes used the notion of voice in several ways. One sense of the term refers to the physical, embodied production of oral texts (e.g.,

Hymes 2003, 247). The related term "vocal realization" directs attention to the acoustic properties of performed texts, as the voice serves as a means to convey affect, to characterize dramatis personae, to organize the oral performance intonationally and prosodically as measured verse, and so on (e.g., Hymes 1981, 321). And, of course, one expression of those individual voices is in the narrative performances of the named verbal artists whose stories Hymes translated, represented, explicated, and celebrated so richly. Some of those "personal" voices (Hymes 2003, 8, 121), such as Hiram Smith and Philip Kahclamet, Hymes heard directly, in their full vocal realizations; others, such as Charles Cultee, Louis Simpson, Frances Johnson, Victoria Howard, and John Rush Buffalo, he engaged at a dialogical remove, through the intertextual mediation of Franz Boas, Edward Sapir, Melville Jacobs, and (like Nevins) Harry Hoijer. At the same time that he championed those individual voices, Hymes, as anthropologist and folklorist, had a fundamental commitment to collective patterns and meanings, insisting that "interpretation that seeks only an individual voice . . . falls short" of full understanding (1981, 9). For him, "Language is . . . a configuration of common understandings and individual voices" (Hymes 1996, 98).

A further sense of voice in Hymes's writings, the one that is foregrounded in these essays, posits the voice as a means of self-realization as a social being in a social world that is "goaded by the spirit of hierarchy," to draw a phrase from one of Hymes's mentors, Kenneth Burke (1996, 16). In this sense, the self, personhood, is a situated communicative accomplishment, but it is also a site of struggle in the face of forces that would constrain or suppress or silence or denigrate its voice (e.g., Hymes 1996, 64, 70).

Ethnopoetics, for the most part, engages the politics of voice in terms of two principal factors. The "ethno-" prefix bespeaks a concern with how affiliation with an "ethnos," a people, a nation, an ethnic group, affects voice, and "poetics" foregrounds artfulness, virtuosity, and the artistic enhancement of experience as a means toward self-realization within a socially constituted matrix of competence and value. And to the degree that ethnopoetics focuses on voice in this third Hymesian sense, it accepts the responsibility of mitigating those forces—racism, colonialism, hegemonic ideologies of language and art—that would erase, ignore, denigrate, or dismiss the artistic voices of any of the world's people. That is an eminently worthy program for us all. But notwithstanding the aesthetic and political motivations for amplifying the voices of those who have struggled against the forces that would silence or ignore them, it is important to bear always in mind that the voices of the speech players and verbal artists celebrated by ethnopoetics are not merely the instruments of personal expression or the outward manifestation of thoughtful minds. One of the unintended effects of a shift from ethnopoetics$_1$ to ethnopoetics$_2$, with its attendant foregrounding of text objects and interiority, is to background the radical insight of the ethnography of speaking—that speakers use their voices to accomplish things in the world. In my view, one of the most valuable lessons of the foregoing essays is that the verbal artists to whom the authors (re)introduce us have social ends in view: to coordinate the temporalities, exigencies, languages, and participation structures of the storyworld and the ongoing interaction; to move an Other to envision a joint future; to induce interlocutors to contemplate the proper comportment of a moral person; to draw children into active participation in the pursuit of cultural knowledge. It is one of the great pleasures of our line of work that we get to listen in and join the conversation.

References Cited

Bauman, Richard, and Joel Sherzer, eds. 1974. *Explorations in the Ethnography of Speaking.* Cambridge: Cambridge University Press.

———. 1975. "The Ethnography of Speaking." *Annual Review of Anthropology* 4:95–119.

Blommaert, Jan. 2006. "Ethnopoetics as Functional Reconstruction." *Functions of Language* 13 (2): 229–49.

Bogoras, Waldemar. 1917. *Koryak Texts.* Publications of the American Ethnological Society 5. Leiden: E. J. Brill.

Briggs, Charles L., and Richard Bauman. 1999. "'The Foundation of All Future Researches': Franz Boas, George Hunt, Native American Texts, and the Construction of Modernity." *American Quarterly* 51 (3): 479–528.

Bühler, Karl. (1934) 2011. *Theory of Language: The Representational Function of Language.* Translated by Donald Fraser Goodwin. Philadelphia: John Benjamins.

Burke, Kenneth. 1966. *Language as Symbolic Action: Essays on Life, Literature, and Method.* Berkeley: University of California Press.

Darnell, Regna. 1974. "Correlates of Cree Narrative Performance." In *Explorations in the Ethnography of Speaking,* edited by Richard Bauman and Joel Sherzer, 315–36. Cambridge: Cambridge University Press.

Gayton, A. H. 1940. "Narrative Style." In *Yokuts and Western Mono Myths,* edited by A. H. Gayton and Stanley S. Newman, 8–11. University of California Publications in Anthropological Records, vol. 5, no. 1. Berkeley: University of California Press.

Goffman, Erving. 1981. *Forms of Talk.* Philadelphia: University of Pennsylvania Press.

Gumperz, John, and Dell Hymes, eds. 1964. "The Ethnography of Communication." Special issue, *American Anthropologist* 66 (6.2).

————, eds. 1972. *Directions in Sociolinguistics: The Ethnography of Communication.* New York: Holt, Rinehart, and Winston.

Hoijer, Harry. 1938. *Chiricahua and Mescalero Apache Texts.* Chicago: University of Chicago Press.

Hymes, Dell, ed. 1964. *Language in Culture and Society: A Reader in Linguistic Anthropology.* New York: Harper and Row.

————. 1968. "Linguistic Problems in Defining the Concept of the 'Tribe'." In *Essays on the Problem of Tribe,* edited by June Helm, 23–48. Proceedings of the American Ethnological Society 1967. Seattle: University of Washington Press.

————. 1972. "The Contribution of Folklore to Sociolinguistic Research." In *Toward New Perspectives in Folklore,* edited by Américo Paredes and Richard Bauman, 42–50. Austin: University of Texas Press.

————. 1974. "Ways of Speaking." In *Explorations in the Ethnography of Speaking,* edited by Richard Bauman and Joel Sherzer, 433–51. Cambridge: Cambridge University Press.

————. 1981. *"In Vain I Tried to Tell You": Essays in Native American Ethnopoetics.* Philadelphia: University of Pennsylvania Press.

————. 1996. *Ethnography, Linguistics, Narrative Inequality: Toward an Understanding of Voice.* Bristol, PA: Taylor and Francis.

————. 2003. *Now I Know Only So Far: Essays in Ethnopoetics.* Norman: University of Oklahoma Press.

Jakobson, Roman. (1957) 1971. "Shifters, Verbal Categories, and the Russian Verb." In *Roman Jakobson: Selected Writings,* 2:130–47. The Hague: Mouton.

Newman, Stanley S. 1940a. "Linguistic Aspects of Yokuts Style." In *Yokuts and Western Mono Myths,* edited by A. H. Gayton and Stanley S. Newman, 4–8. University of California Publications in Anthropological Records, vol. 5, no. 1. Berkeley: University of California Press.

————. 1940b. "Type Myth: Condor Steals Falcon's Wife." In *Yokuts and Western Mono Myths,* edited by A. H. Gayton and Stanley S. Newman, 1–3. University of California Publications in Anthropological Records, vol. 5, no. 1. Berkeley: University of California Press.

Radin, Paul. (1933) 1987. *The Method and Theory of Ethnography: An Essay in Criticism.* South Hadley, MA: Bergin and Garvey.

Sapir, Edward. 1915. *Abnormal Types of Speech in Nootka.* Geological Survey of Canada, Memoir 62. Ottawa: Government Printing Bureau.

Sapir, Edward, and Harry Hoijer, eds. 1942. *Navaho Texts.* Iowa City: Linguistic Society of America.

Silverstein, Michael. 1996. "The Secret Life of Texts." In *Natural Histories of Discourse,* edited by Michael Silverstein and Greg Urban, 81–105. Chicago: University of Chicago Press.

Stocking, George. 1974. "The Boas Plan for the Study of American Indian Languages." In *Studies in the History of Linguistics: Traditions and Paradigms,* edited by Dell Hymes, 454–84. Bloomington: Indiana University Press.

Tedlock, Dennis. 1972. "On the Translation of Style in Oral Narrative." In *Toward New Perspectives in Folklore,* edited by Américo Paredes and Richard Bauman, 114–33. Austin: University of Texas Press.

RICHARD BAUMAN is Distinguished Professor Emeritus of Folklore and Ethnomusicology, Communication and Culture, and Anthropology at Indiana University, Bloomington. Among his publications are *Verbal Art as Performance* (1977), *Story, Performance, and Event* (1986), *Voices of Modernity* (with Charles L. Briggs, 2003), and *A World of Others' Words* (2004).

7   The Poetics of Language Revitalization: Text, Performance, and Change

The term *performance* has reference to the realization of known traditional material, but the emphasis is on the constitution of a social event, quite likely with emergent properties. . . . Two latter considerations will be essential—the performance as situated in a context [and] the performance as emergent, as unfolding or arising within that context.

—Dell Hymes ([1975] 1981, 81)

COLLECTING TEXTS FROM Native American cultures has been a central part of American anthropology since its Boasian beginnings. The Americanist tradition, as this program has been called by Regna Darnell and others (see Valentine and Darnell 1999), differentiated itself from its British counterpart by emphasizing, among other things, the necessity of creating texts (Malinowski's [1935] emphasis on collecting texts being a notable exception). This textualizing tradition targeted Native American/First Nation cultures; its adherents were urged on to "salvage ethnography" by the belief that indigenous peoples would soon succumb to the colonizing forces of the US and Canadian governments. Texts—including mythological narratives, life histories, and elicited linguistic paradigms—would provide materials for the documentation of both the culture and the language of the vanishing tribes. But it was not just for archiving the peculiarities of soon-to-be extinct cultures that texts were to be collected. (En)textualizing practices reflect the Americanists' theoretical focus on studying language and culture together. In the first few decades of the twentieth century, Boas and his students amassed a huge number of texts, many of which would be subjected to new analytical tools by later anthropologists.

Anthropological ethnopoetics is one of the specializations that took great advantage of the text-creating propensity of the Americanist tradition. It began in force with developments by Dell Hymes in the 1960s. At the forefront of a great strengthening of linguistic anthropology based on challenges to Chomskyan formalism, Hymes's various projects included a renewed attention to the Native American/ First Nations texts collected by the first generation of Americanist anthropologists. As Hymes pointed out, ethnopoetics is a metalanguage that addresses a wide variety of issues and features of narrative/ performance that those individuals embedded in the cultural tradition being examined know implicitly or explicitly. Such commentary and performative nuances, however, were just the sort of thing erased by Franz Boas from the texts written down by George Hunt (Briggs and Bauman 1999). Translation itself cannot capture everything that needs to be accounted for, and the gaps remaining lessen not only our analytical understanding, but also our appreciation of the literature.

Boasian entextualization practices have also emerged as a crucial component of language revitalization. The process of rescuing a "dying" language most typically begins with linguistic documentation, primarily because the languages that are most endangered are also unwritten and unanalyzed. It was only later in the development of the field of language revitalization that linguists and language teachers created programs that revitalized unwritten languages without a textual component (such as master-apprentice programs [Hinton et al. 2002] and language nests [Hinton and Hale 2001]). Having emerged out of a tradition of salvage ethnography that emphasized text collection, language revitalization itself has largely been about the creation of texts. Whether for preservation or pedagogy, these entextualization strategies privilege linguistic form (as text) and overlook the significance of performance, erasing the speech errors, individual flourishes, and any other "deviation" imagined by the editor. Yet the ideal goal of language revitalization is to produce more speakers of the language. Therein lies the problem—a theoretical tradition that emphasizes the object and subject of language over the process and performance of language. This intellectual proclivity permeates the groundwork laid for language revitalization in the Yukon, our more specific topic here.

In language revitalization, Americanist entextualization practices have been specifically used in (1) the documentation of historical, literary, and auto- or biographical narratives (e.g., Carr 2004; Hill 1995; Moore 2002; Morgan 2009; Webster 2009); (2) the education and socialization of younger generations and novices through (and into) these texts (e.g., Kroskrity 2012b; Meek 2007, 2010; Paugh 2005; Perley 2011; Urla 2012); and (3) the preservation of particular grammatical patterns and dialect differences (e.g., Frawley et al. 2002; Grenoble and Whaley 2006; Hinton and Hale 2001). To illustrate the centrality of text and poetics to language revitalization, we will discuss and compare four different language projects from the Yukon Territory, Canada: Yukon Native Language Centre texts and teacher training; Kaska Tribal Council and language workshops; Liard First Nation's Aboriginal Head Start program; and the Northern Tutchone Narratives Project of Little Salmon Carmacks First Nation.[1] While we are not the first to recognize the significance of incorporating performance into language revitalization efforts (see, for example, Farnell 2002; Whiteley 2003), our goal is to show the subtle mediations that regimentation, performance, and creativity have on the possibilities and opportunities for language revitalization.

After a brief overview of language revitalization in the Yukon, we begin our analysis by examining educational texts created for Yukon aboriginal language revitalization. We then turn to instances of educational practice, specifically ones that incorporated storytelling. The first example is a Kaska "House of Language" Workshop that used storytelling to teach literacy and social knowledge. The next is from a storytelling event that took place within an Aboriginal Head Start program, in which elders attempted to elicit language use. The final example is an innovative and adaptive use of storytelling for language revitalization—a dramatized version of the Star Husband tale performed by Northern Tutchone speakers. In it, we see the "breakthrough into performance" that Hymes ([1975] 1981) identified. Ultimately, the different strategies for entextualizing and incorporating texts into language revitalization, as well as the various media used for the task, render salient certain aspects of the poetics of these texts while diminishing or erasing others, the most challenging elements being the intertextual links and indexical nods to forgotten texts, fading contexts, and possible futures.

Language Revitalization in the Yukon

Aboriginal language education and revitalization in the Yukon Territory have been ongoing since the 1970s (see Meek 2010).[2] First Nations activists in the Yukon, as part of a broader movement for land claims and educational reform, successfully lobbied to establish aboriginal language education in the schools and to institute territorial support for maintaining or revitalizing their own heritage languages.[3] However, this institutionalization of aboriginal languages became an elaborate, multifaceted process requiring commitment and participation from a range of individuals, organizations, and First Nations communities.[4]

Most prominently, the Yukon Native Language Centre (YNLC) was created in order to document languages, develop curriculum, and train Native language teachers.[5] The initial intervention strategies of YNLC and language advocates resulted in three kinds of texts for reclaiming aboriginal language practices and knowledge: archived grammatical descriptions (not available to the public), commercial language lesson books and pamphlets, and published oral narratives and noun dictionaries (Carr 2004; Cruikshank 1990; Moore 2002; Wheelock and Moore 1997; Yukon Native Language Centre 2012).

Additionally, adults and elders who had some facility with their heritage languages requested aboriginal language literacy classes. These classes became the cornerstone of the teacher-training program and were not intended to assist the instruction of reading and writing among school children. In fact, teachers were discouraged from using texts in the classroom and developing their students' literacy skills (see the 2003 handbook produced by Collynne Bunn and her associates, *Teaching Yukon Indigenous Languages*). To aid the development of literacy skills among adults, state-funded language and literacy workshops were held in Whitehorse and in local communities.

Growing out of experiences with literacy workshops, First Nations adults and elders became disgruntled by the exclusive attention to language form and written text. While certainly an expected component of an institutionalized approach to language curriculum, some individuals with spoken competence in the language failed to see the usefulness of these school-based exercises for encouraging the speaking of these languages by either children or adults. Similarly, First Nations elders and adults became disheartened by the lack of attention to their storytelling practices, their histories, and their oral narratives. They argued that more attention and research needed to be paid to their interpretations of events, their moral narratives and system(s) of value, their socializing practices, and their knowledge generally. Without direct intervention, the general sentiment was that not only would this knowledge be lost, but the health of the community would continue to decline (see Meek 2010, chapter 5). To address this predicament, local communities began to initiate their own language revitalization projects drawing on the same funding sources that supported the Yukon Native Language Centre.

Regimenting Aboriginal Language Instruction: Text

In his article "Breakthrough into Performance," Hymes ([1975] 1981) analyzed oral narrative with the purpose of demonstrating that performance is something that varies. While formal linguistics admitted variation into the equation, it was at that time relegated to the category of speech error and understood as an imperfect reproduction of structure rather than as a creative flourish or innovation. By contrast, the notion of breaking through to performance refers to a storyteller's shift from reporting an account to truly performing it as verbal art, a shift that is evidenced by linguistic cues. This dichotomy of repeating and performing illustrates what Hymes saw as "fundamental to the interpretation of cultural materials," that is, a recognition of "the difference between knowing tradition and presenting it; between knowing *what* and knowing *how*" (84–85; emphasis added). Competence, linguistic or sociolinguistic, entails both knowing what and knowing how.

By showing that performance is substantively different from reporting and that speakers can and do shift between reporting and performing, Hymes (along with scholars such as Milman Parry, Albert B. Lord, and Ruth Finnegan) also illustrated that actual performance is never just a reproduction of a model, but will exhibit emergent qualities. In reality, performances are not all the same; performers often perform extempore and display a great range of creativity within bounds. Ethnopoetics has also been invigorated by Richard Bauman's research on text as performance ([1975] 2001). He, too, corrects one of the limitations of the structuralist method, the assumption that stories are surface-level enactments of deeper, ideal models. Storytelling, analyzed in a performance framework, is recognized as a set of communicative practices and therefore always a social act and always negotiable and contingent. An extensive review of the cross-fertilization of performance theory and poetics can be found in the work of Bauman and Charles L. Briggs (1990). In further distancing performance analysis from structuralism, Bauman and Briggs offer *contextualization* and *entextualization* as replacements for the previously static terms *context* and *text*. Contextualization refers to the emergent and negotiated process of creating interpretive frameworks that human agents are continually engaged in during any communicative event. Entextualization describes the process of rendering a performance as a written text, but also the ways that speakers—including participants and ethnographers—fashion stretches of discourse, transforming thought or experience into objects of analysis or reflection.

The focus on "breakthrough" in language revitalization is a remarkably apt frame for understanding what is at stake and what is desired. Rather than emphasizing (and counting) speakers and bodies, this shift in perspective focuses on performance—not some totalizing, all-encompassing speaker performance over a lifetime, but rather a fleeting instantiation of verbal art by an individual or group of individuals during a particular event or interaction. The goal of language revitalization efforts is to transform individual articulations from *reporting*, or model reproduction, to *performing*, production with all the inherent variation and creative capacity that performance entails. However, Americanist entextualizing practices, and the language revitalization projects based on them, have tended to erase performance, thus curtailing opportunities for successful production.

Our first set of examples focuses on the texts assembled for aboriginal language teaching in the Yukon, the "knowing what" of documentation efforts. Language lesson books have been created for all of the Yukon's aboriginal languages, with separate books for different dialects. This broad representation has been accomplished in part through the aboriginal language teacher training program. As part of their literacy training, student teachers are required to produce a text (or two) using templates provided by the YNLC. The lessons themselves focus on topics such as greetings, weather, relatives, fire, objects, activities, body parts, numbers, colors, feelings, and possession. The activity terms and phrases coordinate (sometimes) with monthly seasonal activities, such as picking berries in September, hunting in October, and tanning hides in May. For example, Southern Tutchone (Aishihik dialect) has a November lesson that conjugates the verb *to drink (–da)* (Workman 1994, 18).

FIGURE 1: Verb Chart: [blank] is/are drinking (tea)

1 person	2 people	3 or more people
(I) ída[nasal]	we (2) iida[nasal]	we (3+) ghàts'äda[nasal]
(you) nda[nasal]	you (2) áda[nasal]	you (3+) ghàáda[nasal]
(he/she) äda[nasal]	they (2) käda[nasal]	they (3+) ghàkäda[nasal]

Most texts illustrate conjugation, or verb morphology, indirectly as imperatives (Workman 1994, 38, 49) and as responses to questions (33, 45):

> (A) Fire (p. 33)
> 9. What is he/she doing?   Ye dà'i[nasal]?
> 10. He/she is making a fire.   Kwän däk'a[nasal].
> 11. What are you doing?   Ye dìn'i[nasal]?
> 12. I am making a fire.   Kwän dìk'à[nasal].
> 13. Make fire!   Kwän dìnk'à[nasal].
>
> (B) Tanning Hides (p. 45)
> 4. What is he/she doing?   Ye dà'i[nasal]?
> 6. What are you doing?   Ye dìn'i[nasal]?

Furthermore, these lesson books are not intended to be read by young students; they are to guide the language teacher's lessons and lesson plans as provided in the instructor's curriculum guidebook *Teaching Yukon Native Languages* (Bunn et al. 2003). The lessons teach basic or novice-level linguistic expressions and are not meant to facilitate literacy or writing. In classroom activities, these phrases elicit minimal response pairs or direct repetition. At the time of our fieldwork in the late 1990s and early 2000s, teachers seldom elaborated on the form, function, framing, or meaning of these verb words. The schematic, referentially focused composition of the texts also did not solicit any additional information.

To ameliorate this limitation, YNLC also began producing narrative texts. As another requirement of the teacher training program, each trainee translated (or transposed) one of four generic activity narratives into his or her heritage language. For example, the story "At Home" begins with the following lines:

> This is John.
> John is packing in wood for his mother.
> John is bringing in water to make tea for his mother.[6]

The nine-line story is presented first in the aboriginal language, then in a bilingual (interlinear) format. While more elaborate composition-ally and technologically, the pedagogical effect remains limited to the lesson's referential expressivity, and therefore, in educational practice the lesson inspired no narrative exegesis.[7]

The textual resources available for revitalization in the Yukon maintained an approach to language delimited to reference and the exposition of nominal categories. Even when more verb-oriented lessons were created, the approach remained the same. The oral dimension in the classroom also followed this format, emphasizing repetition—"modeling"—over performance. By excising performance during the entextualization process, the designers of these learning materials effectively curtail the ability of students and teachers to per-form even novel sentences. Rather than modifying these pedagogical texts to index narrative performances experienced in other contexts, the teachers remained true to the textual genre of the institutionalized materials, reinforced by their own school experiences and their teacher training. That is, the institutionally promoted language-learning mate-rials constituted their own distinct genre, with attendant expectations of use and expression, to which the teachers oriented and attempted to remain faithful. Underscoring the dominance of this generic insti-tutional format, the teachers' authority to instruct in the schools was sanctioned by these dominant institutions (YNLC, Yukon Territorial Government [henceforth YTG]), and thus the textual authority of the institution would tacitly trump, or invalidate, Native language teachers' attempts to deviate from these institutional formats or to in-corporate alternative formats or genres, whether intentionally or not.

Regimenting Performance: Training

The poetics of a performance or of any interactional process involves both historicity and intertextuality. As Bauman and Briggs have noted, "a given performance is tied to a number of speech events that precede and succeed it" (1990, 60; Briggs and Bauman 1992). For language revitalization it is helpful to emphasize the plurality in this statement, that the tying is not limited solely to a previous and future "speech event," but extends to previous and future actors, actions, activities, orientations, perspectives, etc. The narratives used in First Nations' efforts to preserve their languages and cultures may be linked to grandparents who shared these tales with grandchildren, to young men performing for flirtatious admirers, or to adults playfully scolding younger generations; each narrative "carries elements of its history of use within it" (Bauman and Briggs 1990, 73). The "history of use" indexed by the language materials above connected these materials to their institutional origins rather than to the teachers' (and students') heritage, even though the stories were about relevant cultural activities. They did not invoke a history of performances and socializing experiences of the teachers or their students.

Performance art, as communicative practice, must use culture-specific, conventionalized tools to key the appropriate frames. The relativity expressed by the notion that these keys are conventionalized and situated within specific speech communities is extended by adding that even within communities what counts as performance is variable, due to the different contexts of performances and to the individual abilities and preferences of storytellers (e.g., Bunte 2012; Kroskrity 2012a).

Local revitalization efforts—those that are occurring in the communities, away from YNLC's institutional base—have inherited the poetics entextualized in YNLC publications and literacy workshops, yet they attempt to emplace these decontextualized texts, reintegrating them within contexts considered more traditionally appropriate. In the attempt to reestablish genre-based intertextual links, they have expanded these received, published texts, resulting in syncretic approaches to language revitalization that merge institutionally acquired techniques with locally acquired poetics; they have begun to mix genres (Briggs and Bauman 1992).

To illustrate, we turn now to the Kaska "House of Language" workshops. These workshops were sponsored and organized by the Kaska Tribal Council and funded by the territorial and federal governments.[8] They lasted five days and were open to anyone who wanted to participate, including busloads of school children at various times during the week. The mornings were devoted to grammatical elicitation and literacy exercises, interspersed with the performance and recording of elders' narratives. Participants filled out verb charts, provided the missing letter in spelling exercises, and wrote in the missing word for the story-texts provided. In the afternoon, a cultural activity was planned. For the first workshop, moose hide tanning was the focus, so the morning centered on verbs for preparing moose hide, from soaking and dehairing it to tying it up and scraping it. Short conversational prompts were created to aid novice learners as they attempted to speak Kaska with the elders while working on a moose hide.

The literacy components of the workshop especially demonstrate the syncretic dimension of these events. For example, the story-text exercises began with a recording of a narrative performance, an autobiographical reflection, a legend, or a myth. The recording was then transcribed, translated, and formatted for the edited volume *Dene Gudeji* (Moore 1999). For the workshop, these texts were reproduced with words omitted. The workshop students were then expected to follow along in the text as the storyteller performed and to fill in the missing words while the rest of the workshop participants served as an audience.[9]

The modification of the YNLC-style literacy exercises through Kaska narratives served several purposes. This strategy reframed the exercises as communal, shifting them from an institutional context to a locally managed one where local language personnel (re)produced the texts, conducted the exercises, and elicited responses, criticisms, and corrections. It also extended the frame to include a broader spectrum of participants—including anyone interested in enhancing his or her literacy knowledge and practices—rather than limiting participation to those requiring such knowledge as a matter of employment. It also began to blur the distinction between orality and literacy and between "Western" and "First Nations," especially in relation to the storytelling exercise, which developed competence in both domains (oral/literate) and familiarity with two textual traditions (spoken/written). Most significantly, this latter exercise incorporated information deemed significant by the teachers and the elders. Elders were able to introduce social and historical knowledge about the community, knowledge that more typical language classes did not and could not accommodate. This knowledge was also integrated into the workshops through the afternoon activities. Again, elders were provided with a platform to demonstrate their knowledge and socialize more novice participants into and through language, be it spoken Kaska, English, or some combination of the two. Not only were the grammatical forms of (or forms within) the exercises significant, but the generic content was as well.

Unlike the story pamphlets and texts in schools, these workshops began to recognize the histories of interaction associated with the stories and encouraged opportunities to socialize new generations of storytellers qua language learners. The one aspect that this exercise and the workshop structure in general failed to consider or account for was the interactive dimension of storytelling. While we typically think of narrative as a genre, it may be more productive to orient ourselves toward storytelling as a conversational or interactional style (see Carr 2008). Northern Tutchone and Kaska legends are a form of conversation, a way of speaking, and the defining characteristics of this genre really stem from interaction. Unfortunately for the case just examined, the literacy component detracted from the interactional component of these narratives, and though workshop participants may have graduated from this event with a better sense of sound-symbol correspondence, they would not have advanced substantially their understanding of the interactional realm in relation to either conversation or narrative. That is, the intertextual connectedness of this workshop to reiteration-based educational materials overrode the references to previous performances and to future possibilities for new storytelling (interactional) practices; it remained a model of performance (of literacy and storytelling) rather than a "break-through" into performance (of either literacy or storytelling). The next case offers a completely oral performance in which interaction was crucial to its success.

Regimenting Aboriginal Language Development: Teaching

While one aspect of the relationship between breakthrough into performance and intertextuality is the historicity of a narrative, the creative potential of the text–performance linkages can easily move beyond indexical connections to past texts and performances and introduce new connections, approximate generic (re)productions, and unexpected recontextualizations. As Briggs and Bauman (1992, 147) have shown through their comparison of reported speech and genre, "the creation of intertextual relationships through genre simul-taneously renders texts ordered, unified, and bounded, on the one hand, and fragmented, heterogeneous, and open-ended, on the other." This relationship of text to prior discourse (or models of discourse production and reception) can be as complicated as a partially fractal tinker-toy design or as isomorphic as a language map, indexing other performances, other similar texts, and other performers, and creating new indices to otherwise unexpected texts, contexts, and performances. Similarly, the strategies used to manage gaps between texts (maximally or minimally) vary in multiple ways, including within an iteration or performance of a text. That is, the maximal replication of a text—as duplicate—would be the maximizing of the indexical connections between the two texts, such that the duplicate could easily be mistaken for the original (all indices reproduced faithfully, as it were). Minimally managed gaps would minimize links between a previous performance and a current one. In this case, the relationship between texts would seem more allusive and indirect rather than exact and directed. As Bauman (1992) has shown in his examination of the relationship between one Mexican play's written script and its enactment in performance, such indirectness, to the point of complete deviance, might be scripted into the text itself, as part of a genre even, faithfully reproduced in spirit while unfaithfully reproduced in practice. Elements that mediate such variability, however, are not exclusive to text, performance, or genre alone. As Briggs and Bauman (1992) ultimately argue, the social environment of these texts—and the social environment of these breakthroughs into performance—influence the nature of the intertextuality articulated and realized, especially as we broaden our gaze to include the (inter)actions and impact of the audience.

At the Aboriginal Head Start program in Liard River, storytelling events were incorporated into the curriculum to teach children and others directly and indirectly about history, social values, cultural practices, and language. During such events, elders and older adults shared these narratives with a novice audience. These events were intended to mimic socialization experiences familiar to these elders when they were young: they themselves had sat and listened to grandparents and other elders "tell stories" (cf. Bunte 2012; Field 2012; Neely 2012). In Head Start events where children were always a part of the audience, the narrative often addressed the ways in which children and youth should behave, especially toward elders. In the following narrative, the elder switched between Kaska and English, using English to translate her Kaska statements as part of an effort to maintain the children's attention, to encourage participation (interaction), and to facilitate comprehension. The ages of the children ranged from one-and-a-half to five-and-a-half years old.[10] Along with illustrating the instructional function of narrative, this excerpt also demonstrates the effect of the audience on the narrative performance (from Meek 2010, 62–65).

The elder, Mrs. Adele Johnny, began talking in Kaska about her childhood:

ADELE:	*Yā wō˛ gudusdéh sâ˛ géhdi? Heh, heh.*	1
	[What did she say I should talk about? Heh, heh]	
ANN:	*Her?*　　　((referring to a teacher))	2
ADELE:	*Ham.*	3
	[Yes]	
ANN:	*Anything dah gudendéh, kul(a).*	4
	[Talk about anything, ready.]	
ADELE:	*Łááné détséle kú, ts'édāne eslīni—*	5
	[When I was really small, (when) I was a child—]	
ILEANNA:	*Hi*	6
BARB [Meek]:	*Do you know what she said?* (unintelligible)	7
ADELE:	*When I was, long time ago when I was this, you know, little child*	8
	((banging of blocks and toys in background))	
	Dene cho' den(e) dets'į̃į̃´ łén-łéndedē´li, e ts'édāne ts'édān(e)	9
	[When adults people came together, the children children]	
	kē´néht'ē´ de kēndzeht'ē	10
	[everyone (all of us) we did like this]	
	((children sitting in semicircle around Adele))	
	((noise of toys being dumped out of bin))	
	Etígé', etígé' (:02) etígé'one place dene nédzédēts'i', guchō	11
	[(in) one, one, (:02) one one place people, we all sat, our parents]	
	négúdúdē´hí. Ts'édāne nē´gédéts'ek la.	
	[they would be talking (while) we listened.]	
	Dułą´, dułą´ káádzéntąh.	12
	[We didn't play around at all.]	

Interrupted by the children who had begun conversing with each other in English, Adele queried whether or not she should switch to English:

ADELE: *Yeah, maybe I should just talk to them in English; think so?*   26
        Dułą́ nē̃´gédéts'ek gēt'ē.   ((to Ann))   27
        [It seems like they don't hear (understand).]
        ((children talking in background, not paying attention))
ANN: *Kē̃´giht'ē-la.*   28
        [They are like that.]
        ((Meek is trying to get kids to pay attention))
ADELE: *Ī, Ī gáádááscho de , etááne ēdests'es-seg'la, ī ī dédáácho-já?*   29
        How old is he now?
        [That one, that one, when I was that big, I really
        listened (well), that one, that one, how old is he now?
        How old is he now?]
BARB: *How old are you?*   30
JASON: *Five.*   31
BARB: *Five.*   32

Concerned that she may be losing her audience, Mrs. Johnny adjusts
her narrative in two ways. First, she elicits some personal information
about one of the children (the child's age) and uses that information
as a point of departure for her own narrative. Second, she switches
from Kaska to English.

ADELE: *When I was five years old like um five years old like you*   46
        already I had to learn to help help my mom and dad look
        after little little baby like that ((referring to the one-
        year-old child sitting near his brother, Jason)), *we*
        never play aroun' we, we had to help, we don't play aroun',
        sometimes we play aroun', we play aroun' with other—
        ((a child interrupts))
        Listen, sometimes we would play aroun' with other kids   47
        but um a lot of times when we were home we help our mom
        an' mom and dad look after the other kids, you hear?
        ((to children))

The pragmatic elements articulated in the narrative and practiced
as part of its telling reveal the ways in which elders' performances
facilitate both linguistic and cultural instruction—as children "we"
sat and listened, displaying respect to adults and elders. This process
of entextualization—in which elders narrate their childhood experiences, presenting them as a cultural text—is also interactional in that
it both defines and exemplifies interactional protocol, an important

part of this genre. In this way, these texts clearly deviate from the more language- and literacy-focused texts discussed above. The generic intertextuality that elders produce and promote in these performances defines (or naturalizes) the genre itself, regiments a particular interpretation of the past and the present, and establishes the elders' own jurisdiction over storytelling as well as knowledge of the past—that is, knowledge of all things aboriginal.[11]

While this example of using narrative for language revitalization is culturally instructive and highly valued by community members, it failed to result in a breakthrough into performance in either Kaska or English. The elders became weary, distracted by the children, and the children became more restless. As a result, the interactional component remained between adults and failed to engage the younger audience members. The intertextual links to previous tellings and indexical nods to future retellings, a significant dimension of socializing novices into *dene k'eh*,[12] became, in this moment, as evanescent as the interaction, and possibly the stories themselves.

"Star Wife": Breakthrough into Performance

The most provocative examples of breakthrough into performance that we witnessed were of traditional stories staged as plays at language events. These dramatic performances were novel generic experiments, contemporary adaptations of traditional storytelling practices. They evolved from a language revitalization project of Little Salmon Carmacks First Nation (LSCFN), which entextualized Northern Tutchone narratives.[13] In particular, we examine the story/play "Star Wife," performed by Mrs. Agnes Washpan.[14]

Mrs. Washpan's "Star Wife" (*Tthyaw Uts'an*, lit. 'the star's wife') is a version of the Native North American tale "The Star Husband" analyzed by Stith Thompson in his classic historic-geographic study ([1953] 1965).[15] Of the eighty-six versions Thompson analyzed for his study, the Kaska version (version 4, originally collected by James Teit at Dease Lake and published in 1915) most closely resembles Mrs. Washpan's story. This is not surprising, considering that Northern Tutchone and Kaska are neighboring Athabaskan languages and that members of the communities intermarry. A similar version of the story was also collected from Southern Tutchone elders by Julie Cruikshank (1990), who productively defines the broader corpus as the "Stolen Women" genre. Related stories include "Dog Husband" and "Bear Husband" (or "The Woman Who Married the Bear").

In Mrs. Washpan's story, two young women, who may be characterized as acting disrespectfully or at least carelessly, look up at the stars one night and pretend that the pretty ones are their husbands. As they gaze up, those stars look down at them and decide to take the girls for their wives. When the young women awaken, they find that they are no longer in their lands and that there are men sleeping alongside them. Realizing that the star men have brought them to the sky world—that they have gotten what they wished for—they marry the stars, then live happily for many years. The stars are ideal husbands—handsome, loving, and great hunters. Capable of moving at the speed of light, they return with moose meat only moments after leaving to hunt.

But eventually the two young wives get lonely; without their relatives nearby, or children of their own, they only have each other to talk to. So, they plan to get down from the sky by making a rope and lowering themselves while their husbands are away. Using the plentiful supply of moose hide brought by their husbands, the two make *babiche* and begin tying it together into a rope. [16] While they are doing this, they are also digging away at a hole that will allow them to descend back to Earth. When their husbands are around, they hide the rope and cover the hole they are digging. Finally, after perhaps months of work, they see light through the bottom of the hole. They lower themselves down in a moose hide tied to the babiche line.[17]

The two women land on an island in the ocean. They are stranded there and must persuade someone to help them get to the (nearby) mainland before they can head home. With their provisions running low, they begin to call out to people walking along the mainland shore. Many pass by, unwilling to help the young women because they are too lazy to build a raft (in the Yukon, temporary rafts are often made for travel on the large, long lakes). Eventually, Wolverine walks by. Wolverine, or Naye as he is called in Northern Tutchone, is a "long ago" character, from the time "when animals were like humans."[18] When Wolverine passes, the women let out the cry *"Nahumchi-ey"* 'come get us please', lengthening the final vowel for emphasis. Wolverine stops to ponder their request. Intrigued, he replies that he will help if they agree to sleep with him. The women, confident that they can outsmart this fool, collude to trick him. They yell back their answer and Wolverine, excited, throws together a shoddily built raft and heads toward them. He retrieves them, then, as the raft nears the mainland shore, the women jump off and run into the bush. One of the women calls out for the south wind, which soon howls through the forest. The noise confuses Wolverine as he attempts to collect his payment. He runs back and forth to different trees and stumps, holding them, kissing them, perhaps getting a little more involved with them, and commenting that they "don't feel like woman." This is the comic high point of the story: Wolverine is made into a fool by the women, and they enjoy the scene for a while before heading back home to their mother. The contexts where Mrs. Washpan performed these narratives were several, from classroom recountings to public performances at First Nations events. She, along with her sister, also worked to document these stories in writing.

Initially, entextualization practices employed in the Narratives Project derived from the ethnopoetic methods developed by Hymes and also Dennis Tedlock (1972, 1983). Considerable effort was made to break the narratives into lines based on the concept of intonation unit from discourse analysis, where a line is described as a stretch of discourse bounded by pauses and distinguished by intonational contour, a segment within which an interlocutor could not speak without interrupting. Lines are identified in ethnopoetics and conversation analysis by marking the convergence, or near convergence, of completion in the intonational, syntactic, and pragmatic fields (see Ochs, Schegloff, and Thompson 1996). However, the LSCFN community rejected those techniques because the style made the texts look like "poetry" rather than "stories." The members saw no value in breaking the texts into lines based on intonation, breath groups, pauses, and other similar performance elements. They approved of the text when formatted in a prose style because they understood the written text as fundamentally different from the performance of the story. This meant that there was no need to capture performance elements in the written versions.

In addition to a prose version, the elders wanted to produce plays based on some of their stories—first Crow stories, then "Star Wife." These were staged on Aboriginal Language Day and similar occasions. The organizers opted to send the English prose version of "Star Wife" to a playwright in Vancouver, who converted it into a script. Mrs. Washpan, along with Carr and elders Evelyn Skookum and Anne Ranigler, then translated the play back into Northern Tutchone, and created a bilingual version. When performed, a narrator read the English lines while Mrs. Washpan and other elders took on the Northern Tutchone lines. However, these elders did not merely recite the text in their native language; they broke through into performance of their parts. While those reading the English sat, immobile, off to the side (figuratively offstage), the Northern Tutchone speakers moved about the floor, interacting with the audience, gesturing, raising and lowering their voices (and their bodies), using props, and drawing on additional traditional storytelling resources and personal interpretations of what "drama" should entail. The audience—speakers and nonspeakers, elders and children, and even community outsiders invited to the event—enjoyed the storytelling, seeing in it a competent performance intertextually linked to previous iterations.

Hymes envisioned the study of performance as the study of variation in performances—variation across time and space, and across enactments by members of the same culture (cf. Toelken 1996). He criticized the view of variation as deviation from the ideal, something fundamentally suspect, indicative of loss or degradation of tradition or language. Those who see native languages and cultures as dying, judged from imagined past pure forms, often lament that contemporary performances provide evidence for their critiques. But these critics fail to understand that performance follows no universal or inherent template, that performance adapts and even appropriates elements from outside, and that the real judge of success is the extent to which an audience of community members accepts and engages with the performance.

In the context of language revitalization and the significance of storytelling to revived language use, the textual styles and formats relied on for initiating and institutionalizing aboriginal languages often overlook and thus erase this embeddedness, leaving learners and teachers with language reports rather than sociolinguistic performances. Consider again the role of, and strategies for, managing intertextual gaps. These gaps can be used to promote and naturalize a certain perspective or practice, or they can be instrumental in disrupting the same. The mediation of gaps between different texts (and genres) through the mixing of genres/texts can be, as Briggs and Bauman argue, a tool for interrupting hegemonic control over (1) the creation of texts by dominant institutions (illustrated usually by Western-educated non-Indians) and (2) the creation of authority, as instituted through/by the naturalization of texts (and language) in language revitalization projects modeled after Western educational paradigms and the idea that wisdom sits in elders, and elders alone. The cases above illustrate various degrees of mixing and a range of responses, from disgruntlement to appreciation, showing how "breakthrough" in the last case succeeds not merely because of its management of intertextual gaps but because of its shift in management from dominant institutional control to First Nation.

In documenting language and creating texts for language revitalization à la the Americanist tradition, the dominant goal has been to minimize (if not entirely erase) the intertextual gaps inherent in the process, the gap between what has passed (and is passing) and what will be (is becoming) such that the recorded (decontextualized), entextualized, and recontextualized "text" appears identical to its preceding iterations (as with the performance of a play, cf. Bauman 1992), its authority rendered intact by means of intertextual purism. However, the dramatic enactment of "Star Wife" illustrates the importance and potency of breakthrough into performance and the revitalizing force of mixing genres, where possible futures become realizable— performed. In these performances, creativity and variation create intertextual links to previous performances and interdiscursive connections to past socializing events, fusing Western textual traditions with aboriginal innovation and history. They open doors to future sociolinguistic traditions (as with Anthony Webster's [2008, 2009] analyses of Navajo ethnopoetic practices) that may inspire budding performers rather than leaving their aspirations languishing in the margins of Western inscription.

Conclusion

Hymes took seriously the need to simultaneously study linguistic phenomena and translate performances and texts as verbal art. The methodology exemplified in his work stands as a compendium of insights into how poetic structure may be crafted using the linguistic and cultural resources of a society. Furthermore, his work in ethnopoetics shows that fields concerned with language and text would benefit from attention to the discursive features made obvious in socially occurring speech, especially oral narrative. This imperative highlights the challenge for the study and practice of language revitalization. Emerging from a tradition of texts and referential functionality, very little research, or application, has centered on the necessity of language as narrative performance, as verbal artistry, as storytelling (cf. Woodbury 1998; for some recent exceptions, see Debenport 2011; Kroskrity, Bethel, and Reynolds 2002; Kroskrity 2009a; and most exceptionally Kroskrity 2012b). Where Hymes argued that the verse patterning characteristic of Native American oral narratives has been obscured by its textualization as prose, we have similarly argued that language-teaching texts equally obscure socially occurring speech patterns and verbal artistry through their elision in pedagogical prose. Because instruction in and about aboriginal languages adheres so directly to the institutionally based textual genre, we have argued that these instructional texts and pedagogical practices are *reported* language rather than *performed* language; that is, in many language revitalization textbooks and teacher training materials, words and texts have become fetishized and static tokens of a sociolinguistic landscape otherwise in flux.

Furthermore, as several linguistic anthropologists and folklorists mentioned above have noted, evaluation is an equally significant dimension of performance. Whether realized as self-reflection or as audience participation, evaluation mediates the configuration of performance and its interpretation. The act of, and tension with, evaluation is its need for a standard of comparison and expectation, that is, a theory about the object being evaluated. Rachel Fleming (2004) grappled with a similar dilemma in relation to the revitalization of Irish music traditions and the defining of tradition. Her concern was how to preserve (or document) tradition (a bounded, defined convention or genre) given "the challenge of defining [practices] that [are] inherently dynamic, unbounded, and diverse" (2004, 227); in other words, how does one segregate an object of study or object for revitalization without participating in strict regimentation? Our mutual responses have been to turn attention toward vernacular practices and the contexts of their mediation—toward process. For storytelling and language, we have emphasized two analytic elements, intertextuality and genre. In our case, a concern with the intertextual connections across different storytelling contexts within the institutional framework of language revitalization has resulted in a more complicated and richer understanding of the transitional moment affecting aboriginal storytelling and languages in the Yukon, one that relies on a concept of genre that is leaky, shifting, and heterogeneous (cf. Briggs and Bauman 1992).

Finally, through our investigation of the various strategies that individuals have used to incorporate, transform, and overcome certain Western traditions, we have argued that revitalization, like ethnopoetics, is an interactive process. This perspective allows for greater diversity within individual performances (of aboriginal language, storytelling, or Irish music) as well as greater diversity without, as in understanding local genres, habits of circulation, and the regulation of innovation. It underscores Briggs's call for an attention to boundary making, to binding and unbinding, to building fences and to jumping them, and to planning to do otherwise (2008). Thus, the poetics of documentation and revitalization isn't about merely preserving and "speaking the past" (Kroskrity 2009b); it can be and is about articulating a present and, most importantly, a future.

Acknowledgments

Thanks to Tony, Paul, Charles and an anonymous reviewer for their feedback, to the elders who guided the research, and to Fulbright, Wenner-Gren, and NIGMS for research support.

Notes

1. The research for this essay comes out of over ten years of participation by both authors in language revitalization efforts in the Yukon Territory, Canada. Carr's research initially addressed the more quintessentially Hymesian project of documenting ethnopoetic genres and analyzing their structures, while Meek's focused on language development and revitalization in relation to interaction and ideology. Both authors have been concerned with variation and change within and across texts and contexts.

2. There are eight territorially recognized aboriginal languages; seven are Athabaskan, the remaining one is Tlingit. All of these languages are considered endangered, with most speakers fifty years old and older (see Meek 2010 for statistics and discussion).

3. In 1973, representatives from the Yukon Native Brotherhood, predecessor of the Council of Yukon First Nations, traveled to Ottawa to present their document "Together Today for Our Children Tomorrow." In it, they called for aboriginal control of aboriginal education (meaning an end to the residential schools),

control of aboriginal economic development, aboriginal self-government for the Yukon, and the right to preserve their cultural identity and languages. In 1993, after twenty years of negotiating, the Umbrella Final Agreement (UFA) was signed, which set a template for land claims settlement and self-governing agreements across the territory. Most Yukon First Nations now have their own capital agreements under the UFA, and have language programming derived from their agreements.

4. For greater discussion of the emergence of this process, its success, and its influence on the stratification of authority (in relation to aboriginal languages in particular), see Meek 2007, 2009, and 2010.

5. Established initially as the Yukon Native Languages Project, through an agreement between the Council of Yukon Indians (now CYFN) and the Yukon Territorial Government (YTG) the project became the Yukon Native Languages Centre as additional funds were secured in accordance with the Yukon Aboriginal Languages Agreement and participation by all First Nations grew (see Meek 2009). The Centre was and remains under the direction of John Ritter, an MIT-trained linguist.

6. Other thematic templates available online are "At Home," "Fish Camp," and "Camping" (YNLC 2013). While these stories may be based loosely on historical or personal narratives about such activities, neither author has ever heard any of these stories performed as a storytelling event, nor do the templates represent any of the poetic resources found in the narratives documented by Carr or our colleague Patrick Moore (2002).

7. Meek observed the stories in use in a school's computer lab. Each individual student sat at a computer station and played the CD for him- or herself, listening to a narrator and (ideally) following along in the text displayed on the screen. The interaction was between the student and the computer, and the computer-managed narrative never deviated from the text.

8. Patrick Moore codirected these events with Marie Skidmore while Meek helped to facilitate them.

9. See Carr 2008 on Dene audience interaction.

10. Ileana was two years and seven months old, Jason was five-and-a-half years old, Michael was two years and seven months old, John was one-and-a-half years old, Adam was five years and two months old, Tina was four years old, Larry was four years and two months old, and Joy was three years and eleven months old.

11. Meek (2007) discusses the status of elders in greater detail within the context of both the First Nations and the territorial governments.

12. This phrase, loosely translated as "like Kaska, or in the Kaska way," indicates a Kaska way of knowing and doing, of being in the world.

13. The Northern Tutchone Narratives Project was sponsored by the Canada-Yukon Cooperation Agreement for Aboriginal Languages and administered by Aboriginal Languages Services (of the Yukon Territorial Government) and the Little Salmon Carmacks First Nation. It resulted in a bilingual compilation of about seventy narratives from twelve different speakers, privately published for community members.

14. This story was originally recorded in the early 1990s, then translated by Mrs. Washpan, Carr, and elders Evelyn Skookum and Anne Ranigler for the Narratives Project.

15. The tale of the Star Husband has also been analyzed by Reichard (1921), Dundes (1964), and Levi-Strauss ([1963] 1967).

16. Babiche are rawhide strips used for lacing, webbing, and rope, as in making snowshoes.

17. In the Northern Tutchone telling, Mrs. Washpan used the English word *parachute,* saying that the women floated down, but later, during translation, she described the moose hide as "basket-like," saying that the women got inside and lowered it down slowly.

18. Such characters should be imagined as people, not talking animals. In her story, Mrs. Washpan, like other Northern Tutchone storytellers, uses the term *dän,* person or people, to refer to Wolverine, and his motions are described using the verb stem for human locomotion (*-zhi*), instead of the stem *-'ra,* used for animal locomotion.

References Cited

Bauman, Richard. (1975) 2001. "Verbal Art as Performance." In *Linguistic Anthropology: A Reader,* edited by Alessandro Duranti, 165–89. Oxford: Blackwell.

———. 1992. "Transformations of the Word in the Production of Mexican Festival Drama." In *Natural Histories of Discourse,* edited by Michael Silverstein and Greg Urban, 301–29. Chicago: University of Chicago Press.

Bauman, Richard, and Charles L. Briggs. 1990. "Poetics and Performance as Critical Perspectives on Language and Social Life." *Annual Review of Anthropology* 19:59–88.

Briggs, Charles L. 2008. "Disciplining Folkloristics." *Journal of Folklore Research* 45 (1): 91–105.

Briggs, Charles L., and Richard Bauman. 1992. "Genre, Intertextuality, and Social Power." *Journal of Linguistic Anthropology* 2 (2): 131–72.

———. 1999. "'The Foundation of All Future Researches': Franz Boas, Native American Texts, and the Construction of Modernity." *American Quarterly* 51 (3): 479–528.

Bunn, Collynne, Doug Hitch, Jo-Anne Johnson, John Ritter, Gertie Tom, and Margaret Workman. 2003. *Teaching Yukon Native Languages: A Guidebook for Native Language Instructors.* 2nd ed. Whitehorse, Yukon Territory: Yukon Native Language Centre.

Bunte, Pamela A. 2012. "'You're Talking English, Grandma': Language Ideologies, Narratives, and Southern Paiute Linguistic and Cultural Reproduction." In *Telling Stories in the Face of Danger: Language Renewal in Native American Communities,* edited by Paul V. Kroskrity, 44–59. Norman: University of Oklahoma Press.

Carr, Gerald L. 2004. "Northern Tutchone (Athabascan) Poetics." PhD diss., State University of New York, Buffalo.

———. 2008. "The Poetics of Northern Tutchone Storytelling: Highlights from the Northern Tutchone Narratives Project." Paper presented at the Athabascan/Dene Languages Conference, Cold Lake, Alberta.

Cruikshank, Julie. 1990. *Life Lived Like a Story: Life Stories of Three Yukon Native Elders.* Lincoln: University of Nebraska Press.

Debenport, Erin. 2011. "As the Rez Turns: Anomalies within and beyond the Boundaries of a Pueblo Community." *American Indian Culture and Research Journal* 35 (2): 87–110.

Dundes, Alan. 1964. *The Morphology of North American Indian Folktales.* Folklore Fellows Communications 195. Helsinki: Suomalainen Tiedeakatemia.

Farnell, Brenda. 2002. "Dynamic Embodiment in Assiniboine (Nakota) Storytelling." *Anthropological Linguistics* 44 (1): 37–64.

Field, Margaret C. 2012. "Kumiai Stories: Bridges between Oral Tradition and Classroom Practice." In *Telling Stories in the Face of Danger: Language Renewal in Native American Communities,* edited by Paul V. Kroskrity, 115–26. Norman: University of Oklahoma Press.

Fleming, Rachel. 2004. "Resisting Cultural Standardization: Comhaltas Celotoiri Eireann and the Revitalization of Traditional Music in Ireland." *Journal of Folklore Research* 41 (2): 227–57.

Frawley, William, Kenneth C. Hill, and Pamela Munro. 2002. *Making Dictionaries: Preserving Indigenous Languages of the Americas.* Berkeley: University of California Press.

Grenoble, Lenore, and Lindsay Whaley. 2006. *Saving Languages: An Introduction to Language Revitalization.* Cambridge: Cambridge University Press.

Hill, Jane H. 1995. "The Voices of Don Gabriel: Responsibility and Self in a Modern Mexicano Narrative." In *The Dialogic Emergence of Culture,* edited by Dennis Tedlock and Bruce Mannheim, 97–147. Urbana: University of Illinois Press.

Hinton, Leanne, and Ken Hale, eds. 2001. *The Green Book of Language Revitalization in Practice.* New York: Academic Press.

Hinton, Leanne, with Matt Vera and Nancy Steele. 2002. *How to Keep Your Language Alive: A Commonsense Approach to One-on-One Language Learning.* Berkeley, CA: Heyday.

Hymes, Dell. (1975) 1981. "Breakthrough into Performance." In *Folklore: Performance and Communication,* edited by Dan Ben-Amos and Kenneth S. Goldstein, 11–74. The Hague: Mouton.

Kroskrity, Paul V. 2009a. "Embodying the Reversal of Language Shift: Agency, Incorporation, and Language Ideological Change in the Western Mono Community of Central California." In *Native American Language Ideologies: Beliefs, Practices, and Struggles in Indian Country,* edited by Paul V. Kroskrity and Margaret C. Field, 190–211. Tucson: University of Arizona Press.

———. 2009b. "Narrative Reproductions: Ideologies of Storytelling, Authoritative Words, and Generic Regimentation in the Village of Tewa." *Journal of Linguistic Anthropology* 19 (1): 40–56.

———. 2012a. "Growing with Stories: Ideologies of Storytelling and the Narrative Reproduction of Arizona Tewa Identities." In *Telling Stories in the Face of Danger: Language Renewal in Native American Communities,* edited by Paul V. Kroskrity, 151–83. Norman: University of Oklahoma Press.

———. 2012b. *Telling Stories in the Face of Danger: Language Renewal in Native American Communities.* Norman: University of Oklahoma Press.

Kroskrity, Paul V., Rosalie Bethel, and Jennifer Reynolds. 2002. *Taitaduhaan: Western Mono Ways of Speaking.* Norman: University of Oklahoma Press.

Levi-Strauss, Claude. (1963) 1967. "The Structural Study of Myth." In *Structural Anthropology,* 202–28. Garden City, NY: Doubleday Anchor.

Malinowski, Bronislaw. 1935. *Coral Gardens and Their Magic.* Vol. 2. New York: American Book Company.

Meek, Barbra A. 2007. "Respecting the Language of Elders: Ideological Shift and Linguistic Discontinuity in a Northern Athapascan Community." *Journal of Linguistic Anthropology* 17 (1): 23–43.

———. 2009. "Language Ideology and Aboriginal Language Revitalization in Yukon, Canada." In *Native American Language Ideologies: Beliefs, Practices, and Struggles in Indian Country,* edited by Paul V. Kroskrity and Margaret C. Field, 151–71. Tucson: University of Arizona Press.

———. 2010. *"We Are Our Language": An Ethnography of Language Revitalization in a Northern Athabaskan Community.* Tucson: University of Arizona Press.

Moore, Patrick, ed. 1999. *Dene Gudeji.* Whitehorse, Yukon Territory: Queen's Printer.

———. 2002. "Points of View in Kaska Historical Narratives." PhD diss., Indiana University, Bloomington.

Morgan, Mindy J. 2009. *The Bearer of This Letter.* Lincoln: University of Nebraska Press.

Neely, Amber. 2012. "Tales of Tradition and Stories of Syncretism in Kiowa Language Revitalization." In *Telling Stories in the Face of Danger: Language in Renewal in Native American Communities,* edited by Paul V. Kroskrity, 90–114. Norman: University of Oklahoma Press.

Ochs, Elinor, Emanuel A. Schegloff, and Sandra A. Thompson, eds. 1996. *Interaction and Grammar.* Cambridge: Cambridge University Press.

Paugh, Amy. 2005. "Multilingual Play: Children's Code-Switching, Role Play, and Agency in Dominica, West Indies." *Language in Society* 34 (1): 63–86.

Perley, Bernard. 2011. *Defying Maliseet Language Death: Emergent Vitalities of Language, Culture, and Identity in Eastern Canada.* Lincoln: University of Nebraska Press.

Reichard, Gladys. 1921. "Literary Types and Disseminations of Myths." *Journal of American Folklore* 34 (133): 269–307.

Tedlock, Dennis. 1972. *Finding the Center: Narrative Poetry of the Zuni Indians.* Lincoln: University of Nebraska Press.

———. 1983. *The Spoken Word and the Work of Interpretation.* Philadelphia: University of Pennsylvania Press.

Thompson, Stith. (1953) 1965. "The Star Husband Tale." In *The Study of Folklore,* edited by Alan Dundes, 414–74. Englewood Cliffs, NJ: Prentice Hall.

Toelken, Barre. 1996. *The Dynamics of Folklore.* Rev. ed. Logan: Utah State University Press.

Urla, Jacqueline. 2012. *Reclaiming Basque: Language, Nation, and Cultural Activism.* Reno: University of Nevada Press.

Valentine, Lisa Philips, and Regna Darnell, eds. 1999. *Theorizing the Americanist Tradition.* Toronto: University of Toronto Press.

Webster, Anthony. 2008. "'To All the Former Cats and Stomps of the Navajo Nation': Performance, the Individual, and Cultural Poetic Traditions." *Language in Society* 37 (1): 61–89.

———. 2009. *Explorations in Navajo Poetry and Poetics.* Albuquerque: University of New Mexico Press.

Wheelock, Angela, and Patrick Moore. 1997. *Dene Gedeni: Traditional Lifestyles of Kaska Women.* Ross River, Yukon Territory: Ross River Dena Council.

Whiteley, Peter. 2003. "Do Language Rights Serve Indigenous Interests? Some Hopi and Other Queries." *American Anthropologist* 105 (4): 712–22.

Woodbury, Anthony. 1998. "Documenting Rhetorical, Aesthetic, and Expressive Loss in Language Shift." In *Endangered Languages: Language Loss and Community Response*, edited by Lenore A. Grenoble and Lindsay J. Whaley, 234–59. Cambridge: Cambridge University Press.

Workman, Margaret. 1994. *Southern Tutchone Language Lessons: Aishihik Dialect*. Whitehorse, Yukon Territory: YNLC and CYI.

Yukon Native Language Center (YNLC). 2013. "Tagish Story Books." *Yukon Native Language Center*, Materials: Audio Story Books. http://www.ynlc.ca/materials /stories/tg.html.

GERALD L. CARR is a lecturer in Anthropology and American Culture at the University of Michigan. His current research and teaching focus on the institutional and legal contexts that define and constrain indigenous sovereignty, in addition to his work on anthropological folkloristics.

BARBRA MEEK is Associate Professor of Anthropology and Linguistics at the University of Michigan. Her current research and teaching focus on representations and performances of linguistic "otherness," in addition to ongoing work on language endangerment and revitalization.

8 Translating Oral Literature in Indigenous Societies: Ethnic Aesthetic Performances in Multicultural and Multilingual Settings

IN MANY WAYS, the process of translation is one of the most fundamental concerns within the field of anthropology (Becker 1995; Rubel
and Rosman 2003). Even at the outset, one must question the extent
to which translation is possible when passing—as anthropologists so
often do—between distant and often unrelated languages and cultures. What happens to words and other elements of discourse as they
are lifted from one social context and placed in another language, far
from the living subjects who once animated these utterances? When
it comes to writing up these encounters, every anthropologist is faced
with the daunting task of representing these remote worlds of experience in "plain English" or some kind of academic jargon as we attempt
to recreate field interactions in new contexts, for audiences who may
not share the same cultural background or even speak the same language as the original consultants. Thus, in a deep and abiding way,
one wonders how much is lost in the process of translation once the
anthropologist departs from the original language and the context
of shared life experiences.

The majority of professional anthropologists have chosen to stay
close to their sources, working first and foremost with the familiar field
language of their consultants, before moving on to layer upon layer of
translation, often ending with English or some other dominant, colonial tongue. This is true of the founders themselves, such Franz Boas
in America or Bronislaw Malinowski in England, who put together vast
text collections based on their fieldwork, taking great pains to capture
the original words from the mouths of their consultants, even if these
words only ended up in dusty tomes in libraries far from home (see
Boas 1894, 1921; Malinowski [1935] 1978). For many of us, especially

those working within the tradition of linguistic anthropology, this is the received and accepted methodology today. Everything starts with primary source documents of the narrative texts or other types of discourse collected from consultants in the language of their choice. Even as translation comes to a close, one wonders whether this attention to "original words" fully resolves any of the underlying questions about translation. What about the cultural background or the contextual nature of meaning, none of which can be completely addressed in this process?

Translating Oral Literature: Dell Hymes and Edward Sapir

These nagging doubts about the possibility of translation—from one language or one cultural context to the next—become far more pressing when we move from the usual social interactions of everyday life to the heightened aesthetic realm of performing oral literature before an audience. Drawing on the most fundamental meaning of "the culture concept," anthropologists have always been interested in those extensive and almost limitless bodies of stories, songs, and poems that flower in great abundance everywhere on the planet—from Africa to Australia to the Americas and beyond. Oral expression is a powerful human universal—and, as a creative process, it is clearly one that develops in profoundly distinctive ways at every point on the planet.

It was here in the realm of oral literature that Dell Hymes first staked out a career. As Hy mes (2003) has observed, even though Boas insisted on analyzing languages completely on their own terms or strictly within their own internal categories, he hardly stopped to consider the structure of oral narratives. As Edward Sapir (1921, 127) pointed out a generation earlier, oral narratives—and their poetic elements in particular—are often wrapped up in what he called the "genius" of particular languages. Therefore, when translating literature, grave problems present themselves even at the outset. If the poetic elements are based on tone, as in Chinese poetry or Plains Apache narrative, how does the translator represent these in a language that lacks tone, like English, without losing a sense of the original artistry? Similarly, how does one translate a rhyme when there is no close match, especially at the levels of sound and meaning? Hymes spent a good portion of his career entertaining just these questions, often translating the same poem many times in an effort to bring out different aspects of the original artistry, even if everything could not be captured in a single translation.

As Sapir himself noted, one profound question is this: How does a scholar capture the sense of symbolism, or appeal to the sense of collective imagination, built up in entire literary traditions? This, of course, was the real motivation behind his own insistence on what came to be called *linguistic relativity*, which was very much a matter of aesthetics or taste for Sapir. For Benjamin Lee Whorf (1956), on the other hand, the business of linguistic relativity became more a matter of embedded worldviews, which also play an obvious role when translating the poetic elements of oral narrative. In his classic statement on linguistic relativity, first addressed to the Linguistic Society of America in 1928, Sapir ([1929] 1949, 162) said:

> The understanding of a poem, for instance, involves not merely an understanding of the single words in their average significance, but a full comprehension of the whole life of the community as it is mirrored in the words, or as it is suggested by their overtones. Even comparatively simple acts of perception are very much more at the mercy of the social patterns called words than we might suppose.

As Sapir noted, when it comes to understanding a fairly short text, such as a poem, the outside observer must consider the "whole social world" that it reflects (and *refracts*), including its many and perhaps endless meanings for the various participants in the event: the author, the performer, and the immediate audience. Alongside the meanings for the participants in the event, one might also consider the underlying cultural expectations they all carry with them, even if the performers violate some of those expectations.

Given that these texts are generally performed before a live audience, it follows that text is also wrapped up in the moment when it comes to delivering oral literature, tying it to the concerns of the moment and to the actors involved in the performance, which is of course really the point. Thus, in a significant way, this context may not be repeatable (and certainly not within the narrow confines of flat, bookish translation), without an interactive audience or any real aural presence. Contrary to popular opinion, there may be no real "Ur-text," or idealized original text, somehow stripped of context, but thousands of variations on a theme, to be uttered—or recontextualized—once in a solemn way, once in sarcasm, and yet again with mild humor on some other occasion. Translation, in this sense, can of course do violence to the original text, erasing everything from social context to the author and perhaps especially the original language.

Ideologies of Translation: Fidelity versus Stylistic Realism

In a 2003 collection of essays, Hymes suggested that those who appreciate aesthetics are acutely aware how much artistry is lost in the process of translation, as one artistic effort is masked or replaced by another; yet the transformation is unavoidable:

> Still, translation may be the reader's only access to the original lines and relationships. If so, adaptation to the target language may conceal the otherness of the text and some of its interest. There is no single answer to the question, how much to adapt, how much to preserve, but some degree of teaching is often necessary. One must often ask the reader to learn. (2003, 40)

It is well known that, as poets themselves, Sapir and Hymes took translation more seriously than nearly anyone in the generations before or after them. While Boas (1917, 8) was one of the first anthropologists to call for the serious study of both music and poetry, he had his reasons for often settling for clumsy, literal translations, which he felt captured the original text better than amateurish artistic embellishments. In a sense, Boas asked us to prioritize the original text, even forcing the audience to learn another language in order to engage with the material; in Hymes's terms, Boas asked the reader "to learn," to bend a little, to become multilingual. We might label Boas's orientation *fidelity ideology*, since it resonates with a scientific outlook, with a prerogative to document but not distort. Yet as Richard Bauman and Charles Briggs (2003, 281) have pointed out, even Boas, like everyone in his generation, distorted somewhat in his published work, sometimes commissioning primal Ur-texts or even inventing monoliths—standard, uniform languages or literary traditions—out of endless variation.

A separate concern is capturing the sense of artistry in oral or written poetry. To give a name to this impulse, perhaps it could be called *stylistic realism*. This ideological orientation suspends the sense that translation is impossible in every possible aspect, given that we can never find exact equivalents for words and their suggestive overtones or for grammatical categories and their conceptual entailments; it is even harder to find analogs for the genres and stylistic registers of language, for the expectations of a particular audience and its cultural background, or for a particular performance. Instead we might pretend that this or that translation captures some aspect of the original. Even when presenting Zuni poetry strictly in English translation, for instance, Dennis Tedlock (1999) took great pains to devise a sophisticated graphic system for representing subtle, though crucial, textural features of the original oral performances—such as pauses, crescendos, tonal contours, glissando, and various degrees of length when chanting—that are often lost in translation, if noted at all. A fundamental point for Tedlock has always been that the poetic elements, including silences or pauses, are best appreciated when a text is read aloud so that they can be experienced as sound, even in translation (see Tedlock 1983, 124–55).

Hymes apparently felt this impulse very strongly, given the considerable time and labor he devoted to translation over the course of his career; it seemed to drive his almost endless quest to find better translations, those that offer some sense of aesthetics if nothing else. And it is this tension between artistic vision and scientific precision that we see throughout Hymes's extensive body of work on translating poetry. To take one example, consider his classic essay "Some North Pacific Coast Poems: A Study in Anthropological Philology" ([1965] 1981, 35–64), in which he gives multiple translations of the same poems, each one capturing some aspect of the original with the explicit understanding that something will inevitably be lost in English. After presenting the poems in the original languages to give some sense of the phonological character, he provides a brief literal translation to convey a sense of the basic narrative or storyline, without any attempt at capturing the style. These are only the first steps, and the process is painstaking. After introducing the original poem and its storyline, he provides a series of literary translations that represent elements of style before moving on to commentaries in which he provides background on the grammar and vocabulary of the original language, along with a sketch of the relevant cultural assumptions that inform the poem. Layer after layer, Hymes gets closer to conveying a sense of the artistry of the original poem, but it is clear that no single translation can capture every aspect of the initial performance. Thus, like most enduring questions—or unanswerable paradoxes—the underlying tensions are not easily resolved. While the mission is doomed at the outset, it keeps one striving. What artist does not feel these tensions when working out a vision, one that can never be perfected or actually achieved?

Translating Oral Literature in Indigenous Societies

It should go without saying that anthropologists and linguists did not *invent* translation, nor did we invent the related process of moving a text from one social context to another, reframing the original narrative or performance along the way. Clearly, for our own purposes, there are reasons to dwell on the process of translation, since it is often far less transparent than it appears at first blush, with context and social actors pushing in and out of the picture as meanings are shaped and reshaped, even as we give priority to the "original text" itself.

In thinking about our own engagement with translating other people's words and representing their worldviews, anthropologists have in recent times developed a massive inventory of terms for homing in on the many subtle stages in the process, something that Briggs and Bauman branded in their own way in the early 1990s. Recognizing the fundamentally situational nature of all human symbolic action, Briggs and Bauman (1992) gave contemporary names to many necessary stages in the process, such as *entextualization*—the process of removing a strip of discourse from one context and placing it in a new one somewhere else, perhaps giving rise to new meanings. Along the way, some of the original context may be lost (sometimes by becoming irrelevant), giving rise to the concept of *decontextualization,* an almost inevitable part of the process that exists in many degrees. Eventually the discourse finds its way into a new context, thus allowing for a process of *recontextualization,* and so on ad infinitum. This deep concern with the social life of discourse as it passes from one place to another echoes Voloshinov's ([1929] 1972) project of tracing the trajectories of "reported speech," the way that humans everywhere "live in a world of others' words" (Bakhtin 1986, 143) not entirely of their own making.

Yet translation is in no way just a modern question for the professional anthropologist, social scientist, or literary critic. Far from being a strictly theoretical concern for the professional anthropologist or linguist, translation has been—and continues to be—a practical daily affair in many parts of the world, one that resonates with competing ideologies that academics have barely dreamt of, let alone pondered, in much of mainstream anthropology. Now that indigenous cultural contact has come back into view again (Kroskrity 1993; O'Neill 2008), after nearly a century of studying cultures mostly on their own terms, we can safely say that few cultures, now or in the past, could claim to have been untouched or unaffected by outsiders. More often than not, these outsiders trade among, marry, or go to war with their neighbors. Indeed, these foreigners also talk and swap stories, even if their languages impose nearly impossible boundaries. On what continent has this not been the norm?

As we know today, nearly every cultural group occasionally translates some foreign literature and linguistic material, sometimes failing to recognize this obvious fact as a result of purist ideology, or sometimes embracing it with a syncretic outlook. Often there is little concern with the fidelity of the translation, that almost puritanical question that has plagued anthropology from the beginning. Instead, there is often an interest in embellishing the story creatively, imbuing it with something local, laying claim to part of the story, delegitimizing other versions, or even ridiculing the original in some form.

Northwestern California: Multilingualism and Storytelling

In surveying the vast distribution of folktales across enormous geographical regions, folklorists have noted and sometimes attempted to trace the movement of the tale types across space (see Goldberg 1984), even if the human element behind it all has been difficult, if not impossible, to pin down on a face-to-face level. Witness, for instance, the vast spread of Coyote stories across much of western North America, narratives in which Coyote often plays the role of the "bungling host" (Hymes 2003, 203–27), acting the fool in his best efforts to imitate some other more successful "benevolent" host, who provides an example by alleviating suffering and providing the gift of providence, that is, the ability to see the world for the wonderful place it is. Even when the anti-hero or comic-hero Coyote falls short, as he usually does after making many ridiculous mistakes, he still shows a purity of heart and, most of all, provides the ultimate gift—that of humor. Despite the vast distribution of parallel trickster episodes, which are often transformed as they circulate, it is rare indeed to see this process as it unfolds—to glimpse that moment when a story begins to spill over and cross some linguistic boundary, entering into a foreign cultural context.

Nevertheless, I was fortunate enough to observe this presumably pervasive process of translation across cultures while conducting fieldwork in Northwestern California during the late 1990s. Previous generations of scholars, including heavyweights such as Sapir and Alfred Kroeber, had stressed the *uniformity* of the regional culture, which stands out in great relief given the staggering diversity of the area's languages. As Sapir (1921, 213–14) himself once famously pronounced:

> The Hupa are very typical of the culture area to which they belong. Culturally identical with them are the neighboring Yurok and Karok. . . . It is difficult to say what elements in their combined cultures belong in origin to this tribe or that, so much at one are they in communal action, feeling, and thought. But their languages are not merely alien to each other; they belong to three of the major American linguistic groups, each with an immense distribution on the northern continent.

If the culture of the region were somehow uniform, as Sapir and Kroeber both suggested, the major variable from one community to the next would be speech itself, suggesting a kind of relativism that would depend on language alone—a perfect test case for the hypothesis of linguistic relativity, or the impact of language on thought or worldview.

With this in mind, I began translating stories from one tradition into another, assuming that only the language would change, not the content of the stories themselves. To my great surprise, I found that the literary traditions differed as much as the languages, and none of my consultants really wanted to hear the stories told by their closest neighbors. As I came to discover firsthand, Sapir and Kroeber had greatly overestimated the similarities between the tribes, which, as these scholars pointed out, was probably the result of generations of cultural exchange between the tribes, including multilingualism and intermarriage (O'Neill 2008). While both Sapir and Kroeber had rightly detected evidence of widespread historical convergence, the underlying exchanges that brought about these results had just as often produced an insistence on difference at the local level rather than generating outright uniformity.

Inspired by this concept of cultural convergence, which supposedly swept across even the most profound linguistic boundaries, I sought for a time to translate major bodies of Yurok and Karuk texts into the Hupa language, with assistance of a fluent Hupa speaker named Jimmy Jackson. Presumably the stories would be familiar, even if I read him Yurok and Karuk narratives collected early in the twentieth century by some of the biggest names in the business, such as Kroeber and the great field linguist John Peabody Harrington. But every time I read a story from another tribe, even those based on line-by-line English versions of the tales, what inevitably resulted from my attempts to translate these stories was a pervasive focus on local difference.

Imposing Linguistic and Literary Boundaries: Stopping the Translation Short

Much to my surprise, our initial attempts were not always met with great success, despite the seemingly reasonable suspicion that there might be strong similarities in the oral traditions, given the historical background of widespread cultural convergence. At one point early in the process Jackson flatly rejected the tale I presented him, recognizing that it was a Karuk story, and therefore something of a foreign intrusion that he did not care to translate into his own language. "That's a Karuk tale," he announced dismissively, before requesting that we return to our usual business of translating old Hupa stories into a modern form of the vernacular. That day we simply stopped work on the Karuk tale.

This curious rejection of a familiar narrative as it appears in the folklore of a neighboring tribe is similar to what Donald Bahr (2001) has described among the indigenous peoples of the Southwest. Bahr has noted that many episodes in the local storytelling traditions are widely distributed throughout the region, though with an element of inversion or "parody," as Bahr himself calls it, in the spirit of maintaining ethnic distinction. Rather than reporting outright mockery or scorn for the parallel traditions of neighboring peoples, who share similar narratives with slight departures in the characters and storylines, Bahr (2001, 605) instead describes a sense of "compassionate" dissent, not unlike the tension among Catholics and Protestants within the Christian tradition, who often maintain their distinctions on ethnic grounds (as seen in Northern Ireland, for example, in terms of the ethnic Irish Catholics and Anglo-Irish Protestants). On the other hand, rather than simply rejecting material from a neighboring people, even on the basis of some seemingly slight difference of interpretation, a group may adopt material from a neighbor, writing it into history as if it had always been there—much as the blues base of rock-n-roll or even country music has been adopted by Anglo-Americans as a core "American" sound, despite its deep African American roots. Few see this process of borrowing unfold as new material is brought in and *traditionalized*, though Jason Baird Jackson (2003, 211) was witness to the emergence of the Green Corn myth among the Yuchis of Oklahoma in the mid-1990s, when it was introduced before his ears in a ceremony showing clear parallels to the traditions of neighboring tribes such as the Shawnee, where it clearly originated.

Surely both processes—that is, wholesale adoption and parodic mimicry—have been at work in Northwestern California, with some of the material circulating now for centuries even as each group puts its own stamp on those familiar stories, marking them as their own and even creating subtle parodies of the versions that circulate elsewhere. In this way, I suspect that some of the stories I encountered in Northwestern California carried tags or markers that were apparent even when working from line-by-line English transitions, which I simply read out loud, prompting detailed translations into Hupa. Sometimes it was the content of the tale that gave away its foreign origin. For example, we started one day with a Karuk narrative called "Eel with a Swollen Belly," as retold in Julian Lang's (1994) classic book and based on a story Harrington collected in the early twentieth century. Of course, if the culture of the area were uniform, as I had naively expected, then translation would be a simple matter, since a Hupa version probably already existed. I was right that the story was partly familiar and therefore recognizable to my consultant; but rather than being welcome, the story was rejected outright. Among other things, this suggests that not all of the narratives circulated even in traditional times, despite many statements to such effect by many earlier anthropologists, such as Sapir and Kroeber.

Apart from obvious differences in the structure of the tales, so often broadcast by the first mention of the protagonists, other telltale signs of origin were far subtler, relying on a deep inside knowledge of the social conventions surrounding the act of storytelling. I strongly suspect that in some cases speech taboos gave away the story's foreign origin. One day, as Jimmy Jackson and I began to translate a familiar story about Mourning Dove, known to both the Hupas and the Yuroks, he expressed strong hesitation about translating several key lines in story, probably because we were working from a Yurok version of the tale that was not entirely acceptable to him. Though the story was otherwise familiar in almost every other way, including the local variations, he entirely skipped over the part where death was overtly mentioned, answering that line only with silence and refusing to translate it.

As I later discovered, even today there is a strong prohibition against mentioning death in any direct way among many of the elders in Hoopa Valley, despite the fact that death was certainly mentioned in the parallel Yurok version of the story. My notebooks from this time are filled with euphemisms for death in both English and Hupa, showing that some of the traditional wisdom had been translated into English, even if many of the stories had not. Though still observed today, in traditional times violating this speech taboo could result in a stiff fine: speaking of death and uttering the names of the deceased were said to stir the souls of the dead and awaken grief among the living, a double sin against the spiritual community.

In the course of the translation project, it became clear that almost any element of a given performance could be ethnically marked. As parallel narratives were carefully compared line by line, apparently minor differences appeared to act in a profoundly *indexical* fashion, serving as badges of group membership by signaling belonging within a given community. As John Miles Foley (1992) has observed in the performance of Serbo-Croatian epic poetry or even ancient Greek myth, a single word or phrase can be suggestive of a whole tradition, with a recurring figure like "grey-eyed Athena" potentially triggering the world of the ancient Greeks— the character, the city, and the social work around it—for poet and audience alike. Thus, the principle of indexical marking with seemingly subtle features of narrative is a general one, with language itself serving as one of the markers in Northwestern California. For my consultants, the choice of language dictated a whole series of cultural expectations that were not always clear to an outsider like me; they served as markers of identity within the separate speech communities, each with their own social conventions surrounding storytelling or communication in general.

As I came to discover throughout this extended experiment in translation, even something as subtle as the gender of one of the characters could profoundly affect the meaning of a tale—and this was not negotiable within a given linguistic community. As I look over my field notes from the summer of 2000, I see that my consultant politely corrected the gender of one of the characters as we began to translate the story of Mourning Dove. Whereas the protagonist in this tale is generally considered to be female among the Yuroks, the Hupas (who otherwise tell almost exactly the same tale) insist that Mourning Dove was a male. At the time this seemed insignificant, and I actually wondered if my consultant had gotten mixed up or whether the Yurok had simply gotten it wrong. Why, I wondered, would it matter so much? And what is most striking about these failed attempts at translation is the repeated insistence on placing limitations on how far a story (or song) could circulate. Who puts up these barriers and why? The key, in part, may come from outside the region, where tales almost universally bear some kind of local stamp among those familiar with the narrative from past performances. As Brian Stross (1971) has noted, based on his work several hundred miles to the north with the Nez Percé of the Pacific Northwest, the mere mention of the central characters, even in the opening lines or the title, is a highly evocative way to start a tale; to those familiar with the storyline, any characteristic of the protagonist, including their appearance or even their deeds, can potentially trigger entire mythic episodes.

Stressing Local Differences: Performing Identity and Enacting Local Ideology

As our work progressed, Jimmy Jackson and I eventually translated a few of the Yurok and Karuk stories into Hupa, though not without some major changes in the tales, both in the development of the characters and in the transitions between the scenes. At this point, I realized that the languages themselves often marked a boundary that also corresponded to a major literary divide, on each side of which sat very different oral traditions when it came to performing these local stories. Not only were there structural differences in the narrative style, but there were also profound differences in the social conventions surrounding the performance itself—features Hymes characterized as germane to the ethnography of speaking ([1964] 1972; 1974, 53–62). That is, while I had hoped to demonstrate Whorfian effects in terms of grammatical choices, what I was actually encountering were subtle literary divisions that separated communities as profoundly as the differences in the grammatical systems of their massively different languages—much as Bahr (2001) had found in the Southwest.

Later that summer we revisited the Karuk tale of the Eel, and at that point my consultant grudgingly agreed to translate it into Hupa. Looking back, I am not sure why he obliged, after expressing such strong reluctance at the outset—perhaps in part just to have an analog in his language. But, as a connoisseur of the local folklore, he may have been curious to hear this partially unfamiliar story in its entirety; in addition, the process of translation probably offered an intellectual challenge. More than anything else, though, I believe that the process of translation gave him a chance to "correct" the tales and then retell them in proper Hupa, drawing on his considerable authority as an elder statesman for the Hupa storytelling tradition.

Sometimes a simple substitution cleared up the problems in translation from one community to the next; Jackson profoundly altered the tale with a minor change in the wording. When it came to the taboo mention of death, for instance, he merely deleted the scene by repeating the previous line. Presumably his audience could infer that there had been a death, even without saying it, so that his silence in this context was actually filled with meaning. Of course, the deletion immediately gave the narrative a different structure.

In a similar way, we simply substituted one word for another when it came to the gender of one of the main characters: the grandparent who had died. In my notebooks, I see that my consultant initially translated the English word for grandmother, as given in the original Yurok telling of the tale. Then, realizing his mistake, based on the familiar Hupa version of the tale, he quickly corrected this to "grandfather." At the time, I thought it was a minor matter, though it later became clear that that even the subtlest of conceptual distinctions could serve as *diacritica* of ethnicity (see Barth 1969, 31; O'Neill 2012, 76–77), marking a major shift in meaning with only a minor change in the value or status of the characters. As I came to find out, these subtle distinctions acted as platforms for the performance of identity—that is, they could act as statements for the active demonstration of one's membership within a community, as revealed through social inter-action in the telling of a tale.

Whorfian Overtones:
Conceptual Branding and "Hymesian" Linguistic Relativity

When passing from one language to the next, there were also elements that smacked of Whorfanism, where similar words and nearly identical episodes held different conceptual overtones in each of the languages. Obviously the shift in languages was a part of the indexicality of giving a performance, a performer branding the text as belonging to one ethnic group over another by speaking its language and observing local speech taboos. But, as linguists like Roman Jakobson (1960) and Michael Silverstein (1979) have insisted for decades now, language is more than mere reference; rather than simply referring to the world around us, when we use words we are choosing an emotional stance, or selecting a particular perspective, or imbuing language with a sense of the social imagination perhaps based on religion or prior references built up in oral literature. So, when passing from one language to another, my consultant and I were not merely shifting phonological frameworks; translation is more than finding different sounds for the same underlying ideas or worldly referents, more than an enact-ment of the trivial arbitrariness of Saussurean sound-image pairings in the architecture of all languages. Rather, as Wittgenstein used to say, even a simple word can suggest a whole conceptual framework (see Yengoyan 2003, 28). In this sense, strong conceptual overtones sounded throughout our translation process, given that one of the primary functions of language, according to Alton Becker (1995, 288) is to arrive at a shared orientation through the ongoing process of communication, seeing things through the same lens.

Even at the level of vocabulary, one obvious difference between Hupa and Yurok tales is in names given to the characters, which partly reflect the differential status of the characters in the communities as well as the naming schemes of the languages. As we have already seen, a minor shift in worldview occurred when Jackson simply replaced *grandmother* with *grandfather* in telling the story of Mourning Dove. Yet as we moved from Yurok to Hupa (with English as a trans-language) we frequently encountered even greater differences in the content of the shared "social imagination" behind the words. Here, the shift from grandmother to grandfather made all the difference—the status of the characters (as representatives of a gender), the flow of the storyline, and the ethnic overtones of the performance itself were branded by the gender the narrator announced.

In many cases, the names of the characters also held very different meanings in each of the languages (O'Neill 2006), as can be illustrated with the name for a little bird known as the dipper in English, based on its habit of plunging into the water in search of food just below the surface. This much we all can see. Yet for the Hupa and Karuk alike there is an added dimension within the social imagination, in that a story circulates about this bird failing as a parent by hoarding food for itself and not sharing with its children. As punishment for this wrong committed in the ancient past, he is banished from family life and spends his days along the rivers fishing alone. In this particular case, the gender of the character holds constant, while other features shift from one language to the next, based on differences in plot that motivate differences in description. In the Hupa version of the story, the selfish and negligent bird is condemned to having sex with stones, as reflected in the name *tse:-q'eet*, which literally means 'the one who fucks rocks'. In the Karuk version of the tale, the bird is simply left to eat the moss in the beds of rivers; his name, *'asaxvanish'ámvaanich*, means 'the little one who sucks at the floors of the rivers'. In this case, the underlying images suggested by these contrasting names correspond to a slight difference in perspective or worldview.

As Hymes ([1964] 1972; 1966) pointed out early in his career, the Whorfian brand of linguistic relativity is itself dependent on another more fundamental type of relativity in language, namely, those pervasive and often subtle differences in the norms surrounding language use, including poetics and storytelling. As Hymes ([1964] 1972, 32–33) himself said:

> It is essential to notice that Whorf's sort of linguistic relativity is secondary, and dependent upon a primary sociolinguistic relativity, that of differential engagement of languages in social life. For example, descriptions of a language may show that it expresses a certain cognitive style, perhaps implicit metaphysical assumptions, but what chance the language has to make an impress upon individuals and behavior will depend upon the degrees and pattern of its admission into communicative

events. . . . Peoples do not all everywhere use language to the same degree, in the same situations, or for the same things; some peoples focus upon language more than others.

Since communities settle on worldviews in a selective and deeply social way, linguistic relativity in its conventional sense (that is, classic "Whorfian" conceptual relativism as embedded in grammar and vocabulary) is largely a matter of creative differences between languages based on *poetics:* aesthetic choices of interpretation. This of course takes us back to the earliest formulations of linguistic relativity, based on poetics, as proposed by Johann Gottfried Herder in the eighteenth century and later echoed by Paul Friedrich (1986); in this sense, we all live in an inherited stream of words and images by virtue of speaking a particular language passed down from countless generations. In a more active way, a similar thing happens when an audience comes into the grip of a poet or storyteller who is delivering his or her work before a live audience, everyone listening collectively as they socially imagine the narrative at more or less the same time, arriving at a shared orientation.

In this way, the potential impact of the "Whorfian effect" (Lucy 1992a, 1992b) should not be underestimated when it comes to delivering oral literature, given that grammar is both conceptual in nature and highly regular in its overall distribution, affecting almost every construction in any given language. For any poet or storyteller, grammatical categories have an impact—and in some way *shape*—nearly every line in the performance of an oral narrative. To take one telling example, consider briefly how the semantics of time play out in the grammatical systems of the neighboring Hupa, Yurok, and Karuk languages.

Though each of these communities place the creation times in the recent past, perhaps no more than a handful of generations from the present, each group has a very different way of referring to these times when it comes to the practice of storytelling, especially in terms of the underlying conceptual categories of the grammar. When telling stories in Hupa, most speakers prefer to place most events in the imperfective aspect, which emphasizes activities that are ongoing, without a clear beginning or end. Thus, scenes pass before the audience as if they are happening in the moment, even if that moment only exists in the collective imagination. For the Yurok, on the other hand, tense marking becomes critical to the process of storytelling. As a consequence, many (if not most) scenes are clearly situated in the past in Yurok narratives, often with refined distinctions as to overall timeline. For Karuk storytellers, on the other hand, the grammar itself presents an interesting middle ground. While most scenes can be presented as if they are happening right before the audience, a select few, usually at the beginning or end of the performance, are placed squarely in the past. In fact, the Karuk language alone has a special tense for setting scenes specifically within the ancient past (or before recent memory within the community based on first-hand knowledge), but this tense is used sparingly, often at the outset or end of a tale. This kind of tense marking reminds the audience that the story is set long ago, even if the tale is primarily narrated as if the audience were witnessing it in the present. Thus, when telling a story, the narrator must pay close attention to the specific grammatical categories available (and expected) in a given language; when translating, some of this material is inevitably lost or gratuitously added.

English Interlude:
Minimizing Translation in the Mid-Twentieth Century

As illustrated above, there are often limits on what can easily pass between languages among the Native communities of Northwestern California, both today and in the past. Following historical precedent, similar limitations had apparently been placed on what could be translated into English. As I came to discover, few of the stories were familiar to my consultants beyond the bare outlines of the narratives. What was missing they could often fill in with a detailed knowledge of other aspects of precontact culture, such as knowledge of hunting or gambling or fishing, which was far from the rarified register of high oral literature.

Somewhere near the turn of the twentieth century—long before my consultant and I began our work—there was a major rupture in the transmission of oral literature from one generation to the next among the Native communities of Northwestern California. The sudden departure from the past roughly corresponds to the period when the local communities were starting to face the arrival of Anglo-Americans during the gold rush era. Not the least of the problems was the onslaught of English as a dominant language: it had largely replaced the Native languages in most contexts by the turn of the twentieth century, a mere fifty years after Euro-American contact. At the same time, Christianity gradually began to replace indigenous religious concepts, though I am aware of many cases where the two traditions sit side-by-side, and some have found a comfortable common ground between the traditional religion and Christianity. While some of the traditional stories were transmitted in shreds and patches—in other words, *partially*—alongside Christianity and the English language, very few were picked up by the interceding generations in their entirety. In other words, telling traditional stories was apparently not a matter of practice once the communities began to shift to English. Translation into English was apparently not a regular practice, either, though this is obviously possible in the abstract. The limited circulation of traditional lore in the English language today leaves one to wonder: did something ideological block translation into English over the course of the past century?

Even outside the realm of storytelling itself, the absence of translation is striking and deliberate in some other areas of regular social interaction, in part because translation is expressly *forbidden*. In the late 1990s when I was living in Hoopa Valley, I heard that an aspiring healer had been told to learn Hupa before beginning training in the world of traditional medicine. The teacher, a master healer, refused to translate medicinal lore into the English language, which was not deemed appropriate for this accumulated body of wisdom. Whereas Hupa offers many precise words for medicines and medicinal practice, exact equivalents were never developed in English, perhaps because these fell outside of the regular spiritual practice once Hupa speakers began to shift to English. In fact, there was probably enough specialized vocabulary to constitute a shamanic register barely known to the nonspecialist. However, throughout much of the twentieth century translating shamanic concepts into English was apparently considered taboo, perhaps in part because the increasingly Christian culture frowned on traditional medicine, which was gradually being dropped by new generations.

When considered in a broad comparative light, this refusal to translate is not unlike the insistence in many world religions that instruction must be carried out in the language of revelation, since it harkens back to the original moment of divine inspiration and thus preserves some of its sacred character. Such perspectives are common. For Muslims, the transaction between God and Muhammad must be echoed verbatim, as recorded in the Qur'an and recited by believers worldwide every day. In some East Indian ideologies, Sanskrit is seen as a perfect spiritual language, containing the original names for things as given by the gods, while other languages are mere corruptions of this original tongue. Hebrew primers to this day sometimes mention that Hebrew was the language that God spoke. Accordingly, while translations are recognized among Muslims, none can claim to carry the authority of the Qur'an's direct *indexical* link to the first telling of the tale as it passed from God to Muhammad through the angel Gabriel for humanity to recite in worship. Thus, even if translation is possible it can be blocked on ideological grounds, as apparently happened in Northwestern California for similar religious reasons.

Reclaiming Tradition:
Late Twentieth-Century "Language Revitalization"

An important part of my work with the Hupas during the late 1990s consisted of translating a massive body of traditional oral literature into language that contemporary speakers could easily produce in a natural way, without too much effort. This change in the structure of the stories also had the benefit of making them more intelligible to modern-day students of the language. At the time, the Hupas were beginning the process of language revitalization, with both master-apprentice programs and regular classroom instruction during the school year, in conjunction with summer immersion camps. The story collections we produced were immediately brought to bear on the weekly language classes held at the tribal facilities in the center of the Hoopa Valley. Each week a handful of knowledgeable elders met with younger community members to discuss anything of interest within the community; for several months we worked on the traditional stories first collected by Goddard (1904) nearly a century beforehand, as we passed through various stages of the translation. While some of the stories were partially familiar to the younger generations, virtually no one at the time had heard a story performed from beginning to end strictly in the Hupa language.

Within the setting of the language classes, another frequent topic of discussion today is the literal meaning of the words recorded in the dictionaries (see Golla 1996). The vast majority of the nouns in the area's languages are descriptive in content, meaning that they generally derive from verbs and portray elaborate scenes of action associated with a given object of talk. Recall the names ascribed to the little bird known as the dipper, which in turn derive from oral literature. In this way, many learners find that the translations provide a key to the worldview of their ancestors, while the stories often give more background on *why* the characters received a given name in folklore or mythology.

Although translating cultural vocabulary, even into English, is potentially a heuristic process, giving speakers and learners a new and different way of seeing the world, it also sometimes leads to confusion, especially on the ideological plane. For example, the Hupa name for the dipper is sometimes translated as 'rock-fucker', in part because the two roots (*tse:* 'rock' and *q'e:t* 'to copulate') point rather tersely and directly to this image. A more polite translation is 'the one who copulates with stones', but this rendering is quite verbose compared to the original, which is more direct. In cases like this, the elders often explained that in traditional times it really didn't sound so "dirty"; some insisted it was "clean" yet "funny" in days gone by, adopting a stance more difficult to come by given the more puritanical values transmitted in English. In this way, translation was often a cause for reflection on the values imbued in language, what Hymes worked so hard to capture in his work on the ethnography of speaking.

As useful as these materials have been in the classroom, the bulk of our work was carried out in the homes of my consultants, where we spent countless hours carefully translating and retranslating these old stories, often as friends and relatives stopped by for brief visits. In this sense, domestic contexts became a major site for the revitalization of the language, and in this way these private spaces also became key ideological sites (Kroskrity 2004, 505; Silverstein 1998, 136) where respect could be restored for narrative traditions that had been heavily undermined during the era of the boarding school in the early twentieth century. By the mid-1930s, Native languages had largely been dropped from homes altogether as younger speakers became convinced that there was no future in speaking their "ancestral" languages, which were often dismissed as merely "speaking Indian" in the boarding schools. During our weekly meetings, there was an apparent reversal in some of these attitudes as the elders and witnesses began to feel a greater sense of pride in reclaiming their languages. Years later, I heard that the elders were taking these stories into the classroom, using the written texts we produced as a literary guide to the oral narratives.

Contemporary Registers: High Oral Literature and the Vernacular

Looking back, it is clear that many contemporary versions of the narratives were delivered in a style that departed in significant ways from earlier versions of the stories, most of which were collected several generations ago during a time when there were active speech communities for each of the area's languages (see Goddard 1904). Gone today are many of the intricate connectives that used to mark the classic Hupa storytelling register in oral narrative, such as *hayahajid-'ung-q'ud* 'and presently then it (happened) that', and *hayah-mił* 'thereupon'. These were abundantly recorded in the stories collected by Goddard (1904) and Sapir (2001). Traditionally these old connectives conveyed a kind of majesty or eloquence that few speakers were comfortable emulating during my stay, perhaps because they had fallen out of use, much like the stories themselves. In English-language storytelling there are clear parallels, especially in the "high" tradition (or register), which is filled with such genre-marking expressions as "whereupon" and "thereafter." In Hupa storytelling today, less elaborate, contracted forms are far more common, such as *hayaał* 'and then'.

Changing Structures: Couplets and Rhythm Schemes (Borrowed from English?)

Another striking difference between the traditional and contemporary versions of the tales was a shift in poetics, especially with regard to subtle and unconscious elements. One consultant had a strong penchant for rhyming parts of the stories, whenever possible, with matched couplets. I suspect that he picked this up from English, where rhyming was common in the bookish English taught in the classrooms of the early twentieth century, especially in the boarding schools where these values were imparted before the day of e. e. cummings or Dylan Thomas, who avoided such standard flourishes. Rhyming seems to be very rare in traditional Hupa oral literature, so it was a surprise to find it pervasive in the stories I heard in the late 1990s. If the feature was in fact brought over from the example set by schoolroom poetry, it represents a real innovation in Hupa, as well as a classic case of linguistic interference—namely, the transfer of material from one language to another in the performance of a multilingual speaker. Yet the innovative rhyming I observed was an intervention on the level of poetics, rather than the more typical cases of linguistic interference that involve lexical or grammatical borrowings.

Betwixt and Between: Multilingual Speakers and Syncretism

Long before the present, it was clear that a clash of languages, literatures, and ideologies could often be witnessed even in the case of a single person who stood between traditions, feeling the tensions in a visceral way. The case of Jimmy Jackson is telling here, but before him there were presumably many similar individuals who rested precariously between different linguistic and cultural traditions. This calls to mind the Bakhtinian notion of heteroglossia, the notion that societal diversity can be reflected even within a single strip of discourse and of course at the level of the individual, where competing discourses classically collide. In Northwestern California the parallel condition of polyglossia is also relevant, since multiple languages have come into association with a single regional culture.

The Case of Mary Marshall: A Bilingual Storyteller

To take an example of bilingualism from an earlier generation, consider the case of Mary Marshall, who, like many residents of this region going back many generations, had a dual ancestry, meaning that she learned two languages at home, even as she was growing up in Hoopa Valley surrounded mostly by Hupa speakers. As the daughter of a Yurok mother and a Hupa father, she spoke both languages fluently, and she was deeply steeped in each of the corresponding literary traditions, keeping them remarkably separate and therefore heavily compartmentalized (Kroskrity 1993, 210; 2000a, 338–39; O'Neill 2012, 77–84). In practice she was probably not free to pass between the languages purely at will, since the languages were also closely tied to the land in ideological terms.

As I learned during my fieldwork, it was once considered highly improper to transplant a language out of its homeland, and speaking a foreign language like Yurok in Hupa territory was apparently considered offensive in traditional times. In quasi-religious terms, the Hupas observed similar taboos when crossing into Yurok territory along the coast; as one Hupa elder told me, speaking Hupa near the sea was considered dangerous, since it could make the ocean envious. In terms of the surrounding magical realism, it was said that the ocean would rise up and sweep the offender away, a high price to pay for speaking one's language out of place. So, even a fluent Yurok speaker like Mary Marshall probably had few occasions to speak this "foreign" language as a resident of Hoopa Valley, except when visiting Yurok country or when speaking with her mother in the privacy of the home.

Drawing on her knowledge of both traditions, Mary Marshall was able to work as a bilingual consultant to Sapir in the summer of 1927, documenting the storytelling traditions of both the Hupa and Yurok languages in the course of a few short weeks. Here we get a glimpse into the process of compartmentalization, given that she kept the two traditions quite separate in practice, out of respect for a strong localist ideology tying the languages to specific village identities.

On the surface, it is clear that the content of her narratives underwent a dramatic shift as she passed from one language to the next. For example, two of the Yurok stories she shared with Sapir feature Coyote as a religious figure and as an instigator of creation, something that is rare in Hupa oral literature, where he more often serves as a secular buffoon, as a beloved clown, and as the butt of jokes. As one might expect, other tales she recited in Yurok granted special status to sacred sites in Yurok country, as with the formula for procuring wealth, which she set not in Hoopa Valley, but rather in Pek^{w}teł, near the Yurok traditional center of the universe and in the heart of Yurok country. These stories are unknown among most Hupa speakers and do not appear in any of the Hupa story collections. Furthermore, in observing the near prohibition on speaking a language outside of its homeland, it appears that Mary Marshall may have deliberately spoken a faulty variety of Yurok in her work with Sapir. Certainly the Yurok she spoke with him was unusual in many ways, which may be partly explained in terms of both ideology and practice, given the strong ban on outside languages on quasi-religious grounds.

In a far more subtle way, her style of delivery also changed as she passed from one language to the next. When performing stories in Yurok she followed a fairly standard convention in which the characters are introduced by name in the first line, plainly announcing that the story is about Coyote or Crane, for instance. Her Hupa style of delivery, on the other hand, was far more mysterious, though also perfectly consistent with the standard storytelling mode among Hupa speakers. When delivering a story in Hupa, the characters are rarely introduced at the outset, since the audience can usually guess their identities based on their actions. The nouns work in much the same way, since they are also based on a kind of action metonymy.

As discussed in earlier sections, I observed a similar insistence on compartmentalization in my work of translation. The most striking cases were when Hupa speakers quickly rejected Yurok and Karuk versions of the tales. Since nearly everyone in the area was familiar with some of the texts from the neighboring speech communities, each text, and each telling, would be an intertextual event—to be interpreted in the light of prior tellings, though without any single meaning, even within one community. Instead, any of these many local interpretations might echo around in the mind of just one multilingual speaker's imagination, as was the case for Mary Marshall as she considered the clashing Hupa and Yurok versions of a particular tale.

Swapping Songs: Language versus Music

What is true of stories is largely true of songs, which can also shift in subtle ways as one crosses social and linguistic boundaries. As Franz Boas (1917, 8) once observed, oral literature is often delivered in the form of poetry and/or song:

> Undoubtedly problems of native poetry have to be taken up in connection with the study of native music, because there is practically no poetry that is not at the same time song. The literary aspects of this subject, however, fall entirely within the scope of a linguistic journal.

However, when passing between communities, the underlying similarities are sometimes more obvious with song than with oral narratives, in part because the common musical structures are less wrapped up in the peculiarities of the languages. As the great ethnomusicologist George Herzog (1939) often suggested, the differences between musical traditions are more akin those found among dialects rather than languages, in the sense that there may be considerable mutual intelligibility even at the outset, since underlying universals, such rhythmic or melodic elements, may be obvious even to the outside observer (see also Nettl 2005, 49). This principle can be illustrated up to a point in Northwestern California, where music traditions are strikingly parallel, despite the complete lack of mutual intelligibility among languages. Whereas passing from language to language is a labored process of translation, even in the mind of someone who is at least moderately multilingual, the musical traditions are relatively open to all, given that the underlying musical structures are more or less shared among the groups.

When it comes to Northwestern California, the similarities between the musical traditions of the tribes are so striking that trained experts like Kroeber could hardly tell the styles of the tribes apart. As Richard Keeling (1992) points out, much of the music is suffused with a sobbing quality, which (as the performers sometimes explain) gives legitimacy to the underlying feelings expressed in the songs, while also lending authenticity to an individual performance. Yet even here, subtle differences abound, largely in terms of the accentuation of small differences within the larger context of common background tradition. Based on his own years of fieldwork and the wealth of recordings made throughout the twentieth century, Keeling observed that vocal effects like nasalization and tremolo reach an obvious high point in Yurok singing—and while these qualities are certainly found among the neighboring Hupa and Karuk, it is often to a lesser extent.

Similarly, Keeling (1992) notes that the different groups characteristically invoke different genres, in part owing to their separate histories of migration from different homelands long ago. For instance, while animal songs are very popular among the Karuk, for whom Coyote occupies a central place in the creation pantheon, this type of song is far less common among the neighboring Hupa, among whom nonhuman characters such as Coyote play a far lesser role in the mythic tradition. Yet, as Keeling (1992, 231–33) points out, even where animal songs are present, the songs often take on a decidedly different character in terms of their musical texture. Thus, while the animal songs of the Karuk often feature an element of polyphony, with many voices joining forces in a single performance, the animal songs of the neighboring Yurok rely heavily on glottalization in vocal quality. Keeling links the prominence of glottalization to the characteristic animal songs of the northern hunters, whom the Yuroks may have encountered during their migration into California from an original homeland somewhere to the north, where this feature is common. According to Keeling, the animal songs of the Karuk, by contrast, demonstrate affinity with animal songs associated with Paleo-Indians and consequently can also be found throughout much of South America.

The Status of Vocables in Song:
The Unconscious Branding of Sound

Apart from their overwhelmingly parallel musical qualities, many of the songs in Native Northwestern California are also characteristically *wordless*. Rather than having lyrics that provide a sense of narrative, many songs are based in improvised vocables that loosely resemble language in the sense of having phonological segments and even syllables. As Dell Hymes (1981, 36) once suggested, these supposedly meaningless vocables, or nonsense syllables, may actually serve other unexplored functions:

> Here I wish to deal with the largely neglected heritage of poetry, or, more accurately, of the verbal component of song, and to show that it too may yield new knowledge of structure. In particular, I wish to show that poems may have a structural organization, and "nonsense" vocables, or burdens, a structural function, not hitherto perceived.

Thus, while sounding a great deal like language, especially to the outside observer, these meaningless syllables have no regular semantic structure and no particular vocabulary or grammar. Yet I would suggest that in the highly multilingual context of delivering song in Northwestern California, these improvised syllables probably help to move musical meaning beyond the semantics of any single language, allowing members of each speech community to understand some of what is going on in any given performance.

In contemporary times, these vocables also allow the songs to move beyond the semantics of English, creating a far more mysterious auditory effect, perhaps somewhat like the Latin mass in the Catholic

Church. Yet at the most perceptible level, even a wordless song can assume a quasi-linguistic character in terms of the sounds themselves. As is often the case with scat singing, even our best attempts at spontaneous speech sometimes fall back on familiar phonological patterns. In this sense, glottalization, as a vocal effect, is as rare in Karuk singing as it is in the structure of the language, which lacks ejectives. For the most part, this gives Karuk singing a distinctive sound, even when the singer is just using "meaningless" vocables. Similarly, Karuk singers import an [f] sound—or voiceless labio-dental fricative—into their singing, which is absent in the neighboring languages and musical traditions. Yurok speakers, on the other hand, frequently use the shwa in speech and song alike, creating another subtle difference at the level of sound. At the same time, glottalization as a vocal effect reaches an extreme in Yurok that is not matched even in Hupa, despite the fact that both languages use vocal constriction for many speech sounds. Because of these subtle differences in sound, it is probably very clear to speakers just whom they are listening to, much as we would not confuse the karaoke performances of French, English, and German singers, since each one leaves traces of their accents. In this sense, even vocables can index the speech communities from which they originate. Thus even a wordless song bears a strong ethnic mark at the highly perceptible level of the sounds themselves, which inevitably resemble the primary languages of the performers.

The Semiotics of Sound:
Imposing Narrative on "Meaningless" Melody

Even songs without words offer layers of meaning, given that music tends to stir the human imagination, and this process of imposing a narrative unfolds in very personal ways. In this way, listeners often picture nearly a narrative that is associated with the melody, if this suggested storyline is merely broadcasting ethnic identity on the plane of sound. In this sense, few songs in Northwestern California occur without an associated narrative that profoundly affects listeners' interpretations.

Many songs, for instance, are associated with a particular animal, spirit, or force of nature, which is often considered to be the source of the song, a kind of divine inspiration. One common theme expressed

in the religious ceremonies of the region is that the original spirit beings established these dances for humans in the past, giving people a
way to make amends for their sins and restore the world to a state of
grace with the spirits. This premise itself is the basis for much of the
sacred music, but from here the groups rapidly begin to part ways.
Among the Karuk, Coyote is often the protagonist in oral narratives
and the implicit subject of wordless songs; just as he established many
of the visible features of the world, so too he instituted many of the
sacred dances and songs of the region. Among the neighboring Hupa
and Yurok, on the other hand, a figure known as Across-the-Ocean
Widower established many of the songs and stories before abandoning
this world to live in his distant home across the sea. In this way, the
associated narratives, if not the musical structures themselves, sometimes differ significantly from one community to the next, potentially
altering the meanings imposed on a given song, even a wordless one.

Conclusions: Fidelity, Creativity, and Ideology in Translation

Questions of translation will probably always be fundamental to
ethnographic disciplines such as anthropology and folkloristics, not
only because we ourselves bear responsibility as translators of other
cultures, but also because our consultants frequently act as translators
themselves, even if they are rarely credited with such an important role
within disciplinary conventions. In this sense, most of our consultants
have acted as translators for us in the field, at least since the time of
Boas, when legendary collaborators such George Hunt provided massive bodies of oral literature for future generations—cultural insiders,
as well as outsiders—to consult. More recently, John H. McDowell
(2000) has made a case for what he calls "collaborative ethnopoetics,"
in which consultants play an active role in the process of translation
from start to finish—from finding the appropriate stylistic register
in the target language to overseeing the poetic content of the final
translations. As McDowell points out, nearly all of our work in translation hinges on the intuitions of these interlingual and intercultural
consultants, who have acquired a feel for the nuances of structure,
style, and meaning in multiple languages—and are therefore in a
position to advise the translator in the process of transforming a text
from oral to print and from one literary tradition to another. However,

although Boas often acknowledged and sometimes listed George Hunt as a coauthor (Bauman and Briggs 2003; Briggs and Bauman 1999), the contributions of our consultants have often been overlooked in the field as a whole. Yet there have always been translators among us, those who pass between languages and cultures while ably grasping the aesthetic challenges involved in such acts of mediation. In this sense, translation is a profoundly undertheorized aspect of the human condition, one that has faced nearly every language and culture and that takes on increased salience in multilingual communities.

If we can picture Hymes poring over a translation with a deep sense of purpose, trying to convey the artistry in the work he was considering, we must imagine thousands of similar souls throughout the past, many of them equally concerned with aesthetics, but perhaps less so with issues of fidelity. Perhaps especially when the work draws on some established tradition, it often surprises the audience at the same time with a new sense of aesthetics, introducing an unexpected twist and even some subtle inversion in status of one of the characters, such as the gender shifts discussed earlier. In surveying the social life of oral narratives, I think we can safely move beyond fidelity ideology—putting it in its place as just one position among many. Even in Greek mythology, there is a recognition of the curious role of the translator, as exemplified in the case of Hermes who promises *not to outright tell a lie*, even if he must twist and turn words to make them fit within some other distant sense of social reality. Part of the work, of course, is to make the narrative fit into some other aesthetic regime, some other cultural background, some other context, and some other language.

Like literary traditions, religions also find themselves betwixt and between different social realities, languages, ethnicities, and changing times. In this sense, many religions also convey some wisdom on questions of translation. In Buddhist thought, experience is in many ways primary, and it is recognized at the outset that one may not be able to find words for what is often ineffable—for what is beyond the expressive capacity of language in the first place. Underlying this view is a surprisingly modern notion of discourse as human symbolic action that goes well beyond language and is therefore not limited to any one language. There is also an emphasis on experience, which can be transmitted by any means or even lost in translation. When it came to passing on his accumulated wisdom, perhaps gained over many lifetimes, the Buddha entrusted this tradition to the humble Mahakashapa, who understood at once, without extensive training, coming to the realization on his own (Aitken 1991, 52; Reps and Senzaki 1998, 121–22). All that passed between the men was a flower, and perhaps a smile, but no words—and in this way, the Dharma, the deepest truth, was transmitted directly, without translation of any kind. The Buddha himself set an example by insisting that one speak in words that one's audience might easily understand, working in the local vernacular (Nath 1998, 594; cf. 1 Corinthians 14:3, 14:9). In this sense, any language would do—and perhaps the best communication could happen *without any language to muddle the point.* As the Spanish philosopher José Ortega y Gasset (1959) once said in the form of a poem:

> Every utterance is deficient—it says less
> than it wishes to say.
> Every utterance is exuberant—it conveys more
> than it plans. (as quoted in Becker 1995, 370)

Presaging this sentiment many centuries earlier, Zen masters have been known to say that speaking is like pointing, reaching toward some distant truth that is beyond the context of the utterance. And, as we all know, when one points, people are likely to look at the finger, mistaking the words for the message, without translating them into experience!

At the other end of the spectrum, the Islamic tradition is famous for insisting that the Qur'an cannot be faithfully translated, since any departure from its classical form would violate the transaction between God, Gabriel, and Muhammad, which is recorded in exact form (see Baker and Saldanha 2009, 226–28). That is one strong form of fidelity ideology, which even eliminates the possibility of translation as a serious consideration. Of course, there can still be translations, but not without destroying the indexical role language plays in recording this transaction. The Protestants, for their part, insisted that translation could be transparent, and relatively perfect, since all languages were God-given, and therefore in some deep way commensurable, reflecting the underlying architecture of their common source. Perhaps we have been too heavily influenced by their puritanical ways within the field of anthropology, always seeking a good translation, when perhaps that is rarely the point!

In surveying the vast repertoire of human oral literature found in the anthropological record, it is the mischief-makers who really stand out, both as central characters and as the tellers of tales. Quintessentially liminal—by standing between traditions—they often find their voices in a deeply syncretic way, sometimes mocking tradition, sometimes respectfully paying homage, but without losing sight of their own sense of artistic vision, as the Hupa storytellers did in my field experience. In this way, Hymes himself stands out, contributing to our field as both an artist and a scientist—but mostly an artist, who respected the work of other artists in other cultures everywhere. May we all follow in the footsteps of Hymes, giving those artists and translators some of the credit they deserve, for without their assistance and insight there would be no fields of anthropology, folklore, or comparative literature.

References Cited

Aitken, Robert, ed. 1991. *The Gateless Barrier: The Wu-Men Kuan (Mumonkan)*. Translated by Robert Aitken. New York: North Point.

Bahr, Donald M. 2001. "Bad News: The Predicament of Native American Mythology." *Ethnohistory* 48 (4): 587–612.

Baker, Mona, and Gabriela Saldanha, eds. 2009. *Routledge Encyclopedia of Translation Studies*, 2nd ed. New York: Routledge.

Bakhtin, M. M. 1981. *The Dialogic Imagination: Four Essays*. Edited by Michael Holquist. Translated by Caryl Emerson and Michael Holquist. Austin: University of Texas Press.

———. 1986. *Speech Genres and Other Late Essays*. Translated by Vern W. McGee. Edited by Caryl Emerson and Michael Holquist. Austin: University of Texas Press.

Barth, Fredrik. 1969. *Ethnic Groups and Boundaries: The Social Organization of Cultural Difference*. Boston: Little, Brown.

Bauman, Richard, and Charles L. Briggs. 1990. "Poetics and Performance as Critical Perspectives on Language and Social Life." *Annual Review of Anthropology* 19:59–88.

———. 2003. *Voices of Modernity: Language Ideologies and the Politics of Inequality*. Cambridge: Cambridge University Press.

Becker, Alton. 1995. *Beyond Translation: Essays toward a Modern Philology*. Ann Arbor: University of Michigan Press.

Boas, Franz. 1894. *Chinook Texts*. Bureau of American Ethnology, Bulletin 20. Washington, DC: Government Printing Office.

———. 1917. "Introductory." *International Journal of American Linguistics* 1 (1): 1–8.

———. 1921. *Ethnology of the Kwakiutl Indians*. Memoirs of the American Museum of Natural History, Annual Report 35 (1913–1914), pt. 2, 795–1481. Washington, DC: Government Printing Office.

Briggs, Charles L., and Richard Bauman. 1992. "Genre, Intertextuality, and Social Power." *Journal of Linguistic Anthropology* 2 (2): 131–72.

————. 1999. "'The Foundation of All Future Researches': Franz Boas, George Hunt, Native American Texts, and the Construction of Modernity." *American Quarterly* 51 (3): 479–528.

Derrida, Jacques. 1981. "Semiology and Grammatology: Interview with Julia Kristeva." In *Positions*, translated and annotated by Alan Bass, 15–36. Chicago: University of Chicago Press.

Foley, John Miles. 1992. "Word-Power, Performance, and Tradition." *Journal of American Folklore* 105 (417): 275–301.

Friedrich, Paul. 1986. *The Language Parallax: Linguistic Relativism and Poetic Indeterminacy*. Austin: University of Texas Press.

Goddard, Pliny Earle. 1904. "Hupa Texts." *University of California Publications in American Archaeology and Ethnology* 1 (2): 89–368. Berkeley: University of California Press.

Goldberg, Christine. 1984. "The Historic-Geographic Method: Past and Future." *Journal of Folklore Research* 21 (1): 1–18.

Golla, Victor Karl. 1996. *Hupa Language Dictionary: Na:tinixwe Mixine:whe'*. Arcata, CA: Hupa Tribal Education Committee and Humboldt State University.

Herzog, George. 1939. "Music's Dialects: A Non-Universal Language." *Independent Journal of Columbia University* 6:1–2.

Hymes, Dell. (1964) 1972. "Toward Ethnographies of Communication: The Analysis of Communicative Events." In *Language and Social Context*, edited by Pier Paolo Giglioli, 21–44. London: Penguin.

————. (1965) 1981. "Some North Pacific Coast Poems: A Study in Anthropological Philology." In *"In Vain I Tried to Tell You": Essays in Native American Poetics*. Lincoln: University of Nebraska Press.

————. 1966. "Two Types of Linguistic Relativity (with Examples from Amerindian Ethnography)." In *Sociolinguistics, Proceedings of the UCLA Sociolinguistics Conference, 1964*, edited by W. Bright, 114–57. The Hague: Mouton.

————. 1974. *Foundations in Sociolinguistics: An Ethnographic Approach*. Philadelphia: University of Pennsylvania Press.

————. 1981. *"In Vain I Tried to Tell You": Essays in Native American Poetics*. Lincoln: University of Nebraska Press.

————. 2003. *Now I Only Know So Far: Essays in Ethnopoetics*. Lincoln: University of Nebraska Press.

Jackson, Jason Baird. 2003. *Yuchi Ceremonial Life: Performance, Meaning, and Tradition in a Contemporary American Indian Community*. Lincoln: University of Nebraska Press.

Jakobson, Roman. 1960. "Closing Statement: Linguistics and Poetics." In *Style in Language*, edited by Thomas Sebeok, 398–429. Cambridge, MA: MIT Press.

Keeling, Richard. 1992. *Cry for Luck: Sacred Song and Speech among the Yurok, Hupa, and Karok Indians of Northwestern California*. Berkeley: University of California Press.

Kroskrity, Paul V. 1993. *Language, History, and Identity: Ethnolinguistic Studies of the Arizona Tewa*. Tucson: University of Arizona Press.

————. 2000. "Language Ideologies in the Expression and Representation of Arizona Tewa Ethnic Identity." In *Regimes of Language: Ideologies, Polities, and Identities*, edited by Paul V. Kroskrity, 329–59. Santa Fe: School of American Research Press.

————. 2004. "Language Ideologies." In *A Companion to Linguistic Anthropology*, edited by Alessandro Duranti, 496–517. Oxford: Blackwell.

Lang, Julian. 1994. *Ararapíkva: Creation Stories of the People: Traditional Karuk Indian Literature from Northwestern California*. Berkeley, CA: Heyday.

Lucy, John. 1992a. *Grammatical Categories and Cognition: A Case Study in the Linguistic Relativity Hypothesis*. Cambridge: Cambridge University Press.

————. 1992b. *Language Diversity and Thought: A Reformulation of the Linguistic Relativity Hypothesis*. Cambridge: Cambridge University Press.

Malinowski, Bronislaw. (1935) 1978. *Coral Gardens and their Magic*. 2 vols. London: Allan and Urwin.

McDowell, John H. 2000. "Collaborative Ethnopoetics: The View from the Sibundoy Valley." In *Translating Native American Verbal Art: Ethnopoetics and Ethnography of Speaking*, edited by Marta de Gerdes, Kay Sammons, and Joel Sherzer, 211–32. Washington, DC: Smithsonian Institution Press.

Nath, Samir. 1998. *Encyclopedic Dictionary of Buddhism*. Vol. 3. New Dehli: Sarup and Sons.

Nettl, Bruno. 2005. *The Study of Ethnomusicology: Thirty-One Issues and Concepts*. Urbana: University of Illinois Press.

O'Neill, Sean. 2006. "Mythic and Poetic Dimensions of Speech in Northwestern California: From Cultural Vocabulary to Linguistic Relativity." *Anthropological Linguistics* 48 (4): 305–34.

————. 2008. *Cultural Contact and Linguistic Relativity among the Indians of Northwestern California*. Norman: University of Oklahoma Press.

————. 2012. "The Politics of Storytelling in Northwestern California: Ideology, Identity, and Maintaining Narrative Distinction in the Face of Cultural Convergence." In *Telling Stories in the Face of Danger*, edited by Paul V. Kroskrity, 60–89. Norman: University of Oklahoma Press.

Ortega y Gasset, José. 1959. "The Difficulty of Reading." *Diogenes* 7 (28): 1–17.

Reps, Paul, and Nyogen Senzaki, comps. (1955) 1998. *Zen Flesh, Zen Bones: A Collection of Zen and Pre-Zen Writings*. Boston: Tuttle.

Rubel, Paula G., and Abraham Rosman, eds. 2003. *Translating Cultures: Perspectives on Translation and Anthropology*. Oxford: Berg.

Sapir, Edward. 1921. *Language: An Introduction to the Study of Speech*. New York: Harcourt, Brace.

————. (1929) 1949. "The Status of Linguistics as a Science." In *The Selected Writings of Edward Sapir in Language, Culture, and Personality*, edited by David Mandelbaum, 160–66. Berkeley: University of California Press.

————. 2001. *The Collected Works of Edward Sapir XIV: Northwest California Linguistics*, edited by Victor Golla and Sean O'Neill. New York: Mouton de Gruyter.

Silverstein, Michael. 1979. "Language Structure and Linguistic Ideology." In *The Elements: A Parasession on Linguistic Units and Level*, edited by Paul R. Clyne, William F. Hanks, and Carol L. Hofbauer, 193–247. Chicago: Chicago Linguistics Society.

————. 1998. "The Uses and Utilities of Ideology: A Commentary." In *Language Ideologies: Practice and Theory*, edited by Bambi B. Schieffelin, Kathryn A. Woolard, and Paul V. Kroskrity, 123–48. New York: Oxford University Press.

Stross, Brian. 1971. "Serial Order in Nez Percé Myths." *Journal of American Folklore* 84 (331): 104–13.

Tedlock, Dennis. 1983. *The Spoken Word and the Work of Interpretation.* Philadelphia: University of Pennsylvania Press.

———. 1999. *Finding the Center: The Art of Zuni Storytelling.* 2nd ed. Translated by Dennis Tedlock from live performances in Zuni by Andrew Peynetsa and Walter Sanchez. Lincoln: University of Nebraska Press.

Voloshinov, Valentin Nikolaevich. (1929) 1972. *Marxism and the Philosophy of Language.* Translated by Ladislav Matejka and I. R. Titunik. Cambridge, MA: Harvard University Press.

Whorf, Benjamin Lee. 1956. *Language, Thought, and Reality: Selected Writings of Benjamin Lee Whorf.* Edited by John B. Carroll. Cambridge, MA: MIT Press.

Yengoyan, Aram. 2003. "Lyotard and Wittgenstein and the Question of Translation." In *Translating Cultures: Perspectives on Translation in Anthropology,* edited by Paula G. Rubel and Abraham Rosman, 25–44. Oxford: Berg.

SEAN PATRICK O'NEILL is Associate Professor of Anthropology at the University of Oklahoma. His research focuses on the role of language in human social life, including its place in identity politics, storytelling, and song, as well as its influence on worldview. He is author of *Cultural Contact and Linguistic Relativity among the Indians of Northwestern California* (2008).

9   Ethnopoetics and Ideologies of Poetic Truth

I HOLD TWO objectives for the present essay. First, I want to think about the fate of poetic forms in the context of cultural, historical, and spiritual upheaval. My discussion of this fate is based in materials from the Lutheran missionary enterprise on the San Carlos Apache Reservation in southeastern Arizona, especially the work of the Uplegger family, missionaries in San Carlos from Woodrow Wilson's administration through Ronald Reagan's.[1] My second objective is to explore the ethical argument implied in the framework of Dell Hymes's approach to ethnopoetics. The link between these two discussions, in my view, lies in the ways that notions of poetry and notions of truth are caught up in the ethics of both the missionary and the ethnopoetic enterprise. If I may put it briefly at the outset, on the one hand, Lutheran discourses on the truth-value of missionary statements about salvation never escape questions of the poetic and rhetorical forms in which those purported truths are cast. By the same token, Hymesian engagement with poetic form as a culturally coherent expressive presentation of the meaningful world implies a reality-producing force to the appropriately performed utterance.[2]

To put this another way, both Hymes in his presentation of ethnopoetics and Lutheran missionaries in their work on the San Carlos Apache reservation are engaged in ethical arguments about the importance of communicative competence. That is, for both, command of discourse form and a competence demonstrated through performance are part of an individual's claim to being an ethical member of a community. Both are concerned with the discursive constitution of fully socialized and responsible humanity. The relationship between the two projects runs deeper than, for example, the researcher's ability to produce a Hymesian lining-out of Lutheran missionary texts. It is in overlapping concerns with ethical human coparticipation in and

240

with the natural and supernatural worlds, and in the shared focus on proper forms of verbal interaction, that ethnopoetics and Lutheran missionary activity are tied together: each is an approach to what it means to be an ethical person. In the essay that follows I explore the strands of some of these ties. I suggest as well that a further reason for the links between these endeavors is their shared resonance with earlier Christian debates about the ethical relationship of poetry and truth; poetry's place in the world of representation is traceable throughout the history of folklore studies and extends as far back as the Middle Ages.

I begin by outlining the important contribution of Hymes's ethnopoetic theories to an understanding of the effects on expressive culture of missionary encounter. Following this, I describe the activities of the Lutheran church in the communities of the San Carlos Apache Reservation since its first arrival in 1893. I then describe in comparative terms the poetic and rhetorical aspects of two sermons delivered on Easter Sunday 1964—one in English by Alfred Uplegger, the other in Apache by Fergus Sneezy, his Native language interpreter. I conclude with a discussion of how the overlapping aspects of missionary and ethnopoetic projects resonate with earlier Christian poetic theories.[3]

Hymes and Verbal Art

Hymes's insights into the verbal production of Native American poetic expressions fashioned form as the beating heart of socially circulating meaning. His aesthetic sensibility, coupled with analytical rigor, opened new ways for ethnographers to consider questions of culture, socialization, and mediation. The effects of Hymes's observations on the importance of form in considering communication from an ethnographic perspective were simple but consequential: an utterance could not be distinguished from its enunciation. Far from static, form was an emergent aspect of performance, a temporal act by which enunciation was, again, an intrinsic aspect of the social creation of text. By insisting that such expressions were indeed "formally poetry, and also a rhetoric of action" (1996, 120), Hymes argued that narrative practices are constituted by the whole cloth of a community's linguistic, semiotic, and expressive resources, analysis of which is adequately covered neither by a Heideggerian tracing of particularistic semantic denotations of lexical items (Heidegger 1971), nor by a Hoijeresque cultural reading of text (Hoijer 1938). In short, by reading communicative competence as the emergent effect of a range of biographical and social factors external to the linguistic system *per se*, Hymes's model called on researchers to account for the speech act as the acoustic and semiotic signature of the whole person in temporal performance, and to present their accounts as such. Taken as a whole, Hymes's observations thus unite domains of syntax, rhetoric, and poetics under a larger rubric that one might call "eloquence," the process that Gus Palmer, Jr. (2003, 11) has called becoming a "master speaker."

The deep embedding of narrative practice in more widespread cultural forms of circulation and socialization presented different kinds of analytical questions to researchers. The recognition of Native American narrative as poetic form challenged researchers to reassess the means of transcribing an utterance into written media. Evelyn Kendrick Wells had declared in 1950 that "[a] ballad in print is a ballad already dying" (6). Hymes attempted, in his work on ethnopoetics, to set out a means of overcoming the sting of this death. This attempt and the arguments supporting it had ethical implications as well: the new organizations of texts presented by Hymes were meant, in part, to rectify past misrepresentations by researchers whose approaches to text had ended at the prose paragraph. Hymes's reanalysis of the general epistle of James (1986), for example, claimed to solve the problem of the letter's coherence by demonstrating its relation to oral tradition.

Emphasis on the poetic utterance comes at a price, certainly. Hymes's approach to poetics intended to overcome the false dichotomy between poetic and prosaic utterances. "Poetry as such," Hymes (1962, 49) wrote of the range of possible genres in the ethnography of speaking, "would thus be but a principal subtype, proof-reading perhaps a minor one." To be sure, Hymes was hardly the first to have attempted to bridge this gap. Paul Valéry's (1954) theory of poetics, for instance, was built upon erasing the distinction between the supposed polar opposites of "poetry" and "abstract thought," arguing that both are crystallizations of everyday language. And Hans-Georg Gadamer (1986a, 67), citing the "great force" of Valéry's poetic theory, crafted an approach to poetics much more dependent on a distinction, rather than a link, between the poetic and the everyday. For Gadamer (1986b, 133), "poetry and philosophy are both set off from the exchange of language as it takes place in practical activity and in science, but their proximity seems in the end to collapse into the extremes of the word that stands, and the word that fades into the unsayable."[4]

But highlighting narrative performance and verbal art threatens to neglect the analysis of everyday verbal sociability, although a number of scholars have built on Hymes's work in analyzing the poeticity of everyday interactions (Abrahams 2005; Bollinger 1989; Duranti 1997; Ide 1998; Tannen 1998).[5] And the assertion of poetry always carried the possibility of asserting the very distinction Hymes was attempting to overcome (Paul G. Zolbrod [1995] was not alone in preferring the term *literature*), resulting in a number of research agendas geared toward the discovery of utterances containing heightened poeticity. (Is not the linguist's notion of "prosody" closer to the mark?) It is not difficult to imagine, given the symbolic and affective baggage carried by such ideas as "everyday" and "poetic," how the argument that the everyday is redeemed by its containing instances of the poetic results in a conceptual dilemma. The oppositional poles are reinvented at the same time they are dissolved.

That dilemma, dependent on an oppositional relationship between differentially heightened linguistic and expressive practices, perhaps inevitably leads to questions of whether, as Kenneth Burke (1966) might have it, one needs first to understand poetics in order to make sense of everyday interaction, or whether, as Morse Peckham (1977, 803) argued, the task of interpreting "complex literary texts" requires a prior understanding of "interpretational behavior . . . in ordinary, mundane, routine verbal interaction."[6] The thorny relationship between everyday and more overtly poetic expressions, mediated by the moral efficacy implied by the command of genre, pointed to issues of becoming in the human cultural sphere. Hymes consistently emphasized the culturally embedded nature of intersubjectivity in verbal practice, insisting on the quotidian and returning often, for example, to caretaker–child interaction as a key means by which culture is circulated and reproduced, arguing that the way a mother speaks to a child contains as much poetry as the most elaborate ceremony. By emphasizing "the role of speech in socialization," Hymes (1962) committed his theory of communicative competence to an elaboration of the ways in which all linguistic practices were embedded in an ethical discourse about proper socialized intersubjectivity. Communicative competence, in that regard, is overall an idea of propriety, a sense that enables "the distinguishing of what persons will do in particular contexts from what they can do in principle" (Hymes 1981, 83). This distinction between the possible and the appropriate is similarly a lynchpin of Hymes's arguments about competence, poetics, and performance.[7]

Recognizing the role of discourse form in the constitution and circulation of culture enables the ethnographer to reconsider the (re)production of narrative text along two dimensions. First is the socialization to speech. In the process of "ethical becoming" in the social context implied by "a culture," however, speakers acquire control over multiple, interwoven layers of discourse organization and coherence, only one of which is the organization of the semantic import of what one says.[8] The second dimension was the more salient role of the individual agent in performance—that "careful attention to details of language in the context of a theory of . . . poetics . . . makes evident the presence of a narrator" (Hymes 1985, 391). Hymes declined to regard narrative traditions as *objets d'art* taken only "as a collective label and referent" without regard for the individual creative and constitutive speech acts of a narrator (1981, 132). "The words of a single speaker," Hymes scolded, "have been glossed in the name of an entire culture, Victoria Howard as 'Clackamas,' and so on" (1985, 391).

These reconsiderations contribute to the present case in two ways. First, they encourage us to understand the ethical and theological encounter on the San Carlos Reservation as a multidimensional struggle between creatively engaged individual representatives of diverse communities and institutions—not as an encounter between "the Lutheran Church" and "Apache culture," but between, say, Alfred Uplegger, Henry Rosin, or Paul Mayerhoff and, perhaps, Alfred Burdette, Asa Lavender, or Silas John (Watt and Basso 2004, 107–21). Second, by so considering this history, we are able to trace some of the ways in which the process of missionization and Christian conversion on the reservation leaves traces in the ways and means of the production of meaningful discourse form (see Hanks 2010; Keane 2007; Schieffelin 2007, 2008). Hymes (1981, 134) attests as much in his theory of performance, which refuses "any standpoint which divorces the study of tradition from the incursion of time and the consequences of modern history." Although Hymes himself was strongly dedicated to issues of continuity and survival in contemporary circumstances, he had a keen sense, for example, of new contexts (myths told in booths in coffee shops) and new narratives (stories about automobile purchases) in the

Wishram community. Although worried about the disappearance of the "the language of tradition" (1986, 86), his comment about "the interplay of Indian and rural white ways of speaking in the English of the Indians" (1981, 133–34) is suggestive.

Finally, focusing attention on poetics and discourse against the backdrop of Lutheran missionary activities in the communities of the San Carlos reservation contributes to our understanding of the cultural production of narrative inequality as one outcome of these activities. Thinking about poetic form and rhetorical design sharply delineates questions about the role of nonreferential aspects of speech acts in the constitution and circulation of discourse and culture. The overt version of Lutheran discourse ideology disparaged poeticity, insisting that the value of the Lutheran message was in the objective truth-value it contained.[9] This truth was available in all languages, but conveying it was a matter of proper syntax and lexicon, not of narrative, poetic, or rhetorical form. Yet, poetic form could not be erased from view. Although the missionary enterprise focused on the truth claims of competing theologies and set out to replace what its representatives considered to be false beliefs with what they considered true, and while this process was rarely presented as an exercise in poetics, it inevitably produced exemplars of commentary on the proper discursive form for expressions of truth to take. Whether speaking or writing in English or in Apache, the missionaries had to cast their discourse in given forms or create new ones, and they had to engage in comparative discussions of the propriety of one form over another in their efforts to redesign the idea of an ethical approach to the natural, social, and spiritual worlds.

The Wisconsin Lutheran Synod in Apacheland

The first Lutheran missionaries to arrive in San Carlos were two recent seminary graduates of Northwestern College in Watertown, Wisconsin: Johannes Plocher and Thomas Adascheck. Sent by the Wisconsin Synod and arriving in October 1893, they established a church and a school in Peridot, midway between the agency town of San Carlos and the settlement of Rice.[10] Adascheck, experiencing difficulty with the Apache language, returned to Wisconsin, but he was followed into the Southwest by a steady stream of missionaries and schoolteachers who expanded the reach of the Lutheran church across the expanse

of the San Carlos and White Mountain Apache Reservations.[11] Most
were recent seminary graduates. The signal event for San Carlos,
however, was the arrival in 1917 of Alfred Uplegger, followed into the
field two years later by his father Francis, his mother Emma, and his
sisters Johanna, Gertrude, and Dorothea. From 1917 until 1984, when
Alfred passed away, one or another member of the Uplegger family
performed missionary work in the San Carlos Apache community.

William Kessel (n.d.) writes that the volunteers "received absolutely
no special training to work among in [sic] the mission field." They did,
however, come equipped with seminarian knowledge of Latin, Greek,
and Hebrew, which they could apply to learning Apache. Many were
also German speakers. They also brought with them a philological approach to language that was a key aspect of many varieties of Christian
scriptural translation as well as modern linguistic science: the conviction that the propositional matter of a statement was independent
from the form in which it was expressed.[12] For these men and women,
a focus on the truth of scripture, independent of any particular language employed in its enunciation, guided their efforts at rendering
the revealed truth of Christianity in Apache. Francis Uplegger, especially, was a key participant in stabilizing cross-linguistic presentations
of scripture, based on the growing sense of "the inadequacy of entrust-
ing the sacred message to interpreters who themselves did not speak
a correct English, were not grounded in the faith and often were at a
loss as to how to translate words and statements which were not entirely
clear to them" (Hoenecke 1984, 39). This focus on the independent
truth of scripture was accompanied by a de-emphasizing of poeticity
in the name of semantic clarity and, indeed, a preference for translations that had the precision of description rather than the riskiness
of metaphor. And yet this focus on truth at the expense of poetry was
accompanied by massive shifts in poetics at the level of community
experience—new genres of discourse, new semantic loads for lexical
items, new contexts of interaction, new expectations for the roles of
performer(s) and audience(s).

We can get a glimpse at this emphasis on the independent truth-
value of an utterance from Alfred Uplegger's student class notes.[13]
There, mixed in with his extensive notes in German on Hebrew and
Greek philology, a table attempting to calculate the number of years
from Adam to Abraham, distracted drawings of geometric figures,

signet designs of his initials, banners, other desultory doodles and marginalia no doubt executed during boring moments in class, and a somewhat callow collegiate verse, Uplegger suddenly paid exacting attention to James H. Snowden's *The World A Spiritual System: An Outline of Metaphysics* (1910). He produced a twenty-six-page, chapter-by-chapter, section-by-section outline of the entire book. Snowden's popular theology was in the philosophical orbit of Berkeley's Subjective Idealism, and thus dedicated to the search for the objective truth that lies hidden behind appearances and sensory experience. In chapters titled "How We Reach Objective Reality" and "The Nature of Objective Reality," Snowden argued against the solipsistic idea that reality was nothing more than an illusion of the individual subjective mind. Just as the soul, which Snowden earlier defined as "ultimate reality" (1910, 86), is comprised of a "threefold nature of thought, sensibility, and will, and characterized by unity, growth, law, habit, freedom, and purpose" (177), so the world and the universe are "God's consciousness organized into a system of thought and sensibility and will" (223). And because "God is the original, underived, infinite Spirit," his omnipresence guarantees the stable and objective existence of reality. Thus understanding the existence of God and understanding the stability of objective truth are fruit of the same tree. In Snowden's argument, the existence of God and the unity of the three-part structure of the world and of the soul serve to undermine solipsism, exposing it as a logical fallacy.

A link between objective truth and poetic form was made in another class, for which Uplegger wrote a short essay titled "The Subject of an Oration" (A. Uplegger n.d.). Snowden's tripartite framework for the soul and for reality—thought, sensibility, and will—returned in Uplegger's thesis statement about proper and effective oratory: "An oration must appeal to the intellect, the emotion, and the will of its hearers." Because an oration's purpose was to produce some action in its hearers, it needed to touch the will. But because man was a free and rational being, his "free deeds of duty and love" could never be exacted unless he could be "convinced that it was good to do them" through the orator's appeal "to the intellect of the hearers, instruction, explanation, insight, understanding." Convincing a listener with rational argument, however, might not be enough to rouse the will. "The moving of the heart" was a necessary link between the intellect and the will. "An orator, therefore, who would not appeal to his hearers' emotions would be like a farmer that sows corn, and does not cultivate the field." Uplegger found a unity between the thought-sensibility-will trinity that guaranteed the objective existence of truth and the intellect-emotion-will trio undergirding the nature of a rhetorically effective presentation of that truth.

The response of Uplegger's professor in this class reveals the limits of imagining an objective truth outside of the rhetorical form of its enunciation. The marginal comment on the essay, although praising it, asked Uplegger to be more subtle and nuanced in the presentation of his argument. "Well reasoned," the instructor wrote. "Try however *not* to show the mechanical structure of your writing *quite so plainly*, as by the use of then, therefore, &c. For a short paper you have used these words too frequently" (emphasis in original). Poetics and poetry were unavoidable. But as this professor's comments demonstrate, the overt goal of effective rhetoric—the skill of eloquence—was to hide its material construction and make it appear as if there were nothing at stake in an utterance save the referential transparency of the truths embodied in its propositional content (Leff 1986).

In recorded services conducted by the Upleggers in San Carlos, the missionaries' focus on truth can be seen to have run along two main tracks. First was a continual referencing of the truth-value of assertions made from the pulpit. In a regular portion of the worship service, Alfred Uplegger closed the reading of the Gospel and Epistle texts with an acclamation adapted from a verse from the Gospel of John (17:17), a metadiscursive declaration of the certainty of God's word as presented in the Bible: "Sanctify us in thy truth, oh Lord, thy word is truth. Amen." Sermon texts, as well, were salted with truth assertions. In his Easter sermon of 1964, for example, Alfred Uplegger presented key spiritual aspects of the resurrection to his audience and then concluded:

I.a	**That** is the **great**est **event** in **all** the **world**.
I.b	That the Lord Jesus rose from the dead.
II.a.1	And on **this great**est **of all**
II.a.2	**TRUE**
II.a.3	events
II.b	the Christian church is built. (A. Uplegger 1964)[14]

Alfred Uplegger's assertion of absolute truth is organized by syntax, tempo, pause, and stress. Both the regularities and disruptions

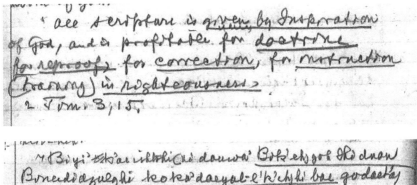

FIGURE 1
Selection from Francis Uplegger's notebooks showing 2 Timothy 3:16.

of regularity and pattern contribute to the poetic organization of his oration. The line break between I.a and I.b occurs at a clause phrase ending that coordinates with a pause break. The lines are coordinated, as well, by repetition of "that" as an appositive conjunction. Uplegger's tempo and rubato are also important to grasp here. I refrain from presenting this passage in musical notation because not everyone reads music. But were I to do so, I would place a metronome marking for this passage at about 75–80 beats per minute, an *andante* marking. At the beginning of line I.a, Uplegger accelerates to his chosen tempo. He treats each line of the passage in a call-and-response fashion, downplaying the regularity of stress and meter in the (b) line of each pair. In line II.a.1, metrical stress comes well to the foreground, as the syllables "this," "great-," and "all" fall on regular pulses at around 77 beats per minute. The intonational and amplitudinal peak of the passage comes on the word "true" in line II.a.2, which is preceded by about a half-beat *fermata*, or pause, that increases the anticipation culminating in the enunciation of the word.[15] Uplegger also emphasizes the focus on this word by contrasting the liquid elongation of the preceding "all" with a staccato rendering of "true."

A second way in which the concept of truth was emphasized by Lutheran missionaries on the reservation can be sensed in translation

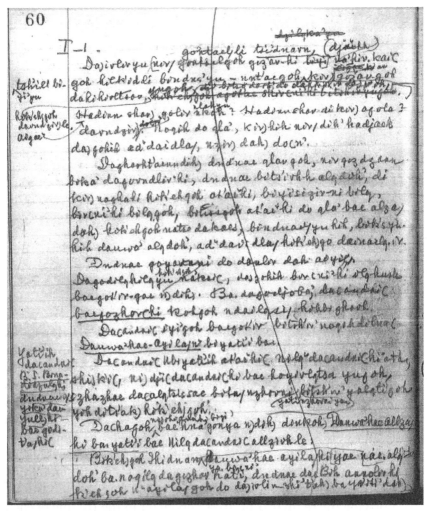

FIGURE 2
Rejected page of sermon translation into Apache from Francis Uplegger's notes.

practices, and especially in the singular focus on transferring semantic values of Gospel texts across to Apache voices and ears in translation. Francis Uplegger's notebooks are filled with page after page of translations of concepts that have life within an evangelical framework but may be difficult to render in a new language. Looking at his translation of St. Paul's second epistle to Timothy (figure 1), for example, reveals that Uplegger was very much invested in a semantic project:

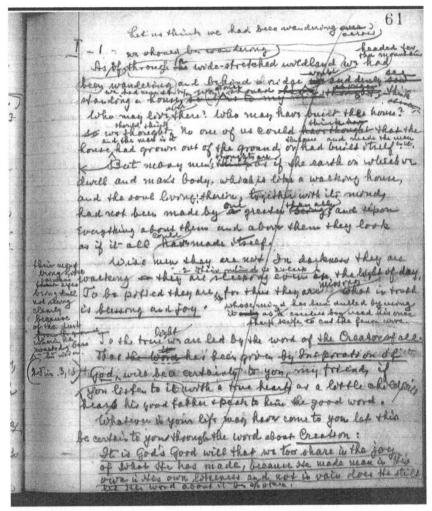

FIGURE 2 (*continued*)

how do you say *righteousness* in Apache? *inspiration*? *doctrine*? *reproof*? *correction*? *instruction*?[16]

This focus on semantics influenced the way even terms with long metaphorical histories in English were rendered in Apache. For example, there are two generally accepted ways of saying *thousand* in Apache. The first is *goneznaadn-goneznadin* 'ten hundreds'. The second is *doholtadgo* 'uncountable,' 'not to be counted'. Of the two, the second

term appears to be more widely used. Francis Uplegger, however, seems
to have preferred the former for its arithmetic precision as compared
with the poetic imagery of the latter, and in his Apache language
notes he characterized the second with the annotation "popularly"
(F. Uplegger n.d.b, 45). He preferred the numerical version despite
the English word's similar etymological history to the Apache term he
balked at: the Indo-European root *tūs* meaning 'multitude' or 'force'.
A leaning toward semanticism influenced a number of translation
choices made by the missionaries in which metaphorical or poetic
relations were submerged beneath a focus on overt description. Representations of the seven days of the week in Apache almost invariably
saddle the names with functional and descriptive meanings: 'day of
rest' (*hana'idzołíí bijįį*) 'day of worship' (*godilziníí bijįį*), '(places of business are) open' (*ch'it'ą́ą́*), and so forth. This functional-descriptive role
of day names was regularly invoked by missionary translators despite
the pagan history of the source-language English days of the week in
days for the Sun, Moon, Saturn, Thor, Wotan, and so forth.[17]

Such clear focus on the semantics of the word might tend to place
form in a subsidiary position, and in fact the missionaries rarely if
ever made use of vernacular Apache poetic or rhetorical forms. But
the formal aspects of Apache discourse were neither ignored nor
unaffected by the missionaries. The importance of the truth meant
that Lutherans often were critical of—and drew contrasts between—
Apache narratives on the one hand and Christian doctrine on the
other. A 1924 mission newsletter article under the byline of Lon Bullis,
the Apache interpreter for the Bylas mission, framed a clear distinction between "a fable story" and "a true story." The former "is a story
that was gotten up for old men and women that do not sleep at nights"
(Bullis 1924, 3). By a similar token, people who worship false gods,
the article states, "pray to something thought out by men," whereas
the true God condemns this behavior in Deuteronomy and especially
in the Gospels. Attached to this dismissal of Apache narratives was a
distrust and semantic derogation of the prominent narrative particle
and verb of speaking *ch'inii*, which the missionaries disapprovingly
compared to the unreliability of gossip.[18] God's word, by comparison,
was not ch'inii, not just something that someone said. It was *danii*: true.

The Lutheran practice of translating Christian theological texts
into Apache did not expend much energy to incorporate already-
existing Apache poetic and rhetorical forms into liturgical practice

on the reservation (see Nevins 2010). Sermons become interesting in this context, for they raise questions of poeticity along two lines. First, they raise questions around the issue first addressed in Alfred Uplegger's college notes, that is, how a speaker produces an understanding of truth and referential transparency for an audience through the mechanisms of poetic organization and rhetorical design. Second, sermons raise questions around issues of the relationship between oral performance and written representation, which I noted in an earlier section as part of Hymes's ethics of ethnopoetics. The preparation of a script for performance in a sense reverses the order of most ethnographic representations of oral narratives. But it is clear that sermons in the Lutheran church were not extemporized or oral-formulaic in composition. This is most clearly shown in Francis Uplegger's preparations for his sermons delivered in Apache, which show him hard at work transferring the referential values of biblical concepts into the vernacular language of adult speakers in San Carlos. Figure 2 shows a page from Uplegger's notebook preparation of a sermon text. It demonstrates the extent to which he preserved the discourse genre of *essay* for his sermon as the text moved from English to Apache. Uplegger displayed a remarkable meticulousness in his search for semantic equivalence. A line through these pages indicates that he rejected this work. He began it anew on the following pages, but a line through those pages indicates that he may have ultimately rejected that version as well. In other instances he returned to original Hebrew and Greek texts to locate his meaning. But his attention to Apache referential detail was not matched by an accompanying sense of preserving or representing Apache poetic or rhetorical forms in either the speech genre of the sermon or its delivery from the pulpit. Indeed, the dismissal of Apache narratives as "fable stories" and the iconic relationship between the structure of truth and the structure of a particular rhetorical structuring of argument almost guaranteed that this would be the case.

Francis Uplegger's translation of Lutheran hymns presents an interesting case in point, as here the desire for objective truth and the demands of poetic form were emphasized by the metrical and periodic setting of liturgical hymns.[19] In arguing for a vernacular mass, Martin Luther ([1525] 1958, 141) also wrote in favor of a vernacular hymnody, the idea that song, "both the text and notes, accent, melody, and manner of rendering ought to grow out of the true mother tongue and

its inflection." Indeed, here Luther was making a case for employing
the poetic potentials of specific vernaculars to house the same objective truth, a struggle to "reconcile . . . the human beauty of linguistic
diversity with the singular and universal message of Christian faith"
that Mary Margaret Steedly (1996, 447) notes is a continuing issue for
Protestantism more generally. Uplegger's hymn translations, however,
make no use of vernacular Apache song forms. Although he quite
skillfully honed Apache language to the meter and melody of German
and other central and western European musical forms—and often
quite ingeniously preserved the semantic import of the text—there
was no attempt to create a vernacular hymnody for the Lutheran community of the San Carlos Apache Reservation. Each Sunday, Uplegger would lead the congregation through a unison recitation of the
hymn text in Apache, which he had written in large letters on a sheet
of oaktag using the Apache orthography he had devised. Replacing
vernacular Apache song with the tunes and harmonic settings of the
Lutheran hymnal went hand-in-hand with a whole series of new forms
of standardization brought about by new religious and educational
institutions sponsored by the mission: group reading of schoolbook
passages and rote memorization of texts were key forms of language
socialization for children in the mission school.

Sermons in Interpretation

So far I have argued that the discourse practices of Uplegger father
and son in their Lutheran Apache mission enterprise in San Carlos
stressed the proper semantic transportation of biblical concepts into
vernacular Apache language but did not devote equivalent attention to
discovering vernacular poetic forms for the circulation of that referential content. Indeed, the very distinction between content and form was
prominent in the Upleggers' approach to their work, with the former
being a matter of objective verification more or less independent of
the latter. Alongside the overt pride of place given the truth-value of
an utterance, however, I have argued that questions of poetic form
remained intact in the background of this discussion about denota-
tion as an additional organizing principle undergirding missionary
work in the community. The effects of this principle manifested in
the denigration of Apache narratives as "fable stories"; the preference
for a particular essay form that engaged the intellect, emotion, and

will of the listener; the sense that this particular form bore an iconic relationship to the threefold nature of reality as thought, sensibility, and will; and the importation of European models of hymnody as the music for worship regardless of the language in which the text was set.

In general, through the 1950s and 1960s and possibly as far back as the 1930s, congregants at the Grace Lutheran church in San Carlos witnessed two sermons. The first, which was delivered in Apache but followed the above-mentioned essay form, was given by Francis Uplegger, whose reputation as the most skilled of the missionaries in the realm of Apache language survives to this day. The other was delivered in English by his son Alfred. These sermons, however, were independent of each other in both topic and scope, the two pastors usually expounding on independent if related themes. A limiting case, then, might be one in which a sermon was delivered in English and was subsequently interpreted in Apache. For many missionaries this was standard practice, as it was on Sundays in San Carlos when Francis Uplegger did not preach. Johannes Plocher's diary contained entries referring to "Oscar Davis" and "Norman" as interpreters (Plocher 2004).[20] Ernest Victor, Wallace Johnson, and Alfred Burdette were prominent interpreters in San Carlos, the first two also traveling with Pastor Albert Meier as he preached in the camp settlements of East Fork in the late 1920s (Guenther 1927). The act of interpretation and the figure of the interpreter were oft-cited symbolic markers of Lutheran missionary work and conversion in the Apache community, especially in the first half of the twentieth century (Guenther 1927; Rosin 1966; Uplegger 1924).

Returning to the Easter Sunday service of 1964, Alfred Uplegger's sermon that day was delivered in English by the pastor and then interpreted for the congregation by Fergus Sneezy, a native speaker of Apache.[21] Uplegger began his textual exegesis with the angels witnessing the resurrection of Christ.[22] Although it was Easter, the sermon was not a treatise on the resurrection itself but rather a commentary on the witnessing of great events by angels and a discussion of how the presence of angels underscores the truth and the greatness of those events. The oration was organized in part by its grammar: Uplegger regularly coordinated pauses with adverbial line openings in his performance. Although these adverbial openings ("now," "and now," "now then") can be used to mark passage of time, Uplegger instead metaphorically mapped temporality onto logic, using these adverbial line openings appositively to offer additional information about the witness of angels to his thesis. In fact, the poetic lining-out of the sermon appears in a way to reverse engineer what might have been Uplegger's original outline of the essay: a topic statement, followed by a selection of examples, followed by a conclusion. The relationship between the topic statement and the conclusion in each episode of the narrative often takes the form of a rhetorical antithesis in the form of "yes, but." Here, for instance, is Uplegger's comparison between the material discoveries of man and the spiritual discovery by angels of the Redeemer and Savior lying in the manger in Bethlehem:

I.a	Those were the greatest events on earth, friends.
I.b.1	The discovery of gold?
I.b.2	Well, that was great,
I.b.3	how to use that,
I.b.4	yes,
I.c	and of silver.
I.d.1	And the discovery of many, many other things,
I.d.2	how to travel fast even through the air,
I.d.3	by trains,
I.d.4	that's great.
II.a	But that's nothing!
II.b.1	The great things were done by God,
II.b.2	by His creation,
II.b.3	by His sending the Lord Jesus.

In this episode, Uplegger makes prevalent use of interlinear repetition, using "discovery" in lines I.b.1 and I.d.1, "great" in I.a, I.b.2, I.d.4, and II.b.1, "how to X" in I.b.3 and I.d.2. The repetition becomes wedded to metrical regularity in lines II.b.2 and II.b.3, where "by His X" is reduplicated as a line-opening phrase in the episode's conclusion.

By comparison, Sneezy's Apache interpretation of Uplegger's sermon directly retells the narrative of the crucifixion and resurrection rather than commenting on one aspect of it, and exhorts the listeners in the congregation to think about it and think about what it means that Christ died as a sacrifice for them. Perhaps because it is a telling of the events and not, as is Uplegger's text, a metadiscourse about the events, the adverbial line- and episode-openings in the Apache version are clearly temporal, marked by the use of adverbials that place the story in time: "now," "then," "today," "a few days ago," "three days from when he was buried."

As with Uplegger's sermon, the line structure takes advantage of repetition. Here Sneezy repeats the phrase *doo iliigo ayilaa da* 'we don't have to pay for it':

I.a.1   akóh
         there

I.a.2   datsaahíí nagonil
         death was paid for

I.a.3   doo iliniigo ayilaa da
            it cost nothing/we don't have to pay for it

I.b.1   Iłch'ideeł golzeeyú doo agot'eehíí
         At the place called Iłch'ideeł what happens there[23]

I.b.2   bee agot'eehí doo iliigo ayilaa da
            how it is, we don't have to pay for it

I.c.1   ch'idn nant'an
         the devil

I.c.2   biyan'isna'nlíí le'at'eehń doo iliigo nohwaa ilaa da
            we could have been his slaves but it doesn't cost us
            anything/we don't have to pay for it

It is interesting to note here that the Apache interpreter, in invoking the name Ch'idn Nant'an to refer to Satan, and in discussing the risk as one of paying what one owes or becoming enslaved, may have made an intertextual link between the story of the crucifixion and resurrection and a vernacular Apache narrative about a man who becomes indebted through gambling to Ndah Ch'ii'n and must work off his debt by performing impossible labor that he can only accomplish with the assistance of Ndah Ch'ii'n's youngest daughter (Ethelbah, Ethelbah, and Nevins 2012). By paying that debt on mankind's behalf, Jesus erases this potential enslavement.

In addition to formal repetition, Sneezy's version also took advantage of the poetic possibilities of sonic iconicity, using Apache phonology for rhetorical effect. In the following five-line section, he used the phonology and morphology of Apache to set up a rhythmic rhyme scheme based on pronoun and verb-root syllabic segments ending in *-aa*:

I.a.1   nohwaa nadidzaa
         he got up again for us

I.a.2   nohwaa goneznaa
         he won it for us

I.a.3   datsąąhíí yaa goneznaa
         he defeated death for us

I.a.4   ch'inyaa goneznaa
         he went through it and won it

I.a.5   nohwaa
         for us

This ends a scene, the next opening marked by a temporal adverbial: "and then new life." The narrator then returns to a new exhortation for the audience to "think about" these events, to think about it "as if it happened this morning," "as if it happened just now," "even though it happened a long time ago think about it as if it just happened."[24] At the same time, it appears that pastor and interpreter employed their rhetorical and poetic skills to different effect. Alfred Uplegger's overall strategies were additive and contrastive. Both the performance features of his sermon and his use of lexical repetition tend to underline his goal of clear presentation of appositive examples and developing sharp contrasts in service of his point. Sneezy, on the other hand, appears to have used repetition as a refrain, amplifying his recurrence to a thematic point.

Poetics and Truth

As an anthropologist, Hymes (1996, 121) was more apt to discuss poetics as "an implicit schema for the organization of experience" than as an implicit model of truth. For those whose experience was organized around the revelations of Christianity, the distinction may have been moot. In any event, Hymes's sense that form and its intelligibility key the discussion of aesthetic and expressive systems draws upon and re-engages an array of arguments about poesis and truth with long histories in the Western-Christian intellectual tradition. These histories have explored the overlapping relationships between a number of binomials: aesthetics and ethics, art and craft, and expressivity and propositionality, this latter implicating a discourse around the truth-value of poetic expressions.[25] The range of positions in this lengthy and ongoing dialogue is extremely broad, of course. Matthew Arnold ([1879] 1922, 4) perhaps reached the pinnacle of Romantic hyperbole with his 1879 claim that "poetry is nothing else than the most perfect speech of man, that in which he comes nearest being able to utter truth." We need only place this sentiment alongside Archibald MacLeish's (1985, 107) modernist caution in his 1926 "Ars Poetica" that

> A poem should be equal to:
> Not true

to get a sense of the gamut of perspectives on poetry and truth available to anyone with the inclination to investigate the matter. Although the dominant tenor of the conversation no doubt shifts across historical and cultural terrains, it cannot be said that a single position is associated with any given social context. It is the continuing existence of the debate, and not any particular position within it, that remains notable. Matthew Arnold's contemporary, Lord Kelvin, appears to have held little store in poetry, minimizing the truth-value of any representational language save numbers. During the 1920s, Owen Barfield participated in a sustained disagreement with C. S. Lewis over the relationship between the poetic imagination and truth. Briefly, Barfield argued that through the workings of poetic diction, the imagination was capable of coming to a perspective on truth by re-experiencing originary and unitary meanings of discourse that had been lost through the ascension of the prosaic and the loss of poetry over time. Lewis's position held truth to be only concrete reality, consistent and objective, in no wise created by the workings of the human imagination (see Adey 1979).

The ethical dimension of the search for representation creates one link between Hymes's ethnopoetic work and the Upleggers' missionary activities at San Carlos. The shared resonance with a history of exploring the proper relationship between an utterance's propositionality and its poeticity is another. I would like to clarify this resonance by exploring some overlapping concerns between ethnopoetics on the one hand and a number of medieval theories about the nature of poetic expression on the other. My choice to focus on this particular resonance is not arbitrary. Rather, I would argue, certain key medieval approaches to poetics share important features with the ethical dimensions of both Hymesian and Lutheran understandings of the import of poetic form. For example, the uniting of syntax, rhetoric, and poetics under the heading of "eloquence" that I attributed to Hymes's ethnopoetic project in an earlier section of this essay was borrowed from the description of the higher arts by the twelfth-century monk Domenico Gundisalvi, and Hymes (1972, 56) noted a relationship between his idea of communicative competence and the relationship between grammar and rhetoric in classical antiquity.[26] By a similar token, Hymes's focus on the role of Jakobsonian equivalences in the crafting of poetic utterances and on recurring numbers such as two and four in the lining-out of Native American narrative texts echoes art historian Henri Focillon's interpretation of the significance of Gothic cathedrals: "A considered arrangement of symmetries and repetitions, a law of numbers, a kind of music of symbols silently co-ordinate these vast encyclopedias of stone" (1963, quoted in Eco 1986, 61–62).

The swath of time and place known as the Middle Ages similarly witnessed a wide range of perspectives on poetry and truth. Conrad of Hirschau, a twelfth-century Benedictine monk, in this sense evinces a "modern" perspective, resonant with Lewis and MacLeish, finding the poet to craft fiction "because he either speaks falsehood instead of truth or mingles the true with the false" (in Eco 1986, 106). In a move that resonates with the Upleggers' distinction between "true" and "fable" stories, Conrad further subdivided these "creative" writers into pagan and Christian. Without the revealed truth of Christianity, the pagan poets could only express truth as if by accident, or inspiration. For his part, Aquinas in the late thirteenth century referred to poetry as "inferior learning" and argued, following a Platonic line, that "poetic matters cannot be grasped by the human reason 'because of their intrinsic lack of truth'" (in Eco 1986, 105). About a half century on, however, Albertino Mussato upended Aquinas's aesthetics and theology by giving primacy to the truths contained in poetic imagery and metaphor over the truths of logical syllogism. Since Mussato was a statesman, playwright, and poet, this shift may well echo a shift in power from monastery to court, and from Latin to the vernacular, as well as new demands made on rhetorical skill in early Renaissance Italy. In the fifteenth century the Spanish court musician Juan Alfonso de Baena, in the prologue to his *Cancionero*, valorized poetry as offering knowledge as valuable as that set forth by the great philosopher Aristotle. This valorization of poetics also implied an ethical reordering of the hierarchical relationship between pagan and Christian poets and philosophers. Yet the simultaneity of multiple perspectives on the relationship of poetry and truth can be seen in the fact that Conrad of Hirschau's early division between truthful and fictive genres, and between Christian and pagan authors, set a curricular agenda for the teaching of Latin that Walter Ong (1959) analyzed as a male rite of passage lasting well into the Renaissance, if not beyond: poetry was for children; philosophy, theology, law, and medicine for adults.

Like medieval aesthetic theorists, the Upleggers and Hymes shared a focus on an organic relationship between part and whole. For the Lutherans, this was manifest in the narrative of salvation, but also contributed to the construction of sermon texts, so that when the speaker reached his conclusion it would appear as a transparent and inevitable consequence of the materials presented in the preceding oration. For Hymes, beauty lay in proportion or, as Aquinas put it, in the tripartite relationships of Integrity, Proportion, and Clarity. Like Aquinas, both Hymes and the Upleggers wedded this sense of proportion to an exacting and rigorous analysis—of line segments for Hymes, of perfect translational equivalents for the Upleggers. For both, as for Aquinas and many other medieval aesthetic theorists, the purpose of such rigor was the discovery of intelligibility: the importance of form was that it be intelligible form. Human sensitivity to beauty, as Hugh of St. Victor had it, was "directed ultimately at the discovery of intelligible beauty" (Eco 1986, 57). More importantly, for all three, the truths uncovered by an exacting analysis carried moral and ethical implications, as experienced in the new organizations of texts presented by Hymes and by Francis Uplegger. For Hymes, certainly, disregard for or distortion of an oral performance's underlying proportions had led to inaccurate and arguably untruthful representations by other researchers.

Like the products of medieval poetics, these new presentations faced the challenge of relating spoken utterance and written text. Estimates of literacy rates in medieval Europe are uniformly miniscule. Furthermore, as a discourse practice, reading itself was not the solitary, silent activity it is commonly framed as today, but a practice of reciting text aloud: "Meaning passed from mouth to ear; transmission was a vocal monopoly" (Zumthor 1992, 19). Medieval textuality overlaps with poetic performance, utterance and enunciation appearing to be similarly inseparable, voice and gesture similarly embossed onto text. Thus medieval poetics shared a challenge with the scribal practices of ethnopoetics and missionary translation. By what means does the recorder or interpreter commit intelligible oral form to written representation without corrupting that intelligibility?[27]

One need not posit an intimate understanding of Hymes's personal background as necessary to explain these links. They percolate up from the mixture of Christian exegesis and attention to the

problems of referential and expressive import in performance seen in
the prominent place medievalism held in twentieth-century arts and
letters. As well, the figure of medievalism reveals an additional trace
of the ethical discourse surrounding the fate of poetry and humanity
in the twentieth century. Some would say, in fact, that modernity was
heralded by T. S. Eliot's inversion of the opening lines of Chaucer's
Canterbury Tales at the beginning of *The Waste Land*.[28] Norman Cantor
(1991) has written that the prominent literary medievalists J. R. R.
Tolkien and C. S. Lewis "used the Middle Ages for therapeutic purposes," that is, as a cure for the disillusionments of industrialization,
capitalism, and the new horrors of modern warfare—what folklorist
Timothy Evans (1988) has called "folklore as utopia."[29] This circulation
of medievalism crucially focused on the poetic and expressive arts,
for example in the emerging popularity of "early music" performance
and a scholarly response to new media that valorized the utterance as
an act of the whole and creative person performing face-to-face in the
small-scale folkloric community. The ethical and political dimensions
of this resistance to the bureaucratization of modernity was early and
sharply drawn in Rousseau's ([1762] 1997, 121) critique of the modern
representative state: "When, among the happiest people in the world,
bands of peasants are seen regulating affairs of State under an oak,
and always acting wisely, can we help scorning the ingenious methods
of other nations, which make themselves illustrious and wretched with
so much art and mystery?" In short, the waters that gave us *The Lord
of the Rings*, the Deller Consort, the orality/literacy theories of Ong
and McLuhan—as well as the validation of non-Western, nonliterate
expressive forms that marks the twinned anxious and celebratory
discourses of twentieth century anthropology, folklore, and ethnomusicology (Feld 2000)—were arguably drawn from the same stream.

A fuller accounting of these eddies and crosscurrents might un-
tangle the thorny relationship between these authors, their theories
of poetics, and their Christian ethics. Ong, McLuhan, and Tolkien, for
example, all professed Roman Catholicism, and Lewis was a member of
the Church of England. Like W. H. Auden, Lewis had reconverted after
an extended period of atheism. Untangling this history would indeed
complicate matters, for it would thereby be substantially more difficult
to argue that the modern disassembly of utterance and enunciation
is predicated on an undifferentiated "Christian" ideology of poetics
and expression.[30] Keane (2007) touches on this in his discussion of

the distinctions between Catholic and Calvinist attitudes regarding prayer books, for example.

Conclusion

In this essay I have argued that Hymes's ethnopoetic project enables analysis of poetic and rhetorical forms undergoing the stresses of post-colonial expropriation and missionary influence. On the one hand, this is because an ethnopoetic approach helps us observe these stresses and shifts through uncovering the rhetorical design of missionary texts purported to be transparent presentations of truth. On the other, it is due to the long-standing dialogue in Western-Christian philosophies about the proper relations between the competing propositional and poetic values of an utterance. The ethical dimensions of this dialogue and its place in an argument about proper human relations within contexts social, natural, and supernatural relate the ethnopoetic and Lutheran missionary perspectives both to each other and to a history of Christian discourse ethics that I sketched out briefly in discussing medieval poetic theory.

The two versions of the 1964 Easter sermon by Alfred Uplegger and Fergus Sneezy contain clear distinctions of poetic and rhetorical strategy. They present differing schemas for the organization of experience and forge different ways of expressing one's ethical humanity. At the same time, however, it would be premature to assume that what we have compared are, on the one hand, an example derived from European, American or English Christian discourse forms and, on the other, an example derived from Apache, non-Christian discourse forms. It may be as plausible to argue that the forms of speech embodied in Apache sermon interpretations were unique to church contexts and other Christian contexts for discourse and interaction. An expanded exploration of these contemporary genres might also account for the massive refraction that the lens of Lutheran missionary presence has likely had on traditional discourse forms in the San Carlos Apache community—not to mention other Christian denominations, including the enduring presence of Catholic theology brought by representatives of Spain in the sixteenth century.

For the Lutheran missionaries, language was problematic so long as it was inextricably linked with socialization practices that would lead speakers to poetic and expressive forms, such as "fable stories," deemed counter to the effective completion of missionary efforts. Meeting this challenge lay in separating the truth-value of the contents of a message from the formal poetic properties of circulating discourse, preserving the former but modifying the latter. For Hymes and those who followed him, on the other hand, a proposition and the material poetic form in which it is made manifest are inextricable, like annealed glass. And yet, as I have tried to demonstrate, both Hymesian ethnopoetics and the Lutheran missionary work of the Upleggers in San Carlos share roots in the ethical discourse of Christianity, encompassing debates on poetics, orality, performance, representation, and truth extending back to the Middle Ages.

Acknowledgments

This essay could not have come close to fruition without patient and productive dialogue with, and the expertise of, many people. I thank Paul Kroskrity and Anthony Webster for inviting me to participate in the session "Ethnopoetics, Narrative Inequality, and Voice: On the Legacy of Dell Hymes" at the 2011 American Anthropological Association meetings in Montreal, as well as the other panel participants and our two discussants. Louise Meintjes, Catherine Chin, and Tom Porcello encountered and helped me grapple with some of the earliest and most loosely formed versions of the ideas in this essay. Willem de Reuse, as well, has been a patient interlocutor through its multiple iterations and has always been generous in lending his ample knowledge of Apachean linguistics to this work. Anthony Webster and Marybeth Nevins read and offered cogent comments on earlier drafts of this essay. A grant from the American Philosophical Society allowed me to spend extended time with the Uplegger papers at the University of Arizona. The staff of the Special Collections division of the University Library were unstintingly helpful. New York University generously paid to transfer the audiotapes contained in the archive to digital media. Cathy Zell, librarian at the Wisconsin Lutheran Seminary in Mequon, helped fill in a number of blanks in Alfred Uplegger's biographical background. The editorial process at the *Journal of Folklore Research*—both editorial and readers' comments—helped me to hone my argument and organization significantly. Joycelene Johnson and Lambert Titla continue to be the models of patient and expert language teachers and consultants they have ever been. All errors remain the sole responsibility of the author.

Notes

1. The Francis J. Uplegger Papers are curated by the Special Collections Department of the Library at the University of Arizona in Tucson. Its five linear feet comprise school records, correspondence, Apache language materials, translations of Old and New Testament texts, and sermon notes and texts. Two boxes contain unarranged audio recordings of church services and other missionary activities of the Uplegger family, dating from the mid-1950s and for about a decade thereafter. The bulk of the Uplegger material discussed in this essay is taken from this archival collection.

2. A mediating figure between the Lutheran approach to truth and the Hymesian approach to poetics, thereby, is something akin to Austin's performative utterances, which would bring the socially mediated world into existence through the assertion of certain kinds of truths in appropriate social contexts for their felicitous completion.

3. Indeed we might say, with Hans-Georg Gadamer (1986b, 131), that "this fruitful tension between poetry and philosophy, is hardly a problem of our immediate or recent history alone, for it has all along accompanied the path of Western thought, which is distinguished from all oriental wisdom precisely by virtue of having to sustain this tension."

4. By Gadamer's (1986b, 136) model, "in general, our [everyday] speech acquires meaningful determinacy and clarity from a living context that is concretely realized in a situation in which we are addressed. The word spoken in such a concrete and pragmatic context does not simply stand for itself: in fact it does not 'stand' at all, but on the contrary, passes over into what is said."

5. I take the term *poeticity* from Roman Jakobson's famous essay, "Poetry of Grammar and Grammar of Poetry" (1981). Indeed, Jakobson (1981, 750) places the value of poeticity at the core of what makes an utterance poetic. "Only when a verbal work acquires poeticity, a poetic function of determinative significance, can we speak of poetry. . . . Poeticity is present when the word is felt as a word and not a mere representation of the object being named or an outburst of emotion, when words and their composition, their meaning, their external and inner form acquire a weight and value of their own instead of referring indifferently to reality."

6. For more on the relationship between Hymes's ethnography of communication and Burke's literary criticism, see Johnstone and Marcellino 2010.

7. Recent work on the circulation of poetic and narrative forms (Prasad 2007), especially as they are implicated in new forms of mediation and listening (Gray 2007; Hirschkind 2009; Miller 2007), has foregrounded this ethical dimension of socially circulating discourse more overtly, although not necessarily by following a path laid down by Hymes.

8. Temporal adverbial phrases and other syntactic markers of line and scene, on which Hymes focused, are additional tools for coherence. Dennis Tedlock (1983) noted pause structure as an organizing principle of discourse, as well as, for instance, inversions of intonational patterns that crosscut multiple speech genres in Zuni, from greetings to prayers. Don Brenneis and Laura Lein (1977) noted how children's schoolyard arguments taught their participants rhyme, assonance, and timing. Joel Sherzer and Anthony C. Woodbury (1987) treat poetic and rhetorical forms as collections of discourse features, logically independent

but mutually influential and indexical of particular genres. Work has emphasized the ways in which nonsemantic features of discourse tend to produce the coherence of an utterance, but Stephen Booth (1998) asserts that these other forms of organization—for instance, grammatical parallelism, clause endings, repetition, breath pauses, patterns of metrical stress, and vocal qualities—often interfere or compete with the purported meaning of the referential text.

9. This goes along with a general Protestant distrust of pomp and ceremony. Webb Keane (2007) explores this ideology in depth with regard to the Calvinist movement.

10. In the 1920s the Federal Government constructed Coolidge Dam at the confluence of the Gila and San Carlos Rivers, and San Carlos—now known as Old San Carlos—was covered over by the gathering reservoir behind the dam. The residents of the town were relocated to Rice, which was renamed San Carlos.

11. Norbert Manthe (1994) notes the arrival of Paul Mayerhoff in 1896, Karl Guenther and Rudolph Jens in 1900, Otto Schoenberg in 1902, Reinhold Kutz in 1903, Henry Hasse in 1904, Gustav Harders in 1905, Emil Recknagel in 1907, Irmgard Harders in 1908, E. Edgar Guenther in 1911, Karl Rotter and Karl Toepel in 1912, Adolf Zuberier in 1913, and H. G. Gurgel in 1914.

12. Joëlle Proust (1989) traces the emergence of this conviction to Kant, with important station stops at Bolzano and Carnap.

13. Alfred Uplegger's educational career was complicated. He was at Lawrence College in Appleton, Wisconsin (where many classes were conducted in German) from 1907–10 but did not graduate. In 1914, he enrolled in the Wisconsin Lutheran Seminary in Mequon, but again did not graduate, his volunteering for service to the Apaches taking precedence. He may have attended Northwestern College in Watertown in the interim. An undated class schedule contains the following courses: "Evol.," "Biol.," "Latin," "Art," "Hist.," "Phil.," "Choral," "Art App.," "Greek," "Lab.," and "Gym."

14. Following is a key to the transcription conventions used in this essay. Line breaks in the transcript are made at pause junctures. The line numbers on the left margin attempt to indicate rhetorical structuring of the strip of discourse, organized as "theme" (designated by Roman numerals), "subtopic" (lower-case letters), and "line" (Arabic numerals). That is, II.b.4 thus indicates the fourth line (delimited by pause break) of the second subtopic of the second theme (both of these delimited by rhetorical or narrative structure). These two should combine to aid the reader in understanding a speaker's coordination, in performance, between discourse features and representational features of an oration. In addition, in this first transcription, I have used boldface type to indicate stress-pattern—a compromise, as I have indicated in the text, between wanting to note stress and not wanting to alienate those readers unfamiliar with musical notation.

15. For example, viewing lines II.a.1 and II.a.2 in the phonetics analysis software Praat (http://www.fon.hum.uva.nl/praat/), the vowel segments of "this," "great-," and "all" hover around a pitch of 240 Hz, between the A-sharp and B below middle C. The /u/ of "true," in distinction, jumps to around 280 Hz, or between the C-sharp and D above middle C.

16. Uplegger's notes, shown in Figure 1, appear to say that this is a translation of 2 Timothy 3:15, but the text is verse 16.

17. This preference for the overtly descriptive when more metaphorical means of translation are available in source or target languages raises a chicken-and-egg

question with regard to Apache being considered by Athabaskanists of many stripes to be "a descriptive language."

18. I do not mean to imply here that the missionaries necessarily substituted a previously nonexistent meaning. It may well be that the use of *ch'inii* as a metapragmatic frame for 'gossip' has always existed, and the missionaries made use of the association. For an outline of San Carlos Apache evidentials and shifting use of narrative particles, see de Reuse 2003.

19. This includes the musical meter of a hymn, generally a strong pulse followed by two weaker pulses (3/4 time), or a strong pulse followed by three weaker pulses (4/4 or "common" time). The structure of each verse, as well, tends to follow a symmetrical pattern of eight measures leading from the tonic or home key to the dominant or fifth degree of the scale; followed by a complementary eight measures leading back to the tonic. These eight-measure halves are often symmetrical in design as well, divisible into complementary halves of four measures each.

20. This was likely Norman Genoway, a San Carlos tribal member who was active in the Lutheran church as interpreter and congregant until his death.

21. Francis Uplegger, who would have sermonized in Apache himself, followed by his son Alfred's sermon in English, passed away in June of 1964 at the age of 97. Easter Sunday that year was on March 29, so he may have already taken ill.

22. In the King James Version of the New Testament (the English text used in Uplegger's sermon), Matthew 28:2 says that "the angel of the Lord" was at the tomb of Jesus; Mark 16:5 calls this figure "a young man . . . clothed in a long white garment"; Luke 24:4 refers to "two men . . . in shining garments"; and John 20:12 reads "two angels in white." Uplegger referred to the Luke passage in his sermon, clarifying for his congregation that the "two men" were "angels."

23. The place-name Iłch'ideeł golzeeyú ('at the place called Iłch'ideeł') proved difficult to interpret. One language expert with whom I consulted rendered it as 'the place of separation', possibly referring to Hell. This would make sense in the context of the theme of the Easter sermon. A second person, though, concluded that it referred to 'a place between heaven and hell', and not Hell itself. A third interpreted it as 'judgment day', observing that it referenced not a place where one has suffered separation, but a place where the process of separating and sorting out would occur.

24. The notion of experiencing past events as if they have occurred in the present is a trope that crosscuts a number of Apache discourse domains. I explore this more fully in Samuels 2004.

25. Music philosopher Michael Szekely discusses how the modern rise of "absolute music" caused "a crisis in the notion of philosophical truth itself." He cites Andrew Bowie's *Aesthetics and Subjectivity*: "From a union of music and language, where language is the senior partner, emerges (with the advent of modernism) a divorce, in which the formerly junior partner becomes autonomous and is no longer bound to represent what a verbal text can express. . . . A potential fundamental change in the idea of truth is the result. . . . If music without words is a higher form than music with words, then music seems able to usurp the word's role as the locus of truth" (Szekely 2001, 1).

26. Gundisalvi (ca. 1105–ca. 1181) was archdeacon of Cuellar and a scholastic philosopher. As such, he oversaw the translation into Latin of a great deal of Arabic scientific knowledge. My thanks to Marybeth Nevins for directing me to the quote from Hymes.

27. In this light it is perhaps unsurprising that Hymes's approach to poetics would have found receptive homes among those who study medieval poetic genres as well as those who continue to work in the field of oral-formulaic composition (Doane 1994; Mitchell 2001; Reichl 2012).

28. Chaucer and Eliot both open their poems in April: "Whan that aprill with his shoures soote/The droghte of march hath perced to the roote"; and "April is the cruellest month, breeding/Lilacs out of the dead land, mixing/Memory and desire, stirring/Dull roots with spring rain."

29. The specter of modern warfare also influenced changing ideas of cultural relativism. Whereas earlier versions of cultural relativism maintained a hierarchy between primitive and modern, the detonation of atomic weapons to end World War II caused a number of mid-century social critics (e.g., Stuart Chase, Dwight MacDonald) to reexamine the idea that "modern" peoples were necessarily more civilized than "primitive" peoples. In a review of Stanley Diamond's *In Search of the Primitive*, Hymes (1979, 491) noted that "even a militant for equality such as Franz Boas . . . and others [e.g. Edward Sapir, Stith Thompson] did not doubt the broad contrast 'primitive' and 'civilized'." Following World War II, Hymes observed, "the contrast was rechristened 'modern' and 'traditional,' 'developed' and 'undeveloped.'"

30. Father Jules Jetté (Jetté and Jones 2000), for example, cited a number of translation choices for theological and spiritual concepts that distinguish Catholic interactions with Koyukon speakers in Alaska from those of the Episcopal Church.

References Cited

Abrahams, Roger. 2005. *Everyday Life: A Poetics of Vernacular Practices*. Philadelphia: University of Pennsylvania Press.

Adey, Lionel. 1979. *C. S. Lewis's "Great War" with Owen Barfield*. Victoria, British Columbia: University of Victoria Press.

Arnold, Matthew. (1879) 1922. "Wordsworth." In *Selected Poems of William Wordsworth*, edited by Harrison Ross Steeves, 1–22. New York: Harcourt, Brace.

Bolliger, Dwight. 1989. *Intonation and Its Uses: Melody in Grammar and Discourse*. Stanford, CA: Stanford University Press.

Booth, Stephen. 1998. *Precious Nonsense: The Gettysburg Address, Ben Jonson's Epitaphs on his Children, and Twelfth Night*. Berkeley: University of California Press.

Brenneis, Donald, and Laura Lein. 1977. "You Fruithead: A Sociolinguistic Approach to Dispute Settlement." In *Child Discourse*, edited by Susan Ervin-Tripp and Claudia Mitchell-Kernan, 49–65. New York: Academic Press.

Bullis, Lon. 1924. "'Good Talk' by Dajida: About False Worship and True Worship." *Apache Scout* 2 (3): 3–4.

Burke, Kenneth. 1966. *Language as Symbolic Action: Essays on Life, Literature, and Method*. Berkeley: University of California Press.

Cantor, Norman F. 1991. *Inventing the Middle Ages: The Lives, Works, and Ideas of the Great Medievalists of the Twentieth Century*. New York: William Morrow.

de Reuse, Willem J. 2003. "Evidentiality in Western Apache." In *Studies in Evidentiality*, edited by Alexandra Y. Aikhenvald and R. M. W. Dixon, 79–100. Amsterdam: John Benjamins.

Doane, A. Nicholas. 1994. "The Ethnography of Scribal Writing and Anglo-Saxon Poetry: Scribe as Performer." *Oral Tradition* 9 (2): 420–39.

Duranti, Alessandro. 1997. "Universal and Culture-Specific Properties of Greetings." *Journal of Linguistic Anthropology* 7 (1): 63–97.

Eco, Umberto. 1986. *Art and Beauty in the Middle Ages.* New Haven, CT: Yale University Press.

Ethelbah, Paul, Genevieve Ethelbah, and M. Eleanor Nevins. 2012. "Ndah Ch'ii'n." In *Inside Dazzling Mountains: Southwest Native Verbal Arts,* edited by David L. Kozak, 197–239. Lincoln: University of Nebraska Press.

Evans, Timothy. 1988. "Folklore as Utopia: English Medievalists and the Ideology of Revivalism." *Western Folklore* 47 (4): 245–68.

Feld, Steven. 2000. "A Sweet Lullaby for World Music." *Public Culture* 12 (1): 145–71.

Gadamer, Hans-Georg. 1986a. "Composition and Interpretation." In *The Relevance of the Beautiful and Other Essays,* 66–73. Cambridge: Cambridge University Press.

———. 1986b. "Philosophy and Poetry." In *The Relevance of the Beautiful and Other Essays,* 131–39. Cambridge: Cambridge University Press.

Gray, Lila E. 2007. "Memories of Empire, Mythologies of the Soul: Fado Performance and the Shaping of Saudade." *Ethnomusicology* 51 (1): 106–30.

Guenther, E. Edgar. 1927. "Native Workers." *Apache Scout* 5 (2): 7.

Hanks, William F. 2010. *Converting Words: Maya in the Age of the Cross.* Berkeley: University of California Press.

Heidegger, Martin. 1971. "A Dialogue on Language." In *On the Way to Language,* 1–54. New York: Harper Collins.

Hirschkind, Charles. 2009. *The Ethical Soundscape: Cassette Sermons and Islamic Counterpublics.* New York: Columbia University Press.

Hoenecke, Edgar. 1984. "The End of an Epoch on the Apache Indian Mission: Alfred M. Uplegger (1892–1984) and Henry E. Rosin (1892–1982)." *WELS Historical Institute Journal* 2 (2): 33–44.

Hoijer, Harry. 1938. *Chiricahua and Mescalero Apache Texts.* Chicago: University of Chicago Press.

Hymes, Dell. 1962. "The Ethnography of Speaking." In *Anthropology and Human Behavior,* edited by Thomas Gladwin and William C. Sturtevant, 13–53. Washington, DC: Anthropological Society of Washington.

———. 1972. "On Communicative Competence." In *Sociolinguistics,* edited by J. B. Pride and Janet Holmes, 269–85. Harmondsworth, UK: Penguin.

———. 1979. "Review of Stanley Diamond, *In Search of the Primitive: A Critique of Civilization.*" *Journal of American Folklore* 92 (366): 491–92.

———. 1981. *"In Vain I Tried to Tell You": Essays in Native American Poetics.* Philadelphia: University of Pennsylvania Press.

———. 1985. "Language, Memory, and Selective Performance: Cultee's 'Salmon's Myth' as Twice Told to Boas." *Journal of American Folklore* 98 (390): 391–434.

———. 1986. "The General Epistle of James." *International Journal of the Sociology of Language* 62:75–103.

———. 1996. *Ethnography, Linguistics, Narrative Inequality: Toward an Understanding of Voice.* London: Taylor and Francis.

Ide, Risako. 1998. "Small Talk and the Presentation of 'Self' in American Public Discourse." *Sociolinguistics Journal of Korea* 6 (2): 31–50.

Jakobson, Roman. 1981. "Poetry of Grammar and Grammar of Poetry." In *Selected Writings,* 3:87–97. The Hague: Mouton de Gruyter.

Jetté, Jules, and Eliza Jones. 2000. *Koyukon Athabaskan Dictionary.* Edited by James Kari. Fairbanks: Alaska Native Language Center, University of Alaska.

Johnstone, Barbara, and William M. Marcellino. 2010. "Dell Hymes and the Ethnography of Communication." In *The Sage Handbook of Sociolinguistics*, edited by Ruth Wodak, Barbara Johnstone, and Paul Kerswill, 57–67. London: Sage.

Keane, Webb. 2007. *Christian Moderns: Freedom and Fetish in the Mission Encounter.* Berkeley: University of California Press.

Kessel, William. n.d. "Paul Mayerhoff in Apacheland." Manuscript. Photocopy in possession of the author.

Leff, Michael. 1986. "Textual Criticism: The Legacy of G. P. Mohrmann." *Quarterly Journal of Speech* 72 (4): 377–89.

Luther, Martin. (1525) 1958. "Against the Heavenly Prophets in the Matter of Images and Sacraments." In *Luther's Works, Volume 40, Church and Ministry*, edited by Conrad Begendorff and translated by Bernhard Erling, 77–223. Minneapolis: Fortress.

MacLeish, Archibald. 1985. *Collected Poems 1917–1982*. Boston: Mariner Books, Houghton Mifflin.

Manthe, Norbert M. 1994. "Missionaries and Teachers Called to Serve in Apacheland During Its First Century as a Mission Field 1893–1993." Wisconsin Evangelical Lutheran Synod, Milwaukee, Wisconsin. http://www.wlsessays.net/node/2885.

Miller, Flagg. 2007. *The Moral Resonance of Arab Media: Audiocassette Poetry and Culture in Yemen.* Cambridge, MA: Harvard University Press.

Mitchell, Stephen A. 2001. "Performance and Norse Poetry: The Hydromel of Praise and the Effluvia of Scorn." *Oral Tradition* 16 (1): 168–202.

Nevins, M. Eleanor. 2010. "The Bible in Two Keys: Traditionalism and Evangelical Christianity on the Fort Apache Reservation." *Language and Communication* 30:19–32.

Ong, Walter J. 1959. "Latin Language Study as a Renaissance Puberty Rite." *Studies in Philology* 56 (2): 103–24.

Palmer, Gus, Jr. 2003. *Telling Stories the Kiowa Way.* Tucson: University of Arizona Press.

Peckham, Morse. 1977. "The Infinitude of Pluralism." *Critical Inquiry* 3 (4): 803–16.

Plocher, Naomi M. 2004. "Holding Up the Prophet's Hands: Anna Dowidat Plocher, A Missionary Wife in the 1890's." *WELS Historical Institute Journal* 22 (1): 24–45.

Prasad, Leela. 2007. *Poetics of Conduct: Oral Narrative and Moral Being in a South Indian Town.* New York: Columbia University Press.

Proust, Joëlle. 1989. *Questions of Form: Logic and the Analytic Proposition from Kant to Carnap.* Translated by Anastasios Albert Brenner. Minneapolis: University of Minnesota Press.

Reichl, Karl, ed. 2012. *Medieval Oral Literature.* Berlin: Walter de Gruyter.

Rosin, Henry E. 1966. "Rankin Rogers." *Apache Lutheran*, June, 2–4.

Rousseau, Jean-Jacques. (1762) 1997. "Of the Social Contract." In *The Social Contract and Other Later Political Writings*, vol. 2, edited by Victor Gourevitch, 39–152. Cambridge: Cambridge University Press.

Samuels, David. 2004. *Putting a Song on Top of It: Expression and Identity on the San Carlos Apache Reservation.* Tucson: University of Arizona Press.

Schieffelin, Bambi B. 2007. "Found in Translating: Reflexive Language across Time and Texts." In *Consequences of Contact: Language Ideologies and Sociocultural*

Transformations in Pacific Societies, edited by Miki Makihara and Bambi B. Schieffelin, 140–65. New York: Oxford University Press.

———. 2008. "Tok Bokis, Tok Piksa: Translating Parables in Papua New Guinea." In *Social Lives in Language—Sociolinguistics and Multilingual Speech Communities: Celebrating the Work of Gillian Sankoff,* edited by Miriam Meyerhoff and Naomi Nagy, 111–34. Amsterdam: John Benjamins.

Sherzer, Joel, and Anthony C. Woodbury, eds. 1987. *Native American Discourse: Poetics and Rhetoric.* Cambridge: Cambridge University Press.

Snowden, James H. 1910. *The World a Spiritual System: An Outline of Metaphysics.* New York: Macmillan.

Steedly, Mary Margaret. 1996. "The Importance of Proper Names: Language and 'National' Identity in Colonial Karoland." *American Anthropologist* 23 (3): 447–75.

Szekely, Michael. 2011. "Jazz Naked Fire Gesture: Improvisation as Surrealism." *Papers of Surrealism* 9:1–12.

Tannen, Deborah. 1998. "'Oh Talking Voice That Is So Sweet': The Poetic Nature of Conversation." *Social Research* 65 (3): 631–51.

Tedlock, Dennis. 1983. *The Spoken Word and the Work of Interpretation.* Philadelphia: University of Pennsylvania Press.

Uplegger, Alfred. 1964. "Easter." Francis J. Uplegger Papers, MS 299, Special Collections, University of Arizona Libraries, box 8, tape 22.

———. n.d. "The Subject of an Oration." Francis J. Uplegger Papers, MS 299, Special Collections, University of Arizona Libraries, box 1, folder 3.

Uplegger, Francis. 1924. "Grains from Rice. Has the Bible Been Changed?" *Apache Scout* 2 (2): 5.

———. n.d.a. Notes for sermon on 2 Timothy. Francis J. Uplegger Papers, MS 299, Special Collections, University of Arizona Libraries, box 5, folder 3.

———. n.d.b. "Thesaurus of Apache Language Forms." Unplublished manuscript, photocopy in possession of the author.

Valéry, Paul. 1954. "Poetry and Abstract Thought." Translated by Charles Guenther. *Kenyon Review* 16 (2): 208–233.

Watt, Eva Tulene, and Keith H. Basso. 2004. *Don't Let the Sun Step over You: A White Mountain Apache Family Life, 1860–1975.* Tucson: University of Arizona Press.

Wells, Evelyn Kendrick. 1950. *The Ballad Tree: A Study of British and American Ballads, Their Folklore, Verse, and Music.* New York: Ronald Press.

Zolbrod, Paul G. 1995. *Reading the Voice: Native American Oral Poetry on the Page.* Salt Lake City: University of Utah Press.

Zumthor, Paul. 1992. *Toward a Medieval Poetics.* Translated by Philip Bennett. Minneapolis: University of Minnesota Press.

DAVID W. SAMUELS, Associate Professor of Music and Director of the Native Studies Forum at New York University, is the author of *Putting a Song on Top of It: Expression and Identity on the San Carlos Apache Reservation* (2004). His work specializes in music and language, and vernacular modernities.

10 Contested Mobilities: On the Politics and Ethnopoetics of Circulation

LIKE FRANZ BOAS and Edward Sapir, Dell Hymes connected linguistic anthropology with social/cultural anthropology. The terms he coined and the perspectives he advanced drew on wider anthropological perspectives, thus bringing linguistic anthropologists into larger conversations and enabling work in linguistic anthropology to gain greater visibility among colleagues with different subdisciplinary allegiances. I would argue that this is precisely the move that has long fostered new spurts of creativity within the subdiscipline and greater visibility for linguistic anthropologists. Work on performance inaugurated in the 1970s by Hymes (1981) and Richard Bauman (1977) energized not only anthropology but also linguistics, communication, and literary studies; the cross-fertilization between linguistic anthropology and folkloristics at this juncture was crucial, as has been true at other points as well. Ideologies of language (Kroskrity 2000; Schieffelin et al. 1998) suddenly transported linguistic anthropology from the relative doldrums of the 1980s to a period when new positions opened up and anthropologists came to see that linguistic anthropologists had a great deal to offer to studies on such topics as colonialism (Hanks 2010; Irvine 2001; Keane 2007), media anthropology (Spitulnik 2002), and more. A crucial feature of these points of intersection is that they did not simply "borrow" from adjacent fields but critically revised concepts in social/cultural anthropology as well as assumptions underpinning linguistic anthropology.

We are, I would argue, at precisely another juncture where a shot of epistemological energy would be particularly valuable. A number of linguistic anthropologists have recently taken on issues that are of interest to other anthropologists by focusing on race, racism, and anti-immigrant discourses (Blommaert and Verschueren 1998;

Hill 2008; Mendoza-Denton 2008), therapeutic regimes (Briggs and Mantini-Briggs 2003; Carr 2011; Dick and Wirtz 2011), globalization (Blommaert 2010), and how languages, linguistic practices, and constructions of language get commodified in neoliberal market schemes (Duchene and Heller 2012). Rather than take up objects framed as "new," these essays by Gerald L. Carr and Barbra Meek, Sean Patrick O'Neill, and David W. Samuels engage a traditional focus of Americanist linguistic anthropology—ethnopoetics—thus requiring a different strategy for building dialogues with other anthropological issues and perspectives. Recently, a great deal of work by anthropologists and other social scientists has focused on circulation and mobility, and here, I think, is a way to extend issues raised by these essays and articulate what they can offer to scholars of other stripes.

Problematizing Circulation and (Im)Mobility

It would be easy to point to stimuli for a shift in emphasis from how cultures inhabit spaces to how they travel, to use the terms posed in James Clifford's (1997) *Routes*. Certainly Arjun Appadurai's (1996) work on globalization and influential reformulations by Saskia Sassen (2006), Aihwa Ong (Ong and Collier 2005), and Ana Tsing (2005) have been important here. For people who think about language and performativity, Jacques Derrida's critique of what he characterized as the analytical limits of J. L. Austin's (1962) "total speech situation" was important. Derrida ([1972] 1977, 40) sought to locate performativity not in originary acts of speaking but in iterative movements in which "something new takes place." Discourse, he suggested, is neither free floating nor locked in contexts. John Urry's (2007) work suggested, however, that mobility is not an intrinsic property of words, images, technologies, bodies, and so forth; such phenomena as walking, bicycles, cars, and airplanes have come to be seen as immanent embodiments of mobility because of the broad transformations of bodies, landscapes, the built environment, and social relations that enabled them. Urry reminded us that the same processes produce forms of *im*mobility simultaneously.

Geoffrey Bowker and Susan Leigh Star (1999) suggest that in the case of diagnostic categories and statistics, producing mobility involves two contradictory processes. First, particular practices, epistemologies, and technologies must be employed in order to enable objects, cultural forms, and other entities to inhabit particular sites. At each location through which they circulate, texts, objects, narratives, and the like get connected indexically to features of these assemblages at the same time that they performatively reshape them, albeit generally in minute ways. Bowker and Star suggest that in order to move on to other sites, however, dimensions of the complex indexical histories generated at each site must be erased. Some actors, interests, languages, conflicts, technologies, and the like must disappear; of the stuff that circulates, some features become figures and others part of the background, some get referentially coded while others are lodged in nonreferential features. Reception, of course, further complicates this process, as some people who get interpellated down the line know enough of the indexical histories to infer elements that have been erased while others are unable to decode even foregrounded elements.

Work in anthropology, science-technology-society (STS) studies, and other areas on circulation thus suggests a number of points. First, scholars often seem to imbibe a sort of naive neoliberal Darwinism of cultural forms and objects, including languages, narratives, and texts—the sense that people always want them to move as far, as fast, as freely, and as long as possible, which Greg Urban (2001) refers to as a metaculture of modernity. Second, mobility is not intrinsic but imbued through complex processes that involve forms of silencing and erasure. Third, forms, objects, and the like do not move evenly or naturally, like water flowing downhill, but, as Tsing (2005) suggests, travel through particular sorts of grooves or channels and often encounter resistance along the way. Fourth, making mobility involves creating immobility; as with secrets and gossip, people are sometime more interested in limiting or stopping circulation than in inducing it. Fifth, people construct cultural or ideological models of circulation at the same time that they engage in complex circulatory practices. Although we may reify our models as faithful maps of how things are actually moving, the two are never identical; here we encounter anew the questions of metapragmatics and pragmatics and of language ideologies that linguistic anthropologists have analyzed so extensively. One final point: scholars have no privileged or disinterested position here; when we construct cartographies of circulation and mobility, we are just as caught up in these processes as anyone else, just as much at the mercy of our own models of mobility and techniques of (im)mobilization.

Recirculating Ethnopoetics

Whence ethnopoetics? In a word, its study has long revealed the complexities of how processes of indexical embedding and making mobile are both invested in narratives. Exploring these processes in a richly ethnographic modality, the three essays in this section critique ways that received, generally implicit models of circulation impede our understanding of how narratives, texts, and languages circulate. They go on to suggest how narratives and translated sermons and language revitalization projects involve complex intersections between competing models and practices. My goal here is to draw attention to the insights they offer into broader questions of circulation and mobility, thereby hoping to increase their value for linguistic anthropologists and their ability to contribute to ways that other anthropologists and social scientists discuss these issues.

Sean Patrick O'Neill usefully repositions the translation of narratives from Northwestern California into the context of relations between Native American nations. His essay seems to suggest that some of the most famous work in the Americanist tradition was informed by a shallow model of circulation that led such scholars as Alfred Kroeber and Sapir to overestimate "the *uniformity* of the regional culture" rather than to see how the people they studied were as interested in imbuing cultural forms with immobility as with fostering their broad dissemination. O'Neill points to the Boasian roots of what he terms a "fidelity ideology," which culturally constructs a trajectory from "the original text" through inscription, translation, and publication, which sounds to me rather like what I have called the image of intertextual transparency (Briggs 1993). This model would lead us to expect that translation practices at least strive to maximize circulation.

O'Neill's ethnographic skill is revealed in the way he listened to his collaborators' refusals—both to translate entire texts as well as to "preserve" such details as the gender of characters. What emerges is a complex construction of circulation that refuses the dictates of a free market of cultural forms, if you will. O'Neill turned what must have been tense moments when translators refused to go along with the assigned task into pedagogical events in which his collaborators could teach him a variety of models and practices of circulation. These seemed to range between "wholesale adoption" to "parodic mimicry" to transformations of the gender identifications of characters to outright rejections of narratives. Reflecting on the way his consultants opened up competing models of circulation, O'Neill looks at other perspectives that problematize what we could call open-source, unrestricted-IP perspectives on the translation and the circulation of texts, especially those framed as religious or spiritual.

The origin stories for tales, songs, and "visible features of the world" that O'Neill's consultants provided were also origin stories of circulatory models, as embodied in such powerful characters as Coyote and Across-the-Ocean Widower. One might suspect that the grammatical properties he identifies, such as tense/aspect forms that projected the temporal contours of narrative events, might also have been modeling circulation as "ongoing, without a clear beginning or end" or, in other cases, as cutting off circulation in the distant past. At times, translators stopped the circulation process right in front of O'Neill's eyes. His discussion of how "speech taboos" posed obstacles to translation is perhaps the most suggestive in this regard. Here translators encountered boundary objects, to use a science studies term,[1] which seemed to suggest how selves, narratives, spaces, and languages were positioned on borders, a theme I will revisit below. And then comes the sucker punch: even as narratives sometimes become immobile, it is songs composed of what are often referred to as "nonsense syllables" that seemed to be designed for circulation across cultural and linguistic borders, "allowing members of each speech community to understand some of what is going on in any given performance."

Echoing the proposition that poetics provides "an implicit schema for the organization of experience" (Hymes 1996, 121), David W. Samuels takes us into a realm of experience that might be acutely uncomfortable for most anthropologists—Christian missionization. Here he traverses the bridge between poetics and social/cultural anthropology that Webb Keane (2007) opened up in *Christian Moderns*. Linguistic anthropologists may participate in Urban's (2001) metaculture of modernity yet at the same time have a bias for stable replication in the circulation of signs classified as traditional. This dual fetishization of circulatory motion can lead to too easy a jump from poetics to ethics, to viewing the imposition of obstacles to circulation as ethical violations; efforts to promote circulation thus become ipso facto confirmations of ethical sanctity. Linda Tuhiwai Smith (1999, 1–2) argues that "the word itself, 'research,' is probably one of the dirtiest words in the indigenous world's vocabulary," adding that it is always "embedded in multiple layers of imperial and colonial practices." Positioning oneself as a champion of traditional circulation thus seems to confer an ethically positive aura on situations where, as Smith suggests, any research project—even when carried out by indigenous researchers—is suspect.

Herein lies, in my view, the potential of Samuels's essay for stimulating rethinkings of both ethnopoetics and circulation. He traces practices of translation that many of his readers would probably like to see *fail*, bringing up the problematics of relationships between linguists and missionaries working in the same sites—and sometimes being one and the same person. By drawing attention to "poetic and rhetorical forms undergoing the stresses of postcolonial expropriation and missionary influence," his essay raises the specter of another form of relativity, which, adding to Whorfian and Hymes forms, I might term *colonial relativity*. I use this term to help us think about how different interpretations of the same forms may reflect their embeddedness in distinct experiences of colonial violence and expropriation. These indexical connections are not "post" (postcolonial) for many indigenous peoples, as Smith (1999, 98) suggests.

Colonial relativity emerges in how missionaries preaching to San Carlos Apaches also embraced, like anthropologists, notions of fidelity or intertextual transparency, similarly framing faux translations as ethical problems. Their focus was not, however, on the transformation of oral texts into written transcriptions and translations but of positioning Scripture in oral performances of sermons. Here transparency went hand-in-hand with the sort of anti-poetic poetics and anti-rhetorical rhetoric that would have made John Locke happy. Samuels explores medieval theories that tied ethics to achieving the proper relationship between poetics and truth, form and content. This discussion also points, I would suggest, to how these histories similarly tie ethical positioning and the politics of performativity to debates about circulation and mobility, about which discursive forms should circulate and which dimensions should be infused with mobility—poetics, logical content, or perfect proportional relations between the two.

In juxtaposing missionary Alfred Uplegger's 1964 Easter Sunday sermon and its translation by Fergus Sneezy, Samuels examines the juxtaposition of competing practices for circulating Christian texts. Suggesting that "Hymes consistently emphasized the culturally embedded nature of intersubjectivity in verbal practice," Samuels draws attention to the "circulation of culture" by detailing cultures of circulation (Lee and LiPuma 2003). He notes Hymes's statement that "the way that a mother speaks to a child contains as much poetry as the most elaborate ceremony." Hymes's (1981) analysis of the Clackamas narrative "Seal and her younger brother dwelt there" might suggest that how children talk back can reveal the importance of competing models of circulation, where insisting on unquestioning replication of the voice of custom and the shushing of efforts to disrupt it can have lethal effects. In the end, Hymes emerges less as an analytical voice that stands outside of history than as an advocate—alongside the Uplegger family, Sneezy, and medieval commentators—for particular perspectives on poetics and truth, practices of translation, and models of circulation.

The essay by Gerald L. Carr and Barbra Meek points to another site for enacting conflicting models of circulation. They extend Hymes's efforts to shift the camera angle, here actually turning it around, focusing less on "language loss" by Yukon aboriginal peoples than the ideologies of language, text, and circulation that shape interventions by linguists and educators into aboriginal language education and revitalization. Here, we might say, a confrontation between object-centered and process-centered models of circulation is evident. In the "rule of experts," to use Timothy Mitchell's (2002) phrase, the circulation of language over time and between generations requires the production of an object that can be exchanged—a text—resulting in a form of text-fetishism, extending Karl Marx's ([1887] 1967) "commodity fetishism," that seemed to dominate in many of the language revitalization projects they describe. What was missed in overlooking "the interactive dimension of storytelling"? Might Hymes's (1981) distinction between "report" and "performance" enter in here? Might the elders have been onto something?

The Yukon elders seemed to grasp problems of scale, a common focus in anthropology and STS, better than the "experts": modeling circulation in interaction might seem to project how it might occur over the longue durée, over lifetimes and generations. Real-time simulations might provide an aura that is lacking in reporting the existence of temporally- and socially-distanced narrative worlds. My allusion to Walter Benjamin (1968) is intentional here, although now I want to shift the focus from "The Work of Art in the Age of Mechanical Reproduction" to "The Storyteller." Benjamin warns about what happens to narrative transmission when it is severed from the material practices in which both the transmission and the performance of stories are embedded. In the eyes of language pedagogy experts, the mobility of language from place to place and generation to generation was centered in the materiality of easily transportable objects, texts; if everyone could just focus on these objects, their intrinsic mobility would guarantee circulation.

Elders, from what I can see, were highly attuned to the processes of erasure required by the production of texts and who controlled their circulation. They rather insisted on the centrality of performance—that is, on imbuing discourse with mobility by the online, real-time creation of new indexical histories. This, in turn, required metapragmatic calibration (Silverstein 1993) of a very specific sort, calibration of relationships between indexical histories and how narratives are embedded in them. Weaving displays of words and knowledge into preschool activities or tanning moose hides required calibrating how the circulation of cultural forms was woven into a succession of indexical histories, not just a single, reified proximal context. Materiality was not exhausted by a text, by spoken words, or by moose hides and blocks; it rather entailed relating these materialities to those concerned with caring for younger siblings or other features of daily life and labor. The elders privileged performance as a site not just for exhibiting narratives but for enacting models of circulation, for putting on display acts that imbue cultural forms with mobility through the collaborative creation of new indexical histories and recovering remembered histories.

Back to Circulation, via Ethnopoetics

In my estimation, these essays provide important sites to reflect on what I would call, following Gregory Bateson (1972), the foundational double-bind of Americanist linguistics. In documenting Kumeyaay language pedagogy, in which he participated, Kalim Smith (2005) documented how linguists declared their firm belief in linguistic diversity at the same time that they were often blind to the wide range of language ideologies in which it was situated. Combine the ethical positioning I cited above and this foundational double-bind and what do you get? "Hi. I have come to help you save your language. But *we* can only succeed if *you* accept *my* definition of language (as embodied in grammars and dictionaries) and materializing strategies, as centered on the production of grammars, dictionaries, and other texts and their use in structuring projects and interactions." Language "preservation" seems to come at the cost of symbolic violence, in Pierre Bourdieu's (1991) terms, of displacing a complex array of language ideologies and related models of circulation in favor of singular, totalizing, seemingly scientific models. These three essays articulate how this violence has been inflicted and how Native Americans have placed obstacles in its path.

Imbuing objects with mobility entails encountering obstacles to circulation and restrictions as well as creatively inventing tactics for navigating the channels or grooves through which particular cultural forms travel in specific directions. Just as reflecting on Urry's work would indicate that producing mobility simultaneously engenders immobility, Bowker and Star would suggest that circulation requires indexical stripping—making tough decisions about what gets entextu-alized and what gets left behind or placed into such obscure features of content and form that only a few future receivers are likely to get it. Anthropological work on mobility and circulation suggests that upholding belief in utopian teleologies for the circulation of cultural forms reflects scientific naïveté as well as ethical self-posturing. As these essays reveal, past generations of linguistic anthropologists may have succeeded less in savaging, as it were, natural circulatory circuits than in buying into rather shallow, monologic models that led them to miss—or even sometimes to suppress—the diversity of practices people were attempting to use in inoculating languages and cultures against successive plagues of colonial violence or, perhaps more humbly, just imbuing translations of sermons with parallelism and other poetic resonances.

What, then, do we make of Native Americans who are generously granted the status of privileged circulators by anthropologists, mis-sionaries, educators, funding agencies, and, one might add, tribal councils, but who then seem to impose impediments obstreperously by refusing to focus exclusively on written texts, pointing out that kids are not listening, or by just saying no—not only to whites (no, you may *not* record that story) but to narratives from neighboring nations as well? Ethnopoetics, as usual, looks closely at these processes, discern-ing how grammatical forms, the gender of a name, a tabooed word, or a cacophonous cascade of blocks can disrupt hegemonic models and practices of circulation. "Just technical issues," other anthropologists may say, but this volume as a whole might suggest to them, if they are listening, how the materiality of objects like high-priced mushrooms (Matsutake 2009) or global pharmaceuticals (Petryna et al. 2006) might be imbricated with such silly things as morphemes, discourse particles, nonsense syllables, and rhetorical patterns.

The return, with Carr and Meek, to performance provides a particularly important lesson here. Bauman and Briggs (1990, 73) emphasized the centrality of entextualization to performance; fashioning "a stretch of linguistic production into a unit—a *text*" can foreground gaps between indexical histories as well as attempts to minimize them, thereby modeling circulation in quite different ways. What Bauman (2008) referred to as *vernacular philology* involves collaboratively recovering what seemed to have been erased and thinking about how to create mobile forms that do not reproduce colonial models of circulation. Drawing attention to intertextuality, heteroglossia, and mixed genres, as linguistic anthropologists have long done, complicates notions of indexical erasure and points to how embedding and disembedding do not stand in complementary distribution. The forms of collaboration in which most of us engage these days involve us directly in the making of indexical histories, the production of written texts, the staging of performances, and the creation of events centered on cross-generational circulation; we thus help shape forms of entextualization that erase or background some indexical features and foreground others. In 2009, Warao communities in eastern Venezuela asked me both to perform curing songs taught me by people who are now deceased and for a copy of my archive. The challenges involved in complying with both requests have increased my awareness that participation in the production of indexical histories now spans generations and can make our own roles somewhat uncomfortably visible.

Thinking dialogically, there is also an important lesson here for folklorists and linguistic anthropologists about being willing to listen to—or rather read—their colleagues. A rich anthropology of documents (Riles 2006), for example, partly advanced by a linguistic anthropologist (Brenneis 2006), and recent work on the intimate place of inscription in bureaucratic practices (Gupta 2012; Hull 2012) might help us think about why written texts so quintessentially embody mobility and modernity. Linguistic anthropologists and folklorists often fail to attend to how colleagues in other areas have critically retheorized the material, medical, legal, environmental, or other objects that constitute the mere referents of the forms they scrutinize. When dialogue is not only reciprocal but critically transformative, as Hymes suggested, creativity and renewal can proliferate.

Conclusion

One of my favorite narratives is a Hopi Coyote story told by Helen Sekaquaptewa (1978) to her grandchildren, filmed by Larry Evers, which has been analyzed by David Shaul (2002) and Andrew Wiget (1987). Observing the birds from a distance, Coyote tries to get close enough to turn them into "a snack." He watches them winnow grass seeds, blow away the husks, and then fly above Old Oraibi. Trying to beguile the birds, Coyote is himself beguiled as he learns their song:

> Pota, pota, pota,
> pota, pota, pota,
> yowa'ini, yowa'ini,
> ph, ph, ph, ph.

Adorning him with their own feathers, the birds then lure Coyote into flying up with them higher and higher, at which point they take back their feathers one by one. He falls to his death.

This narrative suggests what ethnopoetics can offer to the study of circulation and mobility—and also constitutes a cautionary tale. Sekaquaptewa masterfully models the circulation of cultural forms here in multiple ways simultaneously. In showing us how Coyote learned the bird's song, she is also modeling how her grandchildren can learn both song and story. Here models of circulation imbue cultural features with mobility in particularly forceful ways, drawing bodies and voices as well as heads and ears into the process. As Carr and Meek and the elders with whom they worked observed, this process operates as much in performances as in circulating texts. Sekaquaptewa's use of her own voice, face, head, and hands points to the crucial role of intersubjectivity as she moves frequently between a variety of positionalities—a narrator who draws her grandchildren into becoming coperformers as much as an actor who assumes the shifting spatial-temporal-behavioral-linguistic positionalities of Coyote and the birds. The expressive potential of features of the narrative are doubled through use of cante fable (a mixed genre, to use Bakhtin's 1986 term), enabling Sekaquaptewa to infuse the story with drama, bring her characters to life, expose their ethical and subjective complexities, imbue them with possibilities for ethical reflection, and juxtapose a world in which birds can speak and coyotes can fly with the contemporary world confronted by Hopi children.

A different sort of model of circulation is also apparent here, one whose production involved the participation of not only producer Larry Evers but Sekaquaptewa's son Emory—a lawyer, judge, jeweler, University of Arizona faculty member, editor of a Hopi dictionary, and principal consultant on the film project. Originally a video tape, the recording now circulates via the Internet, and English speakers can read the subtitles and learn the song, like Sekaquaptewa's grandchildren, progressively through the four repetitions. We thereby seem to enter directly into the experience of the mobility of culture. The performativity attached to the circulation of a hybrid cultural form, a song embedded within a story, relying (as O'Neill might have predicted) on semantically empty vocables, seems to imbue it with such mobility that it can cross species and engender remarkable forms of physical mobility—a coyote can learn to fly. And this multispecies pedagogical exercise seems to engage us directly in learning the possibilities, limits, and dangers of circulation.

My simple summary of a wonderful narrative is meant to invite linguistic anthropologists to reflect on how they are learning complex and heterogeneous models of circulation and transporting them into scholarly realms. Nevertheless, Sekaquaptewa's Coyote story provides a strong warning. Just when we think that we have become the master cartographers of the circulation of cultural forms, we may, like poor Coyote, be taken in by the very illusions that we help create.

Notes

1. The term was proposed by Star and Griesemer (1989).

References Cited

Appadurai, Arjun. 1996. *Modernity at Large: Cultural Dimensions of Globalization.* Minneapolis: University of Minnesota Press.

Austin, J. L. 1962. *How to Do Things with Words.* Edited by J. O. Urmson and Marina Sbisà. Cambridge, MA: Harvard University Press.

Bakhtin, M. M. 1986. "The Problem of Speech Genres." In *Speech Genres and Other Late Essays,* edited by Caryl Emerson and Michael Holquist, 60–102. Austin: University of Texas Press.

Bateson, Gregory. 1972. *Steps to an Ecology of Mind*. New York: Ballantine.

Bauman, Richard. 1977. *Verbal Art as Performance*. Prospect Heights, IL: Waveland.

———. 2008. "The Philology of the Vernacular." *Journal of Folklore Research* 45 (1): 29–36.

Bauman, Richard, and Charles L. Briggs. 1990. "Poetics and Performance as Critical Perspectives on Language and Social Life." *Annual Review of Anthropology* 19:59–88.

Benjamin, Walter. 1968. *Illuminations*. Edited and with Introduction by Hannah Arendt. Translated by Harry Zohn. New York: Schoken.

Blommaert, Jan. 2010. *The Sociolinguistics of Globalization*. Cambridge: Cambridge University Press.

Blommaert, Jan, and Jef Verschueren. 1998. *Debating Diversity: Analysing the Discourse of Tolerance*. London: Routledge.

Bourdieu, Pierre. 1991. *Language and Symbolic Power*. Translated by Gino Raymond and Matthew Adamson. Cambridge, MA: Harvard University Press.

Bowker, Geoffrey C., and Susan Leigh Star. 1999. *Sorting Things Out: Classification and Its Consequences*. Cambridge, MA: MIT Press.

Brenneis, Don. 2006. "Reforming Promise." In *Documents: Artifacts of Modern Knowledge*, edited by Annelise Riles, 41–70. Ann Arbor: University of Michigan Press.

Briggs, Charles L. 1993. "Metadiscursive Practices and Scholarly Authority in Folkloristics." *Journal of American Folklore* 106 (422): 387–434.

Briggs, Charles L., and Clara Mantini-Briggs. 2003. *Stories in the Time of Cholera: Racial Profiling during a Medical Nightmare*. Berkeley: University of California Press.

Carr, E. Summerson. 2011. *Scripting Addiction: The Politics of Therapeutic Talk and American Sobriety*. Princeton, NJ: Princeton University Press.

Clifford, James. 1997. *Routes: Travel and Translation in the Late Twentieth Century*. Cambridge, MA: Harvard University Press.

Derrida, Jacques. (1972) 1977. *Limited, Inc*. Evanston, IL: Northwestern University Press.

Dick, Hilary Parsons, and Kristina Wirtz, eds. 2011. "Racializing Discourses." Special issue, *Journal of Linguistic Anthropology* 21 (S1).

Duchêne, Alexandre, and Monica Heller, eds. 2012. *Language in Late Capitalism: Pride and Profit*. New York: Routledge.

Gupta, Akhil. 2012. *Red Tape: Bureaucracy, Structural Violence, and Poverty in India*. Durham, NC: Duke University Press.

Hanks, William F. 2010. *Converting Words: Maya in the Age of the Cross*. Berkeley: University of California Press.

Hill, Jane H. 2008. *The Everyday Language of White Racism*. Chichester, UK: Wiley-Blackwell.

Hull, Matthew S. 2012. *Government of Paper: The Materiality of Bureaucracy in Urban Pakistan*. Berkeley: University of California Press.

Hymes, Dell. 1981. *"In Vain I Tried to Tell You": Essays in Native American Ethnopoetics*. Philadelphia: University of Pennsylvania Press.

———. 1996. *Ethnography, Linguistics, Narrative Inequality: Toward an Understanding of Voice*. London: Taylor and Francis.

Irvine, Judith T. 2001. "The Family Romance of Colonial Linguistics: Gender and Family in Nineteenth-Century Representations of African Languages."

In *Languages and Publics: The Making of Authority*, edited by Susan Gal and Kathryn Woolard, 13–29. Manchester, UK: St. Jerome.

Keane, Webb. 2007. *Christian Moderns: Freedom and Fetish in the Mission Encounter.* Berkeley: University of California Press.

Kroskrity, Paul V., ed. 2000. *Regimes of Language: Ideologies, Polities, and Identities.* Santa Fe: School for Advanced Research Press.

Lee, Benjamin, and Edward LiPuma. 2002. "Culture of Circulation: The Imaginations of Modernity." *Public Culture* 14:191–213.

Marx, Karl. (1887) 1967. "The Fetishism of Commodities and the Secret Thereof." In *Capital: A Critique of Political Economy*, 1:71–83. New York: International.

Matsutake Worlds Research Group. 2009. "A New Form of Collaboration in Cultural Anthropology: Matsutake Worlds." *American Ethnologist* 36 (2): 380–403.

Mendoza-Denton, Norma. 2008. *Homegirls: Language and Cultural Practice among Latina Youth Gangs.* Malden, MA: Blackwell.

Mitchell, Timothy. 2002. *Rule of Experts: Egypt, Techno-Politics, Modernity.* Berkeley: University of California Press.

Ong, Aihwa, and Stephen J. Collier, eds. 2005. *Global Assemblages: Technology, Politics, and Ethics as Anthropological Problems.* Malden, MA: Blackwell.

Petryna, Adriana, Andrew Lakoff, and Arthur Kleinman, eds. 2006. *Global Pharmaceuticals: Ethics, Markets, Practices.* Durham, NC: Duke University Press.

Riles, Annelise, ed. 2006. *Documents: Artifacts of Modern Knowledge.* Ann Arbor: University of Michigan Press.

Sassen, Saskia. 2006. *Territory, Authority, Rights: From Medieval to Global Assemblages.* Princeton, NJ: Princeton University Press.

Schieffelin, Bambi, Kathryn A. Woolard, and Paul V. Kroskrity, eds. 1998. *Language Ideologies: Practice and Theory.* New York: Oxford University Press.

Sekaquaptewa, Helen. 1978. "Iisaw: Hopi Coyote Stories." Produced by Larry Evers. Video, 17:47. Words and Place: Native Literature from the American Southwest 4. http://parentseyes.arizona.edu/wordsandplace/sekaquaptewa.html.

Shaul, David Leedom. 2002. *Hopi Traditional Literature.* Albuquerque: University of New Mexico Press.

Silverstein, Michael. 1993. "Metapragmatic Discourse and Metapragmatic Function." In *Reflexive Language: Reported Speech and Metapragmatics*, edited by John A. Lucy, 33–58. Cambridge: Cambridge University Press.

Smith, Kalim H. 2005. "Language Ideology and Hegemony in the Kumeyaay Nation: Returning the Linguistic Gaze." Master's thesis, University of California, San Diego.

Smith, Linda Tuhiwai. 1999. *Decolonizing Methodologies: Research and Indigenous Peoples.* London: Zed.

Spitulnik, Debra. 2002. "Mobile Machines and Fluid Audiences: Rethinking Reception through Zambian Radio Culture." In *Media Worlds: Anthropology on New Terrain*, edited by Faye D. Ginsburg, Lila Abu-Lughod, and Brian Larkin, 337–54. Berkeley: University of California Press.

Star, Susan Leigh, and James Griesemer. 1989. "Institutional Ecology, 'Translations' and Boundary Objects: Amateurs and Professionals in Berkeley's Museum of Vertebrate Zoology, 1907–39." *Social Studies of Science* 19 (3): 387–420.

Tsing, Anna. 2005. *Friction: An Ethnography of Global Connection.* Princeton, NJ: Princeton University Press.

Urban, Greg. 2001. *Metaculture: How Culture Moves through the World.* Minneapolis: University of Minnesota Press.

Urry, John. 2007. *Mobilities.* Cambridge: Polity.

Wiget, Andrew. 1987. "Telling the Tale: A Performance Analysis of a Hopi Coyote Story." In *Recovering the Word*, edited by Brian Swann and Arnold Krupat, 297–336. Berkeley: University of California Press.

CHARLES L. BRIGGS is the Alan Dundes Distinguished Professor in the Department of Anthropology, University of California, Berkeley. Publications include *Learning How to Ask*, *Voices of Modernity* (with Richard Bauman), *Competence in Performance*, *Stories in the Time of Cholera* (with Clara Mantini-Briggs), and *Poéticas de vida en espacios de muerte.*

Index

Lightning Source UK Ltd.
Milton Keynes UK
UKOW06f2315120617
303208UK00007B/789/P